Southern Literary Studies
Louis D. Rubin, Jr., Editor

Erskine Caldwell and the Fiction of Poverty

# Erskine Caldwell
## and the Fiction of Poverty

*The Flesh and the Spirit*

Sylvia Jenkins Cook

LOUISIANA STATE UNIVERSITY PRESS

*Baton Rouge and London*

Copyright © 1991 by Louisiana State University Press
All rights reserved
Manufactured in the United States of America
First printing
00  99  98  97  96  95  94  93  92  91      5  4  3  2  1

Designer: Amanda McDonald Key
Typeface: Caledonia
Typesetter: G&S Typesetters, Inc.
Printer and binder: Thomson-Shore, Inc.

Library of Congress Cataloging-in-Publication Data

Cook, Sylvia Jenkins, 1943–
    Erskine Caldwell and the fiction of poverty : the flesh and the
spirit / Sylvia Jenkins Cook.
        p.   cm.—(Southern literary studies)
    Includes bibliographical references and index.
    ISBN 0-8071-1645-9 (cloth)   ISBN 0-8071-1693-9 (pbk.: alk. paper)
    1. Caldwell, Erskine, 1903–      —Criticism and interpretation.
2. Southern States in literature.   3. Poverty in literature.
4. Poor in literature.   I. Title.   II. Series.
PS3505.A322Z534   1991                                      90-28655
813'.52—dc20                                                CIP

The author is grateful to G. K. Hall and Company for permission to reprint
Chapter 6, which appeared in a different form as "Erskine Caldwell's Nonfiction"
in *Critical Essays on Erskine Caldwell*, edited by Scott MacDonald (Boston:
G. K. Hall, 1981).

The paper in this book meets the guidelines for permanence and durability of the
Committee on Production Guidelines for Book Longevity of the Council on Library
Resources. ∞

*To Dick*

# Contents

# Acknowledgments

I would like to thank the National Endowment for the Humanities for research support while I was writing this book and the University of Missouri–St. Louis for grants from the Weldon Spring and Chancellor's Humanities funds.

I would also like to thank Philip N. Cronenwett, Curator of Manuscripts in the Special Collections Department of the Baker Library of Dartmouth College, and J. Fraser Cocks III, Curator of the Special Collections Department of the Miller Library of Colby College.

# Abbreviations

| | |
|---|---|
| A | *Annette* (New York, 1973). |
| AA | *Around About America* (New York, 1964). |
| AE | *American Earth* (1931; New York, 1946). |
| AM | *Afternoons in Mid-America: Observations and Impressions*, illustrations by Virginia Caldwell (New York, 1976). |
| B | *The Bastard* (1929; London, 1958). |
| CE | *Call It Experience: The Years of Learning How to Write* (New York, 1951). |
| CH | *Close to Home* (New York, 1962). |
| CI | *Claudelle Inglish* (Boston, 1958). |
| CW | *Certain Women* (Boston, 1957). |
| DS | *Deep South: Memory and Observation* (New York, 1968). |
| EN | *The Earnshaw Neighborhood* (New York, 1971). |
| EP | *Episode in Palmetto* (New York, 1950). |
| G | *Gretta* (Boston, 1955). |
| GB | *Georgia Boy* (New York, 1943). |
| GCS | *Gulf Coast Stories* (Boston, 1956). |
| GLA | *God's Little Acre* (1933; New York, 1934). |
| HU | *A House in the Uplands* (New York, 1946). |
| ISB | *In Search of Bisco* (New York, 1965). |
| J | *Jackpot: The Short Stories of Erskine Caldwell* (New York, 1940). |
| JN | *Jenny by Nature* (New York, 1961). |
| JO | *Journeyman* (New York, 1935). |
| KRS | *Kneel to the Rising Sun and Other Stories* (1935; New York, 1951). |
| LM | *Love and Money* (New York, 1954). |
| LN | *A Lamp for Nightfall* (New York, 1952). |
| LNS | *The Last Night of Summer* (New York, 1963). |
| MF | *Moscow Under Fire: A Wartime Diary* (London, 1942). |
| MMA | *Miss Mamma Aimee* (New York, 1967). |
| ND | *North of the Danube*, photographs by Margaret Bourke-White (New York, 1939). |

Abbreviations

PE     *Place Called Estherville* (New York, 1949).

PF     *Poor Fool* (New York, 1930).

RW     *Russia at War*, photographs by Margaret Bourke-White (London, 1942).

S     *Southways* (1938; London, 1953).

SAK     *The Sacrilege of Alan Kent* (Portland, Me., 1936).

SAP     *Some American People* (New York, 1935).

SHG     *The Sure Hand of God* (New York, 1947).

SI     *Summertime Island* (New York, 1968).

SUSA     *Say, Is This the U.S.A.*, photographs by Margaret Bourke-White (New York, 1941).

TG     *Tragic Ground* (New York, 1944).

TJ     *Trouble in July* (New York, 1940).

TR     *Tobacco Road* (New York, 1932).

TVE     *This Very Earth* (New York, 1948).

WA     *Writing in America* (New York, 1967).

WAL     *We Are the Living* (New York, 1933).

WAMM     *With All My Might* (Atlanta, 1987).

WS     *The Weather Shelter* (New York, 1969).

YHSTF     *You Have Seen Their Faces*, photographs by Margaret Bourke-White (New York, 1937).

Erskine Caldwell and the Fiction of Poverty

# Introduction

*The essential characteristic of contemporary American writing is that it is the only literature whose creators are not intellectuals.*

—*André Malraux*

*If I haven't spoken about Erskine Caldwell, it is because he puzzles me. He evades the categories and theories that I am trying to elaborate; . . . and that is all to his credit.*

—*André Gide*

For many years, Erskine Caldwell has been an anomalous and peripheral figure in the realm of American literature. Like one of his own marginal characters, who complained that humans are put into the bodies of animals and then required to act like people, Caldwell balked at the higher role of artist and intellectual, yet revealed just enough of those qualities to make any other labels for him equally unsatisfactory. His long and prolific career as a writer led him into associations with the literary avant-garde, the political radicals, and the social turmoil of much of the twentieth century, as well as into pulp magazines, pornography trials, and dime store promotions of his work. Although he seemed to European scholars and critics, who praised him widely, virtually a blueprint of what was most brash, novel, and fascinating in the American writer, he frequently embarrassed his compatriots into apologies or neglectful silence by his reiterated literary scrutiny of what was most vulgar, violent, and shocking in their civilization. He created a grotesque universe from his imagination and his native South, and then proved himself the most enigmatic part of it. He seemed by turns prophet and profiteer, scourger and exploiter, fabulist and documenter, fatalist and reformer. His style appeared simple, spontaneous, and ingenuous in a way that perhaps only a careful craftsman could contrive. Critical consternation over Caldwell's intentions and methods led initially to lively exchanges on his work during his rapid rise to fame in the 1930s. However, he was soon abandoned to an uneasy limbo when his later career seemed to prove that he had written too much, found "pay dirt" in the lower depths of his native culture, and, as Faulkner bluntly put it, had gradually grown "towards trash."[1]

Yet to write Caldwell off as a second-rate pornographer, a facile humorist, or an outdated proletarian is to make a judgment on a body of work whose most essential quality is its defiance of any such conventional terms of assessment—of literary categories, schools of thought, and ethical and aesthetic labels. When French critics asserted that "no one is more American than Erskine Caldwell," they referred not merely to the hard-boiled style and brutal pessimism associated with American naturalists, but to Caldwell's affinity for the macabre, the irrational, and the subversive that undermined all certainty about the nature of his fiction, tingeing tragedy with farce and comedy with horror.[2] His work thus resists coherent schemes of interpretation, a situation that Caldwell appeared to exacerbate by his continual mocking disparagement of the pursuit of criticism and by his efforts throughout his life to present a simplified and contradictory public image of himself, in interviews and autobiographies, that effectively kept the riddle of his literary world intact.

As the preparation for a career in writing, Caldwell's personal life and experience were particularly and peculiarly American. He was born in Coweta County, Georgia, in 1903, in the heart of a region he later called "a state of mind—a local purgatory or an earthly paradise" (ISB, 17). As the son of a clergyman in the Associated Reformed Presbyterian Church, Caldwell moved frequently around the South with his family during his boyhood. He had the double advantage of intimate exposure to the physical and social sphere that would later be transformed into the imaginary world of his fiction, and observation of the spiritual and emotional yearnings of its inhabitants that would give him some of his central themes. Like many other American writers, he sought his education in experience rather than in books. Such experience meant for him immersing himself in a variety of unskilled jobs, wandering through

---

1. Jonathan Daniels, "American Lower Depths, in *Critical Essays on Erskine Caldwell*, ed. Scott MacDonald (Boston, 1981), 78; William Faulkner, *Faulkner at Nagano* (Tokyo, 1956), 58.
2. Thelma M. Smith and Ward L. Miner, *Transatlantic Migration: The Contemporary American Novel in France* (1955; rpr. New York, 1968), 154.

his native land, and even, when it suited, taking college courses at Erskine College, the University of Virginia, and the University of Pennsylvania. It also meant ultimately four marriages: the first to Helen Lannigan in 1925, the second to the photographer Margaret Bourke-White in 1939, the third to June Johnson in 1942, and the final one to Virginia Fletcher in 1957. However, more than anything else, experience meant for Caldwell constant practice in the art of writing, which he began and returned to frequently, like many other American authors, in journalism and nonfiction. He started in the 1920s by working as a newspaper reporter and writing book reviews, and then rapidly began to try his hand at poems, jokes, essays, short stories, and novels, many of which he viewed quite empirically as tentative rehearsals for a later career as a published writer. This pragmatic approach brought Caldwell, during the twenties, into contact with some of the best experimental writing of his day. Not only did he have the opportunity to review a good deal of contemporary fiction, but in scrutinizing the numerous little literary magazines in search of potential publishers for his own work, Caldwell acquired (perhaps incidentally) an education in the kind of modernist, avant-garde, nativist, and radical writing, and the ideological manifestoes and artistic dicta, that appeared in such periodicals as *transition, Pagany, Hound and Horn, Contact, blues, Clay*, and *Nativity*. During the 1930s, his literary and political concerns for the poorest people of the South led him into closer association with left-wing and proletarian movements, though such novels as *Tobacco Road, God's Little Acre*, and *Journeyman*, and such short story collections as *We Are the Living*, proved rather too earthy even for the committed populists of the *New Masses*. Like many other writers during the Great Depression, Caldwell was drawn to documentary writing; and by the early forties, he had toured and reported on, not just his native South and the United States, but Czechoslovakia and the Soviet Union, producing with Margaret Bourke-White a lively and highly personal variety of the new genre of photojournalism.

When Caldwell returned to the United States from his travels in the early 1940s, he abandoned for some time both short story and nonfiction writing in order to complete a projected ten-novel cyclorama of southern life that he had begun with *Tobacco Road* in the early thirties. He had determined to depict a variety of facets of southern life, and he resumed it by trying, in the remaining six novels, to broaden its range beyond the largely rural and small-town poor whites who had been central to his literary vision during the thirties. He looked now at the same people displaced into urban slums, as well as at the decaying gentility and rising middle class of the South, and especially at the situation of women and blacks and their complicated position within these economic and class structures. When the cyclorama was completed in 1950, Caldwell turned away for a time from the social world of these novels to a more concentrated exploration of people's, and particularly women's, private obsessions and sexual neuroses. He later admitted that dissatisfactions with his own private and marital life might have influenced these novels, but it is significant that there was nothing in the public life of the fifties comparable to the social crisis of the Great Depression to engage Caldwell's partisan sympathies or enable him to use his keen knowledge of southern life. Such an occasion returned, however, with the rise of the civil rights movement, for Caldwell had already written widely of the situation of black people, and now, in the 1960s, he went back to explore this subject with renewed interest. He also returned, for the first time in a quarter century, to nonfiction writing and his memories of racial prejudice and conflict. Though Caldwell protested repeatedly in his many public interviews that he was a writer and not a reformer, and though his literary vision skirts far beyond the usual boundaries of social realism, he was not only sympathetically involved with some of the major political and ideological conflicts of his age; he also produced his liveliest art in those periods when he was most controversially engaged with his society and with efforts to combat injustice and inequity in it.

By the end of Caldwell's long life, in 1987, he had passed through notoriety, fame, neglect, and even, eventually, a certain amount of honorific ceremony. From Poland he received the Order of Cultural Merit; France made him Commander of the Order of Arts and Letters. In Japan, he was honored at a banquet given by the Erskine Caldwell Literary Society; and at home, finally, he was made a member of the American Academy of Arts and Letters. There was also a modest revival of scholarly and critical interest in Caldwell's work, although it still remains largely omitted from the classroom anthologies that mark successful admission into the great tradition of American literature, despite his remarkable skill in producing dozens of short stories that seem eminently suitable for such selection. By being "particularly American," Caldwell had proved perhaps *too* crafty and recalcitrant to be satisfactorily assimilated and classified.

This exclusion of Caldwell means, however, the loss of a unique and audacious voice that explored aspects of life hitherto rarely approached in American literature. He exposed the depravity of poor people's lives with the venom of a naturalist and then held them up to moral irony and incongruous humor. He noted laconically the search for spiritual transcendence in his fellow mortals and the frenzied sexual channels into which it was so often diverted. He observed the powerful instinct of human sexuality and saw how readily it might be bartered or exploited for money, transformed into obsessions, or confused into foolish whims. He portrayed individuals as variously irrational, foolish, and vicious, but he attacked fiercely a social system that exposed them to hunger, disease, and persecution. He envisioned an absurd world, but always insisted that not all of its cruel manifestations were beyond cure. He did this in a style that seemed so simple as continually to risk banality, for only in such a context could his startling dissonances and incongruous juxtapositions have their full impact. He was a powerful imagist and a wildly inventive creator of character and incident. If the greatest successes of his career in short stories, novels, and nonfiction were concentrated largely in the twelve years between the publication of *American Earth* in 1931 and *Georgia Boy* in 1943, his earlier preparation for them was enlightening; and his later work, especially in the 1960s, was often intriguing. Many of these later novels about women and blacks were written well in advance of, and often well beyond the realm of, the verities of current feminist and civil rights thinking; but verities and certainties were never Caldwell's mode, even in his most dedicated proletarian period, unless mixed with more disconcerting and oblique attitudes.

Because Caldwell's literary output was so large (over fifty volumes) and was written over a period of more than half a century and in so many different literary forms, I have tried to organize this book with both his chronological development and his attention to various genres in mind. I have given separate chapters to the short stories, which tended to cluster in the 1930s and 1950s, and to the nonfiction, which dominated in the late 1930s, early 1940s, and again in the 1960s. Caldwell's novel writing, by contrast, was a consistently ongoing endeavor, to which I have devoted four chapters—two to the major work of the southern cyclorama and one each to his apprenticeship and his later work. The novels of these latter two periods are, by virtually unanimous critical assent, awkward and inferior. When Joseph Warren Beach began his chapter on Caldwell in his *American Fiction, 1920–1940*, he confessed that he found himself "inclined to soft-pedal" his early efforts, "hoping that only specialists will come upon them." Likewise, more recent critics of Caldwell have tended to eliminate much consideration of his post-cyclorama novels, finding them both formulaic and sensational. I have deliberately chosen to be more comprehensive, because Caldwell's early and late work, besides its frequent curiosity value, often reveals themes and preoccupations that are pervasive in his fiction, but are sometimes overshadowed by the topicality and social relevance of much of what he did during the 1930s. However, I do not wish to be an apologist for Caldwell's entire opus, whose sight caused Truman Capote to exclaim in awe, "Just to TYPE that much, let alone WRITE." Though there is some risk, in being so inclusive, that readers may find themselves moved (as Malcolm Cowley admitted he sometimes was) "to personal fury against the author" by having to consider the worst of Caldwell, I hope that this larger context of his work may help illuminate what is most bold and artful in the best.[3]

3. Joseph Warren Beach, excerpt from *American Fiction, 1920–1940*, in *Critical Essays*, ed. MacDonald, 186; Truman Capote, as quoted by Herb Caen in "Letter to Victor Dalmas," *Pembroke Magazine*, XI (1979), 30; Malcolm Cowley and T. K. Whipple, "Two Judgments of *American Earth*," in *Critical Essays*, ed. MacDonald, 6.

# 1

# The Apprenticeship

*Fit yourself for writing to the extent that anyone who desires to become successful in his field undergoes a period of apprenticeship. Doctors, lawyers, bakers, barbers, mechanics, engineers, and printers must learn by experience. Why shouldn't writers?*

—*Erskine Caldwell*

*I was trying to start out fresh, as if I had never read a book or no one had ever written a book. Everything was new and unique.*

—*Erskine Caldwell*

In his 1951 autobiography, *Call It Experience*, Erskine Caldwell relates an anecdote about one of his earliest encounters with the New York literary world. It was at a cocktail party given in 1931 by the Macauley Company, which had recently published some of Caldwell's first stories. The party was attended by a stellar group of artists and intellectuals that included Lewis Mumford, Georgia O'Keeffe, Robert Cantwell, Edwin Seaver, Edmund Wilson, and Michael Gold, and for most aspiring young writers would have been an occasion charged with significance. Caldwell describes it thus: "There were two chief attractions, as far as I was concerned, at this party. One of these was a well-provisioned buffet table that provided the only full meal I had had in nearly three months, and the other attraction was Mae West" (*CE*, 105). Sated with feeding and gazing, Caldwell duly records the presence of his influential contemporaries, but if any intellectual exchange among them took place, it does not merit inclusion in his story. It is as crafty an evocation of his own character as writer as anything he created in his fiction. Here is a young artist whose impulse to write is so strong that for three months he has been living alone in a cell-like room, subsisting on bread, cheese, and soup, and working until three or four o'clock each morning. However, when the opportunity arises, his appetite for food and glamour proves stronger than for literary discourse, criticism, or advice. It is a miniature of the image of himself that Caldwell projects and enlarges throughout his autobiographical works—*Call It Experience*, *Writing in America* (1967), *With All My Might* (1987)—and in numerous interviews and public addresses. It depicts a man who is isolated, untutored, perhaps amusingly naïve, but determined to make his own way in his chosen vocation, that of becoming "an accomplished writer" (*CE*, 71). That this accomplishment is defined by Caldwell at least as much in terms of sales, dollars, mass markets, and foreign editions as in artistic integrity to his personal vision of the world is equally suggested in his self-portraits; he candidly enjoys the fruits of his dedicated efforts. He believes that each generation must write its own books *and* deserve its own royalties.

Caldwell's depiction of himself suggests at times a truly Emersonian figure who abandons all obligations to the solitary call of his genius by sacrificing early in life his job, home, family, and all creature comforts. He cut off a promising career in journalism with the Atlanta *Journal* in order to devote himself to fiction; he left his native South for the rigors of the Maine woods in winter in order to find a different perspective on his literary region; he left his wife and children in Maine in order to concentrate exclusively on his writing in New York; and finally, when the cold and damp of his basement room in New York brought chilblains to his hands, he took his pencil and pad on Greyhound bus trips and in this manner completed his famous story "Kneel to the Rising Sun" (*CE*, 50, 103, 154). He read few books, acknowledged no influences, and sought no mentors. He asserts confidently in *Writing in America* that the first "enduring native tradition in fiction" was established in the United States in the 1930s, approximately a hundred years after most literary historians would date it and exactly coincidental with the emergence of writers like himself who found their inspiration in the Great Depression and the hardships of ordinary people (*WA*, 116–17). He repudiates critical responses to his and other authors' work as deprecatory, belittling, jealous, and narcissistic (*WA*, 11, 19, 31, 111, 112, 124), and claims to write for one audience only, the democratic masses, and one severe taskmaster, himself. When reviewers found in his work echoes of Twain and hints of Lawrence, that was their problem, for he was, he said, a writer and not a reader. When he made one of his first trips to New York to encounter the literary world, he took along a first edition of Dreiser's *Sister Carrie*, not, he emphasizes, for the inspiration of the master of

American naturalism, but to sell to defray his expenses (*CE*, 72). He rejects neither tradition nor innovation in literature, but maintains tenaciously his ignorance of both of them and their power to undermine originality. He intends his creative powers to be bounded only by the limitations of his own consciousness and by his physical capacity for work. His ideal writer is "a simple-minded person . . . not a great mind, . . . not a great thinker, . . . not a great philosopher, he's a story-teller." Though he concedes modestly that readers may see in his own work much more than he is capable of seeing,[1] this humility is matched by the confidence with which he broadcasts his opinions to the world: "I am not quiet-spoken and I do not have a velvet touch. I behave like a heavy-handed boilermaker in the literary field. I like to hammer-hammer-hammer and make all the noise I can. The din is not going to produce an euphonious sound, but neither is it going to be a muted dirge of despair" (*WA*, 10).

Malcolm Cowley, who observed Caldwell sympathetically from his earliest writings, felt that this self-made image of Caldwell's as "*homo scribens*" was a "radically simplified picture"; this "Adam in the garden," whose every statement was new, was "not as innocent" as he seemed. Indeed, though all of Caldwell's public actions and pronouncements seem consistent with his autobiographical model, such primitive ingenuousness seems bound to invite a skeptical response from scholars and critics. It is too tempting to search out the obverse side of Caldwell, to uncover a closet intellectual who read Freud, Marx, Whitman, and Bergson, and compiled a private study of the motifs in southwestern tall tales. There is scant evidence for his existence. Though some careful critics have noted the culture and intelligence of Caldwell's parents, the well-filled bookshelves in photographs of his home, the literature and sociology courses he took at the University of Virginia, and the amount of contemporary fiction he must have digested as book reviewer for the Charlotte *Observer* and Houston *Post* during the 1920s—these are small chinks in the armor of innocence. They certainly do not betray Caldwell as a scholar or man of letters, though his concealment of the substance of everything he had ever read, in his discussions of his education and apprenticeship, indicates a willingness to enhance an authentically naïve reputation. Whether Caldwell's aggressively know-nothing attitude had a detrimental effect on his work and

1. Carvel Collins, "Erskine Caldwell at Work: A Conversation with Carvel Collins," *Atlantic*, CCII (July, 1958), 27, 22.

whether indeed he knew and read a good deal more than he acknowledged are questions that obviously can never be fully resolved. Malcolm Cowley traced Caldwell's failure in later life to fulfill his potential as an artist to his willful estrangement from the influences of the literary world: "Writers learn from life, if they are lucky, but they also learn from other writers, and Caldwell was learning less than his contemporaries. . . . Although he lived in an age of experiments, . . . he refused to profit from the experiments of others." Cowley has also suggested, however, that Caldwell learned more than he was willing to admit from Sherwood Anderson, and other critics have argued his indebtedness to Lawrence, Twain, Augustus B. Longstreet, and George Washington Harris, and could undoubtedly have made a good case for Faulkner if only *As I Lay Dying* had predated *Tobacco Road* by a few more years.[2] Caldwell's more extreme claims to ignorance and innocence may well have been formulated in opposition to such critical exercises, though his sense of himself as a writer rather than a reader *is* quite convincing.

The other aspect of Caldwell's self-portrait that might seem initially at odds with the intuitive, unschooled original who goes his solitary way is his shrewd determination to succeed in his particular business and to gain maximum sales and readers for his books. This too, however, is a picture of American individualism, though now more of the Ben Franklin than Emersonian model—where hard work is at least as essential as genius to any possibility of achievement, and astute self-promotion is no cause for embarrassment.[3] Though Caldwell tells comic anecdotes of his early ineptitude with business and financial arrangements, he proved an eager student; and he concludes *Call It Experience* with a bemused account of himself attacked by his fellow authors for bringing their profession into disrepute by autographing 25-cent paperback editions of his work in a Kansas City drugstore (*CE*, 227). Caldwell's willingness to participate in such a publicity scheme is of a piece with his willingness to sit at a typewriter on a winter night, wearing "a sweater, a

2. Malcolm Cowley, "Georgia Boy: A Retrospect of Erskine Caldwell," in *Critical Essays*, ed. MacDonald, 323–24, 316. For literary influences, see Guy Owen, "Erskine Caldwell and D. H. Lawrence," *Pembroke Magazine*, XI (1979), 18–21; Henry Seidel Canby, Introduction to *The Pocket Book of Erskine Caldwell Stories*, in *Critical Essays*, ed. MacDonald, 217; Richard J. Gray, "Southwestern Humor, Erskine Caldwell, and the Comedy of Frustration," in *Critical Essays*, ed. MacDonald, 298–314.

3. See Donald R. Noble, "Erskine Caldwell: A Biographical Sketch," *Pembroke Magazine*, XI (1979), 176.

leather jerkin, and an overcoat," with a blanket wrapped around his feet, writing "story after story, revising, correcting, and rewriting with always a dogged determination, regardless of time or hardship, to keep on trying" (*CE*, 54). This aspiring artist believes in serving his time and fulfilling an arduous apprenticeship, though one whose terms are not dictated by any master. The most important element in this apprenticeship is what Caldwell calls in his autobiography's title "experience," by which he means not so much living as writing—the empirical trial-and-error method he practiced for many years as training for his profession. Often there seems to be more than a hint of a puritan work ethic in his assertion that "impatience, inadequate apprenticeship, or unwillingness to sit at a typewriter day after day and year after year may well outweigh the most intense state of mind or will to succeed" (*CE*, 232). It is as though the rigor and discipline of the writer's preparation are its most important qualities, a moral obligation of diligence that must precede any possibility of accomplishment. Thus *Call It Experience*, subtitled *The Years of Learning How to Write*, and his aptly titled final autobiography, *With All My Might*, concentrate on the independence and pragmatism of Caldwell's early years, largely to the exclusion of any reflection on the ideas and values that were developing simultaneously in the young writer.

However, these two autobiographies reveal incidentally strong evidence of another mode of education, another kind of intellectual background, another set of attitudes and dispositions that qualify any sense of the hungry young man at the Macauley's cocktail party as an ambitious American Adam whose mind is open and unformed. The son of a southern Presbyterian clergyman, Caldwell spent much of his youth traveling with his father into the remote and poverty-stricken byways of his region. He was from the outset exposed to powerful deterministic strains in American life—environmental, historical, religious, and economic—that radically undermine the exuberance of the "heavy-handed boilermaker" refusing to sound "a muted dirge of despair." Because Caldwell's southern background provided the substance as well as the point of view of much of his best work, it is difficult to overstate its importance in his career. He dealt directly with the influence of his father and his region in two autobiographical excursions, *In Search of Bisco* (1965) and *Deep South* (1968), but the impact of the circumstances of his early life in the South is pervasive in his fiction and documentary writing as well. One problem, however, with compiling biographical facts about Caldwell is his obvious creativity with the remembered details of his early life, and a number of potential biographers have been confounded by his selective reticence and inventiveness. He manufactured a colorful account of his career for *Twentieth Century Authors* that included going to sea on a boat running guns for a revolt in South America, though elsewhere he described the same incident as failing to sign aboard a Gulf of Mexico freighter as a deckhand (*CE*, 29). He gave quite different accounts of his youthful Bogalusa arrest and imprisonment in *Call It Experience* and *In Search of Bisco*, though each was skillfully adapted to the separate emphases of these two books. As one of Caldwell's biographers said to another seeking information: "Perhaps I have left you with the impression that no Caldwell statement about himself can be taken as necessarily true. Exactly right."[4] Yet Caldwell's versions of the past are at least as important for understanding his work as what actually happened, and indeed all appear to derive from the continuous revision of a certain solid core of history and experience.

Caldwell's date of birth is one of the many "facts" about his life that has appeared in different versions, although it was finally resolved as December 17, 1903. More important than the precise date is its location in Coweta County, Georgia, in the Deep South, a region he later called "a state of mind—a local purgatory or an earthly paradise—and often an economic iniquity, a social anachronism, a political autocracy, and a racial tyranny" (*ISB*, 17). He was born in a land that provided him with a ready vision of violent incongruities; if his rhetoric evokes similar laments by other southern writers such as Cash, Percy, Couch, Stribling, or even Mencken, it is surely less because of literary influence than because of those pervasive qualities of southern life that seem to demand expression in paradoxes. Caldwell's childhood gave him broad exposure to these varied aspects of southern experience, for his family moved frequently around Tennessee, the Carolinas, Virginia, Florida, and Georgia, wherever his father was sent by the Associated Reformed Presbyterian Church to settle dissension or adjust financial difficulties in troubled congregations.[5] Because the church was not a wealthy one, Caldwell had plenty of opportunity to observe poverty at close hand, as well as acquire an education in Calvinist doctrine

4. Quoted in Cowley, "Georgia Boy," 319.
5. *Ibid.*, 317–18.

and fundamentalist practice, which he considered of more value than any secular education in his early life (*DS*, 1). His father determined to expose his son to as many varieties of religious experience as possible by taking him to visit and observe a host of different faiths and customs, despite his own frequently acknowledged depression after they had witnessed a minister dangling a rattlesnake over his face or hitting himself on the head with a wooden mallet (*DS*, 64). The son was later to recall in his fiction the substance of many of these excursions to "Church of God all-night camp-meetings, Holy Roller exhibitions on splintery wooden floors, Primitive Christian Baptismal immersions in muddy creeks, Seventh Day Adventist foot-washings, Body of Christ blood-drinking communions, Kingdom of God snake-handlings, Full Redeemer glosso-lalia services, [and] Fire Baptized Holiness street-corner rallies" (*DS*, 12).

The Reverend Ira Sylvester Caldwell also provided for his son an indisputable model of impassioned concern for the poor whose lives he witnessed, a concern allied to a bleakly fatalistic sense of their very limited possibilities for improvement. After taking the boy to visit the rotting shack of a tenant farmer, his father, Caldwell recalls, told him: "That poor chap back there hasn't got a chance in the world to get out of the rut he's in as long as he lives. He's as bad off as a toad in a post hole. It's a disgrace that human beings have to live like that" (*CE*, 25). What exactly his father *did* say on the subject is recorded more formally, if less colorfully, in a letter he wrote later in life to the Augusta *Chronicle* in which he restates this deterministic vision, arguing that "thoughtful people are beginning to realize that every individual is to a large extent the product of his environment, of the institutions that men have set up, of the social forces that society lets loose. No man is self-made and no man is self-unmade."[6] The angry ridicule, the pessimistic naturalism, and the ambivalent view of the people caught in the post holes as both human beings and toads are clearly an important part of Caldwell's heritage from his father. An equally important legacy was his interest in storytelling and jokes, and Caldwell's account of his father's return home from a railroad trip to one of his feuding churches is among the most evocative of his personal sketches. The son would sniff his father's smoke-saturated clothing, even rubbing the coal

6. I. S. Caldwell, "Mr. Caldwell Writes," in *Critical Essays*, ed. MacDonald, 132.

cinders he shook from his hatband in an attempt to guess which
railroad line he had traveled, and wait in eager anticipation of his
tale "as if I were listening to a detective or secret agent talk about
an adventure in a far-away place even if all that had happened was
that somebody had stolen his suitcase in a railroad station" (*DS*, 15).
Caldwell's mother, too, was apparently an adept storyteller. She
educated her son at home herself until he was thirteen years old,
and despite his longing for the company of other children at school,
he found his "solitary confinement" made bearable by his fascination with the tales she told him (*WAMM*, 12).

Caldwell dated his desire to be a writer to his midadolescent
years in Wrens, Georgia, when the influence of his father's guided
exposure to the harshness and irrationality of life was powerful on
him. However, because the impulse to write derived primarily from
the appreciation of an oral tradition of storytelling, and because his
goal was "that of becoming a published fiction writer within ten
years' time" (*CE*, 12), he embarked on his conscious apprenticeship
to writing where so many other American writers have—on a newspaper. He began, during a high school vacation, by turning the
handpress of the Jefferson *Reporter*, a weekly paper in Jefferson
County, Georgia, and soon graduated to setting type, collecting
society notes, and actually writing small items. He became a string
correspondent for the Augusta *Chronicle*, the Atlanta *Constitution*,
and the Macon *Telegraph*, and received a classic piece of advice
from Mark Ethridge, the *Telegraph*'s news editor, about the kind of
apprenticeship the determined young author should pursue: "Go
back to Wrens and write about things you see happening," Ethridge
told him. "Don't take anybody's word for anything. See it yourself,
or don't believe it" (*CE*, 22–23). Caldwell apparently took this advice rather literally, embarking on daily trips into the countryside
around Wrens with the local doctor, the county tax assessor, and his
father, and carefully observing the patterns of life there. Although
he enrolled at Erskine College just before his seventeenth birthday,
he found the education there more restrictive than the twofold
training in writing and witnessing life that he had set for himself,
and thence spent as much time off campus as possible. Of his academic record as a freshman, he said, "My grades . . . were so low
that even I was surprised" (*CE*, 28), and he dropped out halfway
through his second year in search of different kinds of experience.
He lived for some months the life of an itinerant laborer, including
his brief term in jail in Louisiana, and continued his string corre-

spondence for newspapers, but did not wholly abandon thoughts of a more formal education. He tried college life again, this time at the University of Virginia, which he entered in 1922. There Caldwell found English and sociology studies most pertinent to his ambitions and began experimenting with many forms of writing (including jokes, which he submitted to the *Virginia Reel*), but he persisted in pursuing his own sense of an education rather than the university's. He switched courses, dropped in and out of school, sought a wide variety of unskilled jobs, and returned to full-time journalism in what seems, retrospectively, a rather coherent amalgam, for a young author, of formal education, worldly experience, and writing practice.

It is very possible that, in remembering these early years, Caldwell imposed a design for his apprenticeship that was less consciously intended at the time. Nevertheless, by immersing himself in all walks of working-class life, as well as in the study of economics and sociology, he managed to acquire a broader context for his early exposure to the remote rural poverty of the South; and by his newspaper experience and his courses in English, he gained both discipline and open-mindedness toward the craft of writing. Caldwell's marriage, in 1925, induced him to acquire a steady job as a reporter for the Atlanta *Journal* and to begin reviewing books for the Charlotte *Observer* and the Houston *Post*. At the *Journal*, he noted admiringly Margaret Mitchell's confidence in abandoning her feature writing job there to concentrate on her future novel *Gone with the Wind*, and listened to vicarious accounts of Frances Newman's meticulous daily progress on *The Hard-Boiled Virgin* (*CE*, 40–41). When he followed Mitchell's example by giving up his job and moving to the state of Maine in 1926, he kept his finger on the pulse of contemporary fiction and of the dramatic developments in that field by continuing his book reviewing. This was for some time virtually his only source of income, though a double one, because he sold his review copies and even attempted to stock his own bookstore in Portland with them. During his time on the *Journal* and in Maine, Caldwell apparently experimented in every genre of writing—poetry, novels, jokes, essays, short stories—with a rather empirical detachment. Believing that "there was only one authentic kind of writer—a writer who could see his stories in print" (*CE*, 47), he determined that the moment he had his first piece accepted for publication, he would make a bonfire of all his previous work. This conflagration actually took place, according to Caldwell, in the summer of 1930, when Maxwell Perkins accepted some of his stories for *Scribner's Magazine*. He describes himself carrying many years' accumulation of unpublished manuscripts to the lake shore by his house for destruction—his poetry, jokes, and essays being the first to go. However, there is evidence that a considerable body of unpublished material, including a novel, a collection of poems, and several volumes of nonfiction, escaped the fire. In addition, Caldwell had already published, before the fire, two novels and two major portions of another complete work that could clearly not have been burned. Nevertheless, he did relegate them to a kind of literary limbo by referring habitually in later years to the 1931 collection of short stories, *American Earth*, as his first book.[7] Thus the fire was clearly a symbolic rite for Caldwell, not merely of his initiation into print, but of the completion of his self-imposed apprenticeship and his arrival at the assurance of a personal style, subject, and audience.

The variety of this cast-off apprenticeship work illustrates both Caldwell's empiricism and his trust in his own intuition, for he got little advice from the editors who rejected his early work, and what there was, was not congenial to him: "I was not adverse to advice in principle, as long as it conformed in the main to what I was going ahead [to] do anyway, but it always seemed to me that the advice I received was surely intended for somebody else" (*CE*, 59). His early work in all genres moves from a tendency to stylistic excess toward those philosophical and social views that would crystallize distinctly only during the years of the Great Depression. Caldwell says that his poetry was the first item to go into the bonfire; but even in the poems that survive, Guy Owen, an astute scholar of all of Caldwell's early work, has demonstrated that the revisions show a definite movement in the author from the manner of a "young romantic, given to mooning about beauty with a capital B" toward directness, control, and realism. The subjects of the poems are traditional and diverse, but already it is noticeable that the most remarkable of them deal with religion, racial violence, and poverty in the South. In fact, one of them, "Southern Nights," in which an unemployed poor white man and an abused and rejected mulatto woman die in each other's arms in a ditch, is almost a blueprint for an essential

7. See Guy Owen, "'The Bogus Ones': A Lost Erskine Caldwell Novel," *Southern Literary Journal*, XI (1978), 32–39, and "Erskine Caldwell's Unpublished Poems," *South Atlantic Bulletin*, XLIII (1978), 53–57; Erskine Caldwell, Introduction to *American Earth*, in *Critical Essays*, ed. MacDonald, 221.

motif of the later fiction. The very significant omission, however, is any incongruous humor in the tone. Caldwell commented many years afterward in an interview, "Everybody has to write poetry sooner or later. I got it out of my system early in life"; but for someone whose later achievements, especially in the short story, were to derive so much from intensity, condensation, and repetitive and rhythmical effects, the early practice of poetry was not such an irrelevant part of his juvenilia.[8]

Caldwell's early unpublished novel "The Bogus Ones" may be a better example of something he had to get out of his system at the beginning, for it is no less than a *Künstlerroman*, a portrait of the artist as a young man, struggling to pursue his craft in a narrow environment of Bohemian artiness and a broader one of New England puritanism. Guy Owen suggests that the protagonist is a self-conscious variation of Caldwell himself, an ambitious young writer in Portland, Maine. He is certainly a character who will not recur again in Caldwell's mature fiction, where the closest he comes to creating an artist, apart from the novelist hero of *Love and Money* (1954), is a skillful con man or a quick-tongued preacher. The New England setting will reappear in his work, but it is generally atypical of an author whose characters, concerns, and even style are later so closely linked to the South. In his treatment of sexuality in "The Bogus Ones," Caldwell anticipates the openness of his later attitude and his distaste for prudery and censorship; Owen notes also one of his favorite future motifs in the use of a witness in a lovemaking scene.[9]

The possible influence of D. H. Lawrence on this and other works by Caldwell is the subject of some interesting speculation by Owen, who has noted not only the similarity between the two in depicting the "life-denying" qualities of the bourgeoisie, but also the careful study Caldwell apparently made of many of Lawrence's works during the 1920s. Caldwell's first wife, Helen Caldwell Cushman, has said that she owned first editions of all Lawrence's books and that she and Caldwell read and discussed them together. In a letter to Owen, she wrote: "I do know that Erskine read with enthusiasm *St. Mawr* in 1925, and that he gave it to me. That winter we also read *Fantasia of the Unconscious*, *Women in Love* and *Aaron's Rod*. The next year we read and discussed two plays, *Touch and*

---

8. Owen, "Erskine Caldwell's Unpublished Poems," 54; Collins, "Erskine Caldwell at Work," 23.

9. Owen, "'The Bogus Ones,'" 32–39 *passim*.

*Go*, and *David*. About that time, too, we read *Kangaroo, Sea and Sardinia* and *Tortoises*. . . . I know, too, that Erskine read *England, My England*. Sometime later, perhaps in 1927, we did read *Plumed Serpent*. Yes, we did read some of the short stories." For someone who averred that he read few books, and then only one by each contemporary author (enough, he believed, to form an opinion), this is an interesting revelation, although it seems that many of these books might have been among his review editions in the midtwenties, and their reading, in part, obligatory.[10] Certainly, both Kenneth Burke and Edwin Rolfe also noticed a Lawrentian echo in Caldwell's work, suggesting again some knowledge of that author's writings. However, it was not enough, apparently, to redeem "The Bogus Ones"; and although Caldwell revised the manuscript (as he had done the poems) in the direction of simplicity and economy, he was not sufficiently satisfied with the results ever to lay claim to the novel in any later discussion of his work.

Caldwell's first two published novels, *The Bastard* (1929) and *Poor Fool* (1930), and his prose poem *The Sacrilege of Alan Kent* (1929–31) show more marked evidence of the development of his unique style and concerns, although, like Faulkner before he found his Yoknapatawpha, there are some curious anomalies. All three are tentative and pragmatic experiments in many forms and ideas, sometimes imitative, sometimes original, frequently jarringly inconsistent. Caldwell shows signs of his later skill in his occasional powerful evocation of a sense of place, but often his preferred setting seems to be a surrealist, modern underworld where characters drift and float without any coherent anchors to an environing society. Organized religion and race, topics so central to his southern fiction, are scarcely touched on, and families and communities are utterly fragmented and estranged, rather than caught in the complicated pattern of intimacy, tension, and betrayal that is his familiar theme. There is increasing evidence of Caldwell's grim humor, shocking violence, antic sexual comedy, and incipient class consciousness, but a less clear vision of the qualified naturalism that imbues his later fiction. Though the plots are generated out of random accidents and coincidences, as well as by the determinist logic of history and biology, the mixture has not yet merged completely into its final grotesque form.

10. Helen Caldwell Cushman, as quoted in Owen, "Erskine Caldwell and D. H. Lawrence," 19–20; Richard B. Sale, "An Interview in Florida with Erskine Caldwell," in *Critical Essays*, ed. MacDonald, 289.

*The Bastard*, which, according to Caldwell, was given its title by the publisher rather than the author (*CE*, 75), has generally embarrassed critics into tactful silence. Maurice Coindreau, his French translator, remarks only that "Erskine Caldwell is not yet himself in *The Bastard*," and Joseph Warren Beach admits he is "inclined to soft-pedal these early efforts, hoping that only specialists will come upon them, or only persons already favorably disposed toward the author from the riper products of his genius."[11] Certainly, in a brief novel notable largely for the range of shocking atrocities it catalogs, not the least unsettling quality is the chaotic variety of writing styles that the young author tries out on his readers. The novel begins in the vein of hard-boiled realism, with a narrative display of worldliness and detachment: "No one knew who was Gene's father. . . . Even his mother did not know—she was a hoochie-coochie dancer then doubling in the Forty-Nine, and she didn't keep books" (*B*, 13). In some chapters, Caldwell pursues a formal and chronological account of events, whereas in others he rejects the narrative mode entirely and moves to terse dialogue of the kind that must have induced F. Scott Fitzgerald, later an admirer of Caldwell, to comment, "more crimes committed in Hemingway's name."[12] Indeed, much of the dialogue is an extended exercise in banality:

> "Kitty wasn't nothing but a slut."
> "That's what most women are, aren't they?"
> "Kitty was a dirty slut."
> "All of them are either dirty or clean."
> "I like 'em clean."
> "No, there ain't much difference." (*B*, 61)

However, Caldwell already seems close to recognizing the possibilities for farce in such degraded conversation and to finding that discomfiting tone between comedy and revulsion that such revelations of human idiocy provoke:

> "But that damn Kitty—"
> "I hope she's smoking now."
> "And stinking."

11. Maurice Coindreau, Preface to *Poor Fool*, in *Critical Essays*, ed. MacDonald, 80; Beach, excerpt from *American Fiction, 1920–1940*, in *Critical Essays*, ed. MacDonald, 186.

12. Andrew Turnbull, ed., *The Letters of F. Scott Fitzgerald* (New York, 1963), 223.

"Kitty was dirty."
"They don't get much dirtier than Kitty."
"Flo was a clean kid, though."
"But that God-damn Kitty was dirty."
"That God-damn Kitty—" (*B*, 65)

In general, the tone of controlled ambiguity still eludes him except in fits and starts; instead of incongruity, his range of styles produces something closer to incredulity, as when Gene Morgan, the man who "likes 'em clean" finally finds a clean woman to appeal to him. When they kiss, Caldwell comments, "The drug from her lips produced an opiatic somnolence in his mind and body" (*B*, 68). It is within the bounds of fictional possibility that Gene might indeed be transformed by his love, but not that the author's language should undergo such an inflated metamorphosis. Caldwell would eventually learn to prune the "opiatic somnolences" from his writing and retain the "dirty sluts" by a conscious effort to concentrate and reduce his literary vocabulary to make it more akin to that of his characters.

Several of the stylistic experiments that appear crude and exaggerated in *The Bastard* are retained in modified or altered forms in Caldwell's mature work. Perhaps the most notable and unusual of these is the combination of southern comic folklore with an ambience of urban crime and anomie, a fusion Faulkner was also attempting at that time in *Sanctuary*. As in that novel, the comic violence involves sex and death—more specifically, prostitutes and funerals, human lust and jealousy, and the violation of the formal propriety of a Christian burial. The interment in *The Bastard* ends with a farcical shoot-up and the desecration of a grave, but the whole affair has a comfortable tradition of folk comedy about it. However, it is followed in the next chapter by the eruption of a much more gruesome kind of violence that is not so easily assimilated into an accepted mode of response. A black sawmill worker is beaten, severed by a ripsaw, and his body then subjected to grisly and curious experiments by his white killers, who comment, "Coons get split open around here every once in awhile, but nobody don't say nothing about it" (*B*, 55). This seems already almost a rehearsal for the episodes in *Tobacco Road*, where horseplay becomes horror with only a slight shift in perspective, although its effectiveness in the later novel comes from the control of the transition. In *The Bastard* the two sensibilities are fragmented into separate chapters that are complete units in themselves, without sufficient reference to the rest of the novel.

Another stylistic innovation in *The Bastard*—which in a later novel like *God's Little Acre* would be more fully integrated into the central theme—is the curious combination of sexual and mechanical imagery to suggest not naturalistic comedy but transcendent, mystical experience. The novel's heroine, Myra Morgan, travels through the night in a juggernautlike truck that thrusts and hurls her vibrating body through peaks and troughs of sensation until she is "breathless in her moments of ecstasy" (*B*, 73). The yoking of a piece of machinery with cogs, chains, and gears to the sensual pleasures of the human body is not a surprising conceit for a naturalist, but it is a supernatural, rather than natural, effect that Caldwell emphasizes. He depicts the truck as demonic, its energy superhuman— "the black monster hurling itself into the white night" (*B*, 73)—and suggests that there is a powerful force abroad that drives and transforms those who submit to it. In later novels, this force continues to be both sexual and spiritual in its manifestations; but Caldwell is able to root it more directly in the cotton mills and churches of his South so that the mysterious connections between erotic, mechanistic, and divine energy derive more logically from the immediate cultural context of his characters.

Although some of the uncertainties and inconsistencies in this first novel stem clearly from Caldwell's experimentation in forms (and perhaps from the residual effect of the hundreds of new books he reviewed between 1926 and 1928), it is also apparent that the looseness and confusion in structure and characters are the consequence of a failure to realize fully the theme implicit in many of the book's incidents and images. Caldwell's publisher heralded the theme by calling the novel *"The Bastard"* with suggestions of both rootlessness and determinism, the absence of a known past and yet the power of that past to assert itself. It is presented in forceful episodes interspersed with incidents that are barely relevant to the determinist emphasis but are more random explorations of human viciousness. They provoked the theory from Guy Owen that Caldwell had "set out deliberately to write a sensational novel and let the ideas fall where they would."[13] Yet the first line of *The Bastard*

13. Guy Owen, "The Apprenticeship of Erskine Caldwell: An Examination of *The Bastard* and *Poor Fool*," in *A Fair Day in the Affections: Literary Essays in Honor of Robert B. White, Jr.*, eds. Jack D. Durant and M. Thomas Hester (Raleigh, 1980), 199.

suggests its potentially central and controlling idea—"When Gene Morgan had last heard of the woman who was his mother . . ." (B, 11)—for Gene's consciousness and actions are dominated by the fact that he does not know who his parents are. He knows that his mother's career has been one of prostitution and degradation in the lower depths of modern society; he hears stories from strangers of the atrocities she has performed; he follows her, whoever she may be—"Norfolk Gertie—Denver Sal—Rose of Scranton—Big Butt Bessie" (B, 12)—for half a night in New Orleans; he has spent the night with her in a Philadelphia hotel; but he does not even know her name. Of his father he knows *only* his name, Morgan, which becomes a taunt to Gene every time he encounters it in another person. He finds a job in a town where the richest man is a Morgan; he mates with a black prostitute called Fanny Morgan; he marries a woman called Myra Morgan; and he even sings a song that goes, "My name is Morgan but it ain't J. P." (B, 17). As any whore may be his mother, so any man may be his father, and anyone he meets may be a potential sibling. Such a realization does not provide Gene with a link to the chain of humanity but rather with a profound estrangement from it. After he has seen a photograph of his mother's knife-scarred belly, he kicks two strange women in the stomach; when he finds himself in a jail with a young girl who is, like himself, alone and homeless, he rapes her brutally.

Caldwell implies indirectly that Gene's abandonment and isolation lead him into a series of destructive relationships that begin when he is drawn back to the southern mill town from which he had run away as a child. Whether by accident or some stranger fate, he meets a woman there who elicits a hitherto completely dormant tenderness in him. She is Myra Morgan, whose father has previously commented on Gene's likeness to one of his missing sons. The stage is thus set for a possibly incestuous marriage between Gene and his sister, and its monstrous offspring in their hirsute and feeble child. When Gene observes the toll this baby is taking on his beloved wife, he drowns it in a misguided act of liberation for her, misunderstanding completely the devotion that binds her to the child, for he has witnessed nothing like it in his own existence. The novel opens and closes with a drowning by Gene, initially of a strange man who had known his mother, finally of his own freakish son, the innocent heir of generations of depravity. A considerable degree of naturalism is implicit in this plot, although it is never explicit in any commentary by the author. He does not say that

Gene and Myra are brother and sister, nor that the child's abnormality is a consequence of this. He does, however, suggest yet another naturalistic cause of the child's illness in Gene's syphilis, a pervasive disease in the novel.

Many of the other incidents in *The Bastard* suggest further variations on this bleakly deterministic vision of human nature. Gene has a friend, John Hunter, also a motherless boy raised largely in a brothel by a series of prostitutes. Like Gene, he is capable of great violence and is the perpetrator, with Gene, of the most gruesome act in the novel, the murder and dissection of a black worker at the sawmill. However, the similarities between John and Gene are given scant attention by Caldwell, and the consequence is that the horror of the murder seems more gratuitous than inevitable—a response that Caldwell's work never completely ceased to provoke. The violence of the act is linked, nevertheless, to another kind of determinism that will become a Caldwell trademark—the effect of devastating heat as a catalyst for savagery. At the beginning of the episode, Caldwell sets the physical scene with care: "In the creek bottom the deep convex sky focused the sun-rays like a burning glass. If there happened to be a hole in the shirt the sun blistered the exposed flesh until it was puffed and raw. The air cooked the earth like oven heat. From early morning until late at night it scorched the lungs and parched the throat. Unless the mouth was kept closed the tongue became dry as a bleached bone and the teeth seared the membrane of the mouth like heated pebbles" (B, 51). This assault of nature against the body provokes Gene and John's countersadism against the black victim. Though Gene is so sick and debilitated he can barely crawl to the water bucket, after the murder he finds that his thirst is quenched by the sight of the swelling pool of blood under the black man's body: "The excitement had revived Gene. He was feeling better and his head was clearing" (B, 53). This episode suggests an immediate kind of environmental determinism, just as Gene's marriage and child suggest that he is the product of his woeful family history; but Caldwell also begins in this novel a contrary process of yoking such controlled responses in his characters to reactions in them that are wholly unpredictable and qualify any simple sense of him as a naturalist.

He depicts the bloodletting of Gene and John as an instinctive retaliation against their own heat-induced agony, but there is no comparable outside stimulus for what then takes place—their foolish efforts to give the dead man a drink and their decision to saw his body in two for easier handling. Naturalism would seem to require a degree of logical inevitability that is certainly not met by this absurdity. Similar, though less grisly, instances of human perversity occur elsewhere in the novel, particularly in the characters' sexual attractions and rivalries. Gene Morgan is for some time obsessed by his desire for the voluptuous wife of the watchman at the cottonseed mill, while the watchman is simultaneously conducting an affair with the foreman's wife, whose face "was so ugly it was hideous" (*B*, 25). The vagaries of human sexual conduct are beyond explanation and frequently bizarre; they culminate here in the night watchman's offer to pay Gene to service his wife for him after all Gene's schemes to get her have failed. This is Caldwell's first rehearsal of the juxtaposition of naturalism and farce that later becomes central to his vision of human affairs. The ridiculous element is not quite intrinsic yet to the narrative, and it is interesting that this kind of comedy only occurs in those parts of *The Bastard* that have a distinctly southern setting. The opening, in an anonymous city, and the closing, in Philadelphia, are of unallayed bleakness and brutality. The intrusion of gothic and exaggerated humor in the southern sections of the novel might suggest a serious qualification of any political or melioristic impulses that derive from its determinism; yet Caldwell's sympathies with the poor, women, and blacks are also most apparent when the location of his work is within a highly structured, class- and race-ridden society. The South provided him with a context for both the grotesque and reformist aspects of his vision, but he did not fully realize these possibilities until he had first experimented with the alienated wastelands of urban anonymity.

Although this first novel deals with the lower depths of modern life, there is little emphasis in it on the kind of material deprivation that characterizes many of Caldwell's later books. Its solitary hero is utterly apolitical, but when the novel was banned in Maine, Caldwell issued a defense of it that already shows a keener consciousness of its potential proletarian implications than anything that is made explicit in the work itself. He says that the book was "conceived and written as an important and untouched phase of American *mores*"; and in discussing its characters, he creates hypothetical ones not present in the novel at all, such as a girl who works in a cotton mill for $11.15 per week, gets laid off, and begins to sell her body for what she can no longer earn in the mill. He writes: "I have an intense sympathy for these people. . . . I have slept with them in jails, I have eaten with them in freight cars. I have sung with them in convict camps, I have helped the women give birth to the living. I have helped the men cover up the dead."[14] There is, of course, a whole new imagination at work in this justification of his novel of atrocities that indicates an awareness in Caldwell of a radical political context that would manifest itself more clearly in his later depression novels.

His proclaimed sympathy for his characters is not advertised in any traditional way in the manner of their portrayal in *The Bastard*; they are inarticulate and banal, and the narrative voice, unlike that of the apologia, is usually flat and disengaged. Brutish behavior in his people is not modified by regret or sensitivity, yet Caldwell already shows that they are not wholly brutes either, a necessity if his book is to achieve more than lurid sensationalism. In the last pages of the novel, Caldwell reaches, for a time, the assurance of both style and imagery that are intermittent elsewhere, as he describes the actions of Gene Morgan after the murder of his child—a murder that is virtually the only planned moral act that he has ever attempted. Before he drowns the baby, he feeds him a bottle of milk and then throws the empty bottle toward the river. It falls short and lands unbroken among some vines; the killing itself is not described. Then Gene Morgan, a man without conscience, without intelligence, a man without sensibility, who must now return abruptly to the vagrant's life from which he emerged into his marriage, goes back instead to stare from the darkness at his wife's silhouette in their window; she is waiting for his return with the child. Three times Gene retraces his steps to the lighted window where the mother rocks in her chair while the father circles outside, unable to break away. His attempts to understand and vindicate himself are as crude as his nature: "Hell, I guess I done right. I couldn't gone away and left her and the kid up there. . . . Maybe she can have some kids what'll turn out right. Jesus, it was God-damn funny about him" (*B*, 89). Yet the images of circling and rocking, light and darkness, the man and woman linked by the empty milk bottle shining on the windowsill and the other bottle among the vines, and the dead child that bore the burden of their history, form a powerful conclusion for a flawed and uncertain book. Caldwell displays here an imagist skill that elevates the lives of his characters and illuminates their concerns without intruding into their private consciousness or dissecting the quaint mystery of what they are.

14. Erskine Caldwell, *In Defense of Myself* (Portland, Me., [1929]).

In an interview many years later with his French translator, Maurice Coindreau, Caldwell made an interesting distinction between what he was attempting to achieve in his first two novels. Of *The Bastard* he said: "I was careful never to get away from the real, or at least the possible. More than anything else I wanted realism with verisimilitude." Of his next novel, published one year later in 1930, he said, "*Poor Fool*, on the other hand, belongs to the literature of dreams. It is something like those diabolical dreams that come out of opium. . . . I simply let my imagination run free, without barriers or restraints . . . and I believe that if [my story] has any interest, the reason is the contrast between the madness of the subject and a style that is cold, concise, and perfectly reasonable in its strict objectivity."[15] This is perhaps an exaggerated and after-the-fact distinction between the aims of these two apprentice novels, but it shows a significant acknowledgment by Caldwell of the strength of two conflicting tendencies in his writing: one toward the feasible and recognizable depiction of typical elements of society, and another toward a distorted, fantastical reflection of particular human perversities. This doubleness was the source of much critical debate, especially during the 1930s, about how "accurate" Caldwell's fiction was, despite his own constant reminders that it was a product of his imagination. In *Poor Fool*, there is certainly no possibility of forgetting that it is fiction, for the novel has indeed all the qualities of a "diabolical dream" in the helpless passivity of its protagonist, the wildly contracting and expanding duration of its episodes, and its evocation of the deepest terrors of the unconscious mind.

Despite the phantasmagoric nature of much of the material, the narrative of *Poor Fool* is more tightly controlled and the structure more artfully designed than that of *The Bastard*. Though there is, as Caldwell suggests, an incongruity between the horrifying subject and the detached style, it is a more controlled disparity than the random disorder of the earlier novel. The setting is again an anonymous urban underworld, unrelieved except for excursions into the city's even grimmer suburbia. Only the lowest class of society is depicted in the novel, although that is divided into victims and exploiters in a reflection of the larger social structure. Caldwell repeatedly disclaimed any interest in creating plots, but the aimless

15. Quoted in Coindreau, Preface to *Poor Fool*, in *Critical Essays*, ed. MacDonald, 81.

wanderings of his protagonist, Blondy Niles, in *Poor Fool* have a significant order imposed on them by the division of the novel into three parallel sections, each of which is dominated by a woman who takes Blondy in temporarily from his homelessness, as well as by constantly recurring motifs and images.

More than any other single image, blood unites and pervades all the events in the narrative of *Poor Fool*, from the bloodthirsty cries of crowds at boxing matches to the atrocities that occur at an abortion clinic and the brutal gang murders that frame the novel. The story of Blondy Niles, a down-and-out boxer, is so soaked in the imagery of blood that its evocation becomes a kind of chorus to the action. At the fight between Blondy and Knockout Harris, "the crowd wanted blood. It wanted to see blood spurt out of Blondy's nose. It wanted to see blood on the ropes. It wanted to see blood spatter down on the ringside seats" (*PF*, 67). At Mrs. Boxx's abortion clinic, women die frequently from graphically described blood poisoning, and in the streets, gangsters shoot people down in pools of blood. The horror of this carnage does not exist, however, merely in its naturalistic or sensational detail, but in its relationship to greed and lust, a relationship further developed through linked patterns of imagery. Boxing matches are shown to satisfy both the lust of the crowd and the greed of the promoters; women's bodies make a double profit for their exploiter both in payment for abortions and in the sale of the corpses; gang murders are committed for the protection of already illicit gains. Caldwell never intrudes in this novel, as he was sometimes later to do, to comment on social evils; but he suggests instead, through clusters of images, the ominous nexus that lies behind such gory manifestations. A typical image pattern is associated with the crooked boxing manager, Salty Banks, who is shown early in the novel selecting a raw steak from a waiter and lingering attentively over the bleeding meat, which must conform to his exact specifications. The process of selection is echoed in Salty's careful examination of prostitutes at a roadhouse, one of whom is later left, like the steak, covered in her own congealed blood. Salty's villainy in the novel is on a much grander scale than these minor encounters with fresh blood, but because it is conveyed in Caldwell's "cold" and "reasonable" manner, the force of this imagist technique in establishing his villain's vicious character is doubly effective.

A similar use of powerful, though indirect, imagist characterization occurs in the novel's female villain, Mrs. Boxx. This former brothel madam, who now deals in abortions and dead bodies, delights in the literal castration of weak men whom she mysteriously enthralls. She is a nightmare vision of female monstrosity, yet the most remarkable hints of her soft and sinister rapaciousness are oblique and imagistic. She sits at breakfast, "eating a soft boiled egg from a coffee cup. She dipped the egg with a spoon and put it between her lips where her tongue rolled it down her throat. Then she swallowed. Her other hand was curled around a plate of toast. The faded green kimono she wore fitted her loosely. It fell open at her throat and the edges were crossed at her waist. Each time she bent over her soft boiled egg her heavy sagging breasts swung away from her chest and hit against the edge of the table rattling the loose lid of the coffee pot" (*PF*, 79–80). This fat, green creature, curling, rolling, and swallowing, suggests the sliminess of slugs and soft eggs, but it also displays the ominousness of those rattling breasts that promise destructive power. Mrs. Boxx's husband, a castrated rapist, has his own impressionist grouping of images, which play with the allusions of the family name: he does tricks with matchboxes and was formerly an assistant to Houdini, presumably to aid him in getting out of boxes. Because the novel's protagonist is a boxer, Caldwell has a broad field for play with the sexual, combative, and entrapping associations of the word *box*, and the play is not merely frivolous. It serves to connect the two worlds of the novel— the brothel turned abortion clinic and the boxing ring—and to suggest, without being didactic, the difficulties of escape from the forces that govern them.

There is also a good deal of whimsical and incongruous imagery in the novel that accompanies the more explicit and naturalistic depiction of horror, though critics have tended to dismiss the playfulness and then to argue, somewhat perversely, that its central emphasis is too unrelieved. Maurice Coindreau, in the preface of his 1945 translation of *Poor Fool*, described the novel as "a chromo illustration of the Oedipus complex and of the castration complex . . . ; one could not study it completely except by using Freudian methods. Psychiatrists will be grateful to Erskine Caldwell for having offered them a naturally savory dish that, for good measure, he has seasoned with a pinch of sadism and necrophilia." Another French reviewer, Jean Vagne, followed Coindreau's line, calling the novel "this nightmare which is closer to psychoanalysis than to literature." An interviewer of Caldwell from *Figaro Littéraire* attempted to link the novel's necrophilia to that of Poe, eliciting from Caldwell the standard response "I never read. In any case, not Poe!" The fascination of French critics with the abnormal in this novel has been countered by a more proletarian emphasis at home: James Korges found the fixed fights in the novel to be metaphors for competition within a free enterprise system, and Guy Owen has argued that Blondy Niles represents the American worker, victimized by forces beyond his control, and that the abortion clinic is a symbol of American capitalism.[16] These explanations are all much more definitive than the novel, which is allusive rather than allegorical in any clearly Freudian or Marxist mode. Psychiatrists might indeed find a rich vein of material in this second motherless, homeless Caldwell hero, defeated as a boxer, passively awaiting the terror of castration by Mrs. Boxx, who exerts a mysterious power over him. Yet what Coindreau calls the additional seasoning of necrophilia is, in fact, a bawdy comic fantasy invented by the deranged Mr. Boxx, who imagines an underworld peopled with hosts of lusty dead who dance, court, and visit each other's coffins, all clad in the strange backless garments in which they were buried. The carefree antics of the dead make for a telling contrast with the sexual ordeals of the living, pointed by the intrusion of Mrs. Boxx with a dying abortion patient into her husband's imaginings. The disruption of the absurd comedy of one by the preposterous cruelty of the other may be a rather heavy moral irony in this episode, but is surely, despite Vagne, closer to literature than psychoanalysis.

A proletarian reading of *Poor Fool* has some evidence to support it, especially as one of the "bottom dog" genre of novels, whose aimless and impotent wanderers are, like Blondy Niles, always "waiting for something to happen" (*PF*, 74). Blondy's passivity is practically his most salient characteristic, rivaled only by an attribute that seems, with constant repetition, to become an actual quality of its possessor—rootlessness. Blondy, a man without a home, is constantly being taken in by women for brief periods of shelter before being rejected again. That he loves some of these women, and that they return this love, is not enough to rescue him from destruction in a world dominated by gangs and organizations, where individuals are easy prey, no matter what their talents or personal attachments. Kroot, a former circus weight lifter, now a café and brothel proprietor, tells Blondy: "You ain't got a chance by yourself. Why don't

16. *Ibid.*, 81–82; Smith and Miner, *Transatlantic Migration*, 152, 155; James Korges, *Erskine Caldwell* (Minneapolis, 1969), 13; Owen, "The Apprenticeship of Erskine Caldwell," 201.

you get a gang together. You can't do nothing alone these days. You got to have a bunch to get anywhere" (*PF*, 149), which is as close as Caldwell comes in this novel to a wry, collectivist homily.

Besides gangs, the main controlling force in the novel lies with pimps, procurers, and promoters who profit doubly from their client-victims, as Salty Banks does in his fixed fights, Kroot in his brothel, and Mrs. Boxx in her clinic. The only time Blondy Niles turns to the official organs of society for help, by reporting a murder to the police, he is arrested and accused of that murder. Thus his final decision to pursue revenge outside the law is, like Gene Morgan's murder of his son in *The Bastard*, a desperate act of perverted idealism by a man who has passively witnessed and abetted atrocities, but who could scarcely be said to have a conscience, or even much consciousness of any kind. His effort at justice ends naturally in bloody failure and with the contemptuous label "poor fool" for a man who could neither understand nor control his fate. It is hardly an auspicious omen for the American worker whom Blondy may represent, although the seeds of an alternative awareness are sown in Kroot's lecture on the power of the group rather than the individual. However, only the barest of hints is given, buried in a vision of people dominated by carnal and bloody instincts, and haunted by nightmare terrors and madness.

This vision is asserted in *Poor Fool* much more effectively than in *The Bastard* by Caldwell's superior handling of imagery to suggest patterns, connections, and parallels between episodes and environments. Although this second novel is longer, it is also more economical than the first. Little is wasted or gratuitous in the narrative, and the simplicity of the style serves to increase the impact of the vivid perceptions. In fact, Caldwell appears to be experimenting with the contrast between narrative banality and powerful imagism, a technique that might seem more appropriate to the short story or even to poetry than to the sustained expository form of the novel; but here Caldwell demonstrates its effective use in the longer form.

The most forceful demonstration of Caldwell's interest in the possibilities of imagism at this stage in his writing comes in his next work, *The Sacrilege of Alan Kent* (1929–31), a piece that most critics have agreed to label a "prose poem" for want of a better category. In fact, it consists entirely of brief prose episodes, from a single sentence to a paragraph in length, separated on the page by roman numerals, so that the effect is of terse chapters in an enigmatic but continuous narrative. These episodes are arranged into three larger parts that were first published separately, but were eventually brought together in a complete book. The first part, "Tracing Life with a Finger," was published in *New American Caravan* (1929); the second, "Inspiration for Greatness," appeared in *Pagany* (1930); and the third, "Hours Before Eternity," was published together with the first two under the title "In the Native Land" in Caldwell's *American Earth* collection of short stories in 1931. In 1936, the three sections were published as a separate book for the first time; in 1976, the work was reissued by Maeght publishers in Paris in an opulent limited edition of one hundred copies each in English and French. It was illustrated by Alexander Calder after a previous arrangement with Picasso had been ended by the artist's death.[17] At $1,500 a copy, it sold out immediately—a sign perhaps of its significance as an art curio rather than a neglected literary masterpiece. Yet in many ways, this strange book deserves a larger audience, revealing as it does how far from conventional and naturalist fiction Caldwell's experiments with technique could take him.

Critics and reviewers who paid attention to *The Sacrilege of Alan Kent* generally found it both engaging in its originality and irritating in its affectation and preciosity—terms otherwise rare in the Caldwell critical canon. Malcolm Cowley found himself moved "to personal fury against the author" by the awfulness of the bad parts, although he found in the "violent poetry" of the rest "a mood unique in American prose." Kenneth Burke found parts of it to be "purest poetry," Gerald Sykes called it "the poetry of unfeeling," Guy Owen "a prose poem," and Cowley again, on reexamination, felt that it corresponded "on a lesser scale to Whitman's 'Song of Myself.'"[18] Because there is no effort at meter, rhythm, or rhyme in these episodes of Caldwell's, and because their topics and sentiments are rarely elevated, the consistency of the critics' response to poetic elements seems to derive largely from an appreciation of Caldwell's imagism and from his remarkable skill here in concentrating lan-

17. Elizabeth Pell Broadwell and Ronald Wesley Hoag, "The Art of Fiction LXII: Erskine Caldwell," *Paris Review*, LXXXVI (1982), 144–45.

18. Cowley and Whipple, "Two Judgments," 6; Kenneth Burke, "Caldwell: Maker of Grotesques," in *Critical Essays*, ed. MacDonald, 167; Gerald Sykes, "The Poetry of Unfeeling," in *Critical Essays*, ed. MacDonald, 7; Guy Owen, "*The Sacrilege of Alan Kent* and the Apprenticeship of Erskine Caldwell," *Southern Literary Journal*, XII (1979), 37; Cowley, "Georgia Boy," 320.

guage into intense statements without sacrificing accessibility or meaning. Caldwell has frequently acknowledged the challenge of condensing and controlling material as a reason for his preference for short story writing, but its benefits are apparent later in his novels and nonfiction writing as well. It is a method that focuses only on certain essentials of experience and response, and is willing to sacrifice both plot and characterization to the creation of motifs and effects.

As in *The Bastard* and *Poor Fool*, the meaning of the casually episodic narrative of *Alan Kent* accumulates from patterns of images, of whose significance the protagonists of all three works and their ingenuous creator seem unaware. Alan Kent shows some advance in consciousness over Gene Morgan and Blondy Niles if only because he is the narrator of his story and must advance beyond them in articulateness. However, despite his capacity to give more colorful voice to his experiences, and even his final recognition of an essential loneliness common to human nature, he is scarcely less naïve than the earlier heroes, a characteristic that begins to appear vital to Caldwell's method. Alan Kent's narrative takes him from birth through childhood, adolescence, and into early maturity. It incorporates many incidents from Caldwell's own life, emphasizing the young man's response to the physical and moral universe he is becoming acquainted with, suggesting the genesis of perceptions and ideas, even containing the embryonic plots and insights of much of his later work. In this sense, it comes much closer to an intellectual or artistic autobiography than the more explicit accounts of his career given in the later *Call It Experience* and *With All My Might*. Although those latter books are prosaic not merely in form but in their conception of a writer's career, *The Sacrilege of Alan Kent* is their gnomic and imaginative counterpart, concerned with emotions, attitudes, and expression rather than the more mundane business of editors, publishers, and profits. Alan Kent is a kind of alter ego for Erskine Caldwell, generated from his own actual experiences and from the incipient consciousness of their meaning and his need to translate it. Thus, like Caldwell, Kent is born in the South; he is a clergyman's son whose childhood is punctuated by the family's constant moves into a variety of different communities. Later, Kent leaves his family to become a wanderer and casual laborer, tries to board a tramp steamer, is arrested and jailed for no obvious cause, and witnesses a "blue Monday" suicide, as Caldwell had done as a reporter for the Atlanta *Journal*. The discoveries that Kent makes during these formative years are both the universal kind that come with every boy's initiation into manhood, and of a much more particular and individual variety that bear witness to the formation of a uniquely imaginative way of perceiving experience.

The common discoveries involve the child's gradually widening awareness of the physical sphere of his life, from bedroom, kitchen, barn, and orchard to railroad track and highway, village store, ball park, and city street. Within that sphere, the child makes a slow, painful, eagerly desired, never-quite-final separation from his parents. He goes to school and is instructed in the schoolyard—"Play games. Don't look through the fence at the girls" (*SAK*, 15)—and thus perversely discovers the route out of childhood. He lingers on the border between the two worlds of innocence and experience, typified in his play with a neighbor's children: "In the morning and in the afternoon I played ball in the courtyard with his two little boys, and in the evening after supper I played in the basement of the new building on the corner with his little girl. We played there alone until dark each night" (*SAK*, 16–17). Thus begins the movement from a daylight world of childhood to a night world, not of maturity, but of experimenting with and observing adult behavior: "We sat up all night drinking two bottles of Coca-Cola and smoking three cigarettes between us" (*SAK*, 18). The adolescent Kent eavesdrops on conversations among white men about black women, spies on people making love, and even watches his classmates while they in turn watch through binoculars trained on the windows of a girls' dormitory. He discovers ideal beauty and lust, injustice, suffering, and poverty, and most acutely, his own isolation in the universe. To this extent, *Alan Kent* shares the theme of a classic *Bildungsroman*.

The hero, however, also experiences a world that is far less typical, one that is permeated from his birth with excesses of violence so extravagant that they finally evoke a surreal vision of a fiendish universe pursuing repeated and malevolent schemes against its inhabitants. The frequency of the violent episodes and their linking by Caldwell's imagist method in fact suggest a grim comic conspiracy of nature against human nature, as in this series of separate but clearly connected accidents that beset the boy narrator: "I chucked a rotten peach into one of the wooden boxes and a bee shot from the hive plumb to my eye. . . . I was barefooted and I stepped on a rotting peach. A bee stung the ball of my foot. It was three miles to the baseball game and I ran down the railway on one foot and the heel of the other. . . . A foul ball shot on a bee-line to my eye" (*SAK*, 8, 9). These accidents are accompanied by "unbearable torment" (*SAK*, 8); the boy is "lame and blind and hurt" (*SAK*, 9), but the playfulness of the language, the punning and permutations of peaches, bees, and eyes evoke detached bemusement rather than great emotion. They shift the emphasis away from the sufferer to the cruel jokes of existence. Besides this impersonal violence, however, Alan Kent observes everywhere men's own taste for torture and destruction and readily participates in it himself: while working in a carnival, he helps to carry a crazy fortune-teller into her tent and to slit her throat. Kent also interprets all manner of physical experiences as harsh assaults on him; in winter the cold is so severe that his fingers freeze around iron bars and have to be bitten away with his teeth; in summer the heat of the sun "scorched my eyes when I wanted to see and . . . seared my tongue when I tried to speak" (*SAK*, 32); away from nature, the sound of streetcars rumbling and crashing attacks his ears, while cigar factories offend his nose with their "vomiting odor[s]" (*SAK*, 12).

The result of this continual mortification of the body, this constant evidence of man's frailty and mortality, and the antagonistic force of the environment might logically be expected to be some qualifying vision of a metaphysical reality underlying the seemingly cruel design of the physical world. Alan Kent hints at it when he says, "Without the painful hunger my body had always known, my soul would have died from lack of food" (*SAK*, 43), but in fact Caldwell does not provide any apparent sustenance for the spirit in the form of supernatural consolation. Though the book is filled with the momentary contemplation of mysteries, the insights they offer reveal only the absence of any divinity and the absolute dominance of the physical world: "One day I was walking through the swamp and I found the skeleton of a man leaning against a tree. When I tapped the skull with a stick, some lizards came out and forked their scarlet tongues at me and ran back inside. When I tapped the ribs, a chipmunk heard the vibrations and began to sing overhead" (*SAK*, 29–30). When a workman in a quarry is blown to pieces, one of the other workers asks Kent's clergyman-father, "Is it true the world is sure enough round?" (*SAK*, 14). His mind is provoked by the disaster to seek some understanding of natural order, but meanwhile his workmate's pieces are buried in a lard pail. Despite humanity's enquiring mind, Caldwell emphasizes always that its fate is in its flesh and is identical to that of the animals: "I reached for and grasped in my hands the large white bowl of smoking-hot sausage grease. The grease flowed down my open collar and ate into my navel. . . . Only after seven months of pain could I sit upright in bed without screaming with agony" (*SAK*, 8). And, "My dog ran from window to window pawing the glass while the flames ate bare his skin. . . . My dog cried all that night and the next and the next" (*SAK*, 11). Kenneth Burke has called this quality of contemplating pain and suffering and then going on "to blaspheme and profane for our enjoyment" a "balked religiosity" in Caldwell.[19] Burke notes it in his later novels, but the underlying philosophical basis for such irreverence is clearly embodied in *Alan Kent*; life itself is a desecration of any ideal of holiness or dignity. The sacrilege is not Alan Kent's or even the author's but a condition of existence.

That there can be anything such as "food for the soul" of people living in this defiled condition seems surprising, yet Alan Kent proves capable of searching for and conceiving ideals that are generated out of the body's suffering. By contrast, in later novels Caldwell is more direct about the need to allay that suffering, and he will certainly never again suggest that lack of food could lead to the enrichment of the spirit rather than to its greater depravity. The few revolts against injustice in this book are personal and instinctual: "A man walked into a restaurant through the front door and ate all he wanted to eat" (*SAK*, 33). Elsewhere, Kent and a black co-worker unite to kill their sadistic employer, but these incidents hardly suggest any context for political action or social change. This point was made with a sledgehammer by Norman Macleod in a 1931 *New Masses* review of *American Earth* entitled "A Hardboiled Idealist." Macleod argued of Caldwell: "His workers are as unaware of Russia as any South Sea Islander and are as isolated from the world as god. And for that matter so is Caldwell." Yet Macleod noted that Caldwell had indeed had much personal experience of poor and lower class people, and concluded his review with the comment "We need writers like Caldwell. He should go left."[20] There may well be the germ of a proletarian writer in the author of *Alan Kent*; certainly, his defense of *Poor Fool* seems to show that his sympathies lay in that direction already. However, this experimental book is clearly not Caldwell's chosen vehicle for exploring the economic or political basis of society, but rather for creating vivid glimpses into a realm of experience that is both more personal and more universal than it is social.

The dreams and ideals that Alan Kent generates out of his bitter

19. Burke, "Caldwell: Maker of Grotesques," 168, 167.
20. Norman Macleod, "A Hardboiled Idealist," in *Critical Essays*, ed. MacDonald, 7.

worldly experience focus on a beautiful and elusive young woman named Florence, scented like flowers. He evokes and pursues her, seeing in her a force for life and fertility comparable in power to the destructive suffering that permeates existence. Because of the book's emphasis on the interaction between Kent and this idealized woman, as well as its concern with desire and memory, death and creation, and Kent's fascination with observing and spying on others, it has been suggested that Florence is in fact Alan Kent's muse, and that the three section titles of the book, "Tracing Life with a Finger," "Inspiration for Greatness," and "Hours Before Eternity," finally make sense as references to the stages of the career of an artist. This is a very attractive speculation, although there is no hint in the text that Kent will transmute his legacy of beauty from the elusive woman into any form that will be available to others. He shows no inclination toward art and is indeed positively opposed to the life of the mind: "I could have been a giant but thoughts made me weak" (*SAK*, 47). Still, there is a strong temptation to translate the fictional Kent into the factual Caldwell: Guy Owen even suggests that the reason Caldwell never returned to this mode of writing again was that perhaps "he felt that he had revealed too much of himself in it."[21] Certainly, this book is as close as Caldwell ever comes in his writing to dealing with aesthetic questions such as the nature of inspiration or the process by which experience takes form and order in the memory.

Although *The Sacrilege of Alan Kent* is distinctly different from the direction that Caldwell's later fiction would take, it is also a rehearsal in experimental form of many of the motifs and methods that recur in that work, though in less fragmentary and self-conscious dissociation from conventional narrative development. Owen notes the use of repetition and exaggeration, of mythology and folklore, of the interest in sexual initiation, mulatto women, lynching, hunger, cruel landlords, and ominous albinos as hints of what is to come; but of most importance, the book anticipates the symbolic and oblique aspects of later novels that are frequently read as simpler realist or naturalist documents. Though Caldwell did not continue to write in the vein of *Alan Kent*, it is also not a direction that he wholly rejected, despite the misgiving of some reviewers that it seemed "not to be the writer's forte," and Caldwell's own later opinion that it "served its purpose at the time, but it was not traditional enough.

21. Owen, "*The Sacrilege of Alan Kent*," 43, 44.

It was not in the great tradition of fiction."[22] Rather, *The Sacrilege of Alan Kent* is a refinement and concentration of ideas and style that later will be expanded in more traditional contexts, and it is also a testament to place beside *Call It Experience* and *With All My Might* to enrich the somewhat limited sensibility revealed in those autobiographies of the origins of Caldwell's creative life.

With the completion and publication of the last two sections of *The Sacrilege of Alan Kent*, Caldwell may be said to have completed the deliberate course of his apprenticeship. In June of 1930, Maxwell Perkins accepted two of his short stories for publication in *Scribner's Magazine*, and Caldwell tasted for the first time the financial rewards of success, as well as the sense of a larger and more popular audience than had belonged to such magazines as *blues*, *Pagany*, and *transition*, and such publishing houses as Heron and Rariora. It was then that he lit the symbolic bonfire of his earlier and unsuccessful efforts: "There were nearly three suitcases full of manuscripts of unpublished work, but after a night of sampling of it, I was so dissatisfied with my past work that the next morning I carried everything down to the shores of the lake and burned it" (*CE*, 87). His later reference to his 1931 collection of short stories, *American Earth*, as his first book ("I am glad *American Earth* is the first book I wrote, and I feel that it is fortunate that it was a book of short stories"), together with his obvious willingness to date his career from that point, suggests that in the short story format and in Scribner's audience he believed he had found the mainstream of his power as a writer.[23] He would never again do something so unrelievedly cruel as *The Bastard*, so wildly fantastic as *Poor Fool*, or so wholly imagistic as *The Sacrilege of Alan Kent*. Yet his later works would by no means represent a moderation of the extreme states of consciousness manifest in these early books. Rather, they would provide increasingly familiar contexts for them, no longer the criminal underworld or the alien surroundings of rootless wanderers, but recognizable social, economic, and geographic communities, particularly those of Caldwell's native South. The uneven hints of philosophic naturalism would sharpen in these settings as well as in the literary and political context of the Great Depression, and the incongruous yoking of humor and horror would seem a deliberate,

22. *Ibid.*, 45; Cowley and Whipple, "Two Judgments," 4; Broadwell and Hoag, "The Art of Fiction LXII," 144.

23. Caldwell, Introduction to *American Earth*, in *Critical Essays*, ed. MacDonald, 221.

rather than a casual, choice in this more mundane environment. Caldwell would continue to test his powers of concentration and condensation, especially in his stories; he would work to perfect a colloquial voice by dispensing with the artifices of dialect; and he would pursue the intense imagism of the wholly poetic *Alan Kent* into the wholly prosaic forms of the novel and the short story. He would venture into new forms as well, in both autobiographical and documentary writing, and revive strains of folklore and comedy from the past that were popular and vulgar in the most literal sense. Perhaps only Caldwell could have considered such a curious blend finally "traditional enough" to signal the end of his apprenticeship. However, in 1930 a check from Maxwell Perkins at Scribner's for $350 was an effective admission ticket for Caldwell to the great tradition and a strong inducement to continue writing, for some time at least, in the vein of this first major success, the short story.

# 2

# The Short Stories

*Short story writing is the essence of writing.*
*—Erskine Caldwell*

*Let us pray, however, that he may be delivered from the highbrows.*
*—T. K. Whipple*

When Maxwell Perkins accepted the first two of Caldwell's stories for *Scribner's* in 1930, the young author, ever intrigued by the statistical side of his profession, set himself a new goal of writing and publishing one hundred short stories. Each story went first to Perkins, then if rejected, to a series of little magazines. Caldwell then decided "when a story was declined by any six magazines, to destroy it and abandon the idea on which it had been based. I never regretted that I followed this plan" (*CE*, 87). With the pragmatism and detachment of a Ben Franklin, Caldwell defined the goals of his career and went about their methodical pursuit; but like Franklin, Caldwell could apparently compromise on principle too. When his short story "Country Full of Swedes" won the *Yale Review* Prize in 1933, Caldwell admitted that it had previously been turned down by "a dozen or more magazine editors," including one who sent a note saying, "This old nag will never reach the post" (*CE*, 149). Clearly, Caldwell could and did apply other standards than editorial rejections and the imprimatur of Perkins on his work in determining its quality. Indeed, the influence of these other standards—derived, according to T. K. Whipple of the *New Republic*, from little experimental and avant-garde magazines, where so much of Caldwell's early work was published—was the subject of an unusual debate in the book review columns of that journal in 1931. It was a debate in many ways symptomatic of the future critical enigma that Caldwell's work would present to his readers.

In the June 17, 1931, issue of the *New Republic*, Whipple and Malcolm Cowley published dissenting opinions of Caldwell's first book of short stories, *American Earth* (1931), a collection of works almost entirely previously published in little magazines. This auspicious disagreement focused primarily on the nature of the new author's talent and the best ways to foster it. To Whipple, Caldwell was an authentic primitive, a common man with a forceful ability to relate simple anecdotes, who could only be tainted by contact with the esoteric little magazines in which he had published most of the stories—*blues, Pagany, transition, Hound and Horn, This Quarter*, and the like. For Whipple, Caldwell's success derived from the immediacy of his stories, their unsophisticated quality, and their sense of lived experience among the people. His occasional preciosity, however, Whipple attributed partly to the influence of Sherwood Anderson and, more provocatively, to Caldwell's deference to those "occult magazines" that printed his work. These journals, "priding themselves on making no compromise with common humanity, these purveyors of caviar, are insidious poison for Mr. Caldwell," Whipple wrote, concluding his review with the prayer that the remarkable young author might yet "be delivered from the highbrows." Whipple's offended populism might well have stemmed from many of the public policies and pronouncements of these magazines, and not least from a manifesto that appeared in *transition*, the Parisian-based journal, in the same issue that published Caldwell's first story. This proclamation advertised a revolution in the English language; a movement away from communication to expression; the right of the artist to "disintegrate the primal matter of words"; and concluded, "The plain reader be damned." Whipple's desire to protect Caldwell's naïve work from the "orchidlike" influence of the little magazines and, perhaps more broadly, from any literary influence at all drew an immediate rebuttal from Malcolm Cowley, then the *New Republic*'s book editor. Cowley defended the magazines for their role, throughout the previous decade, in uncovering new talent and encouraging experiment. Caldwell, he said, was the literary child of "eight foster-parents: 'The American Caravan,' Blues, Front, The Hound and Horn, Nativity, Pagany, This Quarter and Transition," who had aided him in the development of an original style, despite the "affectation, mannerism and unintelligibility" that might be an inevitable stage in that process. Many years later, Cowley, always an astute and sympathetic critic of Caldwell, returned to look at this same question of literary influence, now seen from the other end of Caldwell's career, and concluded that he had suffered from too little of it rather than too much.[1] This

1. Cowley and Whipple, "Two Judgments," 4; Kay Boyle *et al.*, as quoted in

was Cowley's reaction to Caldwell's career by the late 1930s, when his fame was widespread and his stories were appearing in *Esquire, Vanity Fair, Redbook, Harper's Bazaar,* and the *New Yorker,* hardly magazines likely to revolutionize the language or denounce the plain reader.

Although Whipple and Cowley differed over the advantages, for an original and largely untutored stylist like Caldwell, of an association with the literary avant-garde, they agreed on the considerable impact the little magazines had had on his early work. Caldwell, by contrast, scarcely conceded a hint that he was even aware of these experiments by his contemporaries and implied merely that he regarded these magazines as a workshop where he might school himself in the mechanics of getting into print. However, the evidence of Caldwell's correspondence with at least one of the magazines confirms the validity of the issue at dispute between Whipple and Cowley, even if it does not completely resolve the question of the precise effect on Caldwell of his association with the experimenters. During the three years of its existence, from 1929 until 1932, the magazine *Pagany* was one of the most enthusiastic recipients of Caldwell's short stories and of his energetic comments on the work of other writers it was publishing. Caldwell's work appeared in nine of *Pagany's* twelve issues, and during this time Caldwell corresponded with its editor, Richard Johns, not only on the status of his own work, but on his ideas about modern American writing and his detailed responses to *Pagany's* other selections. When he first approached Johns in 1929 with a short story manuscript and *In Defense of Myself,* the leaflet explaining the genesis of *The Bastard,* he wrote bluntly, "You don't know me and neither does anybody else. I've been working for seven or eight years unsuccessfully." Yet when the magazine came to an end three years later, Caldwell had achieved fame, or notoriety, as the author of *Tobacco Road,* and other editors of successive little magazines, such as William Carlos Williams at *Contact,* were writing to Richard Johns in the hope of getting some of Caldwell's work. He had also found favor in the eyes of Ezra Pound, who wrote approvingly to Johns from Rapallo, "This chap Caldwell seems to be a good egg. You seem to know that already," and, echoing the debate between Whipple and Cowley, added, "Wdnt. it be better for people like Caldwell . . . to be able

Dougald McMillan, *"transition": The History of a Literary Era, 1927–1938* (New York, 1976), illustration facing page 48; Cowley and Whipple, "Two Judgments," 5; Cowley, "Georgia Boy," 324.

to afford to stay in a li'erary mag. instead of its being one's human duty to bid 'em god speed for the gate receipts?"[2] Pound, like Cowley, assumed the positive influence of the little magazines for their disrespectfulness toward the values of the literary establishment and their emphasis on originality.

These magazines as a whole encouraged eclecticism and experiment, while individually they promoted exclusive and often antithetical theories of literature; yet Caldwell, like other young writers, appeared ubiquitously in them, often publishing simultaneously in journals of conflicting political ideologies and artistic styles. In 1930 he published stories at the same time in *Hound and Horn*, a magazine that eschewed at that time any involvement with political and social issues, and in *Nativity*, which defined its purpose as "commenting upon America's political and social decline." His first publisher, *transition*, was, under the editorship of Eugene Jolas, an internationally oriented magazine that promoted linguistic innovation and the exploration of the intuitive and irrational aspects of consciousness; it made no compromises with clarity, grammar, syntax, and meaning. *Pagany*, nativist in emphasis, was concerned with articulateness in expression; *blues* advocated radical form; *Front*, radical politics. *Clay* asked humbly, "If the commercial magazines turn your stories down, give them away to *Clay*," but Caldwell broke with its editor because he felt "he wants only a certain kind of writing. Tragedy and tears, for God's sake!"[3] Given the variety of literary creeds and the ease with which many of the little magazines exchanged manuscripts with each other and bequeathed authors as the journals themselves folded, it is questionable how much even the most impressionable young author might be tutored by their advice or proclamations. Caldwell certainly displayed a good deal of self-assurance about the development of his work. However, there is plenty of evidence from Caldwell's correspondence with *Pagany* that he was in fact deeply impressed by the company he kept in its pages—not indeed by editorial pronouncements, and never by poetry and critical writings, which he appears not to have read at all—but constantly and in detail by every new effort in fiction.

2. Quoted in Stephen Halpert, ed., with Richard Johns, *A Return to "Pagany": The History, Correspondence, and Selections from a Little Magazine, 1929–1932* (Boston, 1969), 30, 327–28.

3. See Frederick J. Hoffman, Charles Allen, and Carolyn F. Ulrich, *The Little Magazine: A History and Bibliography* (2nd ed. 1947; rpr. New York, 1967), 285, 206–10, 297, 299; Erskine Caldwell, as quoted in Halpert, *A Return to "Pagany,"* 420.

On the appearance of the first issue of *Pagany*, Caldwell wrote to its editor Johns, offering his theories about what a magazine such as this should try to accomplish: it should not speak for any particular special interest group and should avoid the lure of inferior work by writers with big names. He noted approvingly the clarity of the work in *Pagany*, although he admitted that experimental writing occasionally necessitated unintelligible material, "in a shell like a green walnut"; however, he had little sympathy for deliberate obscurity: "Any man who consciously covers up his work in difficult technicalities is robbing himself and his readers." This preference for simplicity in style was further refined by his response to the first chapter of William Carlos Williams' *White Mule*, which appeared in the third issue of *Pagany*. This graphic biological description of the first few hours in a baby girl's life was pronounced disgusting and tasteless by one reviewer, but Caldwell wrote bluntly to Johns with the comment, "Williams gives me an inelegant puke with his White Mule but he's got *something* (God knows I don't know what it is) that nobody else has ever had." As he read succeeding chapters, his admiration for Williams became unqualified: "White Mule gets better and better. It is apparent to me that the book will be a monumental thing, and the book should place Williams at the head of writers, where he belongs. There is no one else doing what he does." Caldwell's affinity for Williams was reciprocated when Williams and Nathanael West sought out contributions from Caldwell for their revival of *Contact* in 1932, with a plan to emphasize "American super-realism" and to "attempt to cut a trail through the American jungle without the use of a European compass."[4]

Caldwell shared Williams' nativist tendencies, admiring Robert McAlmon but wishing "he would stick to U.S.A." He judged stories frequently by what he called their vitality, rather than by style or subject; he measured and compared writers' stories with each other as well as with their own previous work and with what was being published in other journals such as the *Bookman, New Masses,* and *This Quarter*. He showed an early and significant enthusiasm for the writings of Joe Gould, a near-legendary literary figure who lived as a tramp in New York while working on his "Oral History." The only time Caldwell digressed in his letters from his interest in fiction was to advocate the publication of Gould's anecdotal, highly personal documentary writing. Already, clearly, this non-

---

4. Quoted in Halpert, *A Return to "Pagany,"* 89, 126, 150, 265; quoted in Hugh Ford, *Published in Paris: American and British Writers, Printers, and Publishers in Paris, 1920–1939* (New York, 1975), 89.

fiction mode offered Caldwell an appealing direction to take out-side the traditional forms of fiction. He disliked a parody of Hem-ingway by Albert Halper because it gave him nothing but "a little boyish entertainment": he rejected a story by Eugene Armfield as "pitiful . . . because it missed being good," evidence of a continuing tendency in Caldwell to see stories as effects that either came off or failed.[5] Later he would refer to them as either "humdingers" or "god-awful" (*J*, 125).

It is obviously difficult to proffer any direct consequences in Caldwell's own work stemming from his lively participation in the little magazines, especially because he tended to talk in his corre-spondence about what other writers were doing rather than about his own work in progress, which was considerable during the three years of his *Pagany* connection. He had completed the last two sec-tions of *Alan Kent*, written many short stories, and retired into his isolated room in New York to finish *Tobacco Road*, about which he wrote in a rare comment to Richard Johns, "It's not sensational, experimental, nor important; it is just human."[6] However, this com-ment certainly does not suggest that Caldwell's association with the little magazines was likely to lead him into the decadent, precious, and esoteric realms of avant-gardism that T. K. Whipple had so feared in his *New Republic* commentary. He was neither so mal-leable as Whipple anticipated, nor were the authors he admired and scrutinized most closely so far from Whipple's ingenuous and populist ideal. Many, like Albert Halper, Edward Dahlberg, and Edwin Seaver, were already committed proletarians or were mov-ing steadily leftward in their sympathies; others, like Janet Lewis, William Chapman, and especially William Carlos Williams, were writing in the simple and vital idiom that evoked Caldwell's greatest praise. In addition, Caldwell was reading widely in the works of all of his contemporaries in the little magazines. Some of it was perhaps pragmatic reading to discover the bent of the magazine's editor be-fore submitting his own work, but a good deal was clearly for the pleasure and stimulation it brought him. He scrutinized *Pagany* zealously, as did so many of its contributors, all seeming to share the sense that they were aiding in the creation of an authentic new literature. For an author like Caldwell, who continually protested that he was a writer rather than a reader, who affirmed that he

5. Quoted in Halpert, *A Return to "Pagany,"* 264, 265, 264.
6. *Ibid.*, 221.

would try only one book by the major writers of his time, the little magazines—which were at a high point of their energy and variety in the 1920s and 1930s—were a powerful link to that literary community on whose periphery he later preferred to dwell and from which he became eventually almost completely estranged. In thinking so critically about the questions of style and ideology they raised, Caldwell could not fail to consider the place of his own work in a context for once wholly detached from concerns with popularity or "gate receipts."

A subsidiary result of Caldwell's increasing ease in placing his work in magazines and periodicals was his continuing interest, throughout the 1930s, in the short story, the genre of fiction most obviously encouraged by those organs. Besides setting himself the early and arbitrary goal of writing one hundred publishable short stories, he repeatedly affirmed in his later years his preference for the short story format, one that seems in so many ways the ideal medium for his particular talents. He returned persistently to the topic in his autobiographies, interviews, and introductions to his own work: "I'm an aficionado of short stories"; "short-story writing is the essence of writing"; "I think it's the best form of writing there is"; "I did wish to prove to myself that a short story was capable of being just as interesting and enthralling to a reader as a work of fiction of extended length." Even in his college days at the University of Virginia, he recalled, "my interest . . . [was] with the construction of a short story that had never been written before and that I wanted to write." In explaining the attraction of the short story form for him, Caldwell emphasized one quality of the genre above all others—its demand for contraction, concentration, and intensity of focus: "I have always felt that there were many incidents and episodes in life that could be told more effectively and compellingly in the compact space of a short story than could be related in a chapter or portion of a longer and often artificially extended work of fiction. . . . The most exciting and memorable happenings are usually brief and explosive." He assumed that the purpose of a story was to create an "emotional effect," "an intensity of feeling" (*CE*, 57), and to send the reader off "reeling" and "groggy" (*J*, 521) by ending on a high note. Although Caldwell went on to assert, somewhat paradoxically, that this emphasis on feeling put a greater premium on content rather than on style, in fact many of his comments on the story as an intensified and dynamic form of fiction recall the theories of William Carlos Williams' "super-realism" and those of the imagist manifestoes in the little magazines, with their stylistic concerns for precision, brevity, and force of impact. Caldwell further noted the appeal of the elasticity of the short story for him, and of the variety possible within its flexible limits: it was conducive to both experiment and discipline, qualities that were also promoted in the little magazines in which he first published.[7]

Though many of Caldwell's theories about storytelling coincided with the avant-garde that helped promote him, just as many derived from a more traditional southern source. He believed that stories were innately an oral art form, born of a rural folk culture that reflected the speech, customs, and lore of a particular locality, and that their predominant mode was comic (WA, 36, 53). His interest in the spoken quality of a tale led Caldwell to speculate on the place of dialect in written narrative and to decide decisively against it early in his career, determining instead to work with tone and especially rhythm to create the sense of a colloquial voice without the unnecessary visual distractions to the reader of the quaint spellings and excessive apostrophes that usually mark the texts of such speech. Perhaps a perverse sign of Caldwell's success in evoking regional, accented narration and dialogue is James Thurber's parody of his work in "Bateman Comes Home"; for Thurber's memory of Caldwell's language is reproduced in exactly the kind of dialect Caldwell eschewed, with all its litter of punctuation and intrusive authorial comments on the quality of speech reported: "'Bateman be comin' back any time now wid a thousan' dollas fo' his ol' pappy,' said Birge. 'Bateman ain' goin' let his ol' pappy starve nohow.' A high, cracked voice spoke inside the house, in a toneless singsong."[8] Caldwell's other belief, that storytelling was originally a comic as well as an oral art whose success was measured in part by a belly laugh (WA, 53), led him to begin his early efforts at writing with the submission of jokes to magazines of college humor and to create

7. Jac Tharpe, "Interview with Erskine Caldwell," *Southern Quarterly*, XX (1981), 67; Broadwell and Hoag, "The Art of Fiction LXII," 148; Collins, "Erskine Caldwell at Work," 23; Erskine Caldwell, Introduction to *Kneel to the Rising Sun* in *Critical Essays*, ed. MacDonald, 227; Broadwell and Hoag, "The Art of Fiction LXII," 137; Caldwell, Introduction to *Kneel to the Rising Sun*, in *Critical Essays*, ed. MacDonald, 227–28; Elizabeth Pell Broadwell and Ronald Wesley Hoag, "A Writer First: An Interview with Erskine Caldwell," *Georgia Review*, XXXVI (1982), 100; Caldwell, Introduction to *Kneel to the Rising Sun*, in *Critical Essays*, ed. MacDonald, 228.

8. Sale, "An Interview in Florida," 288; James Thurber, *The Thurber Carnival* (New York, 1945), 70.

many stories that are scarcely more than extensions of the joke form. His attraction to the extravagant yarns of the rural South led many critics to assume the influence of Twain and the old southwestern humorists on his work, but Caldwell staunchly denied this, just as he did any impact of the avant-garde.

Caldwell was open and consistent in his willingness to write and be interviewed repeatedly on his interest in the short story and his theories about it. What he said about his own work is both accurate and helpful, but what he did not say and the questions he repeatedly refused to take up are also significant. Although he was expansive on the virtues of brevity and concentration, he was reticent on the concomitant imagist and symbolist styles to which such methods are conducive. In response to an interviewer's question "Would you admit to there being symbolism in your books?" he answered, like one on trial, "No, not a bit"; when pressed to explain a mysterious character in one of his stories, he replied, even more tersely, "Nope." Interviewers who pursued stylistic and formal questions with him were met with disclaimers of ignorance and outright stonewalling:

Q. Do you consider humor as a device when you're putting a story together?

A. A question like that is a little bit baffling to me, because I don't know the reasons for these things. . . .

Q. In the novel, *Close to Home*, there was a jarring juxtaposing of comedy and the most intense violence. What was your purpose there?

A. Well, you ask a question that embarrasses me because I don't know why I do certain things. . . .

Q. Do you work for an incantation effect by repeating key words or key statements several times? . . .

A. Well, you see it's difficult for me to make a comment even on that.

To the same interviewer's suggestion that there might be artistry in the business of storytelling, Caldwell gave a typical reply: "Well, there's artistry in words, of course, but then you're getting very close to preciousness. You're writing style rather than content, and to me content is far more important than style. . . . I'd rather be more content to be a common practitioner of content in writing."[9]

Despite this repeated emphasis on content, Caldwell was equally

9. Broadwell and Hoag, "The Art of Fiction LXII," 133–34; Sale, "An Interview in Florida," 281, 282, 285, 290–91.

reluctant to be drawn into any discussions of the ideology in his work. Of his association in the early thirties with the *New Masses*, he remarked innocently, "In those days [it] was considered violently Communist, and maybe it was. I don't know." Asked about his social criticism, he replied, "I've never had the ability to be a social critic. I'm only a storyteller." About his familiarity with Nietzsche, he said, "No, no. About the only philosopher, I think, who has ever influenced me is Henry Mencken"; about reading Mark Twain [in 1982], "I haven't yet. It's something to look forward to. I've heard so much about him." [10] Perhaps one of the things Caldwell had heard about Twain was his skill in publicly posing as a genial humorist while concealing a more complicated private personality; certainly, Caldwell carried his avoidance of artistic pretentiousness not merely into his public stance, as a simple and practical storyteller, but into his personal theories on literature, which are skillful evasions of all but a few favorite and nonelitist topics on which he was prepared to repeat himself to a degree worthy of one of his own characters. Whipple's prayer in the *New Republic* that he be preserved from the intellectuals was thus perhaps granted with a vengeance; but in the 1930s, when Caldwell's energies were more devoted to writing stories than to giving interviews about them, he was taken very seriously indeed by those highbrows and critics from whom he later chose to divorce himself so completely.

## American Earth

*Picaresque, proletarian, peasant America . . .*

*—T. K. Whipple*

When Caldwell's first volume of short stories, *American Earth*, was published in 1931, it was reviewed by major national newspapers and literary journals, from the New York *Times* and *Herald Tribune* to the *New Masses* and *Nation*, and it also provoked the Whipple-Cowley debate in the *New Republic*, surely a piece of good fortune for any aspiring writer. In addition, four of the book's two dozen short stories were listed in Edward J. O'Brien's "Roll of Honor" in his *Yearbook of the American Short Story*, and one also was published in O'Brien's *Best Short Stories of 1931*. The reviews were mixed in their responses to the stories, as well as to *The Sacrilege*

10. Tharpe, "Interview with Erskine Caldwell," 72, 64, 73; Broadwell and Hoag, "The Art of Fiction LXII," 154.

*of Alan Kent*, which appeared complete in this volume for the first time, but Caldwell himself was both surprised and disappointed in them. He responded with a bitterness toward both reviewers and literary critics generally that was to set the precedent for his later relations with them; from that point on, he spoke consistently of them with ridicule and contempt as people who helped him understand how little he should care for their opinions, seeking rather the approval of the reading public and his own personal satisfaction. Thus Caldwell placed himself apart, publicly at least, from the literary intelligentsia and theoreticians of art, despite the fact that their reception of him, though contradictory, was often acute and highly interested.

The original 1931 edition of *American Earth* was divided into three sections, the final one of which was *The Sacrilege of Alan Kent*. The rest of the stories were divided under the headings "Far South" and "Farthest East," although Caldwell dropped these titles in the later uniform edition of the book in 1946 and eliminated *Alan Kent* altogether. He explained in the introduction to the later edition that the experiences of the two regions were intended to shed some light on each other by their contrasting perspectives and to make the scene he presented "more truly American than it would otherwise have been." [11] In fact, the main impression that emerges from the juxtaposition of South and Northeast for Caldwell is his greater facility with the southern material. He is so at ease with the social relationships, the customs, and the language of the South that the regional quirks of character and behavior are part of the background of these stories but never the foreground, as they sometimes are in the Maine ones. A direct stylistic sign of this greater intimacy is the fact that while the majority of the southern tales have a first-person narrator, frequently a young or adolescent boy, only two of the Maine stories do, and one of these is about returning home to the South. Thus in *American Earth*, when Caldwell chooses to provide an inside narrative, the milieu he is inside is invariably southern, whereas outside narrators dominate the New England tales; and while the southern stories have a youthful sensibility toward their events, the New England stories have a largely adult perspective. Both regions contribute a share of comic and somber tales to the collection, although the New England humor is of a more

---

11. Caldwell, Introduction to *American Earth*, in *Critical Essays*, ed. MacDonald, 221.

narrowly local color variety than the southern and is rarely over-
laid with any broader social and political implications. It plays on
stereotypical regional characteristics such as stubbornness, penny-
pinching, dourness, and isolation, but rarely takes account of less
personal issues and conflicts.

A taste for macabre and necrophiliac comedy marks the folklore
of both regions, but the difference in Caldwell's application of it may
clearly be seen in two stories that deal with the treatment of a
corpse. In the New England setting, the incident becomes little
more than an amusing tall tale, whereas in the southern one it is
closer to a farcical morality play. In the New England story "John
the Indian and George Hopkins," the ninety-year-old dead man,
George, had been a "mean old scoundrel" in his life, notorious for
his constant scrapping, so that the issue of compassion for him is
diminished from the outset. His body is dug up by John the Indian,
at the behest of one of Hopkins' quarreling daughters, and is subjected to various comic indignities that mostly take the form of pretending he is alive. He is offered fried potatoes and a pipe to smoke;
and finally, propped in a canoe with a baited fishing pole, he is
hooked by a bullheaded salmon and towed down the lake like a
speedboat. By contrast, the southern tale, "Savannah River Payday," is a catalog of gothic horrors made comic only by the ineptitude of its villains; but it is also much more than this, because it
reveals incidentally the poverty, degeneracy, psychology, racial attitudes, and climate that all contribute to the atrocities it depicts.

Though the story is brief, it opens with a suggestive description
of the setting that establishes an ominous atmosphere of heat,
inertia, violence, and decay, as vultures circle over the rotting flesh
of mules killed by heat and work. In this setting, the journey of two
white sawmill workers into town with the body of a black co-worker,
killed accidentally by a falling tree, is primed for disaster. The
whites try first to knock out the corpse's gold teeth with a monkey
wrench and then to rape a black woman chopping cotton by the
roadside, but the dead man is obviously immune to their physical
assaults, the woman escapes, and the two men hurt only each other;
Red knocks out Jake and later slices off his ear. Though the story is
filled with brutality, it is both random and ineffectual. The two
white men are so subject to the rule of casual instinct that they are
continually distracted from one vicious pursuit to another. The
"payday" of the title has thus several implications: of finality for the
black man, of riotous weekend indulgence for the whites, but also

of the larger consequences for all the people in the story of the circumstances that control their lives. This tale is clearly outside the local-color limits that mark such New England stories as "Ten Thousand Blueberry Crates," "An Autumn Courtship," and "The Corduroy Pants," whose observations of human whimsy bear no more demanding social burden than that of presenting local eccentricities, and no more challenging aesthetic response than that to a good-willed joke.

Some of the Maine stories, however, gain from the distinct differences in their setting, especially in the use of social remoteness to explore the sufferings and frustrations of lonely people; in the southern stories, such anxieties are more likely to be the result of too much teeming humanity rather than its absence. In these stories, Caldwell comes closest to Sherwood Anderson, a writer he avowedly admired for a long time—a rare admission for him—although, as with every other writer who has been proposed as an influence on Caldwell, his affinity does not take the form of imitation, but is transformed into a distinctly personal vision.[12] "The Mating of Marjorie," a story about the doomed efforts of a lonely Maine woman to arrange a marriage for herself with an equally lonely Minnesota farmer, is similar to several of the stories in *Winesburg, Ohio* about women who struggle with passions that strike no responsive chord in others. However, whereas stories of Anderson's like "Adventure," "The Teacher," or "Surrender" always provide a history and explanation of his character's anguish or perversity, "The Mating of Marjorie" does not move outside the present moment of the story into exposition or history, but carries its meaning rather by images and exclusions. Marjorie's passionate nature burns with excitement during the visit of the farmer, Nils, but he is as cold and hard as the New England winter, whose imminence hangs over the narrative. The elemental images of fire and ice dominate the affair, suggesting its hopelessness, but Caldwell does not investigate the reasons for its failure. By the end of the story, Marjorie, like one of Anderson's grotesques, is lying in bed stroking the cedar chest in which Nils's crumpled sheets are tenderly folded, whispering to his memory in the dark; but Caldwell offers no theories of causality, no hopes for a new relationship between men and women, no compassionate summary of meaning—nothing but the impact of vivid images embedded in a stark narrative.

12. Tharpe, "Interview with Erskine Caldwell," 69.

When Caldwell drops this stance of detachment and seeks more actively for sympathy for his characters, as he does in another New England story, "The Lonely Day," the result is simple sentimentality. Though Caldwell was accused by one of his early critics of cruel indifference to the fates of his characters, whose activities he oversaw like "a bored and bilious God," it is exactly this aesthetic distance—sometimes achieved by an innocent or callous narrator, sometimes by shocking turns of events, frequently by the intrusion of incongruous humor—that is lacking in "The Lonely Day" and thence unable to moderate the pathos of its plot, an account of a lonely and abused young girl transformed miraculously in her death into a cynosure for tourists' admiring eyes.[13] Caldwell's success in combining pity and grim comedy is illustrated, by contrast, in another story in the collection that uses the same motif of the metamorphosis of a woman in death; but in "Joe Craddock's Old Woman," the only miracle involved is that of the undertaker's art. Julia Craddock has been made ugly by the ugliness of her life, so that "no man had ever seen in Julia anything but the repugnant suggestion of a female" (AE, 86). The victim of toil and poverty, her alteration into a "beautiful lady" just before she is finally laid to rest in the dirt suggests the depths of Caldwell's sympathy with the miserable lives of the poor. However, he refuses to hint at anything romantic or mysterious in the workings of death. Julia is the undertaker's creation: "Julia had been bathed all over, and her hair had been shampooed. Her hands were white, and the fingernails manicured; her face was clean and smooth with powder and rouge, and cotton in her mouth levelled the hollows of her cheeks" (AE, 87–88). Caldwell concentrates on the outward images of a physical change in the body and thus qualifies the pity with an irony that is absent from "The Lonely Day." Interestingly, "Joe Craddock's Old Woman" has a southern setting, consistent again with Caldwell's tendency to maintain a more complicated attitude to his native region, even within a style of great simplicity.

One of the most noticeable innovations in *American Earth*, after the kinds of experiments Caldwell had tried in his two earlier novels, is in the range of narrative voice. Both *The Bastard* and *Poor Fool*, and indeed almost all of Caldwell's later novels, have third-person narrators; but in these short stories, Caldwell tries a much wider range of narrative tone and voice. Besides those related

---

13. Jack Conroy, "Passion and Pellagra," in *Critical Essays*, ed. MacDonald, 18.

by adolescent boys, one is told by a child, and several by mature men, whose characters crucially affect the tale that is told. Those narrated by young people prove among the best vehicles for Caldwell's naïve and dispassionate style, because the narrators are unaware of any ironic dimension in their accounts and are likely to concentrate more feasibly on external details and material images, rather than on the interpretation of their experiences. The voices that narrate are informal, colloquial, and intimate, occasionally confessional, but often clearly relishing their own anecdotes. They reminded reviewers and critics inevitably of Twain, especially in their naïve humor and their closeness to southern folklore and tall tales; but they are almost wholly without regional dialect, in contrast to Twain's painstaking care to record all the subtle variations of local speech. Although, according to Margaret Bourke-White, who toured many southern states with him, Caldwell had a keen ear for dialect, he chose to circumvent the transcription of it, which he felt to be distracting for the reader, by seeking to suggest the quality of a speaker's voice through rhythmical cadences, idioms, and repetition. In the foreword to an edition of Joel Chandler Harris' *On the Plantation*, Caldwell commented: "The first-time reader of Joel Harris is likely to become perplexed and even mildly bewildered by the literal transcription of unfamiliar Georgia plantation Negro-Geechee speech. Although the reader may have mastered the nuances of traditional Deep South accents and inflections, he still will find himself relying upon Harris's rendition for what otherwise might be mistaken for a foreign language." Caldwell thus acknowledges that Harris' artistry is sufficient to temper the difficulty of the dialect, but he notes that other writers, like Ambrose Gonzales, who devoted his life to the most literal transcription of stories in Gullah dialect, produced virtually unintelligible results.[14] Caldwell refuses to make such demands on the reader. His narrative and reported speech suggests the character of the speaker, often the social class and race, but the locale is more forcefully conveyed by the attitudes and actions of the characters than by their accents.

In *American Earth*, one of Caldwell's major achievements in narrative is in capturing the voices of a variety of adolescent boys who do not comprehend the adult meaning of the stories they tell, which are often of early and tentative sexual experiences. The first story in

14. Margaret Bourke-White, *Portrait of Myself* (New York, 1963), 126; Erskine Caldwell, Foreword to Joel Chandler Harris, *On the Plantation* (Athens, Ga., 1980), ix, x.

the book, "The Strawberry Season," is exemplary in illustrating what Caldwell can do with voice, imagery, and brevity. The voice is that of a youthful strawberry picker, innocent and egalitarian in tone, except where he has picked up the expertise of his trade. He admires the girl Fanny, he assures us, because she "could pick all day and never have a single piece of vine among her berries. She used only the thumb and the next two fingers, making a kind of triangle that grasped the berry close to the stem and lifted it off. She never mashed a berry like some people were forever doing" (*AE*, 13). The strawberry itself provides the image around which the tale is clustered; it is lush and sensuous, but also a simple and natural product of the season. It is the subject of a youthful game played by the pickers, in which the boys drop a strawberry down the back of a girl's dress and then try to slap it; but when the young narrator naïvely drops his strawberry down the front of Fanny's dress, he notices that her nipples are "stained like a mashed strawberry." The boy's limited experience of the world intensifies the few images he repeats obsessively in his account—the juicy redness of the crushed berries, the heat of the sun on bare flesh, his confusion over Fanny—but he never understands the evidence of his own emerging sexuality. At the beginning of the story, he says, "We had a lot of fun picking berries" (*AE*, 12), an impersonal and childlike remark; by the end, the boy has entered a different world of pleasure, though his simplicity is unaltered: "Fanny had once said she had never had a sweetheart. I wish she had been mine" (*AE*, 15–16). This intense focus on imagery to carry much of the unspoken meaning of a narrative had been used already by Caldwell in his early novels, but never before so effectively in conjunction with a naïve narrative voice that could lend credence to such exclusive and concentrated emphasis.

In "The Visitor," a similar incipient sensuality is focused on the young narrator's sucking of a beesting from a girl's shoulder, an image traced by Guy Owen to D. H. Lawrence's story "The Shades of Spring."[15] This story was included in Frances Newman's anthology *The Short Story's Mutations*, a book for which Caldwell expressed rare enthusiasm (*CE*, 41), so it seems likely that he was indeed familiar with it. However, compared with the somber discovery Lawrence's fictional hero makes about the power of instinct to overwhelm intellectual aspiration, Caldwell's young lover com-

---

15. Owen, "Erskine Caldwell and D. H. Lawrence," 20.

pletely fails to perceive what is happening to him when he is overcome by desire. The comedy of the tale lies in this lack of an epiphany and in its hero's convenient capacity for ignorance of his own motives. Caldwell often writes of the dilemma of people dominated by primitive and irrational feelings who must nevertheless live in a world that expects rational behavior of them. However, he presents these predicaments more as a bitter cosmic joke for his readers than as a tragic discovery for his characters. This is partially a result of the youthfulness of his protagonists, but it is also a consequence of their remarkable capacity for self-deception, for seeing what they want and need to see in a situation and no more.

A good example of this is another first-person narrative, "Where the Girls Were Different," which opens with the claim from its youthful teller, "Nobody could ever explain exactly why it was, but the girls who lived in all the other parts of Oconee County were different from the ones in our section" (AE, 46). So convinced is Fred that the girls from Rosemark diverge radically from the girls of his native Woodlawn that, when he meets one who tells him her name is Betty, he responds, "No girl up in Woodlawn had a name like that. I was beginning to see why all the boys at home liked to come down to Rosemark" (AE, 49–50). This story proves to be a kind of double joke, revealing the willingness of the boys to persuade themselves that far-off fields are greener or girls are faster, but also showing an accident of fate whereby the hero finds himself with just such a girl, complete with a father armed with a rusty pistol. In a very interesting analysis of this story, Scott MacDonald demonstrates that Caldwell uses increasingly frequent repetitions of the phrase "were different" as a sign of the boy narrator's rising sexual excitement; when he is chased off by the girl's father, the repetition stops abruptly.[16] The reiteration of the phrase is indeed a cleverly used signal to the reader of the impending erotic climax of the tale, but the wording of the phrase itself is equally ingenious. It avoids any overt sexual innuendo but manages to suggest the alternative standards of behavior and morality to be expected from the Rosemark girls; it shows the ease with which Caldwell's characters can rationalize their instincts without ever comprehending their own slyness.

Even the youngest of Caldwell's narrators, in "Molly Cotton-

16. Scott MacDonald, "Repetition as Technique in the Short Stories of Erskine Caldwell," in Critical Essays, ed. MacDonald, 331–33.

Tail," shows a certain expediency in his innocence when faced with his first real crisis of conscience. This child loves to spend his summer vacations at his aunt's house but knows he must pay a price by overcoming his innate revulsion against hunting and killing animals, a practice his aunt believes to be the mark of a southern gentleman. When he decides to resist his scruples and shoot a rabbit, he lays the responsibility squarely on his Aunt Nellie, though in this benevolent tale, the child is rescued from his evil act by his ineptitude in firing the shotgun. It has often been considered something of a critical truism that the comedy in Caldwell's stories derives largely from the innocence of his characters toward their own outrageous conduct; but the evidence of these many first-person stories, of the disparities between characters' behavior and their own commentaries on it, suggests that Caldwell, despite his philosophic naturalism, is not without moral irony in judging his seemingly obtuse people. Though they may speak with great simplicity and act with great simplicity, they are not thereby granted automatic moral absolution by their creator.

Although many of the stories in *American Earth* reveal people acting impulsively and often self-deludingly on their desires, Caldwell also insists on the extent to which large realms of human conduct and fortune are directed by external forces over which individuals have little control. For Caldwell, the son of a Presbyterian minister, a vision of the frailty of human nature, combined with a sense of determinism—not certainly of the divine kind, but of economics, race, culture, and environment—was scarcely a difficult paradox to embrace. The naturalism that was already evidenced in the two early novels, *The Bastard* and *Poor Fool*, is apparent in the short story "Dorothy," a work that reflects on both motivation and personal responsibility in a situation where free choice scarcely exists. The story begins in a classic 1930s mode: "I was standing on the shady side of the street waiting for something. I don't know what I was waiting for. It wasn't important anyway. I didn't have anything to do, and I wasn't going anywhere" (*AE*, 95). However, even in this condition of extreme inertia, the narrator is unable to maintain his moral apathy as he observes an obviously exhausted and poverty-stricken young woman searching the street with the aid of the newspaper want ads. When she asks him to direct her to an employment agency, he sends her instead toward the town's red-light district, a direction to which she quietly accedes. Later, his degree of responsibility for Dorothy's fate becomes an obsessive concern for the narrator: "She knew there was always one way. She knew about Forsyth Street on the other side of the viaduct. Somebody had told her about it. . . . It's a lie! I told her to go down the street and cross the viaduct" (*AE*, 103–104). In this story, the narrator's social and political ignorance makes him take on himself a moral responsibility that Caldwell clearly wishes to place on an economic system in which a young woman eager to work is driven to a practical choice between starvation and prostitution.

Even less ambivalent in its deterministic vision is "Saturday Afternoon," a lynching story that subordinates its potential sensationalism to a wry and disciplined study of motivation. Will Maxie, the black victim, has brought on his fate by doing everything right— growing his cotton well, raising his family conscientiously, behaving deferentially toward whites—and as a result, he is avenged by those whites who have no comparable virtue or restraint. However, "Saturday Afternoon" is no simple racial propaganda story, but rather an imagist meditation on brutality that largely avoids description of the central atrocity in order to focus on the state of mind and the kinds of social values that could foster it. The story opens and closes in Tom Denny's butcher shop, where buzzing flies feast on blood. Amid the stifling heat and odors of decaying meat, Tom dozes on the butcher block, his head resting on a cool steak from the icehouse. Heat, boredom, and blood are the motifs of the story. The lynching provides a welcome interruption to Tom's Saturday afternoon lethargy; however, like the dutiful butcher he is, he is forced to rush away from the killing to slice meat and chop bones for Sunday lunches. Will Maxie is the victim of a dull, hot day as much as of a set of prejudices; he is burned, shot, and hanged to a community chorus on the pleasures of drinking cold Coca-Cola on such a carnival occasion. Though the tale is framed by scenes in the butcher shop, Caldwell relates the murder in antiphonal response to a detailed account of the delivery, chilling, and marketing of the "dopes"; each is given equal prominence:

> Will Maxie was going up in smoke. When he was just about gone they
> gave him the lead. Tom stood back and took good aim and fired away at
> Will with his shotgun as fast as he could breech it and put in a new
> load. About forty or more of the other men had shotguns too. They
> filled him so full of lead that his body sagged from his neck where the
> trace-chain held him up.
> The Cromer boy had sold completely out. All of his ice and dopes

were gone. Doc Cromer would feel pretty good when his boy brought back all that money. Six whole cases he sold, at a dime a bottle. If he had brought along another case or two he could have sold them easily enough. Everybody likes Coca-Cola. There is nothing better to drink on a hot day, if the dopes are nice and cool. (*AE*, 24–25)

Such paragraphs are perfectly balanced throughout the story. Caldwell's narrative detachment is absolute and disinterested, even to according Will Maxie's demise and the Coca-Cola clearance the exact same number of words. Such stories as "Saturday Afternoon" led Norman Macleod, the reviewer for the *New Masses*, to believe that Caldwell was capable of "good proletarian work," but the story is not fully in the proletarian vein of naturalism at all, if that is intended to suggest that the violence done to Will Maxie stems entirely from social and class-related evils.[17] Certainly, the racial hatred in the story has one of its sources in economic resentment, but Caldwell insists on the role of climate, monotony, and sheer randomness in generating the incident, unlikely and unmalleable targets for a dedicated proletarian partisan.

His vision of human nature, dominated by certain powerful instincts, prime among which is the need for food, is certainly a sign that much of his work might be congenial to the literary left wing during the Great Depression; but Caldwell's emphasis on the uncontrollable aspects of the environment, on the natural as well as the social milieu, together with his sense of the unpredictable and eccentric impulses of his characters, suggests, in *American Earth*, that he is still a long way from fitting comfortably into a proletarian mold. A story like "Midsummer Passion" is a prime example of how a Caldwell character, acting out of what seems like brute instinct, is capable of unexpectedly whimsical behavior that does not lend itself readily to logical social analyses. The middle-aged hero of the story, Ben, suffers initially a series of frustrations: rain pours down on his newly gathered hay, and he finds an empty car blocking the narrow lane he is driving his wagon on. He helps himself exasperatedly to a jug of hard cider in the abandoned car and then makes an intriguing find there—a "pinkish," "silkish" (*AE*, 125) woman's undergarment, which he fingers in mounting excitement: it "filled him with the urge to do something out of the ordinary but he didn't know what he could do" (*AE*, 126). He goes to his neighbor's house and looks appraisingly at his good-looking wife: "Watching her while she pulled the peas from the vines, Ben strode around her in a circle,

17. Macleod, "A Hardboiled Idealist," 7.

putting his hand into the pocket where the pink drawers were" (*AE*, 126–27). When the inevitable attack on the wife comes, the two roll around in the garden dirt together until it suddenly becomes apparent that Ben has no sexual designs on the pretty woman but merely wants to put the pink drawers *on* her. Whether Ben is paying her a clumsy compliment or merely trying to restore some sense of order to his disrupted day, Caldwell does not presume to tell us. The neighbor's wife accepts his efforts with decorum, and the story closes on images of harmony as Ben washes, the woman fixes her hair, and they converse politely:

> "It was mighty nice of you to bring the towel and water," he thanked her.
> "You are halfway fit to go home now," she approved, pinning up her hair.
> "Good-day," Ben said.
> "Good-day," said Fred's wife. (*AE*, 128)

The reader's conventional assumptions in the story are neatly undermined: Ben does indeed act instinctively and without regard for normal social inhibitions, but his urge is both comic and generous and is met with appropriate responses. *American Earth* gives ample warning that Caldwell's interest in determinism in human experience may not be easily equated with predictability in his characters' behavior. The hopes of the literary left wing for Caldwell's proletarian conversion were to some considerable extent fulfilled by the emphasis of his reporting and nonfiction writing in the 1930s and increasingly in the concerns of his short stories and novels. However, the eclecticism of the stories in his first collection is a typical sample of what was to come in the three other major short story collections of the decade: *We Are the Living, Kneel to the Rising Sun,* and *Southways.* All of them demonstrate a comparable interest in the narrative voice and tone of a tale, in regional folkways and universal predicaments, in both needless and unavoidable suffering, and in sheer human foolishness.

## We Are the Living

*Caldwell "has yet to learn that the revolution begins above the belt."*
*—Kenneth Burke*

Between the publication of *American Earth* and his second collection of short stories, *We Are the Living* (1933), Caldwell wrote what he sometimes later tended to suggest were his first three novels,

*Tobacco Road,* an early version of *A Lamp for Nightfall,* and *God's Little Acre.* Only after the completion of *God's Little Acre* in late August of 1932 did Caldwell return with renewed enthusiasm to the writing of short stories, some of which were collected, along with a number already published in little magazines in 1931 and 1932, in the new book. Although no effort was made in the formal organization of *We Are the Living* to suggest the regional balance between South and East of *American Earth,* the stories are grouped with some slight reference to geography, with the much smaller portion of New England ones clustered at the end. Surprisingly, although Caldwell had produced since *American Earth* two novels with distinctly left-wing political sympathies, *We Are the Living* has only one clearly proletarian short story, "Rachel." There is, however, a new interest in racial sociology in the collection, a stronger emphasis on power and vulnerability, and one story with a distinctly experimental narrative method; but in general the reiteration of the eclectic mixture of concerns and methods of the first collection now suggests a clear idea of Caldwell's emerging themes and stylistic devices. There are once again a number of comic stories that derive much of their humor from the traditional folklore of the South and New England; a large number of first-person narratives, with even more varied voices than *American Earth;* and a goodly proportion of stories that deal in various modes with suffering, pain, and loss. However, if there is one pervasive subject that links almost every story in the collection, it is sexuality in its most varied manifestations. Indeed, one reviewer suggested the book might have been more aptly titled *We Are the Loving.* An interviewer took up this seeming identification of "living" with "loving" many years later with Caldwell, and in response to the question of whether he believed that "people's sexual relations are sort of a core to everything else," Caldwell tacitly admitted the naturalistic assumptions of the question and replied, "Your first instinct is to have something to eat. Then nature takes over after that and you have this impulse, this built-in impulse or sexual proclivity."[18] This second-place ranking of sex behind hunger as dominant human instincts is obviously not likely to be apparent except in stories that deal specifically with poverty and lack of food, but when the two impulses coincide, Caldwell is at his most discomfiting.

18. Whit Burnett, Review of Erskine Caldwell's *We Are the Living,* in *Books,* September 24, 1933, p. 8; Sale, "An Interview in Florida," 292.

The short story "Rachel" is a blunt examination of the collision of starvation and desire, personified separately in a pair of lovers in the form of a poor young woman who gleans food from trash cans and a young man who adores her. When Rachel accidentally eats food contaminated with rat poison, her lover watches in bewilderment as her desirable body begins to swell and deform. He gazes at her reflected image in a mirror while she urgently requests help. In one of his most effective uses of repetition, Caldwell has the young man turn repeatedly to the sensuous allure of the mirror image and the "grace of her breasts" (WAL, 68), while in the world outside the mirror, the poison is working its destruction in the girl's stomach. After Rachel's death, the young man is tormented by the image of those sinuous breasts bending over a garbage can. He reproaches himself for his inability to have seen Rachel's true predicament, but he remains apparently innocent of the impact of this lingering final image for the reader—not of the youth's helplessness but of the incongruous juxtaposition of his desire and her hunger. Such irony is, of course, inherent in the work of many realist and naturalist writers. A prime example occurs on the deathbed of Flaubert's Madame Bovary, when her husband, Charles, caressingly draws his hands over Emma's poisoned stomach, or when Emma gives her last lustful kiss to the crucifix. But few American writers have chosen to expose the conflicting impulses in such stark nakedness as has Caldwell and to insist equally on the comedy and tragedy of their implications.

He pursues variations on these confused and warring impulses in "Mamma's Little Girl," "The Medicine Man," and "August Afternoon." In the first story, romantic love culminates in an abortion, but even while this is being performed, the carnality of the participants, including the doctor and nurse, arises in mockery of the harrowing procedure. In "The Medicine Man," virtually a classic southern folktale, a thirty-year-old unmarried woman and a traveling purveyor of "Indian Root Tonic" cover their mutual seduction with the proprieties of her virtue and his professionalism until her brother interrupts to force a shotgun wedding on the lusty pair. Though the two acquiesce, he with dignity, she with delight, marriage in Caldwell is rarely a satisfactory solution for containing people's runaway instincts. The marriage in "August Afternoon" between a man and his fifteen-year-old bride is on the point of disintegrating because the two are driven by opposite urges—he toward sloth, she toward sex. When a newcomer arrives who is less inert than the husband, instinct triumphs all round as the stranger and the wife make love while the husband sleeps. The sexual comedy in Caldwell's work arises not solely from the traditional conflict between higher and lower impulses, or the hypocrisy of disguised motives, but often from the clash of two sets of lower impulses, or the perverse and inexplicable ways people go about fulfilling their fancies.

Caldwell writes with considerable comic zest about the numerous possibilities for sexual titillation, using particularly his repetitive technique to insinuate and hint at sexual undercurrents and proving remarkably inventive in creating occasions for literary striptease acts. In both "The Medicine Man" and "August Afternoon," he uses particular repeated refrains to emphasize mounting tension and sexual excitement, far beyond the realistic boundaries of normal reported speech. In the first story, Effie questions every item of clothing she removes, "Do you want me to take—," and is invariably interrupted by Professor Eaton's "Absolutely" (*WAL*, 83, 84). In "August Afternoon," a black observer's half-eager, half-fearful chorus throughout the story is, "We ain't aiming to have no trouble today, is we?" (*WAL*, 145), accompanied by constant references to a stick that the potential lover is gradually whittling to paper thinness.[19] Sometimes actions, rather than phrases, are ritualistically repeated to suggest the erotic arousal. In "Over the Green Mountains," a woman's clothes are progressively removed; in "Indian Summer," two teenage boys decide to "mudcake" a girl who has been teasing them but find that their horseplay is becoming less and less childish with every successive handful of mud they smear over the girl's smooth body. Caldwell's capacity, throughout his short stories, for uncovering women's bodies in ingenious ways is seemingly inexhaustible. Kenneth Burke early noted that he showed a "surprisingly naive delight in all the possible ramifications of the thought that girls may be without panties, and he seems to have searched the length and breadth of the country for new situations whereby some significant part or parts can be exposed for us."[20]

Critics of Caldwell were from the outset divided as to whether to condemn this power of bawdy titillation as obscene or to approve its Rabelaisian temerity. Indeed, Carl Van Doren was able to make fine discriminations between the two, calling "Meddlesome Jack" (a ren-

---

19. See MacDonald, "Repetition as Technique," 333–34.
20. Burke, "Caldwell: Maker of Grotesques," 173.

dition of the folk-belief in the aphrodisiac qualities of a jackass's bray) "a bawdy masterpiece," whereas he argued that "The Medicine Man" belonged "to the shoddy stage of a burlesque theater." Carl Bode agreed that the latter was "really pornography with a horse laugh," but W. M. Frohock felt Caldwell had "an impressive gift for making literary comedy out of the stuff which we most often associate with the irreverently ribald periodical press." Malcolm Cowley noted that there had already been many vain attempts to "introduce the god Pan into American folklore" and acknowledged that Caldwell's characters were certainly representative of "our half-conscious desire for freedom from moral restraints." However, when Cowley regretted the absence of Pan and suggested that "our woods are still unpeopled with fauns, nymphs or satyrs," he was surely referring to the woods of formal literature rather than to the folk traditions of the people among whom Caldwell's stories were set.[21]

The rude characters and situations of many of Caldwell's stories were long familiar as motifs in southern folklore; and in emphasizing their crude and carnal qualities, Caldwell made no attempt to distance himself as author from the vulgar vitality of the tales, as many southern authors had done in the previous decade in their accounts of the same group of people. In the novels and short stories of Jack Bethea, Dorothy Scarborough, Edith Summers Kelley, Elizabeth Madox Roberts, Olive Tilford Dargan, and many more, there is a sympathetic and acute appreciation of the folk culture of the South; and certainly their works constitute a much more comprehensive survey of the language, songs, customs, and legends of the region than do those of Caldwell. He, by contrast, is narrow and selective in his choice of motifs and excludes large areas of traditional activity in southern communities. Instead of trying, like them, to recreate the culture, framed by a knowing author for better understanding and compassion, Caldwell continued to embellish the comic ribaldry of the original tradition and adapt it to his view of the antic dilemma of people with sensual bodies and rationalizing minds, trying to cope with a complicated set of circumstances. Thus quilting bees, barn raisings, taffy pulls, church suppers, and all the other

21. Carl Van Doren, "Made in America: Erskine Caldwell," in *Critical Essays*, ed. MacDonald, 156; Carl Bode, "Erskine Caldwell: A Note for the Negative," in *Critical Essays*, ed. MacDonald, 248; W. M. Frohock, "Erskine Caldwell: Sentimental Gentleman from Georgia," in *Critical Essays*, ed. MacDonald, 201; Malcolm Cowley, "The Two Erskine Caldwells," in *Critical Essays*, ed. MacDonald, 199.

apparatus of the local colorist have no place in Caldwell's fiction; he is aware (sometimes regretfully) that he is working with a version of an oral tradition in a modern setting and that much of the cultural environment of his tales is forgotten, abandoned, or destroyed. However, he is still willing to hazard the risk that he can continue to make the humor of the body—in animalism, violence, death, and particularly sex—reach a modern audience largely insulated from such immediate earthiness, and through it to further his notion of human perversity.

Significantly, the least satisfactory stories in *We Are the Living* are those in which the depiction of romantic love is unmediated by some incongruous or naturalistic intrusion. "Warm River," "The Empty Room," and "After-Image" lack any doubleness of perspective; in contrast, "The First Autumn" is rescued from banality by a single grotesque image of an ant crawling on the face of a dead man who had been loving and vital only a moment earlier. In one of his experimental stories, "We Are Looking at You, Agnes," the female narrator talks obsessively in an interior monologue of the contrast between the formal affection of her family and the revulsion she is certain they feel for her secret life as a prostitute. The story is built on Agnes' anguished tormenting of herself with the taunts that her family refrains from. She wills them repeatedly to ask questions that will elicit a confession, and their silence provokes her to create images of her increasing loathsomeness in their eyes. She notices that "after every meal Mama takes the dishes I have used and scalds them at the sink"; and "Papa takes a cloth soaked in alcohol and wipes the chair I've been sitting in every time I get up and leave the room" (*WAL*, 25). Although Agnes seems close to madness, the story has a closely wrought and controlled tension that comes from the contrast of the feverishly active mind of the narrator and a situation that is marked by silence, inactivity, waiting, and watching. Like so many of the other stories of "loving" in this collection, Caldwell does not try to mediate between the dramatically opposed sets of images—the family at Christmas and the disinfecting of utensils—but creates his tale from their incongruous juxtaposition. When the contrast is missing, the stories are, despite their consistent brevity, monotonous.

Besides the intrinsic variety of meanings implied in the word *love*—from respectable marriage to earthy sex, from affection to abortion, families to prostitution, friends to lovers—and all the whimsical ways in which such meanings may be embodied—from strawberries and silk panties to beestings and jackass's brays—Caldwell also explores some of the complications of love that arise from the particular social setting of his stories. The relative positions of women and blacks in the hierarchy of power that exists in the South, and the ways in which the existence of each group complicates social and sexual relations in general, are a central concern in all of Caldwell's work, in both tragic and comic contexts. In earlier stories, Caldwell showed his fascination with the cruelty, hypocrisy, and farce that derived from the interaction of people with ambivalent kinds of power in their spheres—social status, material wealth, physical strength, sexual allure, racial authority; but now, in this collection, there is new emphasis on the ambivalences and resulting ironies in their most intimate relations.

In "The Picture," a privileged white woman shares and wields her husband's status over her black servants but is threatened by her maid's sensuous beauty into a recognition of her sexual powerlessness. "Yellow Girl" traces a similar dawning awareness of the complicated and contradictory forces of authority and attraction between white and black, though in a crude and unambiguous image. This depicts the discovery by a white woman, Nell, of one brown egg among a basket of white ones from her Leghorns and the knowledge that her private sexual territory is similarly threatened by her black servant, Myrtie. The sexual innuendoes of the story are constantly pointed by interpolated scenarios of the behavior of roosters and hens in the barnyard; but—although some of his detractors would surely deny it—the barnyard image is a vastly simplified metaphor for Caldwell's human society. Instead, elaborate gradations of caste and class counterpoint and qualify any simple naturalistic notion of who is fittest to survive and dominate, even in the practices of mating and marrying. Caldwell would later continue to explore all the permutations of race, sex, and wealth in their more sociological relationships, but in *We Are the Living* the subject becomes another means of meditating on the infinite absurdities encompassed by the notion of human love.

Only two stories in the collection are outside the pervasive concerns of love and sexuality: "The People's Choice," a comic southern tale of fickleness and its shrewd political benefits; and "Country Full of Swedes," a comic Maine tale of rigidity and its chaotic results. Both use and transcend regional stereotypes to comment on universal human folly. Gus Streetman goes on a bender when he hears he has been elected church deacon, rattles the collection basket "as though he were warming up a crap game," yells "Shake it up!" at the female soloist (WAL, 37, 38), and generally imports the wild rituals of Saturday night into the more sedate ones of Sunday morning. The unexpected consequence is a tremendous upsurge in Gus's popularity among the church members, who can now hope for some further entertaining vitality in their religion—a suggestion here of the direction of Caldwell's future investigations into the functioning of the Protestant church in the South.

By contrast, the Maine folks in "Country Full of Swedes" want no hint of novelty entering their daily routine. They are terrified by the invasion of their neighborhood by a family of Swedes so alien to the local mores that they paint their house yellow instead of the prescribed New England white. Panic in the story increases in hysterical proportion to the proliferation of Swedes, who, "like a fired nest of yellow-headed bumble bees, were swarming all over the place as far as the eye could see. . . . There was a Swede everywhere a man could look. Some of them were little Swedes, and women Swedes, to be sure; but little Swedes, in the end, and women Swedes, too, near about, grow up as big as any of them" (WAL, 247–48). Even the Swedes' yellow tomcat is subject to inflation by the xenophobic locals, so that it is at first "as large as an eight-months collie puppy" and later leaps across the lawn "like a devilish calf, new-born" (WAL, 256). Both stories insist on the role of irrationality in human affairs, partly because of the quirky and distorted ways in which people perceive the world around them. When this innate oddity is added to the complicated functioning of environmental and historical determinism, it is more apparent than ever from this collection of stories that, although events in Caldwell's fictional world may well be explained, they can never, with any assurance, be predicted.

## Kneel to the Rising Sun

*I was just on the fringe of Communism, I suppose you would call it.*
*—Erskine Caldwell in 1971*

Kenneth Burke reported in the *New Republic* early in 1935 of having heard a man complain that Caldwell "has yet to learn that the revolution begins above the belt," and indeed, as a left-wing response to *We Are the Living*, the comment is not so unreasonable.[22]

22. Burke, "Caldwell: Maker of Grotesques," 169.

However, shortly after Burke's article, Caldwell published his third collection of short stories, *Kneel to the Rising Sun*, which seemed to offer new hope to literary revolutionaries of an alliance with Caldwell, because the emphasis in so many of the stories was on the radical inequities and injustices in contemporary America. Caldwell's writing had been marked from the outset by a concern and fascination with the lives of poor people, a concern encouraged from his youth by his father and finally developed fully in the left-wing literary milieu of the Great Depression into a newly political consciousness. It never became the kind of intellectual doctrine that Burke's overheard critic might have wished for. Revolt, for Caldwell's characters, is always a gut, rather than a cerebral, response to events. However, the detached irony of the earlier story "Rachel," where the young narrator's attention is focused alternately on a woman's breasts and poisoned stomach, is temporarily suspended in *Kneel to the Rising Sun*, and the revolution ascends, at least into the alimentary organs.

The signs of Caldwell's emerging political sympathies were clearly apparent in his two novels *Tobacco Road* (1932) and *God's Little Acre* (1933)—novels that were published almost simultaneously with their completion—but less obvious in the short stories in *We Are the Living*, many of which had been written and published individually much earlier than their collected publication date. The *New Masses* reviewer of *American Earth*, Norman Macleod, had urged Caldwell in 1931 to place his characters "in the social scheme of things," had seen in "Saturday Afternoon" evidence of good proletarian potential, and had concluded his review by urging Caldwell to go left. There is ample evidence that this is just what Caldwell did, less ambiguously, however, in his actions than in his art, which until *Kneel to the Rising Sun* was a constant source of pique to his left-wing critics for its diversions from their main concerns. In September of 1932, Caldwell supported, along with fifty-two other artists and intellectuals, the candidacy of Foster and Ford, the Communist party nominees for the presidency. Later that same year, he published a review in the *New Masses* of Edward Dahlberg's *From Flushing to Calvary* that displayed, both in form and content, how close he could come to the heart and mind of that journal and its radical ideology. Adopting both Dahlberg's vision and Michael Gold's prose style, he wrote: "We'll continue looking for jobs where there are no jobs and pinching pennies until there is no penny left until the gut-rotting disorganization of unplanned society is thrown bag-and-baggage overboard. . . . We were dumped by a capitalist system on hard ground, and here we lie. Our first step is now being taken; we are scattered, broken, and bewildered; we are lifting our heads and looking ahead into the future." By 1934, Caldwell was being billed by the *New Masses* as a correspondent, reporting on the lynching and terrorizing of southern blacks; and in a letter to the journal that year he wrote, "The Negro, the tenant-farmer, and the mill worker have contributed, involuntarily, to the power of those holding the whip-hand; but the hand grows weak, the oppressed gain strength, and the outcome of the coming struggle cannot be in doubt." In 1937 and 1939 he signed the two proclamations of the League of American Writers, calling for its second and third congresses. Although none of this is compelling evidence that Caldwell ever was a Communist or even a fellow-traveling intellectual, it is certainly sufficient evidence to suggest strong left-wing sympathies and an awareness of what was going on among adherents of a Marxist literary line, even if he was not himself one of them. Caldwell repeatedly downplayed these associations in the interviews he gave, not apparently so much to disavow the ideology as to insist on his isolation, individualism, and innocence of such literary fashions, and his pragmatic desire to place his stories where he could. He commented insistently upon his ignorance and distance from the Communists. To one interviewer he remarked, "I don't know if anybody ever gave me a great fanfare for writing along the Communist line. Maybe they did, but I wasn't aware of it"; to another, "I never, in all the years of my life, considered myself to be a Marxist, Communist, or fellow traveler. . . . But I never fell out with the Marxist critics because I was never in their camp to begin with."[23] Nevertheless, some stories in *Kneel to the Rising Sun* suggest that Caldwell did indeed fulfill Norman Macleod's wish that he "go left." Although there are a significant number of the seventeen stories in the collection that have no obvious political overtones, this third collection of short stories shows Caldwell most directly using his peculiar talents in an ideological and political context.

23. Erskine Caldwell, "Ripe for Revolution," in *Critical Essays*, ed. MacDonald, 21–22; Erskine Caldwell, "Caldwell to Lieber," *New Masses*, January 30, 1934, p. 21; Sale, "An Interview in Florida," 279; Broadwell and Hoag, "A Writer First," 95. See also Sylvia Jenkins Cook, "Erskine Caldwell and the Literary Left Wing," in *Critical Essays*, ed. MacDonald, 361–69, and *From Tobacco Road to Route 66: The Southern Poor White in Fiction* (Chapel Hill, 1976), 76–80.

*Kneel to the Rising Sun* represented for Caldwell an enthusiastic return to short story writing after an interval away from this favored pursuit and into writing of a very different kind. Between the publication of *We Are the Living* in 1933 and *Kneel to the Rising Sun* in 1935, Caldwell found himself not merely "on the fringe of Communism," but he also underwent another experience familiar to many American writers of the 1930s: he found himself on the periphery of Hollywood movie making, as a screen writer. He replaced Faulkner in 1933 on the MGM movie *Bride of the Bayou* with such rapidity after the former's firing that Malcolm Cowley felt they must have been bitten by the same mosquitoes during the Gulf coast shooting of the film. Caldwell too was withdrawn from the script and sent on to Hollywood, where he was to work intermittently over a twenty-year period. He later described it as a "toilsome and far-from-happy career as an off-and-on, in-and-out, sometimes screenwriter at M-G-M, at Warner Brothers in Burbank, and at Twentieth Century-Fox in Westwood,"[24] but it provided him with necessary money when he was making little from his books, especially at the outset, in 1933, when he spent the last of his cash to attend the obscenity trial of *God's Little Acre* (*CE*, 138). To an interviewer's query about whether his Hollywood experiences helped his fiction writing, Caldwell replied, "Not a bit. It was just a waste of time," but an indirect lesson had already come of it by the end of 1933, a year in which Caldwell did not write a novel or a single short story.[25] He decided as a consequence of this that "a writer should set aside ample time for the practice of his profession and guard it zealously" (*CE*, 134), and the hiatus in his own fiction writing apparently renewed his sense of vocation. Early in 1934 he began writing again, reportedly on Greyhound bus trips, bound for "Philadelphia, Baltimore, Washington, Scranton, Pittsburgh, Cleveland, Chicago, Detroit, and Buffalo," completing half-a-dozen short stories en route, including the title one of his new collection, "Kneel to the Rising Sun" (*CE*, 154).

Of the seventeen stories that comprise the book, perhaps half have a central, rather than an incidental, concern with economic misery, social injustice, and the related political issues of individual isolation and detachment or group commitment and action. An even

24. Tharpe, "Interview with Erskine Caldwell," 71; Cowley, "Georgia Boy," 325; Erskine Caldwell, "A Night in November/Beverly Hills, California," *Georgia Review*, XXXVI (1982), 106.

25. Broadwell and Hoag, "The Art of Fiction LXII," 148.

smaller number might be labeled true proletarian stories by the most rigorous definition of the term. Caldwell himself had written earlier, "We cannot expect to write or to read genuinely proletarian novels until we live in a proletarian world."[26] His stories are, like the Dahlberg novel he so much admired, the first steps toward a revolutionary literary consciousness; but they offer virtually none of the optimism that marked the most orthodox left-wing fiction of the thirties and deal candidly with the power of counterrevolutionary forces, not merely in society but in the potential proletariat itself.

One pervasive preoccupation in many of the stories in *Kneel to the Rising Sun* is with solidarity and fragmentation among people who are wholly outside organized institutions, such as unions, or indeed any clearly defined groups that might give them a common identity or goal. In only two stories in the collection, "Daughter" and "Slow Death," does a sense of solidarity assert itself and triumph, in both cases as a bitter rebirth out of a needless death. In "Daughter" it results in a crowd of men acting in unison to free from jail a sharecropper who has despairingly shot his starving child. They act with the apparent collusion of a sympathetic sheriff who departs in the opposite direction. Several of Caldwell's favorite techniques combine in this story to produce its unconventional outcome. The tension in it is built from a series of antiphonal repetitions from the central characters: the sheriff urges his prisoner to eat, to rest, to calm himself, to take it easy; the sharecropper repeats obliviously, "Daughter's been hungry, though—awful hungry" (*KRS*, 153); and the crowd outside the jailhouse window presses closer, roaring and shouting ominously. However, the anticipated mob fury that might, in another story, have produced a lynching, instead acts, contrary to all expectations, to enforce a different kind of justice: "'Pry that jail door open and let Jim out,' somebody said. 'It ain't right for him to be in there'" (*KRS*, 159). It is the same impulse that in earlier comic stories brought about a whimsical surprise ending, but it is now applied to people's capacity to bypass a conventional response in favor of a larger conception of morality.

In "Slow Death," the setting is almost classically proletarian—in an urban Hooverville of dry-goods boxes and packing crates on the banks of the Savannah River, where the grim cycle of birth and death among the poor has neither privacy nor any hint of dignity:

26. Caldwell, "Ripe for Revolution," 22.

"When old men and women, starved and yellow, died in one of them, their bodies were carried down to the river and lowered into the muddy water; when babies were born, people leaned over the railings above and listened to the screams of birth and threw peanut shells over the side" (*KRS*, 173). The images of the story, however, suggest forebodings of change; the roar of traffic in the streets sounds like "an angry mob fighting for their lives" (*KRS*, 174); and there is a constant sense that time is running out, that something must be done "before all of us starve to death and get carried feet first down into that mud-slough of a river" (*KRS*, 175). As the narrator and his friend roam the city in desperation, Dave, the friend, is knocked down and killed while the narrator, in trying to protect him, is knocked unconscious by a policeman's nightstick. However, his return to consciousness is a symbolic one, for he is now being aided by an anonymous member of the crowd, from whose pocket the policeman's stick is protruding. The symbol of authority and repression has shifted sides, and a new fraternity is established between two strangers. The story is more imagist and symbolic than naturalist in its method. There is no analysis of causes or cures, no anticipation of an inevitable revolution, but there is a distinct shift from passivity to action, from victimization to violence, that makes it one of the most overtly political of Caldwell's stories, despite the absence of any group or ideology for these newly awakened mass men to follow.

Much more often in the stories in this collection, Caldwell examines the failure of solidarity between people of common interests, and the bewilderment and guilt that often accompany such a lack of commitment. In "Martha Jean," a group of down-and-out men fail to defend a young girl from the sexual aggression of Nick, into whose poolroom she strays on a bitterly cold night. All of the men are indebted to Nick in some way, and their joint impulses to help the woman collapse before their individual self-interest. A black porter in Nick's Place echoes even more dramatically the impotence of white men. Ordered by Nick to throw one of them out, he is terrified both to obey and to disobey. Out of his powerlessness he becomes not the girl's ally but the main accessory to Nick's brutal schemes for her. "The Cold Winter," which, like so many stories in the collection, uses the ravages of the climate as a symbol of forces that oppose the characters, is a tale of that most passive of all people, an eavesdropper who is drawn vicariously into a family drama with such intensity that he can imagine every facial expression and silent action in the room next to his. He listens to the daily lives of a young woman and her daughter with such empathy that he wills himself to be the father of the child; but when the real father shows up to kill the mother and take the child, he is paralyzed by his long habit of inertia, although he attributes his frozen passivity to the winter cold: "I who would be the father was helpless; my hands and feet were numbed with the cold and I could not move the muscles of my lips" (*KRS*, 124). By the end of the story, he has moved a step closer to acknowledging his complicity: "For a long time I lay against the white plastered wall, trembling because I who was the father had allowed without protest the taking away of the girl, and shaking because I was cold in the unheated room" (*KRS*, 126). Though the world of the story is apolitical, in the wider context of the book it suggests an interesting allegory of a person with the power to enter and evoke the lives of others in the imagination, but unable to act in the real world in which he lives. Vicarious sympathy, no matter how subtle or intense on the part of the storyteller, is finally of no more use than the responses of all the ignorant inhabitants of the rooming house when they finally come running, too late, to the scene of the catastrophe.

Characters who witness action but fail themselves to act are almost a hallmark of Caldwell's fiction, most notably in sexual encounters, but they are present everywhere, looking on and commenting on situations that seem to belie such disengagement. However, in *Kneel to the Rising Sun*, the onlooker, the bystander, the spy, becomes a less comic and more politically significant character whose passivity finally affects the outcome of the story and is thus no longer a neutral or innocent party. This is most dramatically illustrated in the title story of the collection, which opens with a suggestive imagist depiction of what is to follow. The landlord, Arch Gunnard, is sadistically pursuing his favorite hobby of docking the tails of his tenants' dogs and has selected that of his most acquiescent white tenant, Lonnie. While Lonnie looks on in agony, Arch's outspoken black tenant, Clem, has to be held back from protest. A near allegory is thus established among the three characters, of sadism, acquiescence, and protest, but the protester is far more vulnerable as a black than the passive white man, who must choose between loyalty to his race and to his class and common interest. He is the person who may shift the moral balance, though Caldwell does not pretend that this will be more than a symbolic action. However, many forces inhibit Lonnie's capacity to protest, despite the provocations offered him by Arch, which include the starvation of his family because of Arch's meager rations, and the death of his father, who goes wandering one night in search of food, falls into the pig pen, and is greedily devoured by snapping hogs. When Clem questions Lonnie about why he endures such a situation, he can only offer habit as his justification: "I've been loyal to Arch Gunnard for a long time now. . . . I'd hate to haul off and leave him like that" (*KRS*, 223). When Clem can no longer contain himself and attacks Arch, Lonnie is forced to make a choice between his black co-worker and defender and his white exploiter, now rounding up a lynch mob to go after Clem: "He knew he could not take sides with a Negro, in the open, even if Clem had helped him, and especially after Clem had talked to Arch in the way he wished he could himself" (*KRS*, 233). Though he capitulates first to Clem's moral pressure not to reveal his hiding place, Lonnie caves in to Arch's threats and betrays his fellow worker. Clem's ensuing murder produces deathlike throes in Lonnie, but also the stirrings of a new consciousness: "He struggled to his knees, facing the round red sun. The warmth gave him the strength to rise to his feet, and he muttered unintelligibly to himself. He tried to say things he had never thought to say before" (*KRS*, 244). Had Caldwell ended his story on this note, it might have been the social reform tract that some of his partisans welcomed it as, with the rising sun heralding the dawn of the revolution. However, as Lonnie returns again to the world of stale custom, he also retreats from the new awareness that had touched him at sunrise. The final image is neither of him kneeling to the sun nor rising in strength, but slumped inertly with his chin falling on his chest, in mute testimony to Clem's earlier taunt that "if you worked for Arch Gunnard long enough, your face would be sharp enough to split the boards for your own coffin" (*KRS*, 206). Caldwell has posited the revolutionary ideal of solidarity in this story squarely in the rural South and examined its failure and near success with both sympathy and irony. This long story is placed at the end of the collection and thus concludes it with a reminder of the possibility of a new social order, even if it is one that is denied within the setting of the story. Though it is a story of betrayal, it offers a vision of cooperation and thus serves to qualify both the simpler optimistic brotherhood of "Slow Death" and "Daughter" and the utter bleakness of a number of other stories in the collection, which tend to suggest that if any improvement is ever to come to the lives of the poor, it must be generated elsewhere than in their own futile struggles.

Two of the most shocking stories, "Masses of Men" and "Blue

Boy," deal with victims outside the potential embrace of any stirring proletariat—a nine-year-old girl and a retarded black youth—and, perhaps because of their exceptionality, brought down many accusations on Caldwell that he was dealing in pure sensationalism or in the dishonest manipulation of some supposedly objective facts. Certainly, both present appalling incidents in the detached manner of a dispassionate reporter, but the details and images that shape the reader's response to the stories are scarcely the raw material of journalism. Nevertheless, the question, Could these things actually have happened? which seems to have troubled so many of Caldwell's early reviewers and critics—to both resounding affirmations and denials—was to dog Caldwell's fiction perpetually. It was well answered by Hamilton Basso, who, in a response to "Blue Boy" felt that "it could not have happened . . . [but that] idealistically, as a creative and artistic truth, it not only could happen but did." However, despite Basso's effort to focus readers' attention on the aesthetic effect of the stories, many found themselves unable to move beyond challenges to, and defenses of, their authenticity. At one extreme, Arthur Ruhl asked, "Isn't Mr. Caldwell, with his unbroken procession of animalistic negroes, decadent sharecroppers, and sadistic white bosses, leading us on a bit?"; whereas at the other, Oscar Cargill exclaimed passionately, "How any Southerner, after reading this volume and recognizing the shameful truths here told by a native son, can repeat the fatuous nonsense about Southern standards and Southern chivalry, is beyond comprehension."[27] Caldwell, who very likely enjoyed the insinuation that he was leading readers on just as much as the vindication of his view of the South, did not aid in any resolution of this issue, for he insisted continually on the fictiveness of his work, but at the same time encouraged the notion that it was an accurate sociological document.

"Blue Boy" depicts a seventeen-year-old black youth, damaged in mind and body, who is brought in to entertain a group of white people, belching and bloated from their New Year's Day dinner. Though he walks unsteadily—"He dragged his feet sideways over the floor, making a sound like soy beans being poured into a wooden barrel" (KRS, 163)—he is forced to perform a pantomime

27. Hamilton Basso, "Sunny South," in Critical Essays, ed. MacDonald, 38; Arthur Ruhl, "Seventeen Tales by Erskine Caldwell," in Critical Essays, ed. MacDonald, 34; Oscar Cargill, Intellectual America: Ideas on the March (1941; rpr. New York, 1968), 393.

of killing a shoat, to dance, and finally to masturbate for the delight of the company, until he collapses: "With his face pressed against the splintery floor, the grooves in his cheeks began to soften, and his grinning features glistened in the drying perspiration. His breathing became inaudible, and the swollen arteries in his neck were as rigid as taut-drawn ropes" (*KRS*, 169). There is no one in this story to protest, because all the onlookers are in complete complicity; and Blue Boy is no more to them than a grotesque collection of sounds and contortions, a broken toy, but all the more amusing for its defective mechanisms. The imagery in the story alternates skillfully and economically between depicting Blue Boy's barely human physicality—"His once rubbery neck was as rigid as a table-leg" (*KRS*, 168); "He was beginning to droop like a wilting stalk of pig-weed" (*KRS*, 169)—and insisting on the inhumanity that is being displayed toward this wretched person—"The grinning lines on his face had congealed into welt-like scars" (*KRS*, 168). This latter image might stand alone as a response to those critics who felt that Caldwell was dealing in unassimilated shocking material, for it yokes together a naturalistic description (the grinning lines) and an aesthetic and moral response to it (the transformation of those lines into permanent signs of suffering). The lines are what Blue Boy's New Year's audience might see; the response to it is shaped for the reader alone.

The story "Masses of Men" deals with equally appalling material, seemingly unmalleable to an end beyond its own horror. A widowed mother of three starving children, having attempted repeatedly and unsuccessfully to prostitute herself, finally sells the sexual services of her nine-year-old daughter for a quarter. Given such a plot, the opportunities for sensationalism, in the service of whatever cause, seem almost irresistible; but Caldwell provides a curious oblique focus for the story by observing the man who buys the child's services as closely as he depicts the desperate mother who urges the transaction. The man is cowardly as well as lustful, well aware of the legal, if not the ethical, side of his crime. He hangs back and delays, repeatedly suspecting a trap and complaining of the icy coldness of the family's room. To his ritual repetitions, the mother responds only, "Give me the quarter" (*KRS*, 200), until it seems finally as though it is the man who capitulates to her greater pressure. Hunger thus proves to be the most brutally insistent instinct of all, from which every other debasement is derived. When the mother makes her bargain, Caldwell follows her to the store as she races with the money held in her mouth until it can be exchanged for food, and as she leaves the girl to her unobserved fate. There are no witnesses in this story, either in complicity with, or frustrated opposition to, its horrors, except the reader. With nine-year-old Pearl, Caldwell might seem to have reached the final victim of an inhumane system, although seven-year-old Ruby, whimpering, "I'm hungry, Mamma" (*KRS*, 193), will clearly have to serve her turn too.

Although many of the stories in *Kneel to the Rising Sun* that deal with victimization and suffering have some political dimension to them, Caldwell pursues the theme of sacrifice and the potential re-generation that may result from it in other, less partisan contexts. The most notable of these tales is "The Growing Season," a story of physical deprivation and torture, culminating in a sacrificial death that provides neither a new political awareness, as Clem's does briefly in "Kneel to the Rising Sun," nor even a temporary cessation of hunger, as Pearl's sacrifice does in "Masses of Men." Instead, the ritual shedding of blood in "The Growing Season" appears to be an instinctive effort to placate some natural divinity that drives a cotton farmer to such a slaughter. The sacrificial victim in the tale is a crea-ture called Fiddler, whose identity was variously guessed at by early reviewers as a mule, a dog, or even the cotton farmer Jesse's idiot child. The confusion appears as a deliberate design on Caldwell's part to reveal Fiddler only in his role as scapegoat. The imagery for him blurs various forms of human and animal life: he flounders like a fish, thrashes like a headless chicken, wobbles on underdeveloped legs, and pitches forward like a drunk. Though Caldwell depicts the sacrifice of Fiddler as a dubious and debased ritual, his death sates some instinctive need in the farmer. Jesse is revivified by it and afterward feels a breeze blowing against his skin like a gentle rain: "Jesse was not certain, but he felt he might be able to save his crop. The wire-grass could not stand up under a sharp hoe-blade, and he could go back and file his hoe with the rat-tailed file when-ever it wanted sharpening" (*KRS*, 149). Thus Jesse returns, "bare-headed in the hot sun" (*KRS*, 149), to the grueling routine, tempo-rarily purged of the futile anguish of being a cotton farmer. Caldwell was later to investigate and report in some economic and sociologi-cal depth on the plight of desperate southern farmers in *You Have Seen Their Faces*; but this story, which stands entirely outside such a study, is its best companion piece in giving a far different, sym-bolic picture of the degeneration of the once-sacred practice of agriculture.

"The Growing Season" and "Candy-Man Beechum," another tale of sacrifice, are much less concerned than the others in the collection with providing sociological and economic contexts for their action. Though both have subjects—a southern cotton farmer and a black man—that might easily lend themselves to left-wing treatment, both are written in a mode more mythical than political. Just as "The Growing Season" shifts the plight of the cotton farmer away from society and emphasizes instead a man's struggle with the eternal powers of nature, so "Candy-Man Beechum" displaces the conventional terms of a story of racial persecution and creates instead a folk legend of a black man who is himself the embodiment of an exuberant life-force too large for any worldly subjugation. Candy-Man, a seven foot mule skinner, moves throughout this short tale in a single, direct line, from the Ogeechee swamps to his Saturday-night fish fry and meeting with his girl in town. He strides like a giant across the countryside, trumpeting his presence to move lesser mortals out of his path. Everything in the tale is dwarfed by Candy-Man's power and his gargantuan appetites for food and his girl, until Caldwell halts the tide of his progress with the casual inquiry of a policeman, "What's your hurry, Candy-Man?" (*KRS*, 6). By now, however, Candy-Man has built up too much impetus to acknowledge the petty authority of guns and handcuffs: "I'd a heap rather be traveling than standing still," he affirms and by his bravado invites his own destruction. He dies with the same comic grandeur with which he had lived: "There ain't much use in living if that's the way it's going to be. I reckon I'll just have to blow out the light and fade away. . . . Make way for Candy-Man Beechum, because here I come" (*KRS*, 7–8). This story is one of Caldwell's most effective in achieving both a chanting, rhythmic substitute for dialect and in using repetition—"make way for these flapping feet"—to propel the story to its rapid climax. Though it reveals the evidence of racial injustice, it is more memorable for the epic comic energy of its hero than for the puny force that extinguishes him. Although the story is not overtly political, it is significantly placed at the beginning of the collection that culminates in the lynching of the heroic black Clem in "Kneel to the Rising Sun," so that a frame of daredevil black vitality encompasses all of the other tales.

Though the themes of sacrifice, collusion, protest, and solidarity provide links among many of the disparate stories of this collection, it is also quite as eclectic as Caldwell's earlier two in its mixture of concerns and perspectives. Two of the stories, "The Walnut Hunt" and "Maud Island," deal in differing degrees of seriousness with adolescent boys and their discovery of sex; and there are joke stories, such as "A Day's Wooing" and "The Shooting," which derive as much relish as ever from the foolish antics of the characters. In "The Shooting," the absurdly named marshal Toy Shaw disarms a "thin little girl" (*KRS*, 72) with an empty gun, to the enormous entertainment of a small-town crowd as bored as any ever created by Mark Twain: "Somebody fired a pistol two or three times, and the reports shook dust loose from the canned goods on the grocery shelves and woke up some of the flies in the display windows. There had not been so much excitement in town since the morning the bloodhounds tracked the post-office robbers to the vestry of the Methodist church" (*KRS*, 64). This is Caldwell's best economic and comic style. In a collection of stories where a noble brotherhood of people can act in unison to free a wrongfully imprisoned man, or two unemployed comrades can forge an anonymous union against corrupt authority, Caldwell's characters can still be trivial and ridiculous. The not-so-wholesome proletarians in "The Honeymoon" hang around the neighborhood poolroom for "five or six years, maybe ten or twelve" (*KRS*, 74), claiming they are all waiting for a job at the filling station. Their only apparent subjugation to the boss class is their prompt obedience to the ginnery whistle; when it blows at 1:30 P.M., they all go home to dinner, the crowd breaking up "like a rotten egg hitting the side of a barn" (*KRS*, 76). Is this the same crowd that watched Blue Boy perform? That lynched Clem? That freed Jim? Kenneth Burke now began to doubt whether anyone "so apt at entertaining us by *muddling* our judgments" would ever be equally successful at stabilizing those judgments.[28] In publishing *Kneel to the Rising Sun*, Caldwell had both "gone left" to some degree and finally raised the revolution above the belt, but he had still produced an incongruous and "muddling" set of stories. The anomalous and eclectic nature of his vision was by now becoming established as its most consistent feature. Whether there were considerable virtues in this "muddling" of his readers' judgments is a reasonable question; it may be partially answered by Caldwell's later story collections, where he did in fact move toward a stabler and more simplified perspective on his material.

28. Burke, "Caldwell: Maker of Grotesques," 169.

## Southways

*The wild marchgrass of the imagination is thinning, and at the same time*
*a more utilitarian crop, with deeper roots, is being matured.*

—Otis Ferguson

By 1938, when Caldwell published his fourth collection of short stories, *Southways*, he had become a well-known figure in the American literary world. He could place his work profitably in the *Atlantic*, the *New Yorker*, and *Esquire*, rather than give it away to *Clay*
or beg for a few dollars' payment from *Pagany*. His work was now
familiar enough to critics and reviewers for them to scrutinize it for
signs of direction, development, and improvement. Assuming the
eclecticism of his subjects and the incongruity of his tone to be
merely a prelude to a mature style, they began to advise him that
his true métier was folk comedy, not politics, or alternatively, cruel
realism rather than entertainment, or again, fantasy rather than social significance.[29] If any consensus might be said to have emerged
from contemporary and later criticism, it was that Caldwell was least
effective in those stories that seemed to ask for pity or compassion
as responses to the plight of his characters. When they elicited humor, censure, anger, shock, or outrage, Caldwell's exaggeratedly
simple, imagist style would suffice; but if the characters required
sympathy for their human condition, unqualified by incongruity or
irony, the result was, at best, bathos. Yet Caldwell seemed to require of himself some effort to balance tenderness and sensitivity
with the irrational and instinctual impulses that pervade his fictional
people. Every collection of his short stories had contained one or
two such tales, but in *Southways* there is a heavier than usual emphasis on stories in which simple folk are placed in situations of pain
and suffering, largely devoid of any dissonant images that might confuse a reader's simple, compassionate response to them.

Caldwell insisted on his pleasure in creating these sad tales, commenting on one of them, "Wild Flowers": "I derive more satisfaction from the writing of stories such as this one than I do from any
other" (*J*, 289). This story certainly moderates in some important
ways the portrait of the southern poor white that prevails in so much
else of Caldwell's work, including even his documentary writing, by

29. Halpert, *A Return to "Pagany,"* 221. See Dorothy Van Doren, "Out of Georgia," in *Critical Essays*, ed. MacDonald, 68–69; Jonathan Daniels, "From Comedy
to Pity," in *Critical Essays*, ed. MacDonald, 67–68; and Otis Ferguson, "Caldwell's
Stories," in *Critical Essays*, ed. MacDonald, 69–70.

depicting affection and devotion between a man and his pregnant wife as a force more powerful than all the cruelty of the tenant system that oppresses, and usually degrades, such people. The story does have one interesting twist in its depiction of these utterly helpless poor whites; for when the husband rouses a family of blacks in the night to help his wife give birth, the blacks first hide in terror of him and then rush obediently to serve him, making the powerless husband, for once in his life, into a "boss." Though the story ends tragically, with the wife's death, Caldwell picks up essentially the same loving couple again, with only a slight variation in plot, in the story "Man and Woman." Here the two are traveling by foot across the countryside, begging their way in order to visit their dead baby's grave. This latter story is little more than its tear-wrenching plot; but it insists again, not on the more usual dehumanization that poverty brings in Caldwell's world, but on the ways in which the world denies the higher feelings of poor people. "A Knife to Cut the Corn Bread With" also deals with marital devotion and sacrifice, this time between a disabled husband and his seventeen-year-old wife who must carry on his farm labor in order to earn enough for them to survive. However, this story finally submerges its sentimentality under the shocking image that gives it its title—the knife is used not to cut the corn bread but to slice some of the disabled tenant's own flesh so that the starving poor may feed literally, as well as figuratively, upon each other.

Besides these marginally political stories, which depict love in the face of soul-destroying poverty, Caldwell has also several stories in *Southways* that deal with romantic love and loss outside any significant social context. These often seem closer to plot outlines than fully realized stories. The pithiness of Caldwell's style is effective for both humor and shock, and for creating a sense of incongruity and horror, but when it becomes a vehicle for direct statements of pathos, its nakedness seems faintly embarrassing. Caldwell's plots are often slender devices on which to hang his tales, but at best they are whimsical, with sudden unexpected turns that defy anticipation. Often he uses simple character types, together with an unusual incident, to jolt the reader's expectations, as in the surprising behavior of the frustrated farmer with the silk panties in "Midsummer Passion." The same purpose is sometimes effectively accomplished with simple plots but larger-than-life characters, as in "Candy-Man Beechum." However, the combination of ordinary character types with conventional climaxes and denouements is extraordinarily unsatisfactory in his work, for Caldwell is no poet of the ordinary, the average, or the everyday, despite his admiration for Sherwood Anderson. Caldwell's talent is for creating alienating effects rather than mutual sympathy. It can work well for political and satirical purposes or, less didactically, for laughs and shudders, but rarely for pity or empathy, despite his professed satisfaction with such tales.

Jonathan Daniels felt that Caldwell's deliberate striving to be "heart-rending" was only serving to make a "conventional and sentimental . . . moralist" of a writer whose power was for creating disturbing laughter.[30] Certainly, Caldwell's most striking perceptions come in stories where feeling is subordinated to a perverse detail or twisted to an unusual perspective, rather than in those that display the candid didacticism that is aroused from pity. *Southways* has two stories, both about race relations, that illustrate the ways in which Caldwell's special talent and his moral design may work together or become divorced. The story "Return to Lavinia" deals with the love between a white man and a black woman who is both his housekeeper and mistress. This love is first threatened and then reaffirmed by his marriage to a white woman who will provide a respectable front for the affair. The story deals awkwardly in stereotypes of the sensuous high-yellow girl and the frigid old-maid schoolteacher, without either enlarging or challenging them. It makes a formulaic demand for moral indignation in the black woman's behalf, but fails to make her or her situation distinct or memorable. By contrast, the other story, "Runaway," takes what might have been a melodramatic situation—a conflict between a cruel white woman and a courageous black one over a black child abused by the white—and focuses on a character peripheral to that dispute, the white woman's husband. When he is sent to the black woman's home to retrieve the runaway child, he is trapped in one of Caldwell's typical comic moral quandaries between two formidable women, one of whom supplies him with food and shelter. This middle-aged white man is almost as powerless in the story as the nine-year-old black serving girl, and the story creates an interesting tension between her absolute and his qualified impotence, between her desperate rebellion and his timid expediency. The concern with racial injustice in the tale is not minimized by being placed in the context of arbitrary tyranny by an adult over a child, or of the propertied Mrs. Garley over her dependent husband; in fact, the

30. Daniels, "From Comedy to Pity," 67.

Erskine Caldwell and the Fiction of Poverty

oblique focus makes the ethical point more effectively than the tendentious indictment of "Return to Lavinia."

Several of the comic tales in *Southways* also exhibit this ability to include indirect social criticism in a story that focuses primarily on a less overtly political or ideological topic. One of the best of these is "A Small Day," about a landlord's lust for the "hellcat" (*S*, 34) daughter of one of his tenants. This story reveals a social density of details about class and race relationships in a stagnating cotton economy that more than complements its quite insubstantial plot and traditional humor. Governor Gil's efforts to woo Daisy are obviously going to prove as futile as his habitual assaults with his walking stick on the heads of the weeds in the cotton, the tale's opening image. Daisy proves recalcitrant to the "damned old fool" (*S*, 30), despite her father's recognition that a match with the landlord means "not having to go hungry for something to eat, and having enough clothes to cover your nakedness" (*S*, 32), and escaping tedious field labor "tomorrow and every day as long as cotton grows" (*S*, 33). Nevertheless, when she rebuffs the landlord violently, her father enjoys the situation immensely, bringing down upon himself the threat that he will have his head chopped off, presumably with the same effect as the Governor's attack on the weeds. This threat to the tenant is delivered by a nervous black houseboy, terrified of carrying an insult from one white to another, thus hinting indirectly at even more tangled allegiances of caste and class in this small segment of southern society.

While Caldwell was writing the stories that comprise *Southways*, he was also in the process of envisioning a new series of books about American regional life, a series he hoped might "describe and interpret the indigenous quality of life" in areas throughout the United States (*CE*, 182). Caldwell intended to serve merely as editor of this American Folkways series, and to give the writing of the individual books to local experts, but a number of the stories in *Southways* testify to his fascination and expertise with the particular folkways of the South and their embodiment in legends, superstitions, and jokes. One of these stories, "Hamrick's Polar Bear," is an animal tall tale; one, "Nine Dollars Worth of Mumble," is a kind of nocturnal chant about black superstitions; and one, "The Fly in the Coffin," is virtually a ballad of funeral lore. The latter two stories are especially interesting in their narrative voice and tone. "Nine Dollars Worth of Mumble" is set in darkness, lit by sparks from the fires of Sally Lucky, the conjure woman, and pinch-faced Mattie, the guardian of a young woman whom Youster Brown is pursuing with charms and curses. Although the narrator is not an actor in the story, his voice is entirely part of the little community he tells of: "You couldn't see no stars, you couldn't see no moon, you couldn't see nothing much but a measly handful of sparks on the chimley spout. It was a mighty poor beginning for a female courting on a ten o'clock night. Hollering didn't do a bit of good, and stomping up and down did less" (S, 49). The voice almost identifies with Youster Brown, but not quite, because he will eventually be revealed as the comic victim of his own sharp practices; and the narrator, although aware of the joke on Youster, is innocent of any satiric intent on his community's irrational customs.

The tale "The Fly in the Coffin" is an equally remarkable exercise in controlled tone, this time in emulating the cadences of a ballad in its choral and repetitive effects. The plot is undoubtedly common to the folklore of many countries, dealing with a corpse who rises from his death during the funeral in order to secure the right conditions for his permanent rest. In this case, the dead man's obsession has been with pursuing flies—on one occasion on an epic eight-day cross-country flight; on another through the buzz saw at the lumber mill, the occasion of his present decease. The fly is used cleverly in the story as a symptom of Dose's irascibility with the whole world he is leaving behind—the lazy sawmill hands who have not yet dug the grave; the banjo-playing fool, Hap Conson; the jigging, skirt-heisting, high yellow, Goodie; the time-wasting Aunt Marty—all these characters form a repeated refrain to Dose's frustration until finally he can stand it no longer. He rises up to rebuke them for their irresponsibility and to demand a flyswatter: "There wasn't a sound made anywhere. The shovellers didn't shovel, Hap didn't pick a note, and Goodie didn't shake a thing. Marty got the swatter fast as she could, because she knew better than to keep Dose waiting, and handed it down to him. Dose stretched out in the splintery pine box and pulled the lid shut" (S, 96–97). After some violent swishing noises from inside, there is silence, and then the community returns to its normal patterns of misbehavior, having witnessed the genesis of a new legend.

While Caldwell was receiving critical praise for stories predominantly in this comic folk vein, he was simultaneously finding a much greater outlet than hitherto in nonfiction and documentary writing for his most direct political, social, and economic concerns. He had published two nonfiction books of sharply ideological commentary on American life during the depression—*Some American People* (1935) and, with Margaret Bourke-White, *You Have Seen Their Faces* (1937)—and was currently contemplating in 1938 the trip to Czechoslovakia that would result in *North of the Danube* (1939). After *Southways*, he did not publish another collection of short stories for five very busy years, and when the next one, *Georgia Boy*, appeared in 1943, it represented a very different kind of collection from *Southways*, or indeed any of the others of the 1930s, both narrower in range and more consistent in comic tone. This was perhaps the mature style that critics had been seeking, but it was achieved by limiting the chaotic variety that was the hallmark of all the previous short story collections, which, for all the critical frustration they provoked, were nevertheless evidence of a boisterous and fertile talent that had refused to conform to any prescribed notions of form, tone, or genre.

## Georgia Boy

> Georgia Boy is . . . *something like what Mark Twain might have done had he come from Georgia and found himself in a playful mood, and . . . if he had wanted to be sure of not offending his public.*
> —*W. M. Frohock*

*Georgia Boy*, Caldwell's next book of stories, did in many ways fit into a particularly American literary genre, although the author would undoubtedly have disclaimed acquaintance with most of its earlier examples, except perhaps *Winesburg, Ohio*. This is the genre of a cycle of linked short stories, often focusing on one or more recurring characters, in a historical setting or local community that is central to the themes explored. The stories are all capable of standing independently but gain a good deal from their interdependence in the cycle. Other examples of this form of fiction, besides *Winesburg, Ohio*, are Hemingway's *In Our Time*, Faulkner's *The Unvanquished*, Steinbeck's *The Pastures of Heaven*, and Wright's *Uncle Tom's Children*. Caldwell later described this form, in an interview, as possibly an "ideal form" for his own purposes, because "it can be divided into parts and yet the whole put together is a novel."[31] The advantages of the form, however, are greater than mere convenience for the short story writer who wants to emphasize a larger vision of the world surrounding the individual tales. It provides a way of suggesting the density of relationships, customs, and

31. Collins, "Erskine Caldwell at Work," 24.

traditions that form the usual basis of the social novel, while retaining a freedom from their accompanying restrictions, for both characters and author. There need be no continuous plot, for people may appear and move on without explanation, but there may be patterns of action and recurring themes. Though a single narrative voice may be common to all stories, the perspective and point of view may be varied, because such a collection does not demand the tonal consistency of a novel. The form of *Georgia Boy* permits Caldwell to make effective use of some of his best talents—the skillful narrative voice of a naïve, small-town boy, the easy anecdotal tone that relishes the repeated storytelling exercise, the humor that derives from individual crankiness and communal eccentricity, and the keen observation of rival and conflicting authority among people of different ages, classes, sexes, and races. Though the episodes that comprise *Georgia Boy* were written over a five-year period, filled for Caldwell with many of the most dramatic adventures of his life, they are more cohesive than any of his earlier collections of stories, for they are limited by a single time, place, set of characters, narrative voice, and, perhaps most important, comic tone.

The first of the stories was written and published separately in the *New Yorker* in 1937; the remainder were composed in New York, Los Angeles, London, Moscow, China, and back home in Arizona after trips with Margaret Bourke-White to Czechoslovakia, around the United States, and to the Soviet Union between 1938 and 1942. These were both fertile and frantic years for Caldwell: he produced with Bourke-White *North of the Danube* (1939), *Say, Is This the U.S.A.* (1941), and *Russia at War* (1942); and by himself, *Moscow Under Fire* (1942), *All-Out on the Road to Smolensk* (1942), and *All Night Long* (1942). Clearly, *Georgia Boy* belonged to a world apart from the one Caldwell was inhabiting when he wrote the stories. He described them as "a series of sketches about a boy in Georgia growing up in company with his mother, his father, and a Negro playmate of the same age—growing up at that particular time in America when life was a little more leisurely and there was not so much compelling action put upon people."[32] There is in these stories a comforting kernel of security and nostalgia for less complicated times, as well as a tendency to rehearse very frequently the same basic material in various disguises, both qualities probably related to the chaotic circumstances of the book's composition.

Though critics and reviewers found *Georgia Boy* more entertain-

32. *Ibid.*, 24.

ing and less didactic and shocking than earlier Caldwell works—
W. M. Frohock noted the absence of "the rampant sexuality, the
murderous ignorance, the bitterly depressing picture of Georgia
life"—the distancing of these concerns is achieved more through
the innocence of the young narrator than through Caldwell's neglect
of them.[33] In fact, four of the fourteen episodes deal with Pa Stroup's
sexual misadventures, but his son William can only report the consequences of his own naïve eavesdropping, spying, and misunderstanding. When Pa disappears into the locked woodshed with the
gypsy queen, William reports, "I heard him giggle as if he was being
tickled. In a minute the Queen began to giggle, too" (GB, 111).
Similarly, when a traveling saleswoman tries to sell Pa a necktie,
William can only note, "I could see his nose flare open and shut like
a hound sniffing a coon up a tree when he got a whiff of the perfume"
(GB, 160). There is certainly abundant evidence of Caldwell's continuing concern for the abusive treatment of blacks and for the general inequities of the social system to which young William responds
with utter childlike candor and insensitivity. His boundless curiosity
makes him a perceptive, if ignorant, narrator, but his affection for
his dissolute and villainous father apparently infected many reviewers' responses to the satire of the stories. Pa Stroup is depicted as
something of a cross between Rip Van Winkle and Huck Finn's Pap.
His laziness is almost heroic in nature and, like Rip, he has a large
following of dogs; when his ill-treated and unpaid black yardboy
runs away, he feels, like Pap, that somehow *his* rights have been
violated: "It ought to be against the law for a darkey just to pick up
and go without a by-your-leave. He might have owed me some
money" (GB, 118). However, William, unlike Huck, eagerly awaits
the return home of his father from his frequent excursions and as-
pires to accompany him whenever possible. Though Pa and Ma
Stroup wrangle and fight, the family unit of parents, child, and servant is a powerful one in *Georgia Boy;* it shows no signs of dissolu-
tion, no matter how imperfect its members. The exclusiveness of
Caldwell's focus on a single family might seem likely to restrain the
scope of his indictments of society at large, but in fact it serves in
some indirect ways to intensify them by revealing how cruelty, self-
indulgence, deceit, and victimization operate in that most intimate
of settings, between husband and wife, parent and child, master and
servant. Though there are no dismemberments, rapes, or murders

33. Frohock, "Erskine Caldwell: Sentimental Gentleman," 201.

in *Georgia Boy*, Pa's theft of William's savings to see an "unadorned-dancing-girls-of-all-nations" side-show at a carnival (*GB*, 124), his callous willingness to inflict all manner of pain on the serving boy, Handsome Brown, and Ma's harsh revenge on Pa by cooking his favorite fighting cock in a pie so that "my old man hasn't been the same since" (*GB*, 227) appear more brutal in the family context than many more extreme atrocities in other stories. Despite its evident reception as light humorous entertainment, this collection of stories does not signal a retreat for Caldwell from the social concerns of the 1930s, but the resiliency of the characters to suffering and the consistency of the comic tone serve to modify and make more palatable the harshness of the earlier presentation.

Because of the cyclical form of the *Georgia Boy* collection, Caldwell can use individual stories to complement, qualify, and create a more complicated sense of character than in his other short stories, which tend to focus narrowly on situation and incident. Thus, though Pa Stroup is a parodic and exaggerated figure, he is certainly not one dimensional. Though he neglects all the normal responsibilities of providing for his family by abandoning their farm to loaf around town every day, he is capable of the most careful husbandry of his favorite sycamore tree, pruning back its dead limbs and daubing paint around the woodpecker holes until there is nothing left but the trunk, which "jutted straight into the air like a telephone pole" (*GB*, 87). He likes to start his day with a nap after breakfast but is capable of putting wild spurts of energy into futile and fantastic money-making schemes, and will walk for several days to attend a cock fight. He abuses and exploits Handsome Brown with complete lack of concern but proves capable of conscientious and nurturing tenderness to College Boy, his game cock. He is more immature than either of the boys in the household: "My old man, Handsome, and me played marbles sometimes, and Pa was always fudging on Handsome and breaking up the game by taking all his marbles away from him even when we weren't playing for keeps" (*GB*, 118). But he can prove far from innocent in evading the consequences of his actions.

Ma is, by contrast, grim, dutiful, and punitive. She is forced to compensate for Pa's shiftlessness by taking in washing, a responsibility she bears with angry endurance so that William and Handsome are attuned to every gradation of her wrath and its implications: "She was no more mad than usual, but that was enough. When she tapped the woodwork with things like the door key, it

was the only sign anybody needed to know how she was feeling"
(*GB*, 194). Although Pa cannot be induced by all the pressure of the
preacher to attend church, Ma teaches a Sunday School class. Be-
longing to the Ladies Social Circle and the Sycamore Ladies Improvement Society, Ma is the repressive and parental voice of civilization confronting Pa's unredeemed nature; like a poor white
version of Hawthorne's Merry Mount, sobriety and indulgence
struggle for dominion within a single household. However, the format of the book provides Ma, like Pa, with modifications to her
personality that preempt any simple judgment on her. She is capable of seeing, and objecting to, Pa's cruelty to Handsome, but not
her own harshness toward the boy; she has a soft spot for Pretty
Sooky, the calf that Pa outrages her by stealing; and, despite her
disapproval of Pa's dissolute brother Ned, she feeds him with grudg-
ing charity: "The Good Lord will never be able to say that I didn't
lend a helping hand, even though I know it's not the right thing to
do" (*GB*, 219).

Given the choice between his fallible, errant father and his bitter, self-righteous mother, William has no hesitation in preferring
the idler's life of fishing and carnivals; he even emulates, with Handsome, some of his father's dreams of easy money, despite his observation of the drastic consequences of this way of life for the family
and himself. When his father returns in the middle of the night after
a long absence, provoking a furious set-to between Ma and the girl
he has brought back with him, William listens to the fight while
snuggling under his bedcovers and thinking, "It sure felt good being
there in the dark with him" (*GB*, 205). He is happiest when following his father around on any of his foolish pursuits or merely sitting
on the porch with him, smelling the smoke of his cigar stub. Ma,
sensing this empathy, tries her best to keep William from witnessing
his old man's escapades. Her instructions to him to "go inside the
house and pull down all the window shades and shut the doors"
(*GB*, 113) form a constant chorus to the episodes, a chorus that is
matched by the equal repetition of its counterrefrain, "My old man
cut his eyes around and looked up at me" (*GB*, 66), acknowledging
the son's complicit witness of his acts. Though William is clearly
partial to his father, his disinterested child's eye records the burden
that is placed on his mother by Pa's irresponsibility: "All the time
we were out behind the chicken house, Ma was in the backyard
boiling the washing. She was doing Mrs. Taylor's washing then, but
there were six or seven others that she did every week, too. It
looked as if she washed every day and ironed all night" (*GB*, 234).

Elsewhere, he records impassively her comment, "If it's not one thing your Pa's done . . . it's something else. I declare, sometimes I think I'll never have a minute's peace as long as I live" (*GB*, 37).

William's ingenuousness has the effect in *Georgia Boy* of continuing the kind of irony that Caldwell had used so successfully in earlier stories with a naïve narrator; but now it becomes an important agent in the revelation of other characters, because William has, as yet, made few judgments on people and therefore reports on all sides of them with candor. He is an ideal narrator in his passivity and the keenness of his pleasure in observing others, in eavesdropping, spying, racing across town by shortcuts so as not to miss his father's rendezvous, and in the double nature of his delight in hiding, peeping, and listening, because of his father's attempted evasions and his mother's hopeless efforts to forbid his discoveries. William's narrative also proves the most effective means of revealing the character and trials of the fourth member of the Stroup family unit, Handsome Brown, their black servant who came to live with them as an eleven-year-old orphan. William and Handsome have the intimacy of brothers, but William is simultaneously quite unmoved by the ordeals Handsome suffers at Pa's hands, ordeals that are described with precision, detachment, and some relish. His fraternal empathy for Handsome, which can cause him to try to prevent his friend from being scolded, disappears completely when Handsome is being mistreated in his capacity as black servant. When Handsome is forced from his bed by Pa in the middle of the night to scare the woodpeckers out of the sycamore, and sits moaning in the top of the tree, William merely comments: "The funny part of it was that there were woodpeckers all over him. Some of them were roosting on his head and shoulders, and a lot of them were hanging to his arms and legs" (*GB*, 94).

Nevertheless, Handsome is gradually revealed as the most sensible member of the family. He is responsible, like Ma (when the gypsies come, it is Handsome who saves the family's mule, William's train, and his own banjo from them), and he is fun loving, like Pa, ready for fishing, loafing, or a baseball argument on the slenderest pretext. However, all of Handsome's common sense and equable nature can be reduced to idiocy by the burden of coexisting with the warring Stroups; for not only is Handsome forced by their demands to dissimulate and vacillate in his actions (a pattern common to blacks in much of Caldwell's work),[34] but in this case, the two

34. See William A. Sutton, *Black Like It Is/Was: Erskine Caldwell's Treatment of Racial Themes* (Metuchen, N.J., 1974), Chap. 3 *passim*.

opposed whites are themselves both fickle and punitive, so that it is virtually impossible for even the prudent Handsome to find any safe ground. When Pa decides he will go into the scrap iron business and removes neighbors' washpots, ax blades, and pump handles to trade for a new pair of rubber boots, Handsome comments innocently, "I ain't never seen it get muddy enough around here in this sandy country to need knee-high rubber boots" (GB, 78). Threatened by Pa with being left behind from a fishing trip for such talk, Handsome quickly reverses himself: "They're the handsomest rubber boots I ever saw before in all my life. . . . I wish I owned them, because I'd be mighty proud" (GB, 78–79). On another occasion, when Handsome is forced by Pa into evasions and lies to cover Pa's absence, he brings down Ma's wrath on his head and can only defend himself lamely by saying, "Sometimes I get a little mixed up when I try to tell the truth in both directions at the same time" (GB, 140). Ma grimly advises him to keep his mouth shut, or "The first thing you know you'll be telling fibs on your own account" (GB, 150), although it was in fact she who insisted on forcing him to tell Pa's whereabouts in the first place. Even Handsome's eagerness to please becomes a means of entrapment for him, as in his encounter with Pa Stroup's brother Ned:

> "I'll bet he ain't never done enough work, all told, to earn a day's board and keep," Uncle Ned said. "Ain't that right, boy?"
> "I–I–I–" Handsome said, stuttering like he always did when he was scared. "I–I–"
> "See?" Uncle Ned said. "What did I tell you? He ain't even got enough energy to lie about it. All the work that shine's ever done could be counted up and poured into a thimble. Ain't that the truth, boy?"
> "I–I–I–" Handsome said, backing away. (GB, 214)

This kind of humiliation has helped to make Handsome a fairly shrewd anticipator and dodger of trouble, but he is completely vulnerable to the physical pain that results from Pa's disregard of his welfare. He is sent up to the roof to chase down some goats and falls into the well, he is forced up the sycamore to silence the woodpeckers, and his head is made a target in a baseball-throwing game in which Pa proves to have considerable skill.

Indeed, so effectively does Caldwell evoke the plight of Handsome in these stories that one of his most sympathetic critics, William Sutton, appears to think that Handsome is the "Georgia boy" of the title: "Georgia Boy," he says, "is devoted to a teenage yardboy,

Handsome Brown, whose preposterous adventures in the ridiculous Stroup family are a presentation of horseplay by a naive narrator for the purpose of expression of indignation against a maladjusted world."[35] Nevertheless, Handsome is merely an accessory to the revelations of the comic villainy of Pa Stroup, which is the central topic of every story, including many where Handsome does not appear or plays a very minor role. Pa's misbehavior falls into certain recurrent patterns of loafing and flirting, concocting crazy schemes for making easy money, and violating all the civilized norms of the community. Among these is the repeated abuse of Handsome; but the book is both broader in its indictment of the southern poor white male than an attack on his racial practices, and is simultaneously tempered by William Stroup's obvious affection for even this most feckless example of the type.

Reviewers of *Georgia Boy* and many later critics have continually drawn satisfied analogies between this work of Caldwell's and Mark Twain's, especially his *Adventures of Huckleberry Finn*, although their ready praise has also been sprinkled uneasily with terms like "facile," "slight," "amusing," and "featherweight."[36] The comparison to *Huck Finn* is not necessarily an inflated one in terms of the position of *Georgia Boy* in Caldwell's career. Like *Huck Finn*, it represents a milestone in artistic achievement when the author's bitterest social criticisms are modulated by his most genial humor; but like Twain's book too, its very coherence and evenness suggest a reining in of the crazier and more violent reaches of the author's comic vision. Caldwell achieved in it a unified work of art, with valuable social criticism and a successful comic style, but at the expense of limiting himself in both range and mode. That his reviewers noted the minor key of the masterpiece is testimony to the promise of his earlier short stories in all their discordant variety; that the comparisons to Twain were so frequent is evidence that *Georgia Boy*'s achievement was indeed a significant one.

## Gulf Coast Stories and Certain Women

*Sometimes when reading Caldwell I feel as though I were playing with my toes.*

—*Kenneth Burke*

With *Georgia Boy*, most critics would probably prefer to believe Caldwell's career as a short story writer had come to an end. There

35. *Ibid.*, 34.
36. See Frohock, "Erskine Caldwell: Sentimental Gentleman," 203; Canby, In-

was, in fact, a long hiatus in his writing of stories after 1943, although a new collection of previously published work by him was issued almost annually for the next ten years. However, it was not until 1953 that any significant number of new stories began to appear; these were issued in 1956 as *Gulf Coast Stories*. The title of the collection reflects one of Caldwell's main literary interests in the interval—regionalism, illustrated in his cyclorama of novels showing life in various parts of the South, and in his active editorship of the American Folkways series, which extended regionalism beyond the South and throughout the United States. The title also suggests, though not so specifically as *Georgia Boy*, that the stories will have some common denominator; but, in fact, beyond their similar location in small lumber-mill towns and delta farmlands close to the Gulf, there is little effort to suggest a distinctive sense of place or community. Each story is set in a different small town— Crescent, Lancaster, Mingusville, Stillwater, Indianola, Agricola— so that there is no opportunity to develop interaction among a common set of characters. There are no blacks whatsoever in these communities, so that one of Caldwell's better subjects is eliminated; and there is a considerably diminished interest in poverty, injustice, and social inequity. In many ways, the collection is like another version of *We Are the Living* twenty years later, with every one of its twenty-one stories concerned with sexual and romantic relationships between men and women in a variety of comic and tragic situations.

The twenty years show a definite development of Caldwell's interest in and sympathy for women, but a radical reduction otherwise in his narrative range. Only three of the twenty-one are first-person narratives, Caldwell's forte, and none of these is in the ingenuous youthful voice he had perfected by the time he wrote *Georgia Boy*. This is not to suggest that Caldwell has relinquished his naïve and simple narrative method in many of these stories, but rather that he has some difficulty stepping out of this particular mold, even when there is no appropriate character in the story to whom to give the naïve tone. The inordinate bluntness of the narrative now seems less ironic than gauche and less appropriate to the more urban and

---

troduction to *The Pocket Book of Erskine Caldwell Stories*, in *Critical Essays*, ed. MacDonald, 217; and reviews of *Georgia Boy* in *Time*, May 3, 1943, p. 104, and *Weekly Book Review*, April 25, 1943, p. 5.

middle-class characters of these later stories than to the rural poor whites who are by now almost completely abandoned by him. There are again, as in *Southways*, an unfortunate number of tragic tales that prove both banal and melodramatic. There are three suicide stories of young people disillusioned by love: "Her Name Was Amelie," "In Memory of Judith Courtright," and "Girl with Figurines"; an account of a painful crisis in an affair, in "Kathy"; and in "The Last Anniversary" a maudlin tale of a middle-aged woman deserted in her youth by her lover. The situations in the comic stories retain more inventiveness in their details, and Caldwell still has a genial eye for the absurdity of courtship rituals, sexual eccentricities, and the general waywardness of human nature. However, there is little evidence of either the imagist method or the social density of allusion that marked the stories of the 1930s. Even the repetitive and choral effects that suggested the association of the tales with ballads and folklore are gone. There are no tall tales, no animal jokes, nothing that provokes pleasure by its simple denial of credulity or shocks by its insistence on the appalling.

Of the fifteen stories in this collection that were published in periodicals prior to their appearance in book form, five were published in *Manhunt*, two each in *Playboy*, *Esquire*, and *Cavalier*, and the remainder in *Dude*, *Swank*, *Gent*, and *Magasinet*. Of a comparable number of previous periodical publications of stories in *We Are the Living*, four were in *Pagany*, three in *Story*, two each in *Clay* and *Contact*, and the others in *Contempo*, the *New English Weekly*, and the *Yale Review*. Malcolm Cowley had argued vigorously for the positive influence of the little magazines on Caldwell's early work, and it is certainly tempting to connect some of the flatness and indifference of these later stories to the large commercial organs in which they appeared. It is difficult to imagine Caldwell scrutinizing the contributions to *Dude* and *Gent* with the critical fervor he had devoted to *Pagany*. Apparently, it was the policy of these magazines to imitate the success of *Playboy* more economically by scouting out "sexy stories by well-known authors in obscure magazines" and then attempting to buy up the reprint rights as cheaply as possible; *Manhunt* had a reputation as a "men's adventure, crime and sex exploit magazine," and *Cavalier* as a "cross between a pulp and a sophisticated men's magazine."[37] Caldwell of-

37. Scott MacDonald, "An Evaluative Check-List of Erskine Caldwell's Short Fiction," in *Critical Essays*, ed. MacDonald, 342–60 *passim*; Theodore Peterson,

fered these magazines a big name and a reputation for controversial sexual audacity, the two qualities they most desired. Many of these stories are in fact much less risqué than his earlier fiction, but by the mid-1950s, his name alone apparently served as sufficient guarantee of titillation.

The sexual themes of *Gulf Coast Stories* are quite in accord with Caldwell's enduring concern with the dominance of the instincts in human behavior and the perverse ways in which they manifest themselves, so it is unfair to assume that he was pandering to the "sex exploit" element in these journals. However, the absence of so many of the qualities of Caldwell's earlier work suggests that he did indeed both need and benefit from some stimulus that had existed during the 1930s. In terms of the ethical and ideological concerns of his work, this stimulus was clearly the crisis of the Great Depression and the left-wing intellectual milieu it generated; in terms of stylistic originality and variety, a good deal of credit must go to the little magazines that first published his work. They were able to provoke Caldwell to the kind of critical reading of his own work and that of his contemporaries that he was afterward too ready to dismiss as merely an expedient prelude on his own part to his future success. He was the one who had decided in 1930 that he would make no attempt at that time to get into "the mass-circulation periodicals, as I believed that there was more to be gained in the end by first being thoroughly schooled by the literary magazines" (*CE*, 87). His later movement to the mass magazines unfortunately signaled that this "schooling" was complete, and thus he abandoned one of the most vital elements of his literary career.

The most consistent concern in *Gulf Coast Stories* that carries over from *Georgia Boy* and many of his interim novels is Caldwell's continuing depiction of women as overworked, dependent, and self-sacrificing, whereas his men are often childish, exploitative, and selfish. However, the solution proposed for this female dilemma in many of the stories is not a liberation of the woman from her dependency or an improvement in the behavior of the man, but instead either the woman's fortunate discovery of the right man who will protect her from the vagaries of the world or the achievement on her part of a love so transcendent that it accommodates all her part-

---

*Magazines in the Twentieth Century* (2nd ed.; Urbana, 1972), 318; Ronald E. Wolseley, *Understanding Magazines* (Ames, 1965), 270–71.

ner's failings. Outside marriage, women's hopes for fulfilled or even sufficient lives are very limited indeed. Caldwell's only successful career women are brothel madams, although his younger women are often permitted brief stints as secretaries, stenographers, and grade school teachers while waiting for a marriage proposal. Although this is an admittedly narrow range of options, it serves to emphasize both the lack of opportunity for women outside marriage and the reasons for their acceptance of mistreatment within it. However, Caldwell's women are not entirely without advantages in confrontations of the sexes: whereas his men have both economic and physical power over women, women are often able to combat this power through their sexual wiles and a considerable degree of ingenuity in their scheming and bargaining. Men are lured into marriage by pecan pies, driven out as umpires of softball games by girls in tight silk shorts, teased unmercifully by fifteen-year-olds, robbed by seemingly wholesome young college girls, shot by jealous women, dunned out of their money, thwarted from their favorite pursuits, and even pushed to suicide by women's duplicity. Most of the *Gulf Coast Stories* are thus elaborations, with limited sexual metaphors, of Caldwell's interest in the struggle among individuals for dominance over each other and the comic and tragic modes of its achievement.

Almost every story in this collection offers evidence of the power one sex wields over the other and the whimsical ways it may be manifested. Lucy Garner in "Hat on the Bedpost" makes the best pecan pie in Abbeville but looks like "somebody with two pillows stuffed under her skirt" (*GCS*, 231). Floy Rankin, her potential partner, can do all household repairs but is tattered, stooped, and smells of fish. Their coming together is a comic measuring up of dowries and disadvantages. Lujean in "Girl with Figurines" tells of a husband who "used to get a handful of big red beans and tell me to take off my clothes and stand against the wall, and then he'd sit down in a chair and throw beans at my behind, and have himself a laughing fit every time one of them made me jump. . . . That wasn't why I divorced him, though. He spent too much time away from home" (*GCS*, 55–56). These comic stories continue to insist, unlike the tragedies, on the unexpected in human conduct, even in a world that seems predetermined in favor of men against women. However, the surprises finally begin to recur within such a narrow frame of reference, and so repeatedly and predictably, that the unexpected itself hovers on the edge of the mundane.

One year after the publication of *Gulf Coast Stories*, Caldwell brought out what proved to be his last collection of new stories, *Certain Women* (1957), none of which had been previously published. This collection consists of seven stories, all titled with women's names, all individually much longer than Caldwell's previous stories, and all linked by a common setting in the dreary mountain and mill town of Claremore and by a seasonal progression that takes the tales from the grimy drifts of late snow in March to a hard freeze the following January. This town is much more effectively evoked and used to suggest the quality of life in the community than was the Gulf coast environment of the preceding collection, but the sense of a lost vitality and wildness, of a flatness and diminution in Caldwell's stories continues. These stories are once again thematically and ideologically cohesive in their sympathetic concern for the quality of women's lives, but they lack both inventiveness and any novelty of perspective. In one story, a character says, "Men are always making trouble for a young girl, and there seems to be no way to stop it" (*CW*, 171), a comment that might stand as epigraph to the entire collection, together with its foil, "The only thing in life she wanted . . . was to have him put his arms around her and protect her from the harshness of the world" (*CW*, 104). Almost every story is a variation on this theme: an attractive young woman is victimized by a brutal father or lover and forced to make her own way in the world; she is abused by all the men she encounters until finally she is rescued from her vicissitudes by a decent man who is willing to marry or protect her. Anneve and Hilda in their stories both have fathers who beat them and insist that they acquiesce in traditional sexual bartering with men: "I've got no more use for a female who won't please a man than I have for a man who won't go out and earn an honest living," says Anneve's father (*CW*, 9). Hilda's father warns her even more bluntly, "You needn't think I'm going to work for you all my life while you sit around here doing your goddam thinking instead of getting out and rubbing up against somebody till he'll want to marry you" (*CW*, 77). Clementine has witnessed her father's murder of her mother before running away from home at fifteen and being taken into a Claremore brothel; Louellen and Nanette, both fatherless, suffer the exploitations of con men, landlords, and employers; and Vicki, almost choked to death by her lover, remembers how as a child she was threatened by a boy with an ax and was instructed by her father that "there would be many times like that when she grew up to be a big girl, and that as a woman she would have to learn how to persuade a man not to chop off her head" (*CW*, 230). Though the book is titled *Certain Women*, there is little in it to imply that it does not refer to the fate of all women—they must learn to please men. If they are unlucky in their partners, they may at least avoid the uglier consequences of men's worst impulses; if they are lucky, they will be rewarded with the support of their best. Only one female character in the book resists this pattern, the lesbian Nancy Hunter in "Anneve." She, however, merely practices a more cynical and retributive version of it by trading men as little sex for as much money as possible: "Bleed them and leave them. That's my motto" (*CW*, 24).

The most affectionate and sympathetic relationships in *Certain Women* are those between the heroines of the tales and their mothers, or occasionally older women and sisters who play a maternal role. Indeed, these loves are often so intense that they create an impossibly high model for any later heterosexual love to emulate. For Anneve, "every moment she could be in the blessedness of her mother's arms was the most precious escape she could find in life" (*CW*, 6), and Nanette "felt safe and secure in the world when she felt Mrs. Dawson's motherly arms around her" (*CW*, 152). However, the mothers in these stories are also the main agents, both by their example and advice, of the point of view that "being wanted . . . by a man is the most important thing in life for a woman" (*CW*, 36), and that long-suffering and virtuous compliance will be rewarded by true love. Caldwell describes unrelentingly the constant pressures on the young women to separate compliance from virtue, pressures from both lovers and their own impulses, but also the dire consequences if they do so: Nanette is permanently disfigured when her face is slashed by the jealous wife of her employer, and Hilda's secretarial agency is destroyed by vicious gossip from a similar source. The women have one hope—that of meeting good men—but the world of the stories is populated by bad ones, or men like the Reverend Luther Bisbee in "Clementine" or Harvey Ingham in "Selma," who ignore or resist the heroine's lures.

As in *Gulf Coast Stories*, the women have no professional interests beyond an interim employment before marriage; Hilda has established a successful secretarial business, and Selma has taught school, both while looking for the right man, and Louellen's mother is a nurse, an employment necessitated by her husband's death. Besides prostitution in a variety of forms, these are the only professions practiced by women, in contrast to a complete range of jobs for men that encompass all economic and educational levels. Even allowing for its setting in a small factory town, the opportunities for women in this book are clearly even further restricted in order to enhance Caldwell's thesis of the women's dependency and vulnerability. Most of them are working-class women, and the harshness of physical existence for both men and women is integral to many of the tales. Though Caldwell never goes inside the world of the furniture factories, it pervades the stories, toughening the men but also wearing them down. Anneve's father "was still in his early fifties, but after more than thirty years of labor in the wood-turning mills of Claremore he appeared to be many years older" (CW, 5); Louellen's father was killed in a furniture plant accident; and Hilda's father, a millwright in a cedar chest factory, has accumulated so little in his lifetime there that he resents sharing any of it with his daughter. Wives and daughters bear the consequences of the men's anger and frustration. Interestingly, none of the heroines has a brother, for that might complicate the simple pattern of male power and female submission in the family; for the most part, even sisters are kept discreetly beyond aid and appeal. Thus every detail of their lives, from their passive and loving mothers, cruel or absent fathers, low horizons in every direction, worldly pressures and lack of personal support, conspires to throw these heroines back upon accidents of fortune and the mercies of men. From the beginning of his career, Caldwell had acknowledged the primacy of sexuality in his vision of human nature, but it was a sexuality that was broad in various senses of the word—earthy, vulgar, Rabelaisian, and comic as well as intense, violent, and powerful. Its manifestations were as wide as the range of human conduct, from the young man who stared with both horror and longing at the body of his lover, dying of poison, to the blustering southern landlord whose poor white tenant girl was more than a match for his lust; from the hideous exploitation of Blue Boy to the Maine farmer who paid a clumsy tribute to his neighbor's wife by wrestling her into a pair of silk underpants. In *Certain Women*, this scope is finally narrowed to a single theme and an unvarying mode. Told almost without humor, and without even the efforts at whimsy of *Gulf Coast Stories*, the book is the most limited of all Caldwell's short story collections in both form and content, although it is also the most clearly ideological in its vision of the sexual struggle between men and women.

This is clearly no longer the Erskine Caldwell of the "cult of incongruity," "balked religiosity," or "mystifying incoherence," no longer "the two Erskine Caldwells," "the hardboiled idealist," the artist of paradoxes, for whom critics once had strained their coinage of labels to suggest the intriguing misalliance of ideas and forms that seemed to typify his work.[38] When, in 1935, Kenneth Burke had noted Caldwell's capacity for muddling his reader's judgments and had pondered the possibility of his ever stabilizing those judgments, he had added the enigmatic comment, "His very abilities tend to work against him." The implication that Caldwell's talent was conducive to ideological confusion, and that such confusion was not a desirable intellectual goal, proved ominous for Caldwell and his reception by other critics. The obverse of this argument was that the pursuit of a coherent ideology would mean the sacrifice of what was unique and most pleasing in Caldwell's style. Otis Ferguson seemed to complement Burke's theory a few years later, in 1938, when he commented on Caldwell's predicament in the committed ideological decade of the 1930s: "Ideas were afoot and Caldwell knew a writer just couldn't sit around and be delighted."[39] Both critics felt that an increased attention to ideas would direct Caldwell's fiction away from its early polymorphous delight to less pleasing and more restricted purposes of edification. They proved accurate in their predictions of a narrowing of stylistic range and a certain didacticism of focus in his later work, but distinctly less so in their assumptions that Caldwell's ideas were inevitably going to have to be purchased at the cost of aesthetic pleasure. In fact, the range of ideas in Caldwell's tales in the 1930s is far richer and more complex than the occasionally prurient sympathy with the plight of women (and sometimes blacks) that is the main ideological focus of his later stories. In the intellectual context of the Great Depression, and the artistic milieu of the little magazines, Caldwell revealed a range of social sympathies—for the poor and lonely, for women, children, and blacks, for those people most vulnerable and controlled by their circumstances—that existed in the most lively tension with his penchant for recording what was most gross, absurd, and incorrigible in those same people. Though such ideas were dissonant and unstable, they were much more volatile and engaging than the simpler and segmented pity, outrage, and ridicule of the works after *Georgia*

38. Burke, "Caldwell: Maker of Grotesques," 168, 167; Scott MacDonald, Introduction to *Critical Essays on Erskine Caldwell* (Boston, 1981), xxviii; Macleod, "A Hardboiled Idealist," 6.
39. Burke, "Caldwell: Maker of Grotesques," 169; Ferguson, "Caldwell's Stories," 69.

*Boy.* The four story collections of the 1930s— *American Earth, We Are the Living, Kneel to the Rising Sun,* and *Southways*—elicited the complete range of Caldwell's stylistic devices, from naïve narrators and carefully contrived repetitions to stark imagism and bawdy folk-comedy. It was only later, when the ideas began to dwindle, that the craft simultaneously declined, losing the variety, zest, and sometimes chaotic inconsistency that was the mark of Caldwell's best achievement.

# 3

# The Southern Cyclorama I
## The Thirties Novels

---

*Those enjoying the pleasant things in life are fewer than those enduring the unpleasant. When this social condition no longer exists, I'll feel there is no longer any purpose in writing about the effects of poverty on the human spirit.*

*—Erskine Caldwell*

*Caldwell . . . sounds . . . a maniacal hoot for all of us, not one of derision, but of wild recognition of the irrational and the dark.*

*—James Devlin*

---

Although Caldwell took great pleasure in the writing of short stories, which were in so many ways congenial to his talents, his career as a novelist encompassed and went far beyond his work in any other genre and has consequently been largely the source of his reputation. He began writing novels in the late 1920s and continued for the next forty-five years, far beyond the period of both his short stories and his documentary writing. He wrote some twenty-five novels, with the five years between *Journeyman* in 1935 and *Trouble in July* in 1940 (a time when he was preoccupied with traveling and nonfiction writing) the longest he ever went between novels. The enervation and virtual abandonment of the short story after *Certain Women* in 1957 was followed by an, even for him, unusually prodigious number of novels, nine between 1958 and 1973. Although Caldwell spoke often of his delight in the short story and also of his need to return periodically to documentary work, as a means of refreshment and validation of his remembered experiences, it is the novel that sustained his long career and permitted the largest development of his idiosyncratic vision.

After his two early (and sometimes denied) novels, *The Bastard* and *Poor Fool*, Caldwell found his true fictional territory surprisingly quickly. Though he later wrote of his discovery of the southern locale of his novels with an almost Presbyterian sense of its inevitability, it was in fact also something of a pragmatic process of trial and error. In discussing the genesis, late in 1930, of *Tobacco Road*, he wrote: "I had gradually come to realize that I would not be completely satisfied with any of my work until I had written a full-length novel and, moreover, that it was inevitable that the novel was to be concerned with the tenant farmers and sharecropping families I had known in East Georgia" (*CE*, 101). Despite his further comment that this subject was "foreordained" (*CE*, 103) for him, Caldwell's next venture after *Tobacco Road*, in 1932, was into quite different geographical territory, not the Georgia of his childhood but the state of Maine, and he found that his progress was now difficult and unsatisfactory. The finished book, *A Lamp for Nightfall*, published many years later, was rejected in 1932, first by Scribner's and then by Viking. Perhaps the publishers thus had a hand in Caldwell's predestined subject matter, for he began asking himself, "If I really wanted to have the Maine novel published at that time . . . now I was certain I wanted to continue writing about the South" (*CE*, 123). Such certainty led Caldwell to the conception of *God's Little Acre*, about "another phase of life in East Georgia" (*CE*, 123)—the mill towns, now, as well as the backwoods. As he began work on this new Georgia novel, Caldwell experienced a "feeling of complete assurance and satisfaction about it" (*CE*, 126), and by the time he embarked on the writing of his next novel, *Journeyman*, in 1934, a larger vision was beginning to crystallize: "I looked upon it [the subject of *Journeyman*] as being one of the indigenous phases of life in the South which I wanted to include in a series of novels" (*CE*, 155). By the time of his next novel, *Trouble in July*, he had expanded this notion of a series of southern novels both forward and backward, so that it became "another phase of life in the cycloramic depiction of the South begun with *Tobacco Road* and continued with *God's Little Acre* and *Journeyman*" (*CE*, 181). This cyclorama came, by Caldwell's final definition, to include ten novels: *Tobacco Road* (1932), *God's Little Acre* (1933), *Journeyman* (1935), *Trouble in July* (1940), *Tragic Ground* (1944), *A House in the Uplands* (1946), *The Sure Hand of God* (1947), *This Very Earth* (1948), *Place Called Estherville* (1949), and *Episode in Palmetto* (1950). If his uncovering of this southern cyclorama was partially retrospective, Caldwell was nonetheless quick to recognize his proper literary landscape and to pursue his destiny there.

The ten novels of the cyclorama are quite discrete from each other, sharing neither precise location, characters, nor movement in a historical saga. They vary radically in quality, mode, and subject, and even taken collectively do not form a comprehensive vision of southern life and history comparable to Faulkner's Yoknapatawpha novels or Stribling's Vaiden family saga. None is set outside the present day, and, compared with Faulkner's and Stribling's social range, Caldwell's is more restricted to the lower classes, with a best-forgotten venture into the fallen aristocracy in *A House in the Uplands*. Yet there is a clear imaginative vision in these novels— a vision of people trapped by their physical world but lured by ideals that they are unable to pursue in any manner that is not futile or ludicrous. Caldwell's South provides him with a symbolic physical landscape, with carefully selected customs, economic conditions, climate, and environment with which to enclose his characters materially and thus illustrate the radically limited spiritual and ethical possibilities of their existence. It gives him a familiar milieu and intimately observed types of people to adapt to his fascination with the shortcomings and the validity of a purely naturalistic view of the human species. His characters were thus grounded in a poverty-stricken southern setting that was to become, for the public, an increasingly powerful image of national disaster during the Great Depression, when it was also copiously documented, in fact and fiction, by multitudes of other writers. Caldwell contributed vividly to this image by his work in the 1930s; but he was also held hostage to it, because his fiction was scrutinized as though it was sociology and condemned or vindicated on the accuracy of the precise numbers of real families who were found to be starving, per square mile, in rural Georgia. The alternative response to Caldwell's degraded characters was to see him as a writer with a comic vision of human absurdity, and then to puzzle over, or regret, the disjunction between the modes of naturalistic sociology and grotesque comedy in his work. However, in the early novels of the cyclorama, it appears to be just this connection that Caldwell seeks to explore— between the comic futility of the human predicament, reaching for the spirit but mocked by the flesh, and the injustices of society that produce needless and correctable suffering. His realm is the convergence of necessary and unnecessary behavior, of spiritual yearning and physical needs, of irrational existence and rational social improvement.

In the later novels of the cyclorama, Caldwell became increasingly preoccupied with issues of social justice for the poor, women, and blacks, with a corresponding decline in interest in his characters' more visionary aspirations. His comedy in these works is more didactic and less unsettling than the earlier fusion and confusion of metaphysical and social concerns, although his exploration of a variety of facets of southern life as emblems of the larger world remains constant. There is a general movement later in the cyclorama away from rural and into urban settings, most marked between *Trouble in July* and *Tragic Ground*, as well as a definite abandonment of fanatical and mystical religion as a theme, in favor of more conventional satire of organized churches. In terms of their critical reputation, there is a marked distinction between earlier and later works, with *Trouble in July* marking the end of those that were taken most seriously, although one or two of the later ones received isolated favorable attention. It should also be added that, although Caldwell repeatedly referred to *Episode in Palmetto* as the final book in the cyclorama and followed it with the publication of the Maine novel, *A Lamp for Nightfall*, in 1952, nevertheless there are among his later novels quite a number that would not seem out of place as continuations of the southern cyclorama in their setting, style, and concerns. The cyclorama is thus a somewhat arbitrary creation, conveniently confined by its author to ten books, but symptomatic in many ways of his larger output of novels and of the broader evolution of his fictional interests.

Caldwell's account, in *Call It Experience*, of the compelling origins of *Tobacco Road* and consequently of his southern cyclorama, is quite consistent with his self-portrait as a young man determined to improve his craft and discover his true subject almost completely in isolation from the larger literary currents of his time. He wrote: "I wanted to tell the story of the people I knew in the manner in which they actually lived their lives from day to day and year to year, and to tell it without regard for fashions in writing and traditional plots. It seemed to me that the most authentic and enduring materials of fiction were the people themselves, not crafty plots and counterplots designed to manipulate the speech and actions of human beings" (*CE*, 101–102). Such an emphasis, however, on the common people and a new style commensurate with the authenticity of their daily lives was not in fact either unique or eccentric, late in 1930, when Caldwell began *Tobacco Road*. The end of the jazz age and the onset of the Great Depression were already impinging on the literary theory and practice of the period. *Pagany*, the journal to which Caldwell contributed frequently and read avidly at this time, described itself in 1930 as a "native quarterly" interested in "American expression" and "vital" writing. The *New Masses*, in its 1929 rallying cry "Go Left, Young Writers!" described its ideal new author very much as Caldwell presented himself. It evoked a "wild youth" who "writes because he must. . . . His writing is . . . the natural flower of his environment"; his "primitive material" could be found in his native, working-class America. The *New Masses'* prescribed writer was also a "Red," though more by instinct than by intellect; he was a man of few theories, but his political commitment was virtually inseparable from his nativist emphasis and vital style. When Caldwell embarked on *Tobacco Road*, he was certainly committed to both the subject and manner of simple, earthy people he had seen in the Georgia backwoods; and indeed the finished novel might well justify the *New Masses'* assumptions about the political sympathies that must inevitably accompany such an excursion into the world of the poor. Thus Caldwell was not nearly so isolated from contemporary literary and intellectual currents as he suggests in his account of the composition of *Tobacco Road*. Subsisting on seven dollars a week, he lived cramped in a solitary room in a New York brownstone that was soon to be demolished. At that time, he says, his only company was his typewriter and a ream of water-stained paper bought for a quarter (*CE*, 103–105), the only impingement of the literary world being the Macauley's cocktail party at which eating took precedence over meeting Edmund Wilson and Michael Gold. When he wrote to Richard Johns, the editor of *Pagany*, describing his new novel to him, he said: "It's not sensational, experimental, nor important; it is just human. Maybe it's not so good; but I have a sympathy for the people in it."[1] However, he could scarcely have chosen a more modest and appealing set of criteria against which to judge a piece of contemporary fiction in the early years of the depression. Caldwell's experiences, his subject, his background, his sympathies, and his talent were all conducive, whether Caldwell intended them or not, to producing a writer close to the literary spirit of the times, and thus likely to be scrutinized closely for everything he represented.

*Tobacco Road* was not, of course, Caldwell's first novel, though it was sometimes reviewed as such, and he himself later claimed

1. Halpert, *A Return to "Pagany,"* 40; Michael Gold, "Go Left, Young Writers!" (editorial), *New Masses*, IV (January, 1929), 3–4; Caldwell, as quoted in Halpert, *A Return to "Pagany,"* 221.

that it was. However, it was clearly the first one in which he felt
he had found his stride, to judge from his comments on its inevitability: "It was something I was impelled to do. . . . There was
only one possible title for the novel. . . . There was never any doubt
in my mind about the outcome of the novel" (*CE*, 103–104). This
assurance no doubt stemmed from the recognition, hardly unique
to Caldwell, that he could write best about what he knew best, although initially, when he began *Tobacco Road*, he seemed to feel
that its intimately known subject matter was a ghost of his past to
be exorcised before he could go on to other subjects. As with so
many other writers, this ghost became the animating spirit of his
writing, providing a coherent focus for his developing philosophy
and artistic style. In the movement away from the disorderly and
rootless wandering that had formed both the substance and, to some
extent, the technique of *The Bastard* and *Poor Fool*, to the root-
bound festering of the characters in *Tobacco Road*, Caldwell moved
from a chaotic variety of sensationalism to a formally limited setting
in which the impact of extreme states of mind and conduct was
sharpened by the author's newfound control. The surrealism of
many of the episodes in the apprenticeship novels gives way to a
more shocking and highly selective naturalism, less easily dismissed
as mere fantasy because it is so much closer to a documentable
southern social reality. The freakish baby born to the Morgans in
*The Bastard* has a clearly symbolic value in the novel, as a retribution for the past evils of its progenitors; but this hairy little monster is not nearly so disturbing as the harelipped Ellie May or the
noseless Sister Bessie in *Tobacco Road*, for whom there are even
more feasible real-life models. Mr. Boxx's imagined account in *Poor
Fool* of the philanderings of the dead in the underworld gives way
in *Tobacco Road* to Jeeter Lester's grisly memories of the ravages
of rats on his father's dead body; and the miraculous midnight sun-
shine and scarlet-tongued lizards of *Alan Kent* are replaced by the
crazy broom-sedge fire and the "damn-blasted green-gutted turnip
worms" of *Tobacco Road* (*TR*, 12). Caldwell's experience with the
writing of short stories was undoubtedly a powerful factor in his
movement from eclectic disorder to intense control in *Tobacco
Road*, but his discovery of fictional material in his native South gave
him boundaries within which to exercise and intensify his extravagant style, and an authentic context for his grotesque vision. The
concentration on southern material also provided Caldwell with a
milieu within which to develop ideas that had been scattered, im-

plied, and sometimes inconsistent in his earlier writings. Caldwell had, from the beginning of his career, chosen the lives of the poor for his special scrutiny—partly, one may suppose, from a sympathy and familiarity gleaned from his father and his childhood among them, but also from a more thoughtful curiosity that reached beyond compassion and its social and political manifestations to an enquiry into what James Agee was to call, in an almost identical context, "certain normal predicaments of human divinity."[2] For Caldwell among the Georgia poor whites, as for Agee later among the Alabama tenant families who were the subject of *Let Us Now Praise Famous Men*, the nakedness of observed poverty led not merely to ambivalent reformist and Marxist impulses, but also into considerations of the interaction between poverty of the flesh and spirit. In *The Sacrilege of Alan Kent*, Caldwell's early narrator had exclaimed, "Without the painful hunger my body had always known, my soul would have died from lack of food" (*SAK*, 43)—a somewhat traditionally religious response to the value of mortification of the flesh. However, soon after the completion of *Alan Kent*, Caldwell went back to Georgia to look once more at the people he was about to depict in *Tobacco Road* and was profoundly dispirited by what he saw: "Nothing I put down on paper succeeded in conveying the full meaning of poverty and hopelessness and degradation as I had observed it" (*CE*, 103). Thereafter, Caldwell was never again to argue that souls might be sustained by hunger, although the distortion and displacement of spiritual impulses in poor people became a central concern of all his novels written during the 1930s.

There was a similar development in the nature of Caldwell's commitment to social and economic reform in *Tobacco Road* and the later southern novels from the attitudes of the earlier books. He moved away from the estrangement from society that typifies both the setting and approach of the apprenticeship novels and into much more direct criticism of the social systems that contain and share responsibility for his neglected characters. In both *The Bastard* and *Poor Fool*, he presented isolated wanderers in urban underworlds—individuals who had broken almost all links to family, history, and community. With the shift in *Tobacco Road* and later novels to families and communities firmly established in time and place, his formerly anarchistic vision of the modern world became

2. James Agee and Walker Evans, *Let Us Now Praise Famous Men* (1941; rpr. Boston, 1960), xiv.

more specific in its indictments and more politically left-wing in its sympathies, because social injustice could be observed less randomly. Thus Caldwell began in these novels to refine his depiction of the spiritual depravities of the most deprived people and his analysis of the sociological and naturalistic origins of their inequalities. The fact that he chose to pursue a vision of the poor that simultaneously questioned the nature of human divinity and asserted the need for drastic social reforms was the source of bewildered and even cynical responses to these novels. Nevertheless, it was exactly in this fusion of the incorrigible and inexplicable with the socially determined and remediable in his characters that Caldwell's interest and originality resided. In moving to the southern settings, he now had at his disposal the rich literary tradition and the grim social reality of the southern poor white, whose very name was a synonym for incongruity and whose material predicament during the Great Depression was growing annually more dire. He had a class of people who were already the heirs to jarring stereotypes, as both villainously comic and innocently pathetic, and thus, despite their rootedness in history and society, more inherently perplexing than all the strange wanderers of the earlier books. It was just this mystery that Caldwell chose to evoke in the midst of the seemingly deterministic circumstances of the South in the depression.

The first chapters of *Tobacco Road* are a dramatic introduction to Caldwell's newfound stylistic control of disjuncture and dissonance. They reveal a family of people so dominated by primitive instincts that even their most human faculty, that of language, has become no more than a chanting chorus of obsessions that are themselves at odds with the people's behavior. Jeeter Lester, the father, hungers and schemes for his son-in-law Lov's turnips, while he repeats a monotonous chorus to his son Dude to "quit chunking that durn ball at them there weatherboards" (*TR*, 16). Dude continues to slam the baseball against the rotting house while commenting gleefully on the desperate sexual contortions of his harelipped sister, Ellie May, in her efforts to seduce Lov; Ellie May speaks never a word, but squeals as she writhes closer to her prey; Lov tries to defend both his turnips and himself while reiterating to Jeeter a complaint about Jeeter's daughter Pearl's unwifely conduct toward himself. Both speech and action are meticulously choreographed to culminate in Ellie May and Lov's lovemaking and Jeeter's theft of the turnips, a grotesque climax to the dissociation we have witnessed between impulses and speech.

This opening might seem at first to suggest the inevitable dominance of the animal over the human in such debased characters,
but, curiously, their language, though largely ineffectual and formulaic in its repetitiveness, is far from being void of significant content. This content sometimes counters the base, instinctual nature
of their actions by revealing higher aspirations, and sometimes
sheds an ironic light on these apparently simple and brutalized
people, showing them to be as capable of hypocrisy, self-deception,
and guile as their more sophisticated counterparts. For example,
Lov Bensey's complaint to Jeeter about his wife, Pearl, is only superficially a demand that the twelve-year-old girl be ordered into
his bed by her father: what he really wants is to have a more complete communion with the golden-haired child, to have her talk to
him, "ask him if his back were sore, and when was he going to get
his hair cut, and when was it going to rain again. But Pearl would
not say anything" (*TR*, 3). Considering the quality of much of the
conversation of Caldwell's characters, Pearl's silence might not seem
so regrettable, but Lov needs this sign of her humanity as much as
he wants any sexual union. Lov's other desire from Pearl is equally
nonsexual: "Next to wanting to kiss her and talk to her, Lov wanted
to see her eyes" (*TR*, 6). Clearly, Pearl is a mystery as well as a
potential mate to Lov, and he tries, unsuccessfully, to resolve her
puzzle in both material and spiritual terms by alternately buying
her snuff and calico and then speculating on the devil's influence on
her. Lov's bewilderment over Pearl is reflected more broadly in
Caldwell's bemusement over the plight of all the characters in *Tobacco Road*. Are they the victims merely of a deterministic social
system who might have been "saved," as the omniscient author
asserts at one point, by a communal version of snuff and calico,
"Co-operative and corporate farming" (*TR*, 83); or are they, as one
critic neatly phrased it, "God-hungry in a Godforsaken land" and
thence, like Lov, in need of more than bodily comfort?[3] Does their
physical neediness explain their antics, or do they share in a broader
spiritual malaise, merely highlighted by their poverty? The question goes to the heart of Caldwell's naturalism, not in challenging
the verisimilitude of his world, which is highly selective and symbolic, but in explaining his conflicting reformist and fatalist ideas.
These ideas are most clearly illustrated in the character of Jeeter

---

3. Harvey Klevar, "Some Things Holy in a Godforsaken Land," *Pembroke
Magazine*, XI (1979), 66.

Lester, who is, on the one hand, as indolent, wily, and lascivious a poor white as ever emerged from the backwoods, and on the other, a God-fearing but thwarted romantic agrarian. Jeeter's laziness is as epic as his lechery; he will lie on the ground for an hour after he stumbles rather than get up, and he has fathered about half of the Peabody children across the field in addition to his own numerous brood. He steals his son-in-law's food and refuses to share it with his starving family, feeling pangs of conscience for this act only when his own hunger is temporarily abated. Then, "humble and penitent," he picks out "half a dozen of the smallest turnips" to give to his son (*TR*, 52–53). Jeeter's God is clearly a figure of great personal convenience for him, whom he can invoke in various ways as fits the occasion. He troubles Jeeter's conscience after, but not before, an evil act; He offers him easy expiations of his sins and promises him eventually corrections and explanations of all the miseries of existence. Jeeter consoles Ellie May for her harelip by saying, "It ain't no sin to look like that, Ellie May. . . . You came into the world that way from God, and that's the way He intended for you to look. Sometimes I think maybe it would be a sin to change it, because that would be doing over something He made" (*TR*, 81). Jeeter's graceful acquiescence in his daughter's deformity, however, exonerates him from his neglected responsibility to take Ellie May to the hospital to have her lip repaired and challenges the integrity of his devotion to both God and his daughter. Similarly, his certainty that God never meant him to abandon his land and go to work in the cotton mills provides a convenient excuse for his inertia and failure to make any effort to provide for his starving family.

Nevertheless, Jeeter cannot simply be labeled a hypocrite who invokes reverence for God and nature only when it suits him. His lassitude, his dishonesty, his selfishness (together with many socially determined circumstances) all impede his living according to his own reiterated principles of love for God and the land He made, but they do not consequently refute the sincerity of Jeeter's faith. The narrator takes care to confirm repeatedly what the narration itself might be in danger of denying, namely, that "there was an inherited love of the land in Jeeter that all his disastrous experiences with farming had failed to take away" (*TR*, 89). This is asserted directly in the face of Jeeter's family's skepticism about his ideals. In response to his usual spring-time yearnings, his wife, Ada, says: "That's the way you talk every year about this time, but you don't never get started. It's been seven or eight years since you turned a furrow" (*TR*, 77). Even the narrator observes more ambivalently that Jeeter's reaction to the agony of looking at his unplowed fields is that "his head dropped forward on his knees, and sleep soon overcame him and brought a peaceful rest to his tired heart and body" (*TR*, 154). However, the narrator also supplies a wealth of naturalistic reasons for his lethargy and dishonesty, whereas Jeeter's agrarian vision flies in the face of the determinism that is driving all his neighbors to the cotton mills.

Caldwell reinforces Jeeter's ambiguous idealism through the empathy of his son-in-law Lov, already revealed, in his need for Pearl, as something of a visionary himself. Lov speaks a final epitaph for Jeeter that is both absurd, in that the actual circumstances of Jeeter's death prove it false, and profound, in that it acknowledges the power of Jeeter's mystical beliefs: "'I reckon Jeeter done right,' Lov contended. 'He was a man who liked to grow things in the ground. . . . The ground sort of looks out after the people who keeps their feet on it'" (*TR*, 239). This sense of a larger and more intense vision of life, beyond the material, pervades all of the early cyclorama novels and is frequently manifest in such understandings between people who are in other ways disparate and antagonistic. It exists between Will Thompson and Ty Ty Walden in *God's Little Acre*, among the men, including Semon Dye, who look through the crack in the wall in *Journeyman*, and between Sheriff Jeff McCurtain and the black man, Sam Brinson, in *Trouble in July*. Such perverse mysticism inhibits simple pity or ridicule for Caldwell's characters, even in their most extreme conditions.

The frequent episodes of public voyeurism in Caldwell's early novels also seem to be related to a sacramental sense in his characters of the rituals of mating, dying, and coming through that are observed in all their naked physicality. When the Lesters crowd around to watch the consummation of Dude and Bessie's marriage, or the neighbors watch flames consume Jeeter and Ada, they are engaging in a communal act of witnessing rather than a furtive peeping. Though they may giggle and gasp, there is a raw impulse of wonder that later disappears completely from Caldwell's work when he leaves these poverty-stricken Southerners for more middle-class subjects. Their religiosity is a defense neither of primitivism nor of religion on Caldwell's part. He himself remains detached and skeptical of the existence of any transcendent object toward which his people yearn. He is not averse to suggesting that religion is an opiate for the poor in *Tobacco Road*, though it is clearly a self-administered one rather than part of a larger social conspiracy. In treating religious hypocrisy and ecstasy among the poor, Caldwell concedes all the rational and sociological explanations and then insists that his people still have the urge to search for some higher significance in life beyond its physical manifestations that cannot wholly be explained by the methods of naturalism nor dismissed by the application of irony.

Caldwell, nevertheless, shows an intense and simultaneous concern for the natural and material sphere in which his characters' lives are sunk. In choosing to write about the core of existence among the very poor, Caldwell was venturing into literary territory that had formerly been the preserve, among southern writers, of both sentimental and determinist reformers like Dorothy Scarborough, Jack Bethea, and T. S. Stribling, or earlier, of humorists like Augustus B. Longstreet, Johnson J. Hooper, and George Washington Harris, who derived their comic material from a rich tradition of folklore and tall tales. Caldwell's critics have often seen him as trying to weld these two rather unwieldy modes together and have found the fusion incomplete or unsatisfactory. However, Caldwell not only professed repeatedly his ignorance of these traditions but also insisted, somewhat contradictorily, that he was reacting against unnamed fictional versions of poor people's lives with which he was familiar—against artifice, contrivance, "bogus literature," and the "crafty dishonesty of fiction." The result of Caldwell's efforts to write about "people as [he] knew them and about life as [he] saw it" is not a failed effort to synthesize sentimental, reformist, and roguish stereotypes, but rather a careful and discordant image of the irrational longings of the poor conjoined with their innate depravity and social and economic abandonment.[4] The whole question of the deservingness of the poor, which tended to inform the moral vision of so many American chroniclers of poverty during the Great Depression, is irrelevant to Caldwell in his exposés of economic and social injustice. His characters are neither hardworking, honest, wholesome, nor clean, the latter a particularly desirable proletarian quality. In Steinbeck's *The Grapes of Wrath*, the Joad family praises God for washtubs and running water; in *Tobacco Road*, Ada's only housekeeping advice to her future daughter in-law is to encourage her new husband to wear his socks to bed to avoid dirtying up the quilts:

<hr>

4. Erskine Caldwell, Introduction to *Tobacco Road*, in *Critical Essays*, ed. MacDonald, 223.

"Sometimes he don't wash himself all winter long" (*TR*, 107). Caldwell steadfastly refuses to implore pity in return for his characters' worthiness; they are lazy, cruel, lecherous, selfish, and sneaky, but they are also hungry, sick, physically deformed, unclothed, and so weak they can barely lift rocks to hurl at each other. Caldwell is enough of a naturalist to allow for the inevitable connections between their physical and moral predicaments, but he has also enough of a residual Presbyterian vision of human nature to avoid suggesting that there are social and economic cures for *all* that ails his characters.

When Caldwell investigates the historical origins of the Lester family's situation—tracing their rapid decline from a pioneering grandfather, who cleared a tobacco plantation, to their present state as abandoned sharecroppers, without land, stock, food, or even credit for a little snuff to dull the pain—he concludes with the firm authorial assertion "Co-operative and corporate farming would have saved them all" (*TR*, 83). However, just what such salvation would mean to the Lesters is less clearly spelled out. They might have the ability to be self-supporting farmers, but it seems much less likely that such sufficiency would bring with it all the supposedly concomitant self-reliant virtues. Indeed, the employed and more prosperous people in the novel show no gain in virtue over the Lesters, despite their aghast response to these alien poor people. The used-car salesmen call to each other urgently to view Bessie's noseless face: "Come here quick, Harry! I got a real sight to show you" (*TR*, 117); and when they exclaim in delighted derision, "Good God!" it recalls by contrast Jeeter's at least part serious affirmation that Ellie May's harelip is God-given. Other respectable townspeople are just as callous toward the Lesters' oddities: the town clerk who marries Bessie and Dude pries into their personal lives under the guise of being a good Baptist, and the hotel manager exploits Bessie's sexual appetite as a way of making some extra profit from his guests. It may be fairly said that no one in the novel from any higher station in life compares favorably with the Lesters or argues for the virtues of a more comfortable life. Thus Caldwell does not ask for economic justice because his characters deserve it, nor does he condemn poverty as the sole cause of human evil; he simply insists that such excuses are not necessary in order for poverty to be repugnant.

The purported "cure" for the Lesters' poverty—co-operative and corporate farming—is not, however, offered by Caldwell as a viable way to solve their contemporary problem, for it has already gone far beyond the possibility of redemption by such means. Indeed, *Tobacco Road* does not deal directly with solutions at all, much to the disappointment of the *New Masses*, which would have been warmly receptive to some ardent fictional southern proletarians and radical peasants. Ironically, Caldwell's nonfiction writing and his own reviewing at this time show that, in fact, his revolutionary sympathies and his sociology were not at all inimical to those of the *New Masses*. His 1932 *New Masses* attack on the "gut-rotting disorganization of unplanned society" is written from the perspective of hope rather than regret; his series of articles three years later on southern sharecroppers for the New York *Post* proves him quite willing to propose a range of specific solutions, from legalizing birth control to nationalizing the state of Georgia in order to gain access to relief funds. Yet Caldwell finds no appropriate place for such proposals in his fiction, where his poor white characters have the power to mock any simple political answers. His resolution to their plight is thus less positive and more symbolic in nature.

Jeeter and Ada Lester perish finally from neither disease nor starvation, nor are they rescued from their misery by welfare workers and the prospect of a planned economy—the most likely alternatives in the sharecroppers' world depicted in the New York *Post*. Instead they die in a freak accident when the wind changes and carries a broom-sedge fire to engulf the house in which they are sleeping. This disaster has a variety of causes, all of which are inherent in the themes of the novel: it is partially a consequence of Jeeter's and the whole region's loyalty to an outmoded method of farming, the burning of broom-sedge in the spring; it is partly a result of Jeeter's inertia in having neglected the land for the previous ten or fifteen years, so that the fire is uncontrollable; and it is largely the outcome of Jeeter's last desperate effort to make his agrarian dreams come true. As the flames move across his field, Jeeter sleeps with "his mind filled with thoughts of the land and its sweet odors, and with a new determination to stir the earth and cultivate plants of cotton" (*TR*, 232). It is finally, however, a symbol of the lack of control Jeeter and Ada have over their lives and a less-than-encouraging omen for any apocalyptic vision of change wrought by social reform. It is a last irony that the incorrigibly lazy Jeeter should be destroyed when he manages to take some action, but there is an even greater irony in Caldwell's epitaph for his characters: "Ada and Jeeter had not known what had happened" (*TR*, 234). Not only do the older Lesters die with no recognition of what has happened to them, but they leave an even more obtuse heir behind them in the shape of Dude, who ends the novel with an even more foolish echo of Jeeter's obsession: "I reckon I'll get me a mule somewhere and some seed-cotton and guano, and grow me a crop of cotton this year. . . . It feels to me like it's going to be a good year for cotton" (*TR*, 241). This culminating irony in *Tobacco Road* removes it even further from any ideal blueprint for a politically radical novel about the poor. Not only is there no hint of a dawning awareness of potential change among the characters, but they manifest a move in the opposite direction, toward further degeneration. The reader's consciousness is altered, of course, in a different way, toward a larger understanding; but even in this movement, the ironic and grotesque vision tends to militate against any purely material scheme of reform by emphasizing the cosmic and comic, rather than the purely naturalistic, context of the characters.

Caldwell often denied any intentions of being a social critic in his fiction, although there is undoubtedly a powerful, if qualified, strain of such thinking. It is more surprising, perhaps, that he equally resisted the attribution of any comic intentions, despite the fact that the uneasy interaction of these two elements appears to be the dominant feature of his novels. Caldwell's disavowal is only partly explained by his rejection of any clear intention in his writing, which, he always argued, was organic, unplanned, and intuitive, and thus not conducive to categorical approaches. However, because it is patently absurd to deny the presence of social protest and comedy in his fiction, however ambiguous their forms, Caldwell's resistance to the labels seems more likely to derive from the reductive ways in which they were applied to his writing. The social protest was measured against surveys, statistics, and formulas, and the comedy was often viewed as simple and artless farce. Caldwell was judged guilty of writing intrusive propaganda that diluted his humor, and sometimes of exploitation of his poor white subjects. He was accused of pandering to northern tastes for southern atrocities; he was challenged by Donald Davidson to contribute some of his earnings to southern charities and was defended by his parents for doing so. The farcical element in his books brought him the label of a "born humorist" who evoked "cackling laughter" and "native comedy which was excellent for its own sake." Yet when Caldwell told an interviewer, "There is comedy in tragedy and tragedy in comedy; they are inseparable; they're interchangeable," he seemed to imply that no single literary approach in his work could be taken simply "for its own sake," but rather that a continual awareness of contradictions and tension was demanded.[5] In choosing to write in the grotesque mode, Caldwell had to accept from his critics both the benefits and the detriments of uncertainty, although the response was rather more of the latter, except from those few who enjoyed being nonplussed.

The uneasiness of most readers in the presence of a genuinely grotesque mode of vision and their consequent need to resolve paradoxes, resist confusion, and force incongruity into congruous categories is, of course, a measure of the successful operation of that mode. W. M. Frohock, a perceptive and sympathetic critic of Caldwell, demonstrates the exasperation of a reader caught in the spell of such writing, seeking resolution, getting no satisfaction, yet intrigued nevertheless: "Now nobody objects to looking at gargoyles, so long as we know what we are looking at. But the identification of these characters as such should, it seems to me, pretty well cancel out the possibility of reading Caldwell's novels as straight socially-conscious documentaries, and also cancel out the value of the books as serious comedy. . . . Caldwell's novels suffer from a multiplicity of meanings which are incompatible with one another. . . . [Yet] when we take everything into consideration we are likely to feel that, in spite of Caldwell's ambiguity, he is greater than we know."[6] The last clause, which is also the conclusion of Frohock's essay, is an engaging instance of critical humility, but also a piece of comic ambiguity in its own right, an ironic tribute to the power of mystification. Frohock's revelation of his alternating rejection and espousal of ambivalence is a rare example of critical candor. It is comparable to Caldwell's own simple statements of the ambivalence in his vision, captured most neatly in the phrase Caldwell used on a number of occasions to describe what interested him in human nature, namely, its "antics and motivations" (WA, "Introduction"). "Antics" suggests comic and irrational behavior, "motivations" the rational and deterministic origins behind people's conduct. There can never be a fixed balance between the explicable and the inexplicable, only a constantly shifting emphasis among different kinds of causality and the possibility of no causality at all.

5. Donald Davidson, "Erskine Caldwell's Picture Book," in *Critical Essays*, ed. MacDonald, 67; "Erskine Caldwell," Augusta *Chronicle*, March 14, 1935, reprinted in *Critical Essays*, ed. MacDonald, 130; Scott MacDonald, Introduction to *Critical Essays*, ed. MacDonald, xi; Tharpe, "Interview with Erskine Caldwell," 74.

6. Frohock, "Erskine Caldwell: Sentimental Gentleman," 211, 213.

Ada Lester is an example of this "antics and motivations" theory. She is a woman wholly unsocialized into the most primitive of human conventions. She does not talk at all during the first thirty years of her marriage to Jeeter, while she bears numerous and forgotten children, not all of them Jeeter's; she hides snuff from the dying grandmother who searches for it; and she hurls rocks in venom at her own son and his wife. However, for all her erratic wildness, Ada is preoccupied with one of the most minute niceties of the society from which she is an outcast: "Ada had a dress she had been keeping several years to die in, but she was constantly worried for fear that the dress might not be of the correct length. One year it was stylish to have dresses one length, and the next year they were mysteriously lengthened or shortened several inches. It had been impossible for her to keep up with the changes" (*TR*, 93). Thus Ada, dying of pellagra, pleurisy, and starvation, worries like a Georgian Emma Bovary over a fashionable exit from her squalid existence. Her bedroom is devoid of closets, furnishings, and amenities, but Caldwell nevertheless supplies her with a "cracked mirror" (*TR*, 135). This image of Ada, skinny, toothless, ugly, and quaintly vain both invites and defies explanation; it might suggest unlimited human vanity to the comic moralist or dire neediness to the reformer, but it hints at something beyond the power of reason to vindicate.

The other characters in the novel are similarly enigmatic. The aptly named Lov is first seen in the novel confessing his desire to see into the eyes of his golden-haired Pearl, while being lured simultaneously by Ellie May into mating with her like two dogs in the dirt. Ellie May herself, oblivious in her lust to all propriety and conventionality, is still capable of sensitivity and tears over her harelip. Dude is a stupid and vulgar youth who, like Flannery O'Connor's horrible children, exposes adult hypocrisy and concealments; Sister Bessie is the noseless preacher of a nameless religion who looks to God for help for hunger and illness but eschews His sexual council because He has never been a married woman. Even the old Lester grandmother, first seen stumbling among thorns and briars, clad in black rags and whirled by the wind "until it looked as if she were shaking violently with palsy" (*TR*, 17–18), shifts dramatically from this almost biblical image to that of a comic old crone, dodging behind trees to get a better view of a family fight. Finally, she is depicted as a mere sack of flesh and bones, needing immediate disposal: "You help me tote her out in the field and I'll dig a ditch to put her in" (*TR*, 225).

Part of Caldwell's grotesque technique is this attribution of disparate qualities to his characters, so that they are greedy and generous, hateful and loving, sinful and penitent by turns. However, an equally important aspect of his technique is his own shifting perspective on characters and events. Thus the same people and actions may be presented at one moment from a detached comic distance, at the next in more engaged and sympathetic intimacy; at one time his images may be dignified and compassionate, at another degrading—without any intrinsic changes in the characters themselves. The imagery for the grandmother shifts from the mythic black figure falling among thorns to a naturalistic stiffening corpse with a face mashed in the sand, with no essential alteration in the grandmother herself. The doubleness and discrepancy is thus in Caldwell's angle of vision as well as in his people. It is primarily a shift in his perspective that alters the comic horseplay of the Lester family's fight to the serious aftermath of the automobile accident. Bessie and Dude's car knocks down and reverses over the grandmother in the midst of a chaotic free-for-all in which curses, blows, and missiles are exchanged with the inconsequence of cartoon violence. However, Caldwell suddenly shifts away from the burlesque mode, and immediately the antics that seemed so ludicrous are replaced by consequences that recall the suffering of the participants and quickly discomfit any laughter at them. Such shifts are alienating for the reader, who has trouble mustering appropriate responses, but they are also enlightening about the dangers of too ready assimilation of such seemingly comic types.

Perhaps the most easily accepted form of the grotesque in *Tobacco Road* (and, as a consequence, the least disturbing) is the humor derived from traditional southern sources. Many critics have noted how close much of the comedy is to certain strains of southern folklore, and it has been suggested that Caldwell was using even more specific models in the works of the old southwestern humorists such as Augustus B. Longstreet, George Washington Harris, and Mark Twain.[7] Although Caldwell would undoubtedly have denied familiarity with these sources, he always was willing to acknowledge the impact that oral storytelling had on him in his youth, so that indirectly or directly, he had access to the many tall tales of

---

7. Among the critics who have noted Caldwell's affinities to the southwestern humorists are Richard J. Gray, Henry Seidel Canby, and W. M. Frohock (all of whom have essays in *Critical Essays*, ed. MacDonald), and Robert D. Jacobs, "*Tobacco Road*: Lowlife and the Comic Tradition," in *The American South: Portrait of a Culture*, ed. Louis D. Rubin, Jr. (Baton Rouge, 1980), 206–26.

lecherous preachers, country bumpkins, and urban con men, to an extensive strain of funereal comedy, and to the cruel burlesque of sudden death, destruction, and dismemberment. That the tradition already mixed laughter and cruelty, compassion and ridicule, pity and fear, did not deter Caldwell from further adaptations for his own purposes. Many critics have commented on what seems a virtual borrowing from Twain's *Adventures of Huckleberry Finn* of Huck's reply to Aunt Sally, when asked if anyone was hurt in a steamboat accident, "No'm. Killed a nigger," and her reply, "Well, it's lucky; because sometimes people do get hurt."[8] Caldwell's "version" comes in his account of the havoc wreaked by Dude and Bessie's new $800 automobile. Commenting on a black man knocked down by the car, Jeeter observes, "Niggers will get killed. Looks like there ain't no way to stop it" (*TR*, 159). Both Twain and Caldwell appear at first to be exposing satirically the callousness of whites toward blacks, but in fact, in *Tobacco Road* the whites later prove even more indifferent to the killing of their own grandmother. Caldwell points to the comparison by a verbal echo between the two accounts: of the black man's death he writes, "The wagon turned over on him and mashed him" (*TR*, 159); of the grandmother's, "Mother Lester still lay there, her face mashed on the hard white sand" (*TR*, 215). Caldwell's whites do not even value each other, and thus what seemed like an ironic comment on their racism takes on an even more frustrating direction for judgment. The disintegration of the automobile itself recalls the comic folklore genre of dismemberment, such as that of G. W. Harris' Sut Lovingood, but this comedy of wanton destruction is qualified by the knowledge that the Lesters are literally starving to death while they waste a relative fortune on a rampage. Similarly, Jeeter's account of the rats at his father's funeral, the ridicule of the Lesters by the Augusta city slickers, and Sister Bessie's sexual misadventures in the hotel are all versions of traditional folk humor—macabre, cruel, and vulgar. But in every case, Caldwell has made the incidents central to his conception of the characters and their "antics and motivations"— consistently antagonistic to any single line of interpretation yet equally provocative of many questions and answers.

In a recent study of the grotesque as an artistic genre, Geoffrey Galt Harpham has written of it: "Because it calls forth contradic-

---

8. Samuel Langhorne Clemens [Mark Twain], *The Adventures of Huckleberry Finn* (1886; rpr. New York, 1923), 306.

tory interpretations, and interpretations to which it refuses to yield, it disrupts the relationship between art and the meaning of art. We should expect it, therefore, to cause consternation in many camps— among those concerned to relate art and reality, those concerned to establish the basis of 'pure art,' . . . and those who believe that the moral status of art is grounded in reliable and true interpretations." The constant altercations of Caldwell's critics among advocates of a comic vision, of reformist realism, of symbolism, of left-wing propaganda, and of verifiable naturalism bear out Harpham's theory of the disruption of meaning. However, Harpham himself goes on to argue that the consternation aroused by the grotesque is a fruitful kind—that, in the words of William Carlos Williams, whom he quotes: "Dissonance / (if you're interested) / leads to discovery."[9] This discovery enlarges the sense of the strange possibilities of the world but is obtainable only by the sacrifice of certain certainties in exchange for uncertainty and confusion. In Caldwell's case, the problem of uncertainty is compounded by the fact that he deals extensively with economic, racial, and sexual injustices whose province lies at least partly in the realm of rational social reform. Caldwell imagines a world pervaded by incongruity, but that incongruity ranges from conventional and logical moral irony to absurd and meaningless farce. Sometimes the same incident will evoke all of these responses, as in Caldwell's account of the adventures of the $800 car, which initially suggests the moral ills of conspicuous consumption amid starvation but gradually takes on a manic comic energy, independent of any social lesson, as it goes on its crazy, self-destructive way. Caldwell could thus be simultaneously accused of both a surfeit and a lack of meaning, with some real justification, and at the same time be considered by W. M. Frohock to be "greater than we know." *Tobacco Road* indeed elicited mixed and puzzled responses (Wolfgang Kayser has argued that the grotesque applies not merely to the creative process and to the work of art itself, but also to its reception), which in no way deterred Caldwell from pursuing this vision through many of the ensuing novels of his southern cyclorama, certainly through the completion of *Tragic Ground* (1944).[10] It faltered seriously in the next novel, *A House in the Uplands* (1946), where Caldwell abandoned his poor white sub-

9. Geoffrey Galt Harpham, *On the Grotesque: Strategies of Contradiction in Art and Literature* (Princeton, 1982), 179; William Carlos Williams, as quoted *ibid.*, 191. See also Cook, *From Tobacco Road to Route 66*, Chap. 4 *passim.*

10. Wolfgang Kayser, *The Grotesque in Art and Literature*, trans. Ulrich Weisstein (Toronto, 1966), 180.

jects for the first time, and thereafter tended to be limited and intermittent rather than pervasive. However, during the 1930s, when poverty was the most salient characteristic of his subjects, Caldwell maintained most tenaciously his disconcerting vision of the poor, both in *Tobacco Road* and, perhaps even more emphatically, in the novel that followed it, *God's Little Acre*.

After the completion of *Tobacco Road*, Caldwell embarked on a novel about backwoods Maine life in an attempt, he said, to shake off his preoccupation with the South. It did not go well, and although he completed and sent it to Scribner's in 1932, he was apparently already dissatisfied. When it was rejected, first by Scribner's and then by Viking, Caldwell decided to acquiesce pragmatically to his fascination with his native state and begin another book about a somewhat different phase of life in East Georgia (*CE*, 112, 123). Thus he started writing *God's Little Acre* in May, 1932, with a renewed sense that it was the right subject for him—an expansion of the rural world of *Tobacco Road* into the cotton mills that Jeeter Lester had so vehemently resisted. Caldwell recounted later that he wrote the novel rapidly and easily, without revisions, feeling the story and its characters to be so close to the surface of his consciousness that he could abandon his normal process of correction and rewriting (*CE*, 125). It was completed by August, 1932, published early in 1933, and taken to court within a year of its inception by the New York Society for the Suppression of Vice on a charge that it was "obscene, lewd, lascivious, filthy, indecent or disgusting." The artistic merits of the novel were defended in court by a large number of eminent literati whom the Society's lawyer argued to be, *ipso facto*, "abnormal people"; but the presiding magistrate found in the book's favor, judging its extensive sexual preoccupations to be a necessary part of a realistic picture of "a segment of life in the Southern United States." However, many reviewers and critics also found themselves troubled by the seemingly disproportionate attention paid in *God's Little Acre* to the sexual activities of the characters. The *New Masses* reviewer, clearly wishing to encourage Caldwell's new urban proletarian bent, allowed that his approach to sex was "thoroughly healthy," but felt that nevertheless "he ought, in the future, to avoid this over-emphasis," noting the prevalence of scenes that were "as weird and fantastic as the author meant them to be straightforward and genuine."[11] What neither the detractors

---

11. *"People* v. *Viking Press, Inc., et al.,"* in *Critical Essays*, ed. MacDonald, 28, 29, 30; Edwin Rolfe, "God's Little Acre," in *Critical Essays*, ed. MacDonald, 24, 23.

nor the defenders of the novel acknowledged was the absolute centrality of sexual behavior to a grotesque vision of life in *God's Little
Acre* that was as improperly defended for realism as it was attacked
for sexual exploitation.

The irrelevance of such lines of attack and defense may be illustrated in two of the more "weird and fantastic" episodes. Before
Will Thompson makes love to Griselda, near the end of the novel,
he rips her clothing to shreds, not the formulaic tearing of pornographic tradition but an absolute and minute destruction of the cotton fabric that he has woven all his life in the mill, until it is once
more returned to its original lint. The scene discloses not Griselda's
body but Will's obsession. Earlier in the novel, in another strange
sexual episode, the mill girls are described returning to the ivy-
covered walls of the mill, pressing their bodies against them and
kissing them until the men come and beat them for their infidelity.
The women apparently find a symbolic power in their lives displaced into the machinery of the mill, but it would be as absurd to
suggest that the latter incident is realistic as to argue that the former
is an incitement to lust. Every aspect of this novel is pervaded by
sexual associations—with food, machinery, money, work, religion,
disease, and nature. Perhaps most significantly, sexuality is a metaphor for the pursuit of a vision of life that is outside the realm of
conventional, material realism, though certainly for Caldwell's characters this realm has a genuine existence. Sexuality serves as a way
of defining characters, of demonstrating the connections between
seemingly disparate spheres of life, of transferring images, breaking
down categories, and blurring distinctions. Without such an "over-
emphasis," there might remain a comic tale of a hypocritical old
man unwilling to tithe his prospective gold, or a strange account of
life in the cotton mills, but certainly nothing so novel or disturbing
as the book that exists.

*God's Little Acre* initially appears as such an exuberant novel, so
fertile and bizarre in its inventiveness, that it is easy to believe
Caldwell's comment, "I wrote the story as fast as I could wind it
through a typewriter in order to find out what was going to happen next." Caldwell insisted that he had no "preconceived conclusion" in mind for the novel and thus that it followed a kind of self-
generated logic, with the characters taking over their fates from the
author.[12] Nevertheless, the book is one of Caldwell's most tightly

12. Erskine Caldwell, Introduction to *God's Little Acre*, in *Critical Essays*, ed.
MacDonald, 225.

wrought in structure, as it is unified in the ideas that pervade it. Once again, he is interested, as in *Tobacco Road*, in the twists and turns that occur between his characters' "motivations" and their "antics." These motivations may be the fulfillment of basic physical needs (once again Caldwell uses poor people to illustrate this most effectively), or they may be both articulated and unarticulated desires for transcendence from those needs—in the reverence for God, the love of beauty, or even the awe of the inhuman power of machinery. The antics are the quirks of behavior that result not only from these mixed desires but also from the waywardness of the people who pursue them and the constraining sphere of their lives. Once again, the emphasis on material deprivation and the novel's setting in a striking southern cotton mill town raise the possibilities for some proletarian ideology, especially in its 1933 context; but, as in *Tobacco Road*, the politics are both qualified and eccentric.

The artfulness of the design of *God's Little Acre* and even the aptness of its supposedly unanticipated ending appear to deny Caldwell's account of its hurried and unplanned composition, or at least to suggest that he was developing a remarkably intuitive sense of form. Caldwell carefully alternates the setting of the twenty chapters of the book between Ty Ty Walden's farm in rural Georgia and the striking mill town of Scottsville, South Carolina, with a central intrusion of three chapters set in the city world of Augusta. The novel begins and ends on the land, but the settings are constantly linked and juxtaposed, not merely by the characters' journeyings back and forth, but by patterns of images associated with each place. All three are sterile environments where no productive work is taking place and human activity is diverted into oblique channels. Normal farming on Ty Ty's land has been abandoned in a fruitless search for gold, which is aided by the abduction from his home of an albino man to act as a diviner. In the mill town of Scottsville, striking workers have been locked out of the mills for eighteen months, but dream of switching on the power again by taking over the mills for themselves—an action fraught more with the kind of miraculous hopes that Ty Ty holds for the albino than with any practical economic purpose. The urban world of Augusta is characterized by nonproductive labor and decadent moneymaking: cotton brokering, prostitution, and attaching the property of people unable to pay their rent. The settings all betray distortions of normalcy—the holes in the fertile farmland, the silent factories, the unearned wealth; but Caldwell's characters are not looking for the normal, but for ways in which the oppressiveness of the normal may be transcended.

In addition to his careful structuring of geographic settings, Caldwell also creates patterns, repetitions, and echoes among characters and incidents that parallel the larger metaphorical linking of dissatisfied yearnings that underlies the whole novel. Each of the three places in the novel has its own spokesman, and all three voice an oblique version of their philosophies: Ty Ty as a naturalist, Will as an urban proletarian, and Jim Leslie as an urban capitalist. The three women in the novel—Darling Jill, Griselda, and Rosamund—at times appear to represent three different female roles (labeled by one Jungian critic trickster, anima, and nurturer) and at other times to form a composite principle of femaleness.[13] This is most apparent as they move in a harmonic dance to serve Will Thompson his final meal: "He sat down at the table, watching them prepare a place for him hurriedly, easily, lovingly. Darling Jill brought a plate, a cup, and a saucer. Griselda brought a knife, a spoon, and a fork. Rosamund filled a glass of water. They ran over the kitchen, jumping from each other's way, weaving in and out in the small room hurriedly, easily, lovingly" (GLA, 234). The verbal triplings of this passage are echoed in triple repetitions elsewhere in the novel by Ty Ty's tributes to Griselda's beauty and his thrice-repeated request to her to buy herself a "pretty." Even the meals eaten during the novel have a curiously ritual, repetitive quality to them that suggests their larger connection, from Rosamund's peace offering of peach ice cream to Will's last meal and the final somber dinner at the farm that anticipates the tragic ending. The continual pairing and tripling of images, people, and occasions is an important integrating element in a novel whose central concerns seem at first so disparate; it leads to larger thematic associations that are too tentative and intangible to be spelled out in the narrative but that nevertheless permeate the work.

A dominant and controlling metaphor of *God's Little Acre*—as Lawrence Kubie pointed out in his early psychoanalytic study—is hunger, a metaphor that provides a larger nexus for all the varied fields of activity in the novel.[14] Caldwell establishes the connections by constantly transferring imagery from one context to another, linking digging for gold and tending cotton mill machinery with food, sex, death, mystery, and divinity. In both country and town,

13. See David Pugh, "Reading Caldwell Today: Perceiving Craft and Culture," *Pembroke Magazine*, XI (1979), 124.

14. Lawrence S. Kubie, "'God's Little Acre': An Analysis," in *Critical Essays*, ed. MacDonald, 163.

his people have turned a perfectly naturalistic endeavor—earning their daily bread—into a magical rite in ways that are simultaneously ludicrous and charged with significance. On Ty Ty's farm, immediate physical hunger is being subordinated to a larger hunger for gold from the earth, and the rich arable soil is being transformed into a wasteland of mounds and craters that literally undermine the foundations of the family home. Ty Ty's black laborers sense the consequences of this distorted effort in their own lack of food, yet they too are off digging in their own holes at every opportunity. Such perversity is the substance of both folk comedy and classic mythology, and Caldwell pursues both perspectives with zest, from Ty Ty's crazy ambush of the albino Dave to his final wails of "Blood on my land" (*GLA*, 301) after the fratricide on God's little acre.

In the mill town of Scottsville, hunger is an even more painful reality than on the land, for the workers are being starved into submission in their strike against the owners. Yet once again the hunger is transferred and distorted into a desire by the striking men to possess the factory machinery, not so much as an economic protest but rather as a way of reasserting the strange power they feel they have lost to the machines. This power manifests itself in the effects of the machines on the women, who are "in love with the looms and the spindles and the flying lint"; who kiss the mill walls at night and then go home to be beaten for their infidelity; who have the ability to make the machines move more quietly when they are operating them. The mill men's hunger for power, like the farmer's for gold, has both an absurd and mythic aspect to it. The power is on the one hand merely a current of electricity that drives machinery and, on the other, a force worth Will's martyrdom and the ensuing Christ-like division of his shirt, torn to shreds (like Griselda's dress) among the women. Kubie's perceptive theory about the novel is that it "is a story in symbolic language of the struggle of a group of men to win some fantastic kind of sustenance out of the body of the earth, the 'body' of factories, and the bodies of women."[15] This is a neat synthesis of the discrete sets of images in the book, although it does not suggest why the people seek the fantastic rather than the normal, or note the extent to which the people are deprived of the normal—both central concerns for Caldwell in this novel.

His people hunger for beauty, for power, for God, and for mystery, but are limited by their own corporeal beings to actions and

15. *Ibid.*

feelings that can never transcend their brute physical forms. Limited in intellect, education, and experience as they are, they can rarely find a decorous form of sublimation and are thus forced to use "lower" and perverse outlets for what may well be higher impulses. Only in the character of Ty Ty Walden does Caldwell permit the direct articulation of such aspirations, and even then it is inevitably qualified by his blunders and his misunderstandings of the effects of his words on others. His talk is gnomic, both true and silly, profound and simultaneously embarrassing to his listeners. They laugh at and reject it, yet it often seems to be at the heart of their behavior. Many years later, Caldwell commented on Ty Ty that "his life was more spiritually rewarding than the secularly imposed lives most of us live," for "we ourselves are generally too uncourageous, in a circumspect civilization, to allow the spiritual needs of life to take precedence, at all times, over the material." [16] Those who recalled Ty Ty's constant efforts to gyp God of the proceeds of his little acre might wonder at the high calling later ascribed to him; but in fact, in Caldwell's eyes, his foolishness, his greed, and his human failings do not belie his spiritual character. This is revealed in his capacity for wonder at the natural ways of the world. In *Tobacco Road*, Jeeter Lester shared the same passive delight in farming that appears in Ty Ty toward sex. Both men savor these activities more in contemplation than in execution, but their appreciation sets them apart from those who are merely participators in the "secular" world. Early in the novel, Ty Ty criticizes his son Shaw, the most practical and worldly member of his family, for "going rutting every day in the whole year. . . . He ought to be satisfied just to sit at home and look at the girls in the house" (*GLA*, 6), and indeed Ty Ty presides himself like a benevolent spirit over the three women. He extols Griselda's beauty and delights in Darling Jill's sexual precocity; he watches with pleasure as Rosamund and Darling Jill, Buck, and Griselda prepare themselves for bed; he stands holding a lantern over the lovemaking of Darling Jill and the albino Dave, exclaiming in pleasure, "Did you ever see such a sight? . . . Now, ain't that something?" (*GLA*, 137). However, although Ty Ty can appreciate a sacramental element in such acts and insist on their communal nature, the world he lives in operates by the conventions of private property and monogamy, and those who venture to rearrange the conventions are doomed to failure.

16. Caldwell, Introduction to *God's Little Acre*, in *Critical Essays*, ed. MacDonald, 225.

The problem of articulating or finding any appropriate outlet for their higher aspirations or spiritual needs is a pervasive one for the characters in *God's Little Acre* and for Caldwell's people generally. They turn to agricultural fantasies, orgiastic religion, and sexual licence because they have no other means of giving voice to their longings. Nothing else in their culture serves, for Caldwell's people are largely bereft of any folk arts or rituals in which they might give them form. The significance of art as an unavailable form of communication to his characters is indicated in Ty Ty's fascinated response to an artist's rendering in oils of a landscape of trees, which attracts him in Jim Leslie's house: "'The man who painted that knew what he was doing, all right,' Ty Ty said. 'He didn't put in all the limbs on the trees, but I'll be dog-goned if he didn't make the picture more like a real woods than woods really are'" (*GLA*, 175). The notion that a truncated artistic version of reality may be more authentic and truthful than reality itself is clearly an appealing one for Caldwell as well as for Ty Ty, but the illumination of art, or its capacity to give articulation to inchoate feelings, is almost never an option for his characters. The one limited exception in *God's Little Acre* is achieved by Ty Ty's black sharecroppers at the end of the novel, when they turn the story of Will's death into a bawdy, rhythmic chant about the loss of the "male man":

"Lord, Lord!"
"I was born unlucky."
"Ain't it the truth!"
"Trouble in the house."
"Lord, Lord!"
"One man's dead."
"And trouble in the house."
"The male man's gone."
"He can't prick them no more."
"Lord, Lord!"
"Trouble in the house."
"My mammy was a darky—"
"My daddy was too—"
"That white gal's frisky—"
"Good Lord, what to do—" (*GLA*, 278)

However, this chorus does not serve the needs of any of the main characters in the book and is at best a debased and partial form of

articulation. Transcendence for Caldwell's characters is almost always arrived at through the body rather than the mind. Though his
choice of the name Walden for his central family caused a number
of critics to speculate on Thoreauvian ideals in the work, there is no
question in Caldwell of the mind descending into the body in order
to redeem it. If there is any coincidence at all with Thoreau, the
most likely one comes from Caldwell's description of Ty Ty as "a
man who was not afraid to rearrange values in life so that he could
place the true worth on those things men most avidly seek."[17] However, the object of men's search in *God's Little Acre*, though spiritual in nature, finds the body a more feasible conduit than the mind
for its strivings.

This emphasis on sexual impulses, rather than intellect, as the
primary transmitter of deep feelings was again, as in *Tobacco Road*,
an obstacle to the acceptance of *God's Little Acre* by the proponents
of proletarian literature, despite Caldwell's own public political
sympathies and the timeliness of the subject. Caldwell had been
urged by the literary left wing to "go left," to go "deeper into the
life of the working class of the South," and to improve his social
understanding, and there is plenty of evidence in *God's Little Acre*
that this is exactly what he did.[18] Certainly, the urban sections of
the novel focus on some of the favorite topics of left-wing fiction, a
strike among mill workers, the indifference of the union, and the
brutality and decadence of the middle and upper classes. Caldwell
emphasizes the harsh and debilitating quality of mill workers' lives:
spitting their lungs out, pulling plugs of cotton from their ears as
they leave the mill at night, being starved into submission by pater-
nalistic owners who control the rents of their houses as well as their
wages. He evokes the humiliating lack of privacy in their poor
dwellings and the consequent intimacy it fosters among the workers. Darling Jill and Will's lovemaking is interrupted by the woman
next door knocking her dust mop against the thin wall of the company house, though this encroachment also has a positive and uni-
fying effect: "Murmurs passed through the company streets of the
company town, coming in rhythmic tread through the windows of
the company house. It was alive, stirring, moving, and speaking like
a real person." Will describes this communion as a kind of mystical
vibration of common life: "You don't know what a company town is

17. *Ibid.*, 226.
18. Macleod, "A Hardboiled Idealist," 7.

like. . . . But I'll tell you. Have you ever shot a rabbit, and gone and picked him up, and when you lifted him in your hand, felt his heart pounding like—like, God, I don't know what! Have you?" And his listeners are "frightened by the revelation" (*GLA*, 219–20). Will also exhibits plenty of orthodox class consciousness in his attitude to the millowners, and the other workers betray their skepticism of the union's negotiators: "What can you tell that son-of-a-bitch A.F.L.? Nothing! They're drawing pay to keep us from working" (*GLA*, 104). The mill workers are depicted as eager to work, protective of the machinery that is the accessory to their livelihood, and alternately energetic and exhausted by eighteen months of living on coffee and grits. The prosperous bourgeoisie, epitomized by Jim Leslie and his wife, are corrupt and decadent—all elements of what came later in the 1930s to be a veritable formula for left-wing strike novels.

Despite all these correctly left-wing elements, however, *God's Little Acre*, like *Tobacco Road*, refuses to be confined to identifiable social and economic injustices and their political remedies, even though these form such a significant part of the characters' lives. The culminating episode in the novel, the attempt to turn on the power in the mill, is imbued with a symbolism that reaches far outside mere political applications. It certainly suggests sympathy for a revolution from private to collective ownership, but even such a dramatic change is placed in the larger perspective of the significantly named Will's striving for a sense of unity with the entire created world (mill workers, rabbits, streets, machines) in which the communal objective of the strike plays a lesser part. The catalyst for breaking into the mill is a sexual act, and its consequence is death, the only permanent release from such aspirations. Will's act has no political impact except to remove him permanently from the ranks of the workers: "Will Thompson would breathe no more lint into his lungs" (*GLA*, 252). The destruction of Will's vitality means defeat in the mills and trouble on the land, and yet it was also this vitality that precipitated the conflict and caused the trouble. The tragic ending is also incongruous and perplexing, as is Ty Ty's admirable refusal to capitulate to conventions in his extravagant worship of God, gold, and Griselda, which results in desecration and fratricide. Caldwell's understanding of his two main characters' needs to pursue a "spiritually rewarding life" does not mitigate his sense of the inevitably self-defeating nature of such an endeavor. Thus, when Ty Ty says, "There was a mean trick played on us somewhere. God put

us in the bodies of animals and tried to make us act like people"
(*GLA*, 298), Caldwell is not, surely, endorsing a primitivism that
would merely allow his characters to act like animals. Rather, he is
observing the "trick" and the way in which his characters try perpetually to "act like people." James Devlin's term "Dionysiac" for
their consequent behavior is indeed an apt one if its communal and
mystical qualities are evoked as well as its orgiastic; but Caldwell
ultimately depicts this Dionysiac conduct as destructive and death
oriented, an effort to escape the "circumspect" world, but never a
successful one.[19]

It is the certainty of this vision of the longings and shortcomings
of human nature that permitted Caldwell the luxury, and sometimes
the danger, of his organic method of composition, whereby he purported to resign himself to merely observing his characters while
they generated their own incidents and plot. He said in one of his
last interviews, "I never know how anything is going to end" and
added, "Signs and portents indicate . . . that a conclusion is just
around the corner," a curious impersonality of phrasing that suggests that Caldwell was not the originator of those signs.[20] Yet Caldwell also contended that the outcome of his novels was foreordained, and he was understandably contemptuous of the happy
ending given to the Hollywood movie version of *Tobacco Road* and
equally relieved that *God's Little Acre* was left relatively untouched
in that respect. Thus he at least indirectly acknowledged that his
characters were autonomous only within *his* shaping vision; their
balkiness was clearly not readily adaptable to pornographic, proletarian, or romantic primitivist ends, despite the deceptive evidence
of all those strains in his work.

The novel that followed *God's Little Acre, Journeyman* (1935),
was, despite Caldwell's increasing involvement in the social and
economic concerns of the period, one of his least overtly political in
its emphasis and method. It appeared in the same year as the short
story collection *Kneel to the Rising Sun* and the nonfiction book
*Some American People*, each of which was more openly partisan
toward left-wing solutions than any of his previous works. However,
despite a setting once again amid rural southern poor whites, the
new novel deserted the world of hunger, strikes, exploitation, and
class conflict to focus more exclusively than ever before on the hu-

19. James E. Devlin, *Erskine Caldwell* (Boston, 1984), 54–74 *passim*.
20. Broadwell and Hoag, "The Art of Fiction LXII," 131.

man yearning for escape and transcendence from the banalities of daily existence. This important emphasis in *Tobacco Road* and *God's Little Acre* had occurred in conjunction with equal attention to the larger social organism that inadequately maintained its members. In *Journeyman*, although there are telling sociological observations about the relationships between races, sexes, and social ranks, the pervasive malaise that affects the people, although stemming from the boredom, heat, and isolation of a particular southern locale, nevertheless comes to represent a version of modern spiritual desolation, albeit in the form of a burlesque peep show. The method of the novel is more symbolic, allusive, and indeed near allegorical than any of Caldwell's other long fictions. Even the shape of the narrative is suggestive. Unlike the earlier novels, which tend to be highly eventful, *Journeyman* begins and ends with eruptions of energy, but lapses into sluggish doldrums for the large central portion, a method that heightens the climaxes but is perhaps too literally effective in recreating the intervening ennui.

The novel's symbolism focuses especially on its main character, the itinerant clergyman Semon Dye, a character so suggestively named as to invite copious speculation about his significance— semen, for the sexuality he imports and provokes; sermon, for both his climactic tirade and also the entire lesson of his intrusion into a community; simon, for his profane trading of the sacramental; die, for its mortal, lustful, and gambling connotations and also for the suggestion of a mold from which all are cast by a maker: "'Everybody's wicked,' Semon stated grimly" (*JO*, 12). The evocations of Semon's name are extended further in the novel's title, *Journeyman*, which suggests both a traveler and a practitioner of a trade, and his symbolic meaning is explored in every aspect of his appearance and behavior. His great comic intrusion into the sleepy world of the novel, amid deafening explosions and foul-smelling emissions from his rattletrap car, drew from Kenneth Burke a comparison to Wagner's entrance of Siegfried, and from just about everyone else a sense that the devil had arrived.[21] Semon comes in with "an ear-splitting backfire" and a "dense cloud of nauseating black smoke" (*JO*, 5) that is accompanied by an apparatus of images, metaphors, and repetitions that insist on his satanic force. Birds immediately

21. See Gerald W. Johnson, "Saving Souls," in *South-Watching: Selected Essays by Gerald W. Johnson*, ed. Fred Hobson (Chapel Hill, 1983), 22, 24, for an account of evangelists' evocative names. See also Burke, "Caldwell: Maker of Grotesques," 173.

sweep out of the woods, "as if they had discovered a snake in a tree" (*JO*, 5); and women react with fascination: "He's the handsomest thing" (*JO*, 27); "He's the potentest thing" (*JO*, 28); and he is "the most devilish" (*JO*, 29). In appearance, he is utterly grotesque—six feet eight inches tall—gaunt and leather-faced, with slits for eyes and a thumb "sticking up like a nubbin of red corn." He thrusts his hand out in greeting, "pushing it . . . as though it were a pole wrapped in an old coat," and the hand itself looks like "the cured ham of a suckling pig" (*JO*, 7, 16). The sexual and bestial implications of these images are further suggested in Semon's rising in the morning "like a young rooster" (*JO*, 40) and his moving "as restlessly as a fox in a cage" (*JO*, 23). In addition to his sexual power over women, Semon wields a strange authority over men by his articulateness, thereby giving voice to their unspoken feelings. He thus proves to be to both sexes a powerful and magnetic tempter.

Semon is a satyr in black clergyman's garb, but he is also a classic con man and a kind of prophet in wolf's clothing. The plot of the novel follows his violent, trouble-making schemes of extortion and indulgence to their inevitable comic conclusion when he succumbs to his own rhetoric and, instead of taking up a collection at his revival meeting, "comes through" himself and forfeits all profit in his ecstasy. However, instead of anger at this betrayal of his schemes, "He looked then as if he were happy. His face was losing its expression of pain, and a beatific smile spread over his face" (*JO*, 182). As a con man, Semon has all the grim knowledge of human nature necessary to such a calling; as a man of God, he can never be happy with the worldly rewards of his business. Caldwell uses this doublesidedness, as villain and seer, to explore the search for transcendence in a fallen world. When Semon comments of his congregation, "Looks like the people are starved for preaching . . . . These people are ripe for religion" (*JO*, 149), it is obvious that there is indeed a hunger there, as strong as that which drove Ty Ty and Will in *God's Little Acre* or Jeeter in *Tobacco Road*.

The manifestations are different, in worship of land, sexuality, and religious swooning, but all three books insist on an irrational urge for release that is utterly divorced from the moral codes of conventional religious conduct, but has much in common with religious ardor and mysticism. Thus when Lorene, the skeptical prostitute, questions Semon suspiciously, "What are you, anyway? Are you a preacher or a pimp?" the only answer she can logically receive is the completion of the enigma, "I'm a man of God" (*JO*, 78).

Pressed by other characters to define and locate himself either in their world or out of it, he gives consistently ambivalent responses. To Tom Rhodes's suggestion that his conduct is more like the rest of them than of a man of God, he says, "I'm a preacher when I preach, and I'm a sleeper when I sleep" (*JO*, 103), and to Clay Horey's comment, "You're a long way from home, aint you?" Semon demurs, "Yes and no . . . I am and I aint" (*JO*, 8); indeed, he is fundamentally both homeless and at home everywhere in the universe. He is described as "a dirty son of a bitch" (*JO*, 123) and "a fool about God" (*JO*, 154), and Clay Horey acknowledges to him in bewilderment, "There aint no knowing about you" (*JO*, 136)—a tribute both to the unsounded depths of his villainy and to his fanatical determination to save sinners at no matter what cost, even including the risk of being saved himself. The imagery suggests that Semon may be the devil incarnate or a prophet of truth who reveals people in their true colors by exposing their basest instincts. It also suggests that he may be a vital agent in the sociology of a blighted region, providing entertainment and release, like the circus that comes to the sleepy Arkansas town in Twain's *Huckleberry Finn*, transforming criminal boredom to delight and purging base impulse in pleasure. Obviously, the community's values and its response to Semon, just as much as his own personality and conduct, are needed to determine his full meaning, although even when taken in their totality, they are unlikely in Caldwell's world to give any single explanation to so calculatedly ambiguous a character.

The settlement in which Semon arrives is aptly named Rocky Comfort, for indeed it is a community devoid of any signs of redemption—spiritual, moral, or social. The only church has lapsed into a guano shed, a repository for fertilizer in the spring and cottonseed in the fall, whose pulpits have been split for stovewood. The last preacher to visit it, eight or ten years earlier, had done his "damnedest" but concluded, "The folks had gone too far to help any in this life. . . . When it comes to being sinful, I don't know nobody else in Georgia that's in the running" (*JO*, 11–12). Few signs of community spirit or obligation exist there, despite the numerous sexual liaisons between the members: parents neglect children, spouses betray and neighbors cheat one another, and the whole locale is sunk in such torpor that only a jug of corn or the devil himself can shake a man awake. Gerald W. Johnson, in "Saving Souls," described the sociology of such locations thus: "The drab monotony of existence demands some relief. If the poverty and sparseness of the population make it impossible to support theatres and concert-halls, and if the communal *mores* prohibit horse-racing, cock-fighting and dancing, the range of emotional outlets is sharply restricted. Evangelism furnishes one."[22] Caldwell, although clearly not averse to this kind of explanation, nonetheless gives a more symbolic and unworldly context to his community than Johnson's theory permits. His landscape is harsh and scorching, figures appear like illusions in the glare of hot sun on white sand, and everything seems eerily lifeless and becalmed: "There were no clouds in the pale blue sky, there was no breeze to stir the leaves on the magnolia tree, there was no motion in the endless gliding and wheeling of the buzzards overhead, and now the ramshackle automobile and dust-stained stranger were as inert as the row of sagging fence posts beside the road" (*JO*, 4). If Rocky Comfort is, as one critic contended, a postlapsarian paradise with Clay Horey and his fifteen-year-old wife, Dene, as its fallen lovers, the "pastoral peace" that reigns there may be defined largely as an absence of energy to pursue its own innate sinfulness with more zest and imagination.[23] Semon brings a renewal of energy and a revival of enthusiasm—both religious and worldly—into a community hanging in a state of suspension, and his departure finally abandons them to an even more sterile wasteland and a greater relapse into nothingness.

The people of Rocky Comfort can scarcely be said to constitute a true community, because the setting of the novel is confined largely to Clay Horey's farm and the cow shed of his neighbor Tom, and only at the revival meeting do other townsfolk appear. Clay, whose name suggests his mortal and malleable nature, lives in torpor with his fifth wife, Dene, having abrogated the care of his six-year-old syphilitic son to a black servant, Susan, the tilling of his land to the "yellow" man, Hardy, and the functioning of his household to Hardy's wife, Sugar. With all his responsibilities farmed out to the blacks, Clay has nothing to do but sit on his porch, by a road that leads "nowhere" (*JO*, 8), with a clock that is "not far from right" (*JO*, 66), pondering how to wake himself up. Before the novel's conclusion, Clay has been tricked into paying over his scant money in order to be duped, and forced, at the end of Semon's pitchfork, to mate with his ex-wife Lorene; he has gambled away his car, his farm, and his present wife in a contest with Semon's loaded dice;

22. Johnson, "Saving Souls," in *South-Watching*, ed. Hobson, 27.

23. Henry Terrie, "Erskine Caldwell's *Journeyman:* Comedy as Redemption," *Pembroke Magazine*, XI (1979), 26.

and he has "come through" along with every other member of the community but one at Semon's revival meeting. Yet upon Semon's departure, Clay is desolate: "It does sort of leave a hollow feeling inside of me to know he aint here no longer. I feel left high and dry, like a turtle on its back that can't turn over" (*JO*, 193). This feeling of emptiness is echoed at the end by all the other main characters—by the two women, Lorene and Dene, who had hoped to leave with Semon, and by Tom Rhodes, whose whiskey bottle no longer brings him its usual consolation: "He looked down through the hole at the colorless liquor and blew his breath into it. It made a sound like wind at night blowing through a gourd tied to a fence post" (*JO*, 194–95). Everyone except the blacks, who had no share in the preaching, is left aimless, high and dry, facing nada in the hot white sand.

The climactic excitement that Semon's revival brings to Rocky Comfort is not, however, the community's only attempt to escape from the mundane and the worldly. Caldwell establishes another and very different pattern of transcendence in his characters—a pattern that, although equally ludicrous in its manifestations, is as contemplative and quietistic as the other is carnal and orgiastic. This is the practice, first performed in embarrassed isolation by Tom Rhodes, but then eagerly joined by Clay Horey and Semon himself, of sitting on a stool in Tom's cow shed and peering through a crack in the wall at the world outside. In a chapter placed immediately prior to the revival meeting, Caldwell slowly builds both the comic and the mysterious implications of the crack, and he returns to it again afterwards to insist on the connection between the two. To the amazed questions of Clay and Semon, who first discover him in this secret practice, Tom haltingly reveals what he sees: "Well, there's nothing but the woods over there, I reckon. There's that, and something else. I don't know what." He acknowledges that there is not "a bit of sense in it" (*JO*, 141), but Semon is intrigued enough to take a look of several minutes' duration; and when Clay follows suit, he too discovers the spell of the familiar landscape framed from a different angle, and he continues "to look through the crack as though he saw something that he had never seen before in his life" (*JO*, 142). These three men then begin to push each other aside in order to look, and Tom admits, "I can't keep from looking to save my soul. . . . There's not a single thing to see . . . and then again there's the whole world to look at" (*JO*, 144). Semon agrees that "there's something about looking through a crack that nothing else in the whole wide world will give you" (*JO*, 145), and Tom finally concludes, "It's just the sitting there and looking through it that sort of makes me feel like heaven can't be so doggone far away" (*JO*, 147).

The crack allows the watcher to sit in darkness looking at light, to feel no longer immanent in the world but apart from, if not transcending, it; and it orders the external landscape for a moment, like an absurd white trash version of Wallace Stevens' "Anecdote of the Jar": it takes dominion over the "slovenly wilderness" of nature. It is as close as Caldwell's people can come to a visionary experience by their own devices, without the aid of art or religion, although it has obvious affinities with both. While Semon and Tom alternate at looking, Clay plays on his harmonica "as though his life depended upon it" (*JO*, 145); all three men are entranced and transported by the humble music, and Semon is finally moved to tears. Caldwell intersperses their captivation with the banal lyrics of the love song Clay is playing and with the passing of the liquor bottle, so that it is never possible to forget that this is a comic and maudlin group of drunks as well as three humans on the edge of life's mystery. The constant repetition of the words "crack" and "slit" throughout the sequence also evokes Semon's imagery and especially the terms that have been applied to his eyes throughout the novel, "slits in his leather-tight face" (*JO*, 13, 24). They are also connected to a larger pattern of images of staring, gazing, winking, seeing and mis-seeing, so that Semon is directly associated with both the grotesque and visionary aspects of looking through the crack. Indeed, Tom says of the crack in the wall that without it, "I reckon I'd just dry up and die away" (*JO*, 147), a comment echoed almost directly in Clay's remark that Semon's loss leaves him "high and dry," and borne out in the decision of both Tom and Clay to console themselves after Semon's departure by looking through the crack.

This yoking of the earthy Semon (now perhaps also "see man") to an innate desire to penetrate beyond the everyday world anticipates the even stranger misalliance of sexuality and religion that is the culmination of Semon's visit to Rocky Comfort. The backcountry revival meeting is Caldwell's most explicit restatement of the inseparability of profane and sacred impulses in his characters, and Kenneth Burke has described this attitude of Caldwell's in terms of starkest naturalism: "Since the body has less channels of expression than the mind, acute religious ecstasy may be paralleled neurologically by sexual orgasm," but Caldwell also reverses cause and effect in this proposition by suggesting that carnal pleasure may be a means to, as well as a consequence of, divine apprehensions.[24] Thus, as Semon Dye makes love to Dene, she screams hysterically, "I love the Lord!" (*JO*, 133), and one recalls Ty Ty Walden's belief that God is inside the body and in no way separate from the universe of feeling. Caldwell devotes four chapters, or approximately one-fifth of *Journeyman*, to Semon's Sunday revival meeting, which begins at two o'clock in the afternoon with the arrival of thirty or forty adults and their children, some of whom have been traveling with their mules since early morning, and ends late that night with their silent departure in the darkness. In between, the members of the group move from the curious, dispassionate detachment of frequenters of country shows, funerals, and "break-downs" ("He won't get warmed up till about eight o'clock tonight. It'd just be a waste of time sitting in there while he's still cold" [*JO*, 152]) to the abandoned frenzies of shaking, screaming, writhing, and jerking that signal their lonely and private transition to a state of grace.

Caldwell is at his best in these chapters, revealing the group's mores and the tenor of their lives in such subtle conjunction with his themes that they seem inseparable. Families arrive and depart as units, but there is a great divergence of behavior and expectation between the men and the women. The women go immediately indoors, "like a flock of sheep all trying to jump through a gap in a fence" (*JO*, 150), and they sit patiently amidst the heat and buzzing insects while Semon begins his preaching: "Flies and June bugs came in and went out the open doors and windows at will, and in the four corners of the room gray hornets' bags hung precariously. Dotting the walls and ceiling were yellow crusts of clay around which swarmed mud-daubers. At almost regular intervals a woman would slap her leg with a desperate lunge, jerk her dress above her knees, and flick off a red ant that had stung her" (*JO*, 154–55). They have between them a total of twenty cents to contribute to the preacher ("Women never have no money, anyway. It's the men who carry what little there is" [*JO*, 162]), but they are enthralled to sit in discomfort in return for the possibility of what Semon may say about the dark sins that lurk behind beautiful faces and underneath starched and frilled dresses, and by his promise that in heaven they will look even prettier.

When the men and boys come in, much later in the evening,

24. Klevar, "Some Things Holy," 68; Burke, "Caldwell: Maker of Grotesques," 169.

from their whittling, chewing, drinking, and fighting, Semon's tenor changes to more explicit terror, sparked with some salacious testimony of sinfulness. He has no text but preaches an amalgam of sexual innuendo mixed with a Great Awakening theology that might have come straight from Jonathan Edwards: "Tomorrow will be too late. You might die before daybreak tomorrow morning. Nobody ever knows when he's going to do that. . . . Some of you are going to die soon; if you die in sin, you'll smoke in hell till the world comes to an end, and it may never come to an end. . . . It's the only time there'll be for some of you. You might be dead tomorrow, and it'll be too late then to do anything about it. Now's the time!" (*JO*, 165). Caldwell, as might be expected, does not specify which of the two strains is more effective, but soon the sermon is punctuated with cries of "Amen," and when someone screams, Semon's role as instigator is over, and the revival begins to generate its own hysterical momentum.

The manifestations are all of great physical intensity, explicitly sexual in many cases: "Men were prancing up and down like unruly stallions, and women shook themselves in time with [Lucy Nixon's] movements. A man who had been watching her for several minutes suddenly grasped the fly of his breeches with his fist and ran yelling into the crowd. Bursting buttons flew into the air like spit-balls" (*JO*, 176). However, not all the responses are so directly sexual: some of the people writhe and pant in the throes of simulated birth, while others struggle to articulate meaningless sounds like "Unga-unga," "Yee-yow," and other feral grunts and moans. Thus Caldwell insists on a general urge for release that is not exclusively sexual, and he emphasizes throughout both the solitary and the communal aspects of this experience as the people gather to help one of their number come through and then rejoice in the individual's success. Afterwards, there is a solemn peacefulness in their departures: "No one spoke coming out of the schoolhouse. People walked silently on the thick carpet of pine needles towards their wagons and cars" (*JO*, 187).

The frenzy, the rapture, and the calm are not evaluated by Caldwell in a naturalistic or a spiritual context, though such contexts are implicitly juxtaposed throughout the episode. Many years later, in his nonfiction study of such rituals, *Deep South* (1968), Caldwell speculated in somewhat more sociological terms on the reasons for their popularity, noting "the folksy atmosphere of informal religious services, temporary surcease of loneliness, constant reference by the minister to impending death, the promise of instant salvation, a rousing tempo of piano and guitar music, the incitement produced by detailed examples of sexual immorality in sermons, and the opportunity to indulge in emotional spasms in public without inhibition" (DS, 52). However, even these reasons suggest that something inexplicable and irrational, as well as naturalistically grounded, lies behind the power of this ecstatic ritual. The forms may lay themselves open to ridicule—such as watching a "Sanctified preacher hit his head with an axe handle until he had achieved a state of semiconscious delirium" (DS, 12), or a "minister dangling a rattlesnake above his face" (DS, 64), or floor rolling, blood drinking, head banging, or glossolalia. However, Caldwell grants these ceremonies a vital role in bringing a sense of the sublime, albeit entwined with the absurd, into such human deserts as Rocky Comfort. This is unlikely to save the citizenry of Rocky Comfort any more than collective farming might have saved the inhabitants of *Tobacco Road*, but it seems vital to sustaining them.

Semon, in keeping with his dual role in the novel as con man and shaman, comes through at the revival but is left with other dissatisfactions and for appropriately double-edged reasons. His oblivion causes him to omit taking a final collection, ostensibly his prime purpose there, and he is depressed by his inability to save the prostitute Lorene: "He felt sick and discouraged. He had saved perhaps forty people that night; but the most hardened sinner he could not help" (JO, 187). Lorene scoffs and withdraws from the orgiastic behavior of the community, but her skepticism carries little authority in the novel except insofar as it damages Semon's pride as a true professional. Elsewhere in the novel, Lorene opposes Semon and even suffers a beating for it, but she is not a strong or sympathetic enough character, either ethically or emotionally, to rival Semon. Caldwell offers no serious counterforce in the novel to the magnetism of the journeyman preacher. When he departs silently as the people sleep, Lorene is among those left devastated by his disappearance. As his loss is discovered, each member of the group left behind in Rocky Comfort slowly lapses back into the passivity and dullness of the novel's opening, with no consolation but the jug and the crack and the rusting hulk of Semon's old automobile for remembrance.

Such a depiction of anomie among poor whites might be expected, in a writer with Caldwell's demonstrated left-wing political sympathies, to be linked to the slough of capitalism and the energiz-

ing and visionary aspects of revolution, especially in a work published in the same year as *Kneel to the Rising Sun* and *Some American People*, which, in short story and documentary, emphasized the
social and economic roots of despair. However, *Journeyman* is
largely lacking in such concerns. We know that Clay Horey's farm is
mortgaged to the bank, and we know the people in Rocky Comfort
do not have much money, but such economic details are not given
much weight. Clay also has a new car and a number of black sharecroppers; no one in the novel is starving; and the only physical illness in the novel is not pellagra or malnutrition but a child's inherited venereal disease. The milieu of the novel is a spiritual and
emotional desert, and the people are, as Semon says, "ripe for religion" rather than, as Caldwell had earlier written of Dahlberg's
characters, "ripe for revolution." His simultaneous and continued
literary interest, in the other works of 1935, in social exposés and
reform suggests that *Journeyman* was not a harbinger of a sudden
change in Caldwell's perspective, away from such political concerns,
but rather that this novel was a reaffirmation of the centrality to his
vision of the human need for sublimation and transcendence that
might show itself in comic, terrifying and sometimes ridiculous
forms. *Journeyman* was not well received by contemporary reviewers, although it has tended to provoke increasing interest among
later critics; and on its publication in France in 1950, it was ac-
claimed one of Caldwell's best, "a master work," "perhaps his chef-
d'oeuvre," "one of the summits." James T. Farrell, reviewing it for
the *New Masses* in 1935, found it "merely a picture of the life of
primitive and undeveloped American folk" but not a novel that
contributed to the understanding of a section or a sense of the
people in this milieu. Those readers who looked to southern fiction
in 1935 for regional education or social muckraking were certainly
less likely to appreciate *Journeyman* than was a French audience in
1950, by then about to embrace Beckett's *Waiting for Godot* (1952)
and its preoccupation with a world where "nothing happens, nobody comes, nobody goes, it's awful."[25]

After the publication of *Journeyman* in 1935, Caldwell took a
long leave from his southern cyclorama in order to engage extensively in traveling and documentary writing with his then wife, the
photographer Margaret Bourke-White. They toured the South to

25. Smith and Miner, *Transatlantic Migration*, 159; James T. Farrell, "Heavenly
Visitation," in *Critical Essays*, ed. MacDonald, 41; Samuel Beckett, *Waiting for
Godot* (New York, 1954), 27.

produce the picture-text *You Have Seen Their Faces* (1937), and Czechoslovakia for *North of the Danube* (1939). When he returned to novel writing with *Trouble in July* (1940), Caldwell produced his first full-length book about race and showed signs of a shift in his ideological interests, along with this change in subject matter. Caldwell had, of course, already shown a considerable interest, both in and out of fiction, in black people and their vital and ambivalent position in southern culture. As early as 1926, in a book review for the Charlotte *Observer* of *Folk Beliefs of the Southern Negro*, he acknowledged that "those of us who live in the south are as deeply interested in superstitions and folk lore as the negroes who make them," and he insisted on the common heritage shared by black and white, where "we read our own lives and thoughts, as well as our neighbors." In the same year, he reviewed *The Negro in American Life*, arguing that "no one who is interested in the advancement of society can afford to be without [this] book"; and a few years later, in 1931, Caldwell applied for a Guggenheim fellowship, with the intention of writing about the relevance of blacks' economic conditions to the rest of the nation.[26] Many of his short stories throughout the 1930s dealt with racial topics: with lynching ("Saturday Afternoon" and "Kneel to the Rising Sun"); with folk culture ("Nine Dollars Worth of Mumble" and "Candy-Man Beechum"); with sex and miscegenation ("Yellow Girl" and "Return to Lavinia"); with atrocities committed by whites on blacks ("Blue Boy"); with comic dealings between the races ("The Negro in the Well"); and with the stunted communication and prevarication forced out of blacks ("A Small Day" and "August Afternoon").

Blacks had played minor roles in the novels before *Journeyman*, but in that novel he had broken new ground with the fifteen-year-old white girl Dene's account of her desperate attraction to the black sharecropper Hardy and her insistence that he make love to her. Semon's angry response to her confession—"Pretty soon everyone will be the same yellowish color if this keeps up" (*JO*, 131)—is a sardonic comment on a double standard (he himself has made an assignation with Hardy's black wife, Sugar). However, it is also one of the earliest statements of what Caldwell on various occasions suggested as the only natural solution to racial antagonism

26. Erskine Caldwell, Review of Newbell Niles Puckett's *Folk Beliefs of the Southern Negro*, in Charlotte *Observer*, August 15, 1926, p. 9; Erskine Caldwell, Review of Jerome Dowd's *The Negro in American Life*, in Charlotte *Observer*, November 21, 1926, p. 10; Sutton, *Black Like It Is/Was*, 120.

in the United States. When asked by an interviewer in 1973 if he prescribed "miscegenation" for racial integration, Caldwell denied direct advocacy but agreed it was "nature's way" of erasing distinctions. In his reportorial career, Caldwell had also shown a continuing interest in racial conflict and black oppression. In 1934, he had for a time acted as a correspondent for the *New Masses* while he was at home in Georgia, sending accounts of a barbaric lynching episode in which three black men died. In 1936, when he had traveled through the South with Margaret Bourke-White in preparation for *You Have Seen Their Faces*, she reported that they had again come across the trail of a lynching at Kelley, Georgia; a white girl with a reputation as a prostitute was reportedly raped by a black man, and a race was on between a lynch mob and a sheriff.[27] Caldwell's new novel, *Trouble in July*, took up many of these issues; it dealt with the supposed rape of a promiscuous white girl, Katy Barlow, by a black youth, Sonny Clark, in a small southern community, and with the subsequent pursuit and execution of Sonny by a lynch mob with the acquiescence of the community's sheriff, Jeff McCurtain.

On the immediate level of its plot, the novel appeared to many critics to be a standard retelling of a well-known piece of southern mythology that dealt in such stereotypes as the innocent black victim, the seductive and tainted white woman, the lustful mob, and the self-serving sheriff. Many of the responses to it were highly ideological, from Oscar Cargill's assertion that "if conditions are ever better in the South, if the treatment of the colored man is ever more humane, we are going to owe a very great debt to Erskine Caldwell," to Burton Rascoe's amusing contention that "the Arvin Hickses and Freeman Cantwells of the League of American Writers had creased Caldwell with their Marxian dumdum bullets, . . . branded this literary Meddlesome Jack with the hammer and sickle, [and] rechristened him Social Significance." Rascoe went on to cite southern rape and lynch statistics in an effort to forestall the shaking of "smug, pharisaical Northern heads" in their inevitable response to the novel. In fact, *Trouble in July* follows no party line on either lynching or class conflict. Indeed, in some major ways, it undermines the *New Masses'* insistence that lynch mobs were composed of "local representatives of the upper classes" who saddled the poor whites with the blame.[28] However, the melodramatic ingredients of

27. Tharpe, "Interview with Erskine Caldwell," 65; Erskine Caldwell, [Untitled], *New Masses*, January 16, 1934, p. 13; Sutton, *Black Like It Is/Was*, 66.

28. Cargill, *Intellectual America*, 396; Burton Rascoe, "Caldwell Lynches Two

the novel provoked reactions to a well-known type of story rather than to the darkly absurd tragicomedy that Caldwell actually told.

Only one contemporary reviewer, Richard Wright, saw that the novel might be something other than a conventional account of white villainy. He found the moral dilemma of the community's sheriff, Jeff McCurtain, to be the foreground of the novel and described the book as "a picture of an unheroic man who is pitiably human."[29] Up to this point in his southern cyclorama, Caldwell had tended to diminish the significance of personal ethical choices of his characters by emphasizing the extent to which they were both predetermined and perverse; but in this three-hundred-pound comfort-loving sheriff, he created someone who was clearly conscious of the consequences of his actions in terms of others' suffering and his obligations to his society, as well, of course, as his own self-interest. Caldwell had never, certainly, permitted his characters the excuse of complete moral innocence, no matter how naïve and obtuse they were, but he had shown their common lack of consideration of their own motives and their indifference toward responsibilities to one another. In *Trouble in July*, he connects his characters, and especially the unheroic Sheriff Jeff, much more closely than ever before to the legal, political, and religious institutions of their society, so that their ethical conduct can no longer be so readily viewed as a mere feature of their isolation and quaintness.

Jeff McCurtain is a creature of ambivalences, a man with innately decent sensibilities who is also a thoroughly lazy coward. He is continually thrust into the midst of community conflicts in which his moral perceptions are directly at odds with his sense of his material welfare. As a consequence, he can find no peace, despite the high priority he assigns to sleep, inertia, and abstention: His "soul is worried limp from one day's end to the next" (*TJ*, 30). He avoids crises of conscience by fleeing from town on fishing trips that have become grim ordeals for him: "He had had to force himself to catch fish in every known manner. He had snared them with a wire-loop; he had seined them; he had shot them with a rifle; and, when he had been unable to catch them any other way, he had dynamited them" (*TJ*, 11). The sheriff is dogged by moral perceptions that he is unwilling to face, believing of his jail that "the people on the inside were no

Negroes," in *Critical Essays*, ed. MacDonald, 74, 76; "Editorial," *New Masses*, January 16, 1934, p. 3.

29. Richard Wright, "Lynching Bee," in *Critical Essays*, ed. MacDonald, 72.

different than those on the outside, except that they had been caught" (*TJ*, 4); and, of the controversy over the sale of Black Jesus Bibles, "The niggers has got just as much right to say Christ was a black as the brother whites has to say he was a white" (*TJ*, 122). He knows instinctively that Sonny is innocent, yet his grimly comic goal throughout the novel is "to see this lynching kept politically clean" (*TJ*, 74). The result of this dubious ambition is that McCurtain moves in a literal and symbolic maze, constantly circling, doubling back, and getting trapped, once in his own jail. Subjected to assault, harassment, and conflicting orders from his superiors, the sheriff is simultaneously despicable and sympathetic, a man who never seriously considers the possibility of acting on principle but who suffers the pains as well as the comforts of his gross self-indulgence. He serves Caldwell as a typical, or perhaps a better than typical, member of the body politic of Andrewjones, a man with both power and responsibility who nevertheless likes to think of himself as "as innocent of wrong-doing as a newborn pup" (*TJ*, 116). However, McCurtain is one of Caldwell's least innocent creations. He is no Jeeter Lester or Ty Ty Walden, obsessed with a peculiar teleological vision of existence, but a man who must work actively not to see the evidence of his continuous daily betrayal of his own moral vision of the world.

Caldwell's view of the society that abets, permits, or fails to stop the lynching, and of the mob that actually perpetrates it, is equally complicated. When a writer commented in the *New York Times Book Review* in 1984, "I'm still waiting for the white writer to write a novel about lynching from the point of view of the lyncher," a prompt letter to the editor cited Caldwell's "Saturday Afternoon" as a short story, at least, with such a perspective.[30] However, *Trouble in July* does more than present the murderers' attitudes; it ranges through an entire community, exploring the preoccupations of every individual who is associated with the lynching in any way. Thus Caldwell reveals that people engage in it as a consequence of boredom, personal failure, and powerlessness, as well as hatred and lust; and they oppose it from selfish concerns for their cotton crops or their family safety. Such a broadly ranging survey of community motives and concerns might, in another writer, risk invoking the axiom that understanding brings forgiveness, but Caldwell's ironic detachment works against this. He focuses on issues among the people that

30. Julius Lester, "James Baldwin—Reflections of a Maverick," *New York Times Book Review*, May 27, 1984, p. 23; Letter in *New York Times Book Review*, July 1, 1984, p. 27.

may be viewed as by turns profoundly deterministic in shaping the lynching and by turns trivial and coincidental. The effect of these incongruities is less to create understanding than to insist on its limitations.

The novel is in part a restatement of the incorrigibility and irrationality of human nature, but in a context that is much more secularized and socialized than any of the earlier novels. It is the beginning of a process much more apparent in Caldwell's later novels, and of qualified artistic success, of grounding grotesque and exaggerated types in a reasonably familiar social context. In *Trouble in July*, it still works effectively because Caldwell has a topic and types of characters that are capable of being adapted to the abstract, near allegorical level of representation on which Caldwell's fiction works well. In later novels, when he moves into a mode that might be mistaken for realism, his ironic detachment disappears and is replaced by more didactic sympathies. *Trouble in July* is more concerned with social and ethical conduct than with spiritual cravings; but Caldwell does not pretend in it to be able to resolve, rather than reveal, the mysteries of human conduct by adopting a particular political line or posing as a psychologist or sociologist, as he was sometimes later to do.

Caldwell uses a number of devices in *Trouble in July* to shift from the kind of perspective he had in *Journeyman* on Rocky Comfort as a peripheral place, apart from, though symbolic of, the contemporary world, to Andrewjones, a community with all its channels of communication, dependency, and interaction open to the larger society of which it is a part. It is a more sizable, organized town with a wide range of social classes, occupations, institutions, and special interests. Besides the sheriff, with his symbolic legal status, Caldwell introduces, in turn and somewhat schematically, the other representative characters. Bob Watson, the victim's employer, is a man most concerned with his investments and therefore wants the lynching stopped. Mrs. Narcissa Calhoun is gathering signatures on a petition to send blacks back to Africa and is thus first to cry "rape." Senator Ashley Dukes and Judge Ben Allen are amoral and self-serving politicians, testing the direction of the wind in order to determine their responses to the lynch fervor. Finally, the lynchers themselves are introduced in their unsavory variety, from Oscar Dent, who has lost count of his black victims, to Milo Scroggins, whose salacious account of a sadomasochistic episode fuels the mob's lust for both Sonny and Katy.

Such an evocation of familiar types comes close to allegory and caricature, both apt methods for Caldwell's oblique vision, but it is rescued from tendentiousness by Caldwell's skill as a humorous raconteur. Many of the characters are introduced by way of exaggerated comic anecdotes that nevertheless serve to reveal details that later prove of great importance in the plot. Shep Barlow, the father of Katy, is the subject of a classic piece of macabre Caldwell humor. Reputedly "the quickest-tempered man ever known" (*TJ*, 81), he is so furious when his wife falls down the well and drowns that he throws his entire woodpile down after her. The story is akin to the tall tales that the characters trade among themselves, but it also reveals a significant fact that proves crucial later, when it becomes apparent that the fifteen-year-old Katy's wild behavior, which incites the lynching and her own grisly death, stems from the loss of her mother at this time. As with the tall tales, Caldwell also uses a familiar and predictable plot in this novel as a means of exploring the more important values of the community. Although many reviewers objected to Sonny's transparent innocence and the inevitability of his sacrifice, it is just this sense of certainty that shifts the focus of the novel away from the suspense involved in the chase and the brutality of its culmination. Because the outcome is predetermined, the interest must be in the players rather than the action, which is notably circular, digressive, and given to lulls and starts rather than building to a climax.

The lynchers are presented as a quarreling and indecisive bunch, divided by tensions between town and country men, and delayed, but not deterred, by titillating stories of Katy Barlow's previous sexual adventures. Caldwell's attitude to the mob is quite complicated and certainly not a clear illustration of upper-class manipulation of poor whites, which the *New Masses* might have approved. As in his earlier lynching story, "Saturday Afternoon," part of the mob's motivation consists of a transference to one black man (and immediately afterwards to one white woman) of a variety of failings in the character of the killers: a resentment of hard work in the light of their laziness; a jealousy of sexual innocence in the light of their own lust; and finally, in the stoning of Katy, a horror of the naked truth when they have all endorsed duplicity. As Joseph Warren Beach noted, "The negro becomes a physical symbol for men's consciousness of sin," as, of course, does the woman as a symbol of lust, and the slaughters are purgations of evil through these scapegoats.[31]

31. Beach, excerpt from *American Fiction, 1920–1940*, in *Critical Essays*, ed. MacDonald, 190.

The lynching is also, as in "Saturday Afternoon," a diversion, an entertainment more thrilling than a weekly possum hunt, and a release from the tensions of the midsummer heat. There are no ruling-class villains controlling the episode, though Judge Allen and Senator Dukes watch it carefully for political gain and Mrs. Calhoun certainly helps provoke it. Narcissa's supposedly Christian principles spur her to prevent the sale of Black Jesus Bibles, which are competing with her own distribution of a book about Jesus returning to earth as a salesman of secondhand cars. Mrs. Calhoun is certainly a sinister figure in helping to incite the mob; but beyond her there are forces in the community, less easily personified or countered, that affect the actions of these sawmill workers, tradesmen, and farmers, such as their dependency on cotton, the inheritance of slavery, and the punitive and guilt-ridden morality of a decadent Protestantism.

Even as the farmers gather round a smudge fire to plan the imminent execution of Sonny, their conversation is of the price of cotton, and Caldwell reveals how precarious their own lives are, how utterly beyond their control: "If the price dropped under eight cents a pound, it meant that a lot of them would have to live on short rations for the next twelve months; but if the price went above ten cents a pound, they would not only be able to eat well, but also be able to buy some new clothes and a few pieces of new furniture. Day in and day out, the price of cotton was the most important thing in their lives" (*TJ*, 80). Shep Barlow hopes to be the one to catch Sonny single-handed, but this ambition has less to do with the rumored rape of Shep's daughter than the fact that "his cotton was stunted and starved. In another few days his crop would be too far gone to save," and the men to whom he hopes to deliver Sonny "looked at the grass-choked cotton without comment" (*TJ*, 138). After the mob has tortured and laid waste to a black community, one of them remarks, perhaps too pointedly: "It was getting about time to clamp down on a nigger again. . . . A week ago I was in a store in Andrewjones, and I'll be damned if a black buck didn't come in with more money in his pocket than I've had in mine all summer long" (*TJ*, 190). In response to Mrs. Calhoun's petition, one of them asks rhetorically, "Who'd do all the work, if the niggers was sent away?" (*TJ*, 191). The excessive violence that Caldwell depicts in his mob and throughout the community has clear affinities with that of the people of Jefferson in Faulkner's *Light in August*, meting out death and destruction to purge their joyless lives. It is one consequence of a dour and repressive religion, and because there is in *Trouble in July* no search for other forms of ecstasy, this grisly behavior has to suffice.

The victims, Sonny Clark and Katy Barlow, are detached from the mob of men not merely by their race and sex or even their actions, but by the act of accusation itself, and thus they become fair game for the ritual hunting and taunting to which they are subjected. Sonny finds himself an instant and threatening pariah in his own black community. His arbitrary selection as the accused thrusts him outside the tightly knit group in a symbolic scene in which his friend Henry disengages Sonny's clutching arms from him and pushes him out into the darkness, whence Sonny returns repeatedly to beg for shelter, comfort, and food. Sonny is also an orphan, and Katy is motherless and in some ways less than fatherless as Shep's daughter, so that the two are already, by past accidents of fate, loners. Sonny lavishes his affections innocently on pet rabbits; Katy, less innocently but still in search of love, uses her sexuality to seek men's attention and responses. Caldwell draws careful parallels between the two that were largely ignored by those critics and reviewers who felt Caldwell was merely rehearsing a formulaic southern myth in the novel. Both spend the last night before their separate deaths fleeing in darkness through weeds and briars, and both bodies are juxtaposed in death, Katy's on the ground by the river and Sonny's slowly turning at the end of a rope on the tree above. Katy's complicity in Sonny's death, followed by her own subsequent sacrifice for exposing the injustice of his murder, aligns her symbolically on both sides of the conflict between white men's oppression and their victims. Caldwell's stories and novels up to this point in his career had always revealed his keen eye for the tricky and ambivalent relationships of blacks and women in southern society, but with the double lynching in *Trouble in July*, their situation is more explicitly compared than ever before. Caldwell had hitherto confined himself to more feasible images of the personal violence of individual confrontations between men and women, while noting the communal violence that society endorsed between blacks and whites. However, in Katy's death he created a much more audacious image of impersonal animosity toward Katy's sex, on a par with Sonny's race in provoking irrational and generic punishment.

Katy is not comparable in innocence or ignorance to Sonny, even though she is only fifteen years old, but Caldwell permits her in the end a kind of moral heroism reserved for few of his characters. She is more friendless even than Sonny after her mother's death, abused by her father, used by Mrs. Calhoun, and rejected by her lover, Leroy Luggit, for her desperate promiscuity. Yet Leroy's taunt— "You ought to be ashamed of yourself for letting people lynch a little nigger boy that's as innocent as the day is long" (*TJ*, 150–51)—precipitates a crisis of conscience in Katy that sends her running off like Sonny through a dark night of terror in which she flees guiltily from an intangible assailant, while Sonny hides innocently from his very real pursuers. Katy's flight, which culminates in her honest confession to the lynchers, "He didn't do it! . . . It was a lie! . . . Nobody done it" (*TJ*, 237), has the same grim conclusion as Sonny's, but her battle with her guilty conscience parallels the sheriff's flight from his duty the same night. All three wander in a wilderness (the sheriff with convenient pauses for naps and meals) from which the innocent black man and the repentant woman emerge to the deaths they now long for, while Sheriff Jeff lives on in the world he has helped to make. Although Katy Barlow seems at first to come from the mold of such other Caldwell nymphomaniacs as Sister Bessie and Darling Jill, she is both more a creature of her circumstances even than they are, and at the same time the final determiner of her own fate through a deliberate act of principle. As such, she presages the much more detailed absorption in women's psychology and circumstances that characterizes so much of Caldwell's subsequent fiction, while still retaining much of the fabulous quality of his extravagant earlier heroines.

In describing Sonny's ordeal, Caldwell represents the absolute entrapment of the black community, once more, in terms of whites' manipulation of language as a way of cornering their victims. When Sonny protests his innocence of Mrs. Calhoun's charges, Harvey Glenn says, "You wouldn't call a white woman a liar, would you?" to which Sonny can only reply, hopelessly, "No sir . . . I sure wouldn't" (*TJ*, 217). When the lynch mob invades a black settlement, they say to a black woman, "You'd want your own man shot down if he raped a white girl, wouldn't you?" (*TJ*, 189), and to a black man, supposing his own wife were attacked, "You'd shoot him down even if he was a white man, wouldn't you, nigger?" (*TJ*, 182). There can be no response to these questions but evasion, obtuseness, and prevarication, which serve to fuel the contempt and sadism of the questioners and allow the lynchers to set aside their own reservations about the particular guilt of Sonny in order to indulge in a general frenzy of racial hatred.

In the actual capture of Sonny by the white farmer Harvey Glenn, Caldwell suggests a potential act of conscience that is diffused into another kind of irony. Glenn hesitates at first between revulsion from his betrayal of an innocent man and tribal loyalty to men who will endorse his act: "It was difficult for him to make up his mind. First he would tell himself that he was a white man. Then he would gaze at Sonny's black face. After that he would stare down upon the fields in the flatlands and wonder what would happen after it was all over. The men in the hunt-hungry mob would slap him on the back and praise him for having captured the Negro single-handed. But after the boy had been lynched, he knew he would probably hate himself as long as he lived" (*TJ*, 220). Sonny begs Harvey to shoot him instead of turning him over to the mob, but Harvey "shook his head from side to side, every muscle in his neck aching painfully. . . . 'I ain't got a gun to do it with,' he said, stumbling over the ground" (*TJ*, 226). The episode ends in the patent absurdity of the fleet-footed Sonny following obediently along behind the stumbling and unarmed Glenn to his ghastly death, for Sonny does not know how to act like a criminal any more than Glenn has the taste to be an executioner.

The novel is full of such incongruous and convincing moments, when people fall into patterns of habitual conduct in the midst of a crisis. The lynchers break off their chase to go home and eat dinner; the sheriff manages to catch a long, uninterrupted nap; several members of the mob pause in the pursuit of a supposed rapist to rape a black woman; and talk of revenge is constantly deflected to talk of cotton. Such incidents inevitably qualify any tragic irony in the central event of the novel—the revenge lynching of an innocent man—and evoke a sense of the ludicrous, in which all values are distorted in strange ways and people's behavior is curiously at odds with their own principles. When the astonishing story of the stoning of Katy is added to these other episodes, it gives to the plot of the novel what Kenneth Burke called "the logic of dreams."[32] In this sense, the world of *Trouble in July* is still grotesque and founded on no solid explanatory principles, but it is a different variety of incongruity from that of the three previous cyclorama novels. None of the characters seeks any escape from the immanence of the material world; and though there may well be some distorted spiritual urges in the lynching, rather than depicting these as the thwarted un-

32. Burke, "Caldwell: Maker of Grotesques," 172.

leashing of an inherent religious impulse, Caldwell presents them as (in part) the social inheritance of a punitive Protestantism, led by the community's official church leaders. There are no folk priests of nature, sex, or mystery here, but instead the bigoted and repressive Preacher Felts and the prurient tract saleswoman, Narcissa Calhoun—two characters who point the way toward Caldwell's increasingly hostile future satire of formal, organized religion. Caldwell's political concerns with poverty, inequity, and injustice are still strongly felt in this novel, but now in conjunction with a stronger emphasis on social agencies than with an alternative and more teleological view of human aspiration. The novels that follow *Trouble in July* are more and more occupied with the political and economic operations of southern society and with the predicament of "ordinary" (which in Caldwell's world eschews a wholly conventional meaning) people, caught up in these larger currents over which they have no control. The increasing tendency to focus on the lives of women and blacks and to abandon rural for urban settings is first apparent in this novel. The later novels become more sensational in the everyday terms of their plots, but at the same time less extravagant and inventive. *Trouble in July*, which looks both backward and forward in these areas, is, like the short story collection *Georgia Boy*, poised at a significant transitional point in Caldwell's career, as he begins to move away from ecstasy and frenzy among rural poor whites and to shift his focus from their isolated tobacco roads and mill villages to the strange but less startling activities of people in the larger and more cosmopolitan southern community.

# 4

## The Southern Cyclorama II
### *The Forties Novels*

---

*Erskine had a favorite saying which he repeated very often—so often that I think he convinced himself of its truth. "The life of a writer is just ten years," he would say.*
*—Margaret Bourke-White*

*He was substituting extensity for intensity.*
*—Malcolm Cowley*

---

The cyclorama novel that followed *Trouble in July* was *Tragic Ground*, published four years later in 1944, not a particularly long interval, but one that was crammed for Caldwell with a host of new writing commitments that took him far afield from the familiar realm of southern fiction. In 1939, he had negotiated with his publishers the editorship of a series of nonfiction books on regional life in the United States, under the general title American Folkways, and had launched his editorial efforts with a cross-country trip to search for writers for the series. In early 1940, he began the task of assembling the seventy-five short stories that would comprise the *Jackpot* collection and of writing prefaces for each of them. In September of 1940, he embarked on another cross-country trip with Margaret Bourke-White to prepare for the picture-text *Say, Is This the U.S.A.*; and almost immediately afterwards, in 1941, he and Bourke-White began to plan a similar expedition to the Soviet Union. They were there when the Russian-German war began in June of 1941, and Caldwell was immediately besieged by requests from American news organizations for his services as a reporter. He agreed to "file daily radiogram reports for North American Newspaper Alliance; . . . to broadcast twice daily to New York via shortwave for Columbia Broadcasting System; and, finally, to write articles for *Life*" (*CE*, 203). He did this in addition to observing and preparing the material for the four books that would shortly emerge from his Soviet experience, the picture-text with Bourke-White, *Russia at War* (1942); his wartime diary, *Moscow Under Fire* (1942); a book based on his newspaper and radio correspondence, *All-Out on the Road to Smolensk* (1942); and a novel about guerrilla warfare, *All Night Long* (1942). Even after his return to the United States, Caldwell ignored his doctor's advice to rest and went to Hollywood in late 1942 to work on the screenplay for the film *Mission to Moscow*, although his name was later removed from the credits after he became "unwittingly" involved in the heated political controversy over it (*WAMM*, 198–99).

When Caldwell finally emerged from the last of these wartime writing engagements, he made the transition back to his more familiar literary territory by completing the short story cycle *Georgia Boy* in 1942. This book, however, is less a return to his native imaginative landscape than a farewell to it; for after *Georgia Boy*, Caldwell's southern fiction no longer leads the reader into the strange and remote country that houses the Ty Tys, Jeeters, Semon Dyes, and Pa Stroups as integrated members of a grotesque universe, but instead into something more akin to a radically reduced model of our own world. One signal of the change in the rest of the cyclorama novels is an alteration in their setting that displays a general movement from rural to urban, from containment and stasis to uprooting and change, and from hazy timelessness to more precise contemporaneity. Although it is true that the settings of the earlier novels were neither exclusively rural (*God's Little Acre*) nor isolated from contemporary issues in society (*Tobacco Road, Trouble in July*), they nevertheless belong to a vision of human affairs that is self-contained, coherent, and independent—oblique perhaps in relation to the actual world it represents but internally quite consistent. There is no disjunction between the characters and their environment, no confusion on Caldwell's part at least about the exact distance at which they exist from contemporary social, political, and psychological facts. However, in the cyclorama novels that follow *Trouble in July*, Caldwell begins to place comically distorted poor white types in settings that mimic modern urban reality or, alternatively, to set characters who conform increasingly to conventional norms in milieus more apt for tall tales and gothic thrills. There is a general leveling off of extravagance in the later novels, not so much in terms of distorted personalities and shocking events, but in the larger conception of the universe in which the characters move. Caldwell maintains and increases his zeal for social satires; his sense of determinism is keener than ever; and there is still bawdy laughter and lurid sensation; but Caldwell now seems more likely to create social villains and victims who provoke outrage and pity rather than bewilderment at their essentially mysterious natures. Caldwell's reviewers reacted with increased misgivings to these novels, arguing that he had "changed his tune with no profit to his art"; that he was performing like "a once-talented dancer who still remembers all the steps . . . but has forgotten how to dance"; and, perhaps most ominously of all, that he had moved from his former laudable artistic detachment from his creations to a stance of sheer indifference.[1]

The change in direction of Caldwell's novels after *Georgia Boy* is neither so abrupt nor irrevocable as to suggest a dramatic alteration in the author's consciousness or talents at this time. Caldwell's sympathy for the underdogs of society is, if anything, increasingly evident and his capacity to write direct and simple prose is undiminished. He continues to explore the paradoxical mixture of social neglect and original sin that determines the predicament of his poor white characters; but now these characters are moved increasingly out of their own element into a struggle for survival in urban slums, where their manners and morals are more obvious objects of ridicule and pity, and their oddities are a sociological phenomenon but no longer a spiritual mystery. Caldwell's preoccupation with the irrational in human nature becomes more reductive. Religious ecstasy appears more hypocritical, and sexuality is reduced to "complexes" and "hang-ups," such as the need of the neurotic heroine of *Gretta* to kiss the genitals of strange men, or the more frivolous talent of Mrs. Medora Earnshaw for cutting heart shapes in pubic hair—a considerable falling off in grandeur of design from the Dionysiac lust of Will Thompson in *God's Little Acre* or even the bestial seduction of Lov by Ellie May in *Tobacco Road*. Also, the characters' obsessions diminish in significance, from Jeeter Lester's dream of cultivating the land to Native Hunnicutt's yearning and bargaining for cold sweet potato pie.

The consequence of Caldwell's declining interest in that incongruous realm where the souls, as well as the bodies, of the poor whites hungered for satisfaction is the substitution in his later novels

1. Harrison Smith, "Well-Controlled Anger," in *Critical Essays*, ed. MacDonald, 83; "Caldwell's Collapse," in *Critical Essays*, ed. MacDonald, 87; Lon Tinkle, "Crumbled Georgia Crackers," in *Critical Essays*, ed. MacDonald, 87. See also Sylvia J. Cook, "Caldwell's Fiction: Growing Towards Trash?" *Southern Quarterly*, XXVII (Spring, 1989), 49–58.

of more limited social criticism and satire for the larger fusion of political, social, and spiritual concerns that had so frustrated critics of his earlier work. They had frequently urged him not to dilute his politics with farce or his comic vision of human nature with sociology, but when Caldwell now separates out these strands that had been so mutually dependent, his moralizing begins to appear too obvious, his humor too contrived. Now, in addition to his simple narrative and simple people, the ideas seem equally simple, so that we are encouraged to deplore brutal white men, reject the injustices inflicted on noble blacks, pity the sufferings of vulnerable women, and laugh at the antics of comic types, without the qualifying misgivings that complicate any such direct response to the characters of *Tobacco Road*, *Trouble in July*, or even *Georgia Boy*. Caldwell's gradual abandonment of the poor white as a subject may be either a cause or an effect of this altering vision; but certainly, as he focuses increasingly on the plight of women and, even more markedly, of blacks, he tends to create moral melodramas, which, for all their ideological decency, nevertheless reduce female and black characters to similar paradigms of suffering virtue inconceivable among the flawed and festering ranks of his white trash.

Of the six remaining cyclorama novels, the greater fictional flexibility afforded Caldwell by the traditionally grotesque figure of the poor white may still be seen in *Tragic Ground* (1944), *The Sure Hand of God* (1947), and *This Very Earth* (1948), in contrast to the stilted formality of those works dealing with less vulgar types, such as the decayed southern aristocrat in *House in the Uplands* (1946), the admirable black siblings in *Place Called Estherville* (1949), or the middle-class white woman in *Episode in Palmetto* (1950). The former three all demand the kind of descriptive contradictions embodied in such terms as absurd naturalism, grim comedy, or tragic farce, whereas the latter are more simply characterized as melodrama, tragedy, and satire, none of them genres in which Caldwell had as yet revealed great adeptness.

Caldwell's next cyclorama novel, *Tragic Ground* (1944), is interesting as an attempt to retain the associations of his poor white characters from earlier works—promiscuity, laziness, physical debility, poverty, foolishness—and at the same time to shift these alien characters into a more familiar setting. This is the slum neighborhood of a big Gulf coast city where they have been lured from their rural homes to work in a wartime powder plant. With the closing of the plant, they are left to fester, uprooted, unskilled, and unemploy-

able, having tasted enough of city living to deter them from returning home, but at the same time resenting the appalling quality of
their lives in the slum and thinking nostalgically of their former rural
ways. As in many of Caldwell's earlier novels, there is a central concern with determinism, both with the larger circumstances of the
war and the more immediate manipulation of these poor people by
the government in order to lure them into munitions plants, only to
abandon them casually when they have served their purpose. There
is, in addition, an even more fatalist vision of a class of people whose
poverty is as much moral and spiritual as material, and so long-
standing as to blur all distinctions between cause and effect. At first
sight, Caldwell would seem to be back in the grotesque world of
*Tobacco Road* and *God's Little Acre;* but the tone of *Tragic Ground*,
much more erratic than these earlier novels, reveals inconsistencies, contradictions, and disquieting lapses of thought, not only in
the characters but in the narration. Although Caldwell formerly had
seemed to relish overturning and reversing any stereotyped notions
of noble and deserving poor folk while at the same time exposing
and berating a society that permitted and even exploited their poverty, by the time he writes *Tragic Ground*, his ironies at the expense of the lowest class have become so anarchically distributed
that they subvert any sense of moral values. Caldwell's subject had
always been immoral man in immoral society, yet his works hitherto
had rarely seemed cynical except to those who felt he was mining
the lower depths for "pay dirt."[2] The line between scourging satire
and contemptuous disgust at human nature is obviously a tenuous
one for any writer, but especially so in an author like Caldwell, who
had tended not to emphasize redemptive moral capacities in his
individual characters, but had pursued, instead, certain unworldly
qualities in the poor in the form of their fanatical obsessions and
their desire for mystery and transcendence.

In *Tragic Ground*, the satiric exposure of the hypocrisies and
selfishness of the poor is as sharp as ever, but the emphasis on their
dreams and obsessions is diminished, for they themselves grow first
skeptical about their own lives and then cynical about their conduct.
In *Tobacco Road*, Jeeter Lester could maintain his irrepressible and
foolish faith in a good Lord who would arbitrarily "bust loose with a
heap of bounty" (*TR*, 13); but in *Tragic Ground*, the more worldly
Spence Douthit knows from the outset, "I was born poor, and I'll

2. Daniels, "American Lower Depths," 78.

die poor, and I won't be nothing but poor in between" (*TG*, 21). When Spence invests a windfall gift of thirty dollars from a social worker in a crap game, he comments sardonically, "We'll never get rich if we don't work for it" (*TG*, 182)—a level of conscious disingenuousness inconceivable in Jeeter, Ty Ty, or even Jeff McCurtain. Caldwell's comic characters depend to such an extent on the melding of unscrupulousness and innocence that any tendency toward reflection or self-analysis in them, any insight into their own moral logic, risks forfeiting their artistic integrity as naïve types. Even Semon Dye, the con man in *Journeyman*, who is certainly a manipulator of others for his own profit, is sufficiently "innocent" to be duped in the end by his own rhetoric and the power of religious fervor he has himself stirred up. With the first steps toward a more cynical awareness taken by the comic hero of *Tragic Ground*, Caldwell simultaneously disengages his sympathies from Spence Douthit's predicament and focuses them instead on Spence's friend Floyd Sharp, a more tragic figure who still retains a desperate and naïve idealism in the same circumstances that have educated Spence to his more worldly adjustment. This unusual division of comedy and tragedy, unwholesomeness and pathos, between Spence and Floyd is a new departure for Caldwell and one that, together with the diminishing power of obsession, hints at the decline of the grotesque mode that had been so fruitful in his fiction.

Spence and Floyd, who constitute the rather rare phenomenon of two middle-aged male friends in Caldwell's work, are each (allowing for some irony) family men. Both are the fathers of adolescent daughters for whom, in such circumstances, a career in prostitution is virtually axiomatic by Caldwell's rules. Floyd's wife is pregnant with their ninth child; Spence's is sick beyond the ministrations of everything but Dr. Munday's patent tonic, which brings her no cure but plenty of consolation. The families have been drawn to the city by lures promised to prospective "patriotic" employees of a now-defunct wartime powder plant. For a brief period, they have liquor and luxuries in return for the daily boredom and alienation of their assemblyline jobs, but when these become obsolete, they are quickly told that "it's just as patriotic now to go back where you came from" (*TG*, 22). Instead, they squat in the aptly named slum of Poor Boy—a topographical equivalent of its inhabitants—abandoned as worthless for profit and then taken over and wholly neglected by the city administration. There they are quickly bereft of their consumer goods and decline into the abject indignity of sifting garbage dumps for reclaimable items or, without laws to protect or regulate them, turning to duplicity, crime, and desperate measures to ensure their survival.

Despite the similarity of their predicaments, the reactions of Floyd and Spence are diametrically different and anticipate the conflicting attitudes in the novel about the responsibility for such degraded lives and the best response to them. Floyd from the beginning leans toward drastic and nihilistic symbolic acts. Having founded and named Poor Boy in the first place, he feels his current suffering is a divine punishment for that and contemplates burning it; he debates drowning his children in the canal and hesitates only because "those girls of mine are the only thing I've got to show for living, so far" (*TG*, 57). Finally, he commits an ax murder that is a perfect travesty of his own apparent ideological sympathies. Spence, by contrast, is both less class-conscious in his outlook and less violent in his reactions, finding wiliness, deception, and passivity more satisfactory ways to survive than grandiose gestures of conscience. He steals from his sick wife, dupes social workers, and tries to marry his thirteen-year-old daughter to a pimp. In the end, he is rescued from Poor Boy by a *deus ex machina* in the form of his son-in-law, while Floyd seems headed for the electric chair for his confessed murder. Floyd takes upon himself both the guilt and the crazy, incongruous retribution for a world he never made; Spence blames, evades, and exploits those people to whom he has real obligations. The paradoxes embodied in the two men seem at first reasonably simple: the conscientious, hard-working man is the sufferer; the wily man is the lucky escapee from Poor Boy and its horrors. Fate seems to parody conventional notions of justice. However, there are so many anomalies within these contradictory types that any political or ideological conclusions about human nature that are based on them must finally be so qualified as to be negligible.

The most dramatic anomaly is Floyd's choice of victim for his ax murder—the pimp Bubber. Bubber is certainly a theoretical threat to a father who anticipates and dreads the prostitution of his daughters, but even Floyd cannot fail to see that this moronic youth is an effect, and a pathetic one at that, rather than a cause of slum life. Not only is Bubber weak and feebleminded, but his sexual crime with Floyd's twelve-year-old daughter, Justine, is the clear culmination of her urging and begging. Thus the reader can scarcely fail to see the inappropriateness of Floyd's outrage at "what he made Justine do" (*TG*, 174) and of his conclusion that "it's what happens everytime the poor run up against the rich" (*TG*, 171), surely a quizzical reversal of the kind of irony that gave such force to other stories of class-biased sexual abuse, like "Blue Boy" and "Masses of Men." One of Caldwell's great achievements in the comic depiction of poor people is his balancing of indignation at their imposed predicament with bemused exposure of their flawed natures; but it is a yoking that continually risks disintegration into simple inconsistency of characterization, and no novel demonstrates this better than *Tragic Ground*. When Floyd later decides to confess his murder of Bubber in order to draw the attention of the world to the injustices of Poor Boy, his prospects of being effectively understood seem only a little worse than those of Caldwell in creating such a quandary. With Spence Douthit, his main character, Caldwell is equally enigmatic. Spence is clearly an unscrupulous man, but apparently, like Floyd, he resents his thirteen-year-old daughter Mavis' being driven to promiscuity. He reviles his neighbor Chet for initiating his daughter into sex, but he later ponders its advantages in helping Mavis find and please a rich man who will subsidize Spence and his wife: "It looks now like it was a good thing what Chet Mitchell done to her, after all. . . . But, just the same, it aint going to stop me from getting even with him, because it's the right thing to do" (*TG*, 80). Any misgivings that the reader may have about whether Spence can possibly have any notion of "the right thing to do" are furthered by his responses to Mavis' young friend Florabelle, who moves him first to pity and then to lust. Spence's hypocrisy finally becomes a means of questioning how seriously Poor Boy is responsible for the ugly lives of the novel's characters, for despite his convincing exposés of Poor Boy's horrors and his nostalgic effusions of loyalty for the rural lives he and his family left behind in Beasley County, Spence actively resists the final return to the country and is already planning at the end to come back to the urban slum that seemed to be the symbolic villain of the novel.

Every moral stance that Spence takes in the novel, every social insight, every decent impulse, is directly countermanded by a contrary one; but unlike Jeeter Lester and the fanatical heroes of earlier novels, there is no larger vision in Spence's life that has the effect of diminishing these contradictions in his nature. He has become a Caldwell type without a distinguishing obsession. He is more banal in his depraved nature than Jeeter, Ty Ty, or Semon, and is a man with no transcendent dimension, no matter how absurd, to his life and no purpose in living beyond the easiest mode of survival. In this context, the friendship with the more teleological Floyd permits Caldwell to create these two separate types from the elements of his former grotesque characters and to scrutinize the place of such types in a more familiar social setting than Walden Farm or Rocky Comfort. The social conclusions of this scrutiny have a good deal in common with the earlier novels: Caldwell's people continue to be pushed and pulled, lured and rejected, rewarded and exploited by a callous government, by obtuse social workers, by opportunistic landlords, and by enterprising criminals, most of whom are conveniently offstage during the novel. However, the main focus is no longer on the earlier conjunction of the circumspect and the spiritual in the lives of the poor, but more narrowly on the means by which they survive, retaliate, and glean what pleasure they may from an environment that seems to collaborate with their innate dispositions to ensure a vicious existence.

Though the grim world of Poor Boy is indicted by a variety of voices in the novel as the "tragic ground" of the title, Caldwell does not endorse the simple sociological determinism that would hold the urban slum wholly responsible for its degraded inhabitants. The solution proposed by all those in the novel who accuse Poor Boy—Spence's family, his son-in-law, the city social workers—is a return to rural life and agrarian roots that Caldwell shows to have been contaminated long before the movement to the city. The rural world, despite people's distorted memories, is certainly not the domain of unfallen human nature—a realm that has no existence in Caldwell's fiction, not even in his stories of childhood and adolescence. His naturalism insists always on the interaction of human and societal evil so that, if the city seems worse than the country, it is only because the latter is more sparsely populated. Despite the fragmentation and inconsistency of his conclusions on Floyd and Spence, Caldwell continued in several of the later cyclorama novels to explore the situation of transplanted rural people and their new-found urban existence, and to delve further into the whole question of causality in their lives. These novels concern themselves increasingly with relationships between the material and moral aspects of his characters' lives and finally abandon completely both the hunger for God and the ardor for revolutionary social change that held Caldwell's allegiance during so much of the 1930s.

The two remaining cyclorama novels that manifest Caldwell's continuing concern with uprooted poor whites, *The Sure Hand of God* (1947) and *This Very Earth* (1948), also begin to reveal his increasing fascination with the dilemmas of women. *The Sure Hand of God*, the first novel to focus exclusively on a woman as protagonist, is also one of Caldwell's most deterministic works. Its heroine, the vulgar and monstrous Molly Bowser, is revealed in a variety of comic, self-indulgent, and self-pitying situations. Then, when her repellant and ridiculous behavior is firmly established, Caldwell begins a grim investigation of her history that provides a naturalistic basis in environment, education, and biology for her present condition and for the values she is trying to inculcate into her sixteen-year-old daughter, Lily. Through an elaborate network of plots connecting Molly to the social, professional, and religious community of the curiously named town of Agricola, Caldwell explores his ironic theories on the interaction between the sexual and economic bases of society and the place of a single woman within that context.

Molly Bowser is certainly one of the most Rabelaisian of Caldwell's heroines in the sense of the absolute centrality and tyranny of her body and its biological functions in her existence. She is enormously fat, a favorite image in Caldwell for both gross sensuality and the loss of allure; she is addicted to both alcohol and an unnamed drug, which she injects into herself; and she is given to bouts of uncontrollable giggling that result in the loss of bladder control. Her body dominates not merely her physical world, demanding continuous infusions of food, drink, and drugs, release from the constriction of clothes, and escape in sleep from the pain of consciousness; it also is the focus of her emotional and moral existence. Three glasses of wine before breakfast can cheer her, whereas a glance at her reflection in the mirror can reduce her to mercifully blinding tears. Her body is also her only capital for business, and so she must market and sell it by whatever means she can, whether in the legitimate arena of marriage or the illegitimate one of prostitution. Molly has tried both and chosen marriage; but when a freak accident leaves her widowed, she is unhappily back in the marketplace at the beginning of the novel, pondering how to make provision for her own and her daughter's future. Surveying her grotesque body, limp hair, and aging face, she articulates her economic survival theory: "My hair won't take a curl and I can't find a girdle that helps my figure and my brassiere won't hold me up and men've got the notion that they can't have the kind of good time they want with widows past thirty-five, anyway" (*SHG*, 2–3). Her solution is to market her beautiful sixteen-year-old daughter, Lily, instead, trying to ensure that Lily wins a husband from among the wealthy families of Agricola and does not waste her charm in unrewarding romantic affairs with unsuitable prospects. The context of the novel suggests that Molly is eminently realistic in her intentions and certainly no more deserving of moral censure than other citizens who pursue similar material goals just as blatantly. However, Molly proves a good deal too candid for both the citizens and for Lily and her fickle admirers. She also underestimates the lust for money in her community and its capacity to subordinate even the lust for sex.

For all the energy that Caldwell pours in this novel into chronicling the more distasteful manifestations of human carnality, his harshest irony is directed not against lubricious lovers but against the business ethic of Agricola's leaders, who control all desires but that of acquisitiveness. Jamie Denton, Molly's landlord, is a prime example. Twice married to elderly rich widows, he owns most of the rental property in town, although his great regret is that he has not invested exclusively in rentals to black people, who can be exploited and intimidated most unreservedly. He controls poor white housing in the Slum Hollow, too, but finds poor whites much more truculent tenants, chopping up porches for kindling wood and digging for fishing worms in the cold damp earth around the foundations. Immune to Molly's predicament, and especially to her efforts at seduction, he is determined to force her and Lily into moving to the Hollow for fear her reputation may reduce the property values in her current neighborhood. He argues, "There's a place for women on both sides of town, but down there's where you belong" (*SHG*, 128). Indeed, he conspires eventually to force Molly to take up her rightful dwelling in the worst part of town, where he invests some of his money in helping her fix up a brothel, presenting her with a nude painting and an ornate glass chandelier to help lure men without his own qualms. Jamie Denton's business and world view is based on a caste system that assumes an absolute division between respectable and disreputable people, and profits by its perpetuation. Molly's view is more democratic, based on a belief in the universal needs of the body that all people must provide for, whether in alcohol, drugs, brothels, or the institution of marriage.

The other prime spokesman for the business ethic in the novel is the town's banker, Frank Stevens, whose nephew Claude is the future husband Molly has selected for her daughter, despite his engagement to someone more suitable in the banker's eyes. When Claude falls in love with Lily, the banker is at considerable pains to destroy the relationship, arguing of Molly: "There'll always be women like her, but we do not have to accept them as our social equals. Molly Bowser would sell herself with no more thought than you or I would take a drink of water" (*SHG*, 161). By a combination of persuasion, innuendo, and, most important, bribery, Frank succeeds in returning Claude to his former fiancée, thus accomplishing the selling of his nephew with perhaps somewhat more thought than taking a drink of water; but then this property is a great deal more valuable. Caldwell thus demonstrates the extent to which Molly's exchange theories are thwarted by the laws of profit and convention, although he offers as well plenty of vindication for them at all levels of Agricola's society.

The churchwomen of the community, and particularly Molly's neighbor, Lucy Trotter, are among her most violent censurers. Lucy, who teaches the women's Bible class at the Methodist church, avers that she will no longer teach if Molly is present. However, Christine Bigbee, the minister's wife, is in fact a prime specimen of Molly's world view; sexually frustrated by her husband's puritanical coldness, she turns secretly to Molly for friendship and, of more importance, for her "vitamin" shots. The two shoot each other up and lie smoking cigarettes, and Christine eventually elopes with a salesman.

The depiction of the Reverend Bigbee and the churchwomen is a far cry from the ecstatic rural religionists of *Tobacco Road* and *Journeyman*. The clergyman who reads aloud in bed from the gospel of Luke and turns out the lights before permitting his wife to undress is clearly for Caldwell a more warped man of God than any of his bawdy country preachers. He kills himself after his wife's elopement, not because of her loss but because of his own disgrace in the eyes of his parishioners. Like Christine Bigbee, other members of Agricola's middle-class community are revealed as frustrated or secret lovers who pursue their gratification underhandedly while relegating Molly and her candor to what they profess to see see as her God-appointed place at the bottom of the social order. Doctor Logan makes a practice of luring young women to his office with narcotics, but unlike Molly, he is able to avoid detection and remain an important member of the community. The novel in certain ways seems to revert to the theories of Ty Ty Walden in *God's Little Acre* regarding the conflict between conventional social and moral edicts and people's God-given bodies, which urge them in a contrary direction; but the world of Agricola makes the conflict not simply a moral one but a clash of nature with profit and social advantage. It also depicts the workings of nature in a much more sordid fashion.

Molly Bowser has an earthy and simple philosophy like Ty Ty's, but her naturalism is more stringently measured against the complicated values of Agricola, an urban world that distorts, subverts, and profits from the remaining vestiges of natural instinct in its members. Molly's presence in Agricola is like the intrusion of a more primitive principle; she awakens some members of the community, disturbs and threatens others, and is finally safely institutionalized in its economic system. Molly brings to the city a simple version of sexual determinism learned in her girlhood experiences as a poor farm servant: a woman's only useful capital, her main source of consolation, resides in her body, so she must invest it prudently in order to maintain her comfort. A reasonably satisfactory marriage might seem an adequate solution for her, but there is not a single example of this among the many pairings in the novel, except for Molly's own to Putt Bowser, whose funeral opens the first chapter. All the other marriages exist for convention, respectability, or profit, whereas sexual pleasure is taken only illicitly. Molly's strategies are not, of course, a whit more ethical than those of the community's leaders; her strategies are merely less devious and cynical. By the end of the novel, when she is firmly ensconced in the Hollow, with chandelier and nude painting, she says of her future brothel, "I feel more at home down here than I ever did anywhere else, and maybe it's where I belonged all the time" (*SHG*, 243). The target of Caldwell's irony here is, as in so many of his later novels, ambiguous. Perhaps it is Molly herself, comically acknowledging that prostitution was her real métier from the start; perhaps it is the respectable world of Agricola that has finally forced a woman into its preconceived mold for the disreputable, out of sight of the respectable but not beyond the reach of their furtive misbehavior.

The "sure hand of God" that brings Molly to this pass turns out to be less divine than accidental and human in origin. Molly's fate is determined equally by the accident of her birth, as poor and female, and by the various people who condemn and exploit her, from her first wealthy employers on a farm where she is programmed for future promiscuity, to those who laugh her to scorn when she tries to get other work as a sales clerk or doing alterations in a clothing store. Yet for all the emphasis of this novel on the entrapment of a woman like Molly in inevitable squalor, the novel retains some comic vitality. This emerges largely through the incorrigible nature of its heroine, who is at work making "black lace step-ins" (*SHG*, 15) as mourning clothes and whose enthusiastic response to her final brothel home is, "It's like—like—fairyland" (*SHG*, 239). Caldwell leaves the reader in no doubt about this enchanted dwelling place: "It was a dilapidated, unpainted, frame dwelling with a rusty tin roof. Some of the windows had been broken and boarded up, and a rank growth of pigweeds reached almost to the level of the porch. . . . The streets were unpaved and potted with mudholes that never quite dried up the year around" (*SHG*, 234). Yet for Molly, when the chandelier is switched on, a transformation takes place in this sordid setting: "Dozens of iridescent cut-glass figures of cupids and mermaids were suspended from the chandelier on invisible threads, and the slightest disturbance of the air started them twisting and turning. Slivers of reflected light danced on the walls and ceiling, and the huge oil painting came to life in the bright illumination" (*SHG*, 239). Caldwell's dramatic shift in perspective here undermines any easy moral judgments on either the community or Molly. Is she to be pitied, dismissed, or envied her capacity for aesthetic delight? If she believes her situation to be "almost too good to be true" (*SHG*, 239), who has the right to insist on improvement?

As in *Tragic Ground*, we are left to puzzle over the "correct" response to people's damaged lives when the people themselves may be indifferent or hostile to any reforms. A somewhat similar situation had provoked James Agee, in *Let Us Now Praise Famous Men*, to challenge the arrogance of reformers who might violate more than they improved, through their ignorance of the integrity of lives based on values very different from their own. Caldwell poses the same problem as does Agee, but comically rather than compassionately. Agee's defense of the dignity or holiness of his tenant farmers tends to be enhanced by his description of their tawdry possessions, whereas Caldwell's portrait of Molly delighting in the accoutrements of her whorehouse is much more ambivalent in directing the reader's sympathies. Such ethical pluralism on Caldwell's part proved upsetting to reviewers seeking "honest social concern" and finding what one characterized as belligerent mindlessness.[3] In many ways, *The Sure Hand of God* recalls the ambivalences of *Tobacco Road* toward the poor, but now they are no longer part of a larger portrait of the southern poor whites with all their

3. Tinkle, "Crumbled Georgia Crackers," 87.

innate traditions and contradictions. Unlike Caldwell's novels of the 1930s, *The Sure Hand of God* provides neither an arena conducive to social reform (no striking mill workers, lynch mobs, or starving sharecroppers) nor a context for grotesque comedy (no obsessive or wildly idiosyncratic characters). Its emphasis on biological and psychological determinism points the direction for later comic and tragic novels with female protagonists, but it also anticipates a certain banality that enters Caldwell's work as he gradually refrains from exploring those aspects of his characters that struggle to escape from a purely material sphere.

Caldwell's cyclorama novel immediately following *The Sure Hand of God* was *This Very Earth* (1948), which once again dealt with a poor family that had abandoned its rural origins for the ambiguous rewards of urban life. Despite a devastating *Time* review, which claimed that the novel followed Caldwell's preordained formula of rape, murder, and stupidity, without any motivating idea, *This Very Earth* is in fact virtually a bible of Caldwell's *idées fixes*, admittedly illustrated in his typically sensational images.[4] By 1948, these images may have seemed gratuitous in terms of any aesthetic ideal of subtlety, refinement, or even novelty of example, but they are never irrelevant to the themes that continue to preoccupy Caldwell—the degeneracy of primitive codes of conduct, the power of the irrational in people's characters, and the brutal struggles for dominance between young and old, male and female, black and white, and all their more complicated permutations. The novel explores the abuses of power in a variety of relationships, but especially those of its protagonist, Chism Crockett, to his son, to his daughters, to his father, and to black women. *This Very Earth* is much less concerned with the material poverty of this family—who appear to have a paltry enough sufficiency of food and shelter—than with the moral and spiritual decline of the father, Chism, and its consequences for the rest of them.

Crockett is, as his name suggests, a debased version of the frontier type who has brought into his urban existence a distorted pioneer masculinity whereby he uses his strength to bully the weak and his wiliness to blackmail the powerful. His great residual passion from his early life is his love of hunting and his disproportionate affection for his hounds over his family—a subject that is elsewhere a favorite for Caldwell's amused satire. The novel opens with Chism

---

4. "Caldwell's Collapse," 86.

about to initiate his eager eleven-year-old son, Jarvis, into the joys of the hunt, but the father immediately feels he must extend the boy's ritual into a forced bout of drinking corn whiskey, which causes Jarvis to pass out, followed some time later by an introduction to the sexual exploitation of black girls. This is all done in the name of making a "real man" of Jarvis and preventing him from becoming a "sissy" (*TVE*, 82). The result is that these pursuits of hunting, drinking, and casual sex become identified with a brute masculinity that is presented as both ludicrous and sadistic—a judgment very different from the Hemingway world view that Caldwell was sometimes accused of imitating. All the villains in *This Very Earth* are men who act out traditionally male cultural roles: the ironically named Noble Hair, husband of Chism's daughter Dorisse, is a former football player whose sole legacy from his brief career of fame is aggressive physical cruelty; Daniel Boone Blalock, lover of Chism's second daughter, Vickie, is a florid, back-slapping senator who trades alternately on folksiness and sophistication for political capital (contrary to the integrity of his pioneer namesake); and Russ Thornton, admirer of Chism's youngest daughter Jane, is the successful coach of the high school football team. His private idea of good sportsmanship is to seduce a sixteen-year-old schoolgirl with pleas of his wife's indifference. All three men are clearly variations on Chism Crockett in their distortion of power and skill into selfishness. Their attraction for Chism's three daughters suggests that, whatever the reasons for the father's degeneracy, the daughters may suffer the consequences doubly, both from their father and their lovers.

The other men in the novel are, by contrast, gentle and protective; in fact, Chism's father, Grandpa Crockett, represents a radically new departure in characterization for Caldwell in that he seems to be virtually a direct spokesman for the author's opinions. There was some anticipation of this in the character of Jim Howard Vance in *Tragic Ground*, but he was a minor figure compared with Grandpa, who is central to both the action and meaning of *This Very Earth*. Grandpa is a snowy-bearded patriarch who extols the virtues of country living, country hams, motherhood, and innocence; he defines the good in life as "something you feel deep down in your heart most of the time, and you know it's there even though you can't find a name for it. Some people would call it God, I suppose, but I think it's much more than that. It's like being kind and thoughtful, and striving to be honest and truthful" (*TVE*, 53). This Pollyannaish version of Ty Ty distorts the novel, because Caldwell's fictional universe does not normally admit moral philosophers who are untainted with the folly and self-indulgence of their fellow mortals. The other clearly approved male character, Chism's oldest son, Ross, is also a detached and perceptive moralist who speaks the kind of common sense that normally works only through its absence in Caldwell's novels, which are not easily amenable to personal representatives of humanist virtues, no matter how strongly their endorsement may be otherwise implied.

Caldwell's clear distaste for aggressive masculinity in all its formulaic manifestations and his abounding sympathy for the female victims of it raises again, as in the later short stories, the questionable nature of his feminist sympathies. Chism's three daughters represent varying degrees of resistance and acquiescence to suffering in "a man's world" (*TVE*, 149), as one of them characterizes it, but they are clearly all unable or unwilling to imagine anything else. Dorisse, the oldest, is abused and finally beaten to death with a flatiron by her husband, Noble, on whom she lavishes affection and loyalty. Caldwell depicts forcefully the humiliation of women who must rely on men for material support in Dorisse's entreaties to her husband to get a job and move out of her father's house: "I'll do anything in the world you tell me if you'll only let us have a home of our own. I don't care what it's like, inside or outside. I'd rather live in a tent or under a tree than have to stay here another day. Won't you go to work, Noble, for my sake?" (*TVE*, 34). Nobby's reply, though callous, reveals the obverse side of the problem: "I know all about you women. You don't care how a guy gets money as long as he hands most of it over to you" (*TVE*, 35). All relationships between the sexes in Caldwell's world are based on various exchanges of sex and money, affection and provender, domestic care and financial protection. Prostitutes offer the same kinds of exchange as wives, though with adjustments in the rates; they have greater independence but a consequent reduction in the man's obligations. The incessant repetition of this theme throughout Caldwell's work suggests that he holds a bleak view of the institution of marriage in the midtwentieth century. Not only is there no sense in his work of the possibility of alternatives, there is also no evidence that his women characters would seek them.

Chism's second daughter, Vickie, is a telling case. A waitress at the Rainbow Café, self-supporting and far more assertive and worldly than Dorisse, she trades on Blalock's obvious attraction to her to ask for advancement for her brother, a job for her father, and a diamond ring for herself before bestowing any return favors. In the end, Vickie leaves home to follow the congressman to Washington as his mistress. However, in response to her boss's taunt at the Rainbow Café that "deep down in your heart you want a home of your own and babies and a good, kind, providing husband," she replies, "You're so right I could murder you for knowing how I feel" (*TVE*, 151). Ironically, Chism's daughter Jane, the most domesticated of the Crockett girls, is the only one who finally makes a choice against marriage, even running away from her home and lover so that she will not be tempted to accept his proposal. However, she runs with her grandfather's parting dictum in her ears that "marriage can be one of the good things of life" (*TVE*, 240), and she certainly has no alternative goal. Such attitudes seem to place Caldwell in a curious halfway house between feminist sympathies and traditional "happy marriage" solutions. It was a position from which there was little possibility of advance, and so instead he continued to reiterate multiple variations on this restricted theme.

If *This Very Earth* offers a melodramatic and somewhat didactic treatment of the power struggle between the sexes and the predicament of women trapped by their narrow options, it provides by contrast such an unresolved and open-ended vision of determinism in the male characters, and especially in Chism Crockett, that it seems at times to mock all efforts to search for causality in human affairs. Caldwell presents such a multiplicity of explanations for Chism's present condition—and then proceeds to show how distorted, partial, hypocritical, and conflicting these explanations are—that he creates a kind of causal anarchy in the novel. This is a far cry from the coherently grotesque vision of *Tobacco Road* or *God's Little Acre*, although it is a logical next step beyond the confusions of *Tragic Ground*. The variety of reasons offered in *This Very Earth* for Chism's and his family's decline include the death of his wife, Alice, and the loss of her decent and unselfish influence on the family; the move from a hardworking rural life to city aimlessness and easy vice; the errors of Chism's father and, in turn, *his* father, in each forcing his son, against the son's inclination, into a life for which he was ill-suited; the role of the Ku Klux Klan in making Chism abandon his farm and move into town to suit the Klan's purposes; the suggestion that the Crockett family was already disintegrating in the country and mistakenly tried to stay together amid such conflicts. The fact that many of the reasons are retrospective excuses given by Chism for his misbehavior lessens their deterministic persuasiveness. For example, the Klan is regularly invoked as his favorite ally for threatening black girls and white politicians and for justifying his unpopular acts to his family, although there is absolutely no evidence of this alliance in the novel.

Of all Chism's explanations, the only ones taken seriously by the family are the loss of their mother and the subsequent move away from the farm. Jarvis recalls the pleasure of driving home the cows and going fishing after school, and dreams of a return to the land; Grandpa remembers the family's former pride and self-sufficiency; and Dorisse insists that "things like this never happened when we lived on the farm. . . . But Mama was alive then. That made all the difference in the world" (*TVE*, 58). If we ask how seriously Caldwell is proposing motherhood and the agrarian way as the best bulwarks against modern decadence, the entire body of his work up to this point makes the corroborating evidence seem at best ironic, at worst cynical. If his towns and cities have been centers of sloth, crime, and vice, his Tobacco Roads and Rocky Comforts have hardly been stalwart or pristine in their ambience; and if his motherless families have fallen on hard times, they would scarcely have been better off with Ada Lester or Maud Douthit to nurture them. Certainly, the only good mothers in Caldwell are the dead ones, the only good farms the ones that have been left behind, and whether this is meretricious nostalgia on Caldwell's part or a sardonic comment on the dishonesty of his characters is not always clear. *This Very Earth* shows a group of people all desperately searching for why their lives went wrong, with the most villainous and self-serving of them (Chism, Blalock, and Russ Thornton) coming up with the greatest variety of excuses. Caldwell does not wholly dismiss these reasons, but because of their pluralism and sometimes doubtful authenticity, they can no longer serve, as in the earlier novels, as the basis for a political or social critique of his world.

The characters in *This Very Earth* continue to display irrational and obsessive behavior—Chism's with hunting, Grandpa's with his farm, Nobby's with gambling, Blalock's with sex, Dorisse's with love; but even their most intense manifestations seem diminished in comparison with earlier novels. Grandpa Crockett's pride in his well-run farm can scarcely compare with Jeeter Lester's urge to "stir the earth" each spring, nor can Blalock's smooth philanderings match the frenzies of Semon Dye. This change has been defined and mourned by Harvey Klevar as one from transcendentalism to humanism in Caldwell, and explained as a consequence of his long separation, by this stage of his career, in both time and immediacy of experience, from the roots of his inspiration in the "God-hungry" people of Georgia.[5] Accompanying the gradual abandonment of his "God-hungry" people was an uneven relinquishment of the grotesque comic mode that had both intrigued and frustrated Caldwell's earlier critics. The complex yoking of determinism and irrationality that had pervaded the early cyclorama novels began to dissipate. As *Tragic Ground* had distributed wiliness and idealism between two separate characters rather than merging them in a single one, so *The Sure Hand of God* and *This Very Earth* divide their vision of determinism between sincere victims, especially women, and hypocritical and self-serving types, largely men, who appear to be more in control of their fates. As melodrama and satire came increasingly to dominate as vehicles for this didacticism, Caldwell's work provoked, first, bitter critical tirades and, then, increasing neglect.

In 1946, Caldwell revealed his penchant for melodrama, formerly confined to his short stories and brief portions of his novels, in one of his weakest full-length novels, *A House in the Uplands*. The book was clearly an effort on his part to cover an aspect of southern life hitherto excluded from the cyclorama—the decline of an aristocratic southern family into brutality, self-indulgence, and self-destruction. In the introduction to a later edition of the novel, Caldwell wrote that his cyclorama "would be incomplete and prejudiced without this particular picture" and that the subject of the novel was "an inherent part of a people's heritage."[6] His former omission of the decline of the southern aristocracy was not in fact a particularly glaring one, because the whole series of novels was so whimsically and personally conceived outside the broader field of southern social history. He had certainly displayed a fascination with the subject of degeneracy within a family, most notably in *Tobacco Road* and *This Very Earth;* but at their highest social point, these had been yeoman farmers or plain folks rather than plantation owners and lords of the *ancien régime*. In *A House in the Uplands*, Caldwell plunged, quite far on in his career and with little evidence of any prior interest, into the material of Faulkner and Stribling.

The theme of the novel is announced as explicitly as a sociological text: "Most of the old families still clung obstinately to their decay-

5. Klevar, "Some Things Holy," 74–75.
6. Erskine Caldwell, Introduction to *A House in the Uplands*, in *Critical Essays*, ed. MacDonald, 233–34.

ing and dilapidated manor houses and stubbornly maintained an outmoded way of life at the expense of Negroes and uneducated whites who were kept in some form of peonage" (*HU*, 149). However, the outmoded way of life of aristocrats does not include the preservation of a mode of speech and manners that allows them to be distinguished from Caldwell's more typical characters. These characters had always had a remarkable capacity for stating normally private thoughts in their crudest and most blatant terms, but in earlier novels this linguistic vulgarity was used for startling effects. What the characters said was so nakedly self-evident or so necessarily a subject for discretion that the articulation itself revealed a jarring simplemindedness or strangeness in the speaker. However, when Grady Dunbar, scion of the declining family in *A House in the Uplands*, says to a sharecropper, "Keep your low-white hands off my wife" (*HU*, 118), or when his neurotic mother comments, "It's a shame the way awful people are moving into our part of the country from the outside and trying to mingle with us on our own level" (*HU*, 20), they provoke not amazement, like Dude, Ty Ty, or Semon, but mere disbelief in their vitality as characters. We are willing to accept much more outrageous statements from simpletons, eccentrics, prophets, and outsiders than from those who not only are in the social mainstream but presumably set the standards for the other characters to violate.

Despite the fact that *A House in the Uplands* was Caldwell's first venture into this literary territory, much about it seems secondhand and stale, from its Poe-like thunderstorm and Stowe-like race relationships to its gothic romance plot and flat characters. The novel is ideologically a compendium of received standard ideas on what was wrong with the Old South and its upper class, with none of the novelty or ambivalence of Caldwell's usual treatment of lower-class people. The land of the Dunbar family has been decimated and destroyed by the debaucheries of the owners and their unenlightened methods of farming; the drinking and gambling of Grady Dunbar have reduced the property from five thousand to two hundred acres of "depleted and eroded cotton fields and cut-over timber lands" (*HU*, 27); the family is down to its last direct heir in Grady, who has not been able to consummate his ten-month marriage to Lucyanne because he has known only black women hitherto, and, "after sleeping with nigger girls for ten years, you just can't switch to a white girl" (156). Grady's wife, Lucyanne, is long-suffering, whereas his quadroon mistress is a light-skinned she-devil; his white sharecroppers are the very epitome of good plain folks, whereas his blacks are servile and whining. There is a stalwart generation in the novel that has as its representatives Grady's cousin Ben Baxter, an idealist lawyer; Brad Harrison, class-conscious son of the white tenants; and Sammy Jackson, ambitious son of the blacks. This creates a kind of schematic ideological balance in the complete cast but fails to compensate for the narrow inflexibility of the individual characters.

Caldwell's retrospective introduction to the novel suggests that he had in mind for it a larger philosophical view of human suffering than the hackneyed sociological analysis that emerges. He refers to the cumulative effect of the story as "tragic and overpowering" and continues, "It is not surprising that the innocent suffer to as great a degree as the guilty, and the suffering of the innocent in *A House in the Uplands*, while not a justifiable atonement for a whole people, at least serves to ease the pain of violent vengeance for the guilty and unguilty alike."[7] This rather obscure remark suggests an ambitious seriousness in the book, but it also suggests an about-face in much of Caldwell's world view of innocence and guilt, which even in his left-wing fiction in the thirties stopped far short of any clear notion of the innocence of victims. The belief in some variety of innate depravity in human nature had always been central to Caldwell's work, whether it emerged as uncontrolled carnality, selfishness, or more mysterious obsessive behavior. The movement into a less morally ambiguous vision of human affairs is still not complete in *A House in the Uplands*. The villainous Grady Dunbar is capable of a certain insight into his own nature that qualifies his viciousness: "I crooked my wife, and she didn't deserve it. . . . I'm the dirty dog" (*HU*, 197). Similarly, his seemingly virtuous wife suggests that she has been "not quite good . . . a different kind of girl" (*HU*, 181) in the past, but these hints of ambivalence are certainly not central to the conception of the characters. This conception reinforces a clear division between guilty and innocent, evil and good—a division quite foreign to Caldwell's earlier theories.

The novel is not the death knell of the old Erskine Caldwell so much as a failed experiment and at the same time a continuing symptom of a change in his work that every critic of it has noted and characterized in a variety of ways—as self-parody, exhaustion, or the final division of the two warring strains in his fiction into comedy and sociology or didacticism and sensationalism. The change was

7. *Ibid.*, 233.

explained by critics just as variously: as a consequence of Caldwell's desire to feed too fast the public's taste for his peculiar thrills; as a result of his boredom with regional writing after his international travels; as a result of his loss of connection with the South that had fueled his imagination; and as the inevitable outcome of his abandonment of the spiritual concerns of his characters for a more realistic and worldly treatment of their predicaments.[8] Caldwell's decision to give up both nonfiction writing and short stories in favor of the novel might be added to the list, and undoubtedly his rejection of the poor white as the character who had seemed the most fatal symbolic embodiment of his world view. *A House in the Uplands* was not a final turning point in Caldwell's treatment of poor whites, for it was followed chronologically by *The Sure Hand of God* and *This Very Earth;* but it certainly indicates a sense on his part that the cyclorama needed changes in the form of new themes and new social classes. These were indeed what he chose to pursue further in the final two novels of the series, *Place Called Estherville* (1949) and *Episode in Palmetto* (1950).

The question of Caldwell's exhausted fictional territory was taken up in a review of *The Sure Hand of God* by Harrison Smith, in which he urged the author to abandon his current topics in favor of "the great theme which he must eventually undertake. . . . Racial prejudice remains. Twelve million colored people of the South remain subject to dangerous economic hazards in the next decade. . . . Mr. Caldwell, . . . [y]ou have been a powerful propagandist, disguised as a novelist and satirist. Get to work!"[9] Although Smith disliked *Place Called Estherville* even more, it is in almost complete compliance with his advice, albeit the propaganda is more thinly veiled and the economic hazards more fraught with sexual dangers than Smith probably would have specified. Caldwell had already written copiously on blacks in his short stories and his novel *Trouble in July*, but he had not yet taken the final step, still rare enough for a white writer in the 1940s, of making blacks the unrivaled central characters of a long work of fiction. His decision to focus the novel equally on the economic and sexual exploitation of blacks by whites immediately places it in a category quite distinct

8. The following critics and reviewers have speculated interestingly on Caldwell's decline and the reasons for it: Malcolm Cowley, Richard J. Gray, Lon Tinkle (all of whom have essays in *Critical Esssays*, ed. MacDonald), James Korges, and Harvey Klevar.

9. Smith, "Well-Controlled Anger," 84.

from that of his earlier works on the victimization of poor whites. In those works, the sexual adventurings of his characters could suggest both the degradation and resilience of their natural instincts and could be vehicles for humor, horror, and even heroism, as in *God's Little Acre*. However, when Caldwell turns to black protagonists, their sexuality takes the much more passive form of their unintended allure for the unwanted responses of whites, with minimal emphasis on their own carnal desires. Thus, although the two central characters of *Place Called Estherville*—the black brother and sister Ganus and Kathyanne Bazemore—have reached maturity, they are closer to the innocent, simple, or preadolescent blacks like Handsome Brown and Sonny Clark than to the sexually precocious Darling Jill, the aggressive Ellie May Lester, or the twelve- and thirteen-year-old prostitutes of *Tragic Ground*.

Curiously enough, Caldwell's libidinous poor whites had struck Ralph Ellison in the 1930s as audacious parodies of the most common stereotypes then applied to blacks. He recalled that when he first saw the dramatized version of *Tobacco Road*, he felt it must have been written by a black man who had "read Mark Twain, George Washington Harris, Rabelais, Groucho Marx and Voltaire" and then passed for white in order to put over his outrageous humor.[10] The temerity of conception and characterization that made such twists of perception possible has disappeared entirely from the black protagonists of *Place Called Estherville*. The result is a more sentimental and less complicated novel, a consequence of Caldwell's more timid delicacy in fearing to exacerbate racial stereotypes of blacks and of his increasing tendency at this stage to diffuse the elements of his grotesque vision into simpler social statements. Despite the clear evidence of Caldwell's desire not to further notions of blacks as lustful, passionate, or hot-blooded, the novel certainly fails to challenge other invidious stereotypes. Most prominent is that of the mulatto heroine, Kathyanne, of whom "few would have known, by looking casually at her, that she was a mulatto" (*PE*, 26), because her beauty consists primarily of her "straight hair" and "softly tinted skin" (*PE*, 203). Although Caldwell is capable of parodying with distaste the lascivious looks and talk of white men about "high yellow" women, black women in his novels consistently approach physical attractiveness as they approach lightness in color. In *A House in the Uplands*, Grady Dunbar's quadroon mistress Sal-

10. Ralph Ellison, *Going to the Territory* (New York, 1986), 181.

lie John has "delicately tinted skin and naturally straight black hair" (*HU*, 73); Sugar, the "high yellow" in *Journeyman*, is alluring, whereas the black-skinned Susan in the same novel is nurturing and maternal; when the lynch mob invades the black quarters in *Trouble in July*, they pour turpentine on the body of a black woman and choose a lighter one for their sexual "games." In the later novel *Close to Home*, Josene, whom Native Hunnicutt prefers to his new white wife, is "light octoroon in color" with straight dark hair (*CH*, 44); Kathlee in *The Weather Shelter* first attracts her potential white lover because she has "unusual coloring" for a white girl (*WS*, 40); in *The Earnshaw Neighborhood*, Suze, the winner of a beauty contest, is either a quadroon or octoroon. Although Caldwell may be describing the preferences of his fictional males, there is not much evidence of irony in them. It may be argued that this preference for light-skinned black women over both black and white is consistent with Caldwell's endorsement of intermarriage and crossbreeding between the races as a way to produce a superior mixed strain; but in his fiction, this sexual coupling tends to occur only in one combination, between white men and beautiful mulatto women. There are a number of mutual love affairs between these two groups, as well as many forced liaisons between them, that result in children largely ignored and disowned by their fathers; but the only instance of a black man and a white woman willingly making love is that reported by Dene with the "yellow" Hardy, who acts as if he is "just as good as a white man" (*JO*, 38). There are many other instances in Caldwell's fiction, and especially in *Place Called Estherville*, of white women taunting and tantalizing black men sexually, but generally those who are most interested in black men are also most cruel and desperate themselves. In his early work, *The Sacrilege of Alan Kent*, Caldwell had written in a fictional conversation, "It's all right for a white man to lay with a nigger woman, but I'll be damned if it's right for a nigger man to lay all night with a white woman, now is it?" (*SAK*, 19). Although Caldwell clearly questions this double standard, his novels seem to suggest that any advances toward his biologically integrated society are likely to come without much participation by either black men or white women.

In other aspects of black characterization in *Place Called Estherville*, Caldwell tries to counter old stereotypes. The black brother and sister, Ganus and Kathyanne, speak in grammatically correct and formal English, whereas whites speak a debased and vulgarized version of the language. This is an effective device for revealing the resentment of the whites toward educated blacks—"You talk mighty big for a nigger" (*PE*, 46)—but it results in stilted and mechanical speech and consequent woodenness in the black characters. Ganus, when attacked in an alley, says to his assailants, "I wish you'd let me go now. I wasn't bothering anybody. You white boys oughtn't to chunk rocks at folks like that" (*PE*, 45). Kathyanne, abducted to a shed and forced to strip by a group of white boys, notices that one of them is upset. She "put her arm around Jimmy protectingly. 'He's too little to be going around at night with big boys,' she said" (*PE*, 115). After this well-nigh incredible display of self-possession and charity, in the face of imminent rape and possible murder, Kathyanne then repels the advances of a white policeman with the candid but hardly tactful remark that she is "too good" for him (*PE*, 121). To say that such behavior seems uncharacteristic of any young black woman in either situation, and certainly inconsistent for the same character in both situations, is to require a sense of feasibility that is quite foreign to Caldwell's new black heroes and heroines. Not only is their sexuality, color, and language reduced, but also, unfortunately, their fascination as curious specimens of human nature in all its varied unregenerateness. They are types of virtue and victimization who, unlike the beleaguered poor whites, never exploit or betray each other, never fall prey to irrational whims and obsessions, and are uncontaminated by the evils inflicted upon them. There is also, of course, the danger that such counterstereotyping may backfire, creating incredulous amusement in the reader, as was the case with one of the novel's first reviewers, who wrote of it: "Oddly enough he succeeds in making fun of the miserable colored boy and his almost white sister."[11] Ironically, the reviewer was Harrison Smith.

If there is a positive side to this novel's heavy didacticism, it lies in Caldwell's ingeniously detailed accounts of the everyday trials to which the black characters are subjected, rather than the more sensational sexual assaults and murders. Kathyanne is urged to accept old clothes in lieu of wages from her female employer and is threatened with a bad reputation if she refuses them. Her brother is trapped into taking a loan at exorbitant interest to pay for a bicycle he needs in order to get a job delivering groceries, which in turn will finance the payments on the bicycle. This double bind for

11. Harrison Smith, "Comic Citizens of the South," in *Critical Essays*, ed. MacDonald, 90.

blacks, whereby they are trapped by every course of action that they have open to them, is illustrated by the Sphinx-like riddle some of the white town boys put to Ganus: "Boy, which are the best, white girls or nigger girls? . . . You'd better be careful what you say" (*PE*, 53–54). Ganus' attempt to justify his confused response, "Please, sir, I only meant what I ought to" (*PE*, 54), encapsulates Caldwell's black people's enigmas. They are led repeatedly to express preferences, opinions, and desires, and then denied choices, or they are lured into acting like autonomous people and then quickly reminded of their dependency. The motives of the whites who orchestrate this entrapment are not simply sadistic (though there are goodly examples of that) but often originate in genuine impulses of interest and affection toward the appealing brother and sister. These gestures threaten the relative status of the two races and are consequently perverted into hostility. Kathyanne Bazemore's first employer in the novel, the banker George Swayne, works very hard to convince himself that the strong attraction he feels for her is a result of saucy "Negress" behavior. He is constantly reassuring himself that he saw a "knowing smile on her face" (*PE*, 28) and "an impudent sparkle in her eyes" (*PE*, 33). The dignity of her actual reaction to him leaves him feeling "embarrassed," "inferior," and "shamed by a mulatto girl," so that "he felt that he had to dominate her at any cost" (*PE*, 42). The cost for Kathyanne is rape and the later birth of George's first child; for George, it is a legacy of guilt and the loss of both Kathyanne and the child, to whom he later sends some conscience money. Similarly, among the many white women in the novel who attempt intimacy with the black youth Ganus, there are several who are clearly driven by their own loneliness and even by compassion for his situation. Nevertheless, even those individuals with other than cruel intentions inevitably become the agents of more suffering for Ganus, because he is always forced to bear the brunt of their unacceptable actions. Caldwell intimates through these characters that there may be a longing for better feelings between the races, but not in the near future. For the time being, it is thwarted into suffering for blacks and occasional guilt for whites.

The novel ends with a return to the heaviest symbols of the disharmony between the races in the birth of Kathyanne's child and the death of Ganus. The young man's death is by an ax murder (itself rapidly becoming formulaic) on a false accusation of assaulting a white woman; the birth of Kathyanne's daughter precedes her imminent marriage to a decent black man. In order to make this rape-begotten birth into a positive symbol, Caldwell needs a spokesman in this unlikely setting for the benefits of racial intermixing, and he produces one on demand in the person of Dr. Horatio Plowden, a hitherto unrevealed white doctor who embodies every virtue that Caldwell might ever be assumed to espouse. Of the baby he comments, "Nature's been striving for perfection for a long time now, and this's just about as close to perfection as I'll live to see" (*PE,* 236). As with Grandpa Crockett in *This Very Earth,* though in even more arbitrary fashion, Caldwell departs radically from his normal mode of detachment to insert a character who speaks for the author and indeed has no other function in the plot. This not only underscores the novel's tendentiousness, but it also indicates the book's limited success in embodying the novel's ideas in its fictional form. His argument in favor of racial integration is given no support among the people involved in the interracial sexual couplings, nor does it seem likely that this single infant born of them can do anything other than suffer, like her mother, for her "perfection." Unlike his venture into the world of the Old South in *A House in the Uplands,* however, his concern with the dilemma of southern blacks was not a transient one for Caldwell; and despite the many problems of *Place Called Estherville,* the subject was one to which he would return again and again in his later fiction and nonfiction.

In 1950, Caldwell published what was technically the last book in his ten-volume cyclorama, *Episode in Palmetto,* which returned in some measure to the comic mode. An account of the trials of a glamorous young schoolteacher in a small town, condensed for effect into a very short period of time, it deals with a favorite theme of Caldwell's from the earliest days of his career—the various acceptable and unacceptable social manifestations of an essentially antisocial instinct, sexuality. However, for almost the first time, Caldwell exhibits this instinct among a community of people not noted for their Dionysiac urges or for their capacity for earthy articulation, the *petit bourgeois* rank of society. Whether this collection of small shopkeepers and minor professionals was a last effort to modify the social imbalance of the cyclorama or to select a class ripe for sexual burlesque, Caldwell needed an approach to them distinctly different from his habitual depiction of bawdiness and outrage among the rural poor. *Episode in Palmetto* shows a few efforts to move from exaggerated lower-class whites to more rounded, urban, middle-class types; but these moves run counter to Caldwell's previously displayed humorous mode, and he frequently lapses into the cruder manner of depiction with which he is most familiar. This is most evident in the dialogue of the novel, frequently notable in Caldwell's work for its punctuations of idiocy with profundity, simplicity with wiliness, and innocence with vulgarity. This kind of talk, which is central to the conception of a Jeeter Lester or a Ty Ty Walden, does not trip easily off the tongue of the school principal's wife in Palmetto. Although it enhances grotesquely conceived characters, it diminishes more realistic ones with its inappropriateness.

The satirical direction of the novel also calls for a greater subtlety than Caldwell's admittedly "heavy-handed boilermaker" technique, dealing as it does with the disruption of a tiny community's fixed norms by a stranger who refuses to conform to them and with the psychological self-discoveries the stranger makes in the process. The novel has no large didactic or political theme comparable to Caldwell's usual concerns with poverty and racism. Instead, it focuses not on evil and injustice but on the compromises, dissatisfactions, and frustrated expectations of men and women in their ordinary domestic, economic, and sexual relationships. It is an apt context for moral irony, and the novel has an array of minor comic types and situations that contribute effectively to its satire of love and marriage. These include Jenny Mustard, who refuses to bail her husband out of jail because she finally has unlimited access to the family car; Em Gee Sheedwood, a parsimonious progressive farmer, who judges the heroine's attractions exactly as he would those of a new piece of stock for his farm; and Thurston Mustard, the county agricultural agent whose idea of elopement to Chicago with her encompasses a tour of the stockyards and grain elevators. As in *The Sure Hand of God*, men and women enter into partnerships and liaisons with each other for reasons that are whimsical, self-defeating, and rarely mutual, and they live grimly with the consequences. Ash Neff has traded his independence for the financial support of his wife's boarding house, and Jenny Mustard has given up a career for the dubious status of a marriage she regrets. The novel is populated by single people trying desperately to marry and married people living bitterly or rebelliously in their joint estate.

The new schoolteacher, Vernona Stevens, triggers discontent in single and married alike, and is consequently the recipient of six proposals, variously ethical and legal, during her first two weeks in Palmetto. Vernona, however, unlike her comic suitors, is clearly marked for more detailed psychological treatment, and therein lies a problem, for Caldwell attempts this analysis by exposition rather than the suggestive imagery that worked effectively in *God's Little Acre* and *Journeyman* to evoke extreme modes of behavior. On her arrival in Palmetto, Vernona plans to challenge herself to one year of teaching and then hopes to follow it with an early marriage and a home where she will be "protected and secure" (*EP*, 13). This is not, as might appear, because she is a domestic woman who wants to toy briefly with a career, but rather because she is a highly sexed woman who fears the consequences of remaining single and available to any man who solicits her. She already has before her the ominous example of her older sister, who is "kept" by a wealthy retired rear admiral in Washington; and she intends to prove to herself "that it was not inevitable for her to live like her sister, much less be like her, even though they were so much alike in many ways that they were often mistakenly thought to be twins" (*EP*, 10). The novel bears out this seemingly deterministic connection between the sisters by leading Vernona through a series of sexual encounters to the eventual acknowledgment on her part that she is incapable of conventional love, must always try to have men she can't have, and is thus, by Caldwell's logic, destined to be a "successful prostitute. I can't keep on pretending any longer. I've got to be what I am—I can't help myself!" (*EP*, 248). When one of the least sympathetic characters in the novel responds, "What a peculiar thing to say" (*EP*, 248), it is difficult to disagree. Even within the novel's fictional world, Vernona's predicament and analysis ring false, or at least too hasty, because the two mature unmarried men who propose to her, and whom she finds unacceptable, are indeed clearly ludicrous and repulsive, whereas the two unavailable men she favors, a tenth-grade schoolboy and a married politician, are depicted as more obviously attractive. Her responses to them, if somewhat impulsive and extreme, are not unreasonable, and Caldwell's effort to make of this somewhat cruel social and sexual comedy a psychodrama, complete with an infatuated adolescent's suicide and a neurotic woman's shocking self-discovery, is not convincing and damages any moral edge that the comic sexual maneuverings might have had.

Although the heroine is never specifically labeled a nymphomaniac, Caldwell appears here and elsewhere intrigued with female characters who are promiscuous and lured by what is taboo in their societies. In the early novels, this fascination was part of a general assertion that what might be conventionally considered abnormal psychology was very normal indeed in unrepressed human nature.

Thus a character like Darling Jill in *God's Little Acre* is clearly a child of nature whose difficulties will arise only in a society that imposes unnatural moral standards. However, in *Episode in Palmetto* and a number of later novels, such as *Claudelle Inglish* and *Gretta*, the heroines' sexual predilections are not integral to any larger theory of human conduct, but appear to be linked uniquely to their own personal circumstances; thus they lend themselves more readily to the suggestion that their intent is titillating or shocking. At the end of *Episode in Palmetto*, Caldwell abandons somewhat abruptly his depiction of the antics and dubious motivations of all the other characters in order to focus on Vernona's discovery and confession that she is a whore at heart, a repeated motif in the later novels. Caldwell effects a not very satisfactory escape for his heroine and himself from the tangles of everyday craziness in Palmetto by having her elope to Chicago with the agricultural agent, but this provides a conclusion rather than a resolution to Vernona's oddly unconvincing predicament. Caldwell's much-noted detachment from his characters, which had served his grotesque comic vision well, here appears to dwindle, as many critics noted, to indifference, as his characters rise in the social scale and their problems become stranger and more contrived. A young schoolteacher's accelerated journey into self-knowledge when she finds herself alone in a new community is not intrinsically a negligible topic, but the nature of the heroine's perversity, the narrowness of its analysis, and the lack of any larger social significance all suggest a falling off of Caldwell's talent and his cohesive vision when it is applied to the private dilemmas of his fictional bourgeoisie.

Like the short stories that Caldwell was publishing at this time, *Episode in Palmetto* portrays the limited options available to women in their efforts to reconcile their demands for emotional pleasure and economic security in their lives, options almost exclusively of unhappy marriages, stultifying careers as secretaries and teachers, or some form of prostitution. This might seem to suggest the larger social and economic naturalism behind the discovery by so many of Caldwell's later heroines that they are "whores at heart"; certainly, it is of considerable significance in Molly Bowser's decision to set up her brothel in *The Sure Hand of God*. However, running counter to this material pattern of determinism is the psychological drive of these women toward promiscuity, detached from any need for payment, sometimes in conjunction with loving husbands and financial stability. In this sense, the middle-class, small-town setting of *Epi-*

*sode in Palmetto* shows a distinct movement away from the kind of naturalism that might offer multiple explanations for Sister Bessie's pleasure in her night in the Augusta hotel in *Tobacco Road* or even Katy Barlow's desperate sexuality in *Trouble in July. Episode in Palmetto* avoids the more obvious determinism of poverty and primitivism in rural settings and in the sinister temptations of the big city in order to concentrate wholly on the psychology of its middle-class heroine. Such aspects of the small town as are evoked indicate a pettiness and surface propriety and the marked absence of any larger vision of human affairs such as those that occur among Caldwell's less respectable types. People in Palmetto live lives devoid of mystery and obsession; they do not try to peep into eternity through holes in walls or dream of turning on the power in cotton mills. Their social and economic advantages over Caldwell's former characters take them further from the crucial relationships between deprivation, depravity, and spiritual hunger that had so intrigued him, and their sexual peculiarities are robbed of both their material and their divine context.

With the completion of *Episode in Palmetto*, Caldwell had finished the ten novels of the southern cyclorama, which he was to define and describe the following year, 1951, in his first autobiography, *Call It Experience*. Thus, when Caldwell discussed the cyclorama there, he was not only summarizing most of his fiction to date but perhaps also imposing on it a scheme that was not quite so precise in its conception as it may have appeared to him retroactively. Nor at this point in his career could he know how close some of his later novels might come to fitting under the cyclorama umbrella. He himself marked the conclusion of the cyclorama at this point in his career by turning somewhat arbitrarily to very different topics for some time and by simply asserting that it was done. The publication in 1952 of *A Lamp for Nightfall*, the novel set in Maine that had been rejected by Caldwell's publishers before he embarked on *God's Little Acre* in 1933, provides a convenient punctuation point but by no means signals the end of Caldwell's interest in southern material or his use of southern settings as emblematic of the larger universe. Caldwell returned in his later novels to various regions of the South and repeatedly to themes that had dominated in the last few years of the cyclorama, to the preoccupation with family decadence and the decline of once vital clans, to the problems of women and especially to their more sensational sexual neuroses, and, most insistently, to race relationships and their impact on every facet of personal and public life. His interest in rural and lower-class people continued to wane, although there were some lively resurgences of comic, outrageous poor white types, but never again in the political and spiritual context that had permitted them to evoke anger and wonder as well as comedy, pity, and contempt.

# 5

# The Later Novels

## Sex, Race, and Degeneracy

---

*No man as yet has reached the depths to which a woman can sink; and I doubt very much if the Negro will ever fall to the lowest depths of the white race.*

　　　　　　　　　　　　　　　　　*—Erskine Caldwell*

　　　　　*Just to TYPE that much, let alone WRITE.*
　　　　　　*—Truman Capote, of Caldwell's opus*

---

After the conclusion of his southern cyclorama, Caldwell's decision to publish his early Maine novel, *A Lamp for Nightfall*, seems like a pragmatic pause in his career to allow himself the opportunity to seek new directions for his fiction. This novel is both a curious anachronism, evoking as it does the rural milieu and images of his earlier work, and a significant reminder that no matter what the setting, certain preoccupations dominated in Caldwell's novels from start to finish. *A Lamp for Nightfall* recalls, twenty years on, the New England regionalism of his early stories and, even more strikingly, the elemental patterns of imagery from which there was such a falling off as Caldwell moved in his fiction further away from simple, land-bound people. It is the only one of Caldwell's novels to have a minutely detailed environment that is not southern and yet displays the intimate knowledge of landscape, social relationships, customs, climate, and local types that characterizes the best of his early work. Though not one of his most memorable novels, it suggests again how well he could integrate character, theme, and setting, how acutely he could draw on the implications of the weather and the physical terrain, and how disturbingly his irony might operate. At the same time, this early novel anticipates many of the issues that dominate Caldwell's later work: the enervation of pioneer populations, the self-destructive effects of their ethnic and national prejudices, and the degeneration of relations between the sexes. Although written early in the Great Depression, it displays no hint of topicality, no economic concerns, no hunger or poverty, but is much more broadly modern in its desolate view of spiritual and emotional exhaustion among descendants of the first American settlers.

The native Maine farmers, with their slyly symbolic literary names (Emerson, Frost, and Robinson), who people the town of Clearwater, watch grimly as French Canadian and Scandinavian immigrants thrive while they decay, and Indians with Ph.D.'s teach in colleges to which they are too parsimonious to send their children. They resent their womenfolk's betrayal of them and their daughters' abandonment of them for the newcomers but acknowledge that they are themselves "petered out" (*LN*, 9)—drained of sexual energy, vitality, and ambition. They conserve all of the capital they have left in these areas, refusing to invest any of it in the future yet regretting their decline to their present condition from their former triumphs as clearers of the wilderness who held nature at bay while they established their model farms. The situation is not quite analogous to that of blacks and whites in the South, because the Maine "Canucks," "hunkies," and "squareheads" (*LN*, 5) are immune to the curses of the WASPS and are quite successfully replacing them in farms, government, and business. However, Caldwell suggests that, like southern whites, the only hope for the Maine Yankees lies in intermarriage and crossbreeding with more potent minorities, and indeed the instincts of the majority seem to lead them often in this direction, no matter how strong their social prejudices against it.

In *A Lamp for Nightfall*, Thede Emerson consents to his daughter's marriage to a French Canadian farmer as a way of easing himself from her financial support, even though he is extremely wealthy. His family life is certainly heavily laden with the symptoms of pioneer decadence: Thede is asexual, miserly, and sadistic to his children; his wife is promiscuous and matches him in parental cruelty; their son and daughter, Howard and Jean, have a near incestuous relationship; and Howard is also suicidally depressed. In the end, Jean escapes the degeneracy of the Emersons by her marriage, whereas Howard ends the male line of the family by killing himself. Though obviously lacking in subtlety, the novel's thesis is worked out against a New England background that uses the landscape and the seasons to good effect in suggesting the ongoing contest between people and nature, and the ominous consequences, for the people, when they withdraw from the competition and try merely to hoard their acquisitions.

Jean's October wedding, with its display of the harvest bounty of the Emersons' Autumn Hill farm, comes at the annual testing time for these old Maine residents. The wedding is the last chance to affirm life before the death of winter sets in to obliterate the signs of human endeavor from the countryside, when the snow will cover stone walls and hedges and all but the hardy newcomers will give up their struggle with nature. On her wedding day, Jean collects red and gold maple leaves and strews them on her white silk dress before preserving them in her jewel box; but while her thoughts are of the future with her French husband and their own children, for her parents the occasion is merely a last reminder of a more generous way of life, of the hospitality, satisfaction, and pleasure that they have sacrificed to their bitterness and frugality. Nature has become wholly malevolent for her parents and their compatriots, now that they no longer work with it and reap from it. The roof of their house collapses under the weight of snow, the paint peels and cracks under the onslaught of frost and sun, and even a family burial ground is in a short time "covered by the creeping forest" (LN, 30). These images are, as James Devlin has noted, a New England version of the insidious broom-sedge of Tobacco Road, but the Emersons and Frosts have lost the last connection to the land that enables even Jeeter Lester to recognize a certain divinity in the pursuit of agriculture, despite his neglect of his own land.[1] Jeeter still believes in God, but the New England Yankees have long forsaken any religion: the Congregational church has gone; Thede has never attended religious services, for "he had always tried to evade what he was incapable of comprehending" (LN, 147); and when one of the other families makes plans for a wedding, they forget, significantly, to arrange for a minister to perform the ceremony. The novel is an intriguing one to have been written so close in time to Tobacco Road, because it notes the similar decline of old rural families into lassitude and degeneracy. However, it wholly avoids any economic or political explanations, suggesting rather that the bitter struggle with the elements has sapped the vitality of the farmers and that their exclusiveness has prevented its regeneration with new blood or fresh points of view. This is suggested in sly comic fashion at the Grange hall dance, where the three-piece orchestra has learned

1. Devlin, Erskine Caldwell, 84.

only two pieces of modern dance music, which it performs alternately all evening, while the musicians cling to a large repertoire of square dances that the old people dance to but the young sit out. The other relic of the old rural traditions is the charivari at Jean's wedding. As part of the joke playing, a chamber pot is rolled down the stairs to the feet of the newlyweds, bumping on every step. The reaction of the guests to this lowly prank is a classic example of Caldwell's inscrutable irony: "A shout went up all over the house, louder than any before then. It was the climax of the wedding and the only entertaining part of the evening. This was what everybody had been waiting for two hours or more to see. And some of the guests had traveled a long way to get to Autumn Hill" (*LN*, 186). The reenacting of the old country ritual reveals not just the foolishness of those performing it but the emptiness of the lives of those who enjoy it. They cling to these symbols of a remembered bucolic way of life, but their nostalgia is vitiated by their refusal to pursue its essence anymore. Thede Emerson ritually places a light in his farm window every night at dark as a symbol of his family pride and endurance, while he simultaneously abandons his farming and drives his family one by one from their home. Like the Dunbar family in *A House in the Uplands*, the old settlers are trapped in a decadence that they recognize but are incapable of resisting, a theme present in much of Caldwell's work, but usually in his southern novels in such close juxtaposition to economic and social determinism that the sense of human waste is not nearly so naked and unqualified.

The decline of a once vital family into enervation or decadence was a topic to which Caldwell returned often throughout his long career and one that reveals by its varying treatment both his constant and his changing concerns. He had first taken up the subject in *Tobacco Road* and almost simultaneously in *A Lamp for Nightfall* (though it was published much later). He returned to a family of formerly wealthy, upper-class Southerners in *A House in the Uplands* and to their poverty-stricken lower-class compatriots in *This Very Earth*. In one of his last novels, *The Weather Shelter* (1969), he would examine again a prosperous family of white Southerners who would survive only in their illegitimate and unacknowledged black offspring; and in *Miss Mamma Aimee* (1967), he would bring together many of his lifelong concerns in a comic novel about family disintegration that provoked a renewal of critical interest in him late in his career. C. Hugh Holman found the latter "possibly his best novel since *Georgia Boy*," and James Korges thought it "grandly rendered in the comic mode, as though in his full maturity Caldwell had returned to his major themes with renewed vigor."[2] The novel did indeed take this favorite topic and apply to it much of his old extravagant humor, though now in a context that was recognizably contemporary. A number of characters are straight out of the classic Caldwell mold—a lecherous hillbilly preacher with a backfiring car; an incestuous family with a promiscuous daughter, a crazy son, and a number of parasitical relatives so lazy that they cannot even get themselves breakfast when the black maid quits. However, there are changes as well as reversions. The government now requires employers to pay their black workers minimum wages; these workers abandon the white employers for better jobs and quote Martin Luther King in justification of their actions. The novel has the Vietnam War in the distant background, as well as bearded folk singers, shopping centers, Billy Graham, and urban developers invading the decayed remnants of the older South. The central character, Miss Mamma Aimee, is not so much the beloved mother her name implies but a more misguided version of Ty Ty Walden in *God's Little Acre*. Her efforts to control and keep her family under her roof are rewarded with their resentment of her dubious generosity, and with violence and betrayal. The Mangrum family—which has given its name to an Augusta street, a creek, and a schoolhouse, and boasts war heroes and plantation owners in its past—is now reduced to a final core of squatters in the family mansion who lack the initiative or ability to strike out for themselves. They are willingly, if meagerly, supported by Miss Mamma Aimee, who has been selling off parcels of the original plantation in piecemeal fashion while resisting the complete surrender of her estate to a developer who plans to use it for "Woolworth's, Grant's, Penney's, the A.&P., the E-Z, the I-X-L, the Do-Rite, the coin laundry, liquor store, barber shop, beauty parlor, loan company, pizza bar" (*MMA*, 16). Miss Mamma is in the tradition of Caldwell's obsessive and irrational characters, blinkered in her determination to hold together a family she is helping destroy. Contradictory in her mean-spirited generosity, by turns affectionate and manipulative, stubborn and erratic, she is a grand comic creation who provides an effective foil for the simpler hypocrisy of the other characters—for her worthless, sponging brother-

2. C. Hugh Holman, "Detached Laughter in the South," in *Comic Relief: Humor in Contemporary American Literature*, ed. Sarah Blacher Cohen (Urbana, 1978), 97; Korges, *Erskine Caldwell*, 44.

in-law, who complains of people who "think the world owes them a living" (*MMA*, 54); for his wife, Katie Snoddyhouse, who bitterly criticizes the hospitality she exploits; and for her folk-singing son-in-law, Woody Woodruff, who composes songs about the constipation and gas they all get from eating Mamma's greasy fatback sausage, but never refuses the free food.

Although the Mangrum family members recall much of the behavior of Caldwell's poor whites, in their violence, sexual antics, lassitude, and self-centeredness, they are in fact very far from being members of that class, in either social rank or material circumstances. Thus Caldwell does not offer any of the standard economic or naturalistic explanations for their degeneracy. Like the pioneer New England Emersons, they have exhausted their original energy and ambition as a family unit, and now their only hope lies in dispersal and independence; like the Emersons, too, incest marks the final stages of the family's effort to preserve its identity, for Miss Mamma was already a Mangrum before she married her first cousin Ralph Mangrum. Caldwell seems to suggest a fatality inherent in the very ideal of family pride and cohesion personified in Miss Mamma Aimee, although he unfortunately undermines the paradoxes she represents by attempting finally in the novel to provide a psychological explanation for this incongruous person, in terms that inevitably reduce her grotesque comic stature to that of a normal person who "had worked herself into a dangerous state of mind over the years and finally . . . was on the verge of a complete emotional and mental collapse" (*MMA*, 203). By suggesting, in the end, reasonable and scientific causes for a disordered personality, Caldwell undermines the power of the unreasonableness, exaggeration, and outrage that worked better in the novel than his unsatisfactory psychology.

The method by which explanatory theories are introduced in the novel is a relatively late innovation in Caldwell's work. He adopts the device of an italicized voice that interrupts the standard narrative at occasional intervals to give a second commentary on what is being said. Often the voice, though disembodied, seems to belong to one of the characters in the novel. Sometimes it seems an unspecified voice from the community, and just once it seems a barely disguised authorial commentator who finally explains Miss Mamma's problem to us. Most often, the voice seems that of Cato Boykin, the Mangrum family's lawyer and thus a somewhat more educated and analytical voice than Caldwell usually allows in his fiction. However, the effect of this slight expansion of narrative perspective is not as complicating as might be anticipated. It does not, as in Faulkner, suggest the elusiveness of knowing and understanding what happens, but is used instead to reinforce, emphasize, and amplify the main line of the narrative.

The one area of the novel in which Caldwell returns most fully to an early concern and reveals the later development of his thinking is in the recurrence of a genuine poor white preacher, who is largely extraneous to the Mangrum family's decadence and is something of a quaint outsider to the 1960s urban milieu. He is the self-styled Reverend Raley Purdy, founder and only minister of the Supreme Being Missionary Church, a Tennessee hillbilly who has been inspired by the radio broadcasts of Billy Graham ("He's everywhere like God is" [MMA, 79]) to emulate the master. Raley's religious fervor is allied both to his poverty-stricken origins and his desperately repressed sexuality. Like one of Flannery O'Connor's fanatical religionists, he is capable of extremes of asceticism and excess in the service of his passion. His only possessions, besides his ten-year-old car, are his radio, his Bible, and a large, pearl-handled revolver. He takes up residence in Augusta in a single bleak room that is this modern monk's cell: "The window had neither a curtain nor a shade over it, there was no rug on the plank floor, and the ceiling was rain-stained and sagging in two of the corners. On a shelf above the cold-water basin was a rusty hot-plate, and on the floor under the basin was a dented tin pan and a chipped china plate and a discolored coffee cup. Raley's black suit was hanging on a nail in the wall" (MMA, 49).

Like O'Connor's crazed founder and sole member of the Church Without Christ, Haze Motes in *Wise Blood*, Raley serves to reveal the false values of the more conventional preachers by his fanatical candor. He has learned from observation that the best churches are against, rather than for, things, and that "God wants people to listen to preaching and praying the way me and Billy Graham do it and pay in money for it" (MMA, 98). Like Haze, Raley is torn between committing himself to sin (by buying some provocative underwear as a courting gift for Connie Mangrum) or battling absolutely against it (by preaching a sermon against the very existence of such garments). Trapped between his imperial church-building fantasies and his libido, he brings to mind Caldwell's earlier fiction about the paradoxes of religious obsession; but Raley is isolated from any believers other than those who toy with him, unlike Sister Bessie and

Semon Dye, who symbolize a larger power and neediness in their communities. Raley is finally quite unlike O'Connor's Haze Motes in that he is ultimately no "Christian *malgré lui*"; if there is a genuine truth in him behind the posturing, it is certainly not an orthodox Christian one.[3] Caldwell's early characters had consistently sought transcendence from their grim earthly lives, but for Caldwell, this constituted no evidence whatsoever that a true Christianity was the real, if unrecognized, end of their desires. Nonetheless, there was a communal impulse that might genuinely be designated a religious one, which seems to have all but disappeared in the formal churchgoing of the characters in the later works.

Caldwell's almost simultaneous publication, with *Miss Mamma Aimee*, of his nonfiction work *Deep South* (1968), which explores all the facets of southern religion that he had noted in his youth, indicates that his thoughts were turning again at this time to the backcountry evangelists with their meager, poverty-ridden origins, who had earlier been so central to his work. One of the minor characters in the novel suggests that their continuing presence in southern towns is a commonplace enough occurrence, but Caldwell's later novels no longer explore the rural poor white communities where they were central. Thus Caldwell uses his poor white preacher effectively in *Miss Mamma Aimee* as a vehicle for satirizing the values of respectable churchgoing society, but the personal power of Raley Purdy as a literary character seems almost wasted in this more secularized context. By the end of Caldwell's career, such characters had dwindled to a very small number and had become, in his more prosperous urban communities, the eccentrics rather than the focal points of his people's inchoate aspirations.

*Miss Mamma Aimee*'s Georgia setting and emphasis on southern customs and characters make it one of quite a number of novels written later in Caldwell's career in which he returned to a partially and curiously modernized version of the native material that had helped establish his early reputation. However, immediately after the completion of the last of the ten books of the southern cyclorama in 1950, he appeared to make a concerted and largely unrewarded effort to seek new subjects and settings for his fiction, or at least to rest the old ones. In addition to the two new short story collections, *Gulf Coast Stories* (1956) and *Certain Women* (1957), he published three novels during the 1950s, *Love and Money* (1954), *Gretta*

3. Flannery O'Connor, Introduction to *Wise Blood* (2nd ed.; New York, 1962).

(1955), and *Claudelle Inglish* (1958), which, with the exception of the latest of the novels, attempt to shake off any specific regional emphasis and turn from social concerns to the private, and especially the sexual, problems of increasingly middle-class and professional characters. Race, poverty, and class are temporarily abandoned as subjects of concern, and along with them the comic mode, so that the decade of the fifties in Caldwell's stories and novels consists largely of humorless sexual psychodramas among a rather awkwardly realized bourgeoisie.

The first of the three novels, *Love and Money*, is the furthest departure from Caldwell's norm in that it has as narrator a successful writer of popular novels who is at a temporary impasse in his writing. This protagonist, Roderick Sutter, is between novels, between wives, and between priorities. Having fallen in love with an elusive cocktail waitress, he engages in a cross-country quest for her while his agent, his publisher, and a variety of acquaintances urge him to get down to the real business of his life, the production of his annual best-selling book. Thus Caldwell's *Künstlerroman* is a version of the struggle between perfection of the life and of the work, though with both sides in the conflict reduced to their lowest common denominators—sexual conquest and royalty checks. Though the novel ends in the failure of the pursuit of love and the resumption of the solitary business of writing, there is a final effort to connect the two by suggesting that the desired girl, Tess, was a kind of muse whose allure lay in her evasiveness: "For the first time in almost a month I wondered if I loved Tess as I thought I did, or if actually she merely represented the unobtainable that I felt a need to strive for" (*LM*, 212). There is a hint here of a fable of the birth of art similar to that in the early *Sacrilege of Alan Kent*, but in this novel, the fable is so mundanely grounded that it loses both its mythical element and any sense of conviction behind the myth. Instead of the early flower-scented goddess who haunted Alan Kent across a blasted landscape, Roderick Sutter hunts through the bars of Sarasota, Houston, and Colorado Springs and encounters any number of willing and nubile women, all virtually indistinguishable. Of Charlotte he says, "The mold of her breasts and the flare of her thighs were arresting and conspicuously feminine" (*LM*, 233); of Nancy, "The smooth, soft flesh of her feminine hips responded in a slight ripple with each movement of her body" (*LM*, 155); and of Tess, "Her flexuous hips . . . were rounded and responsive and firmly molded" (*LM*, 31). There is a good deal of discussion by Roderick's friends of the inability of artists to live in the real world because of their transference to it of ideals born in the imaginary one, but the evidence of this literary author's adventures and of his images of love suggests that his conceptions are a good deal more base and circumscribed than those of people who dwell only in the real world. Whether or not the novel is self-consciously autobiographical, it is not a sympathetic portrait of the artist as a middle-aged man, either in his life or in his work.

*Love and Money* has, however, a certain curiosity value among Caldwell's works because of its educated, first-person narrative voice and its array of professional, upper-middle-class characters. It represents another occasion in his fiction when Caldwell's prosaic vocabulary, plain style, and naïve repetitions seem to need to be altered in the service of credibility for a presumably more articulate and fluent speaker. The narrative language *is* indeed different in that it is unusually verbose, with choral repetitions now replaced by strings of synonyms: "I was glum and downcast and thoroughly unhappy" (*LM*, 24); "Normal, average, ordinary, everyday people" (*LM*, 239); "I'm selfish and cruel and scoundrelly" (*LM*, 209). Although the narrator's prose can be both purple and stilted, the language of some of his professional friends varies unevenly between formal speech and vulgar mindlessness, as though Caldwell had difficulty in striking an authentic, or at least a consistent, tone for them. The language of Caldwell's characters in many of the cyclorama novels had had a shocking and incongruous quality; but for the most part he had not been attempting a mode of social realism, and his settings were in a sphere deliberately distanced and set apart, rather than in the familiar and at least superficially decorous world of this novel.

Caldwell later wrote in his final autobiography that he had worked on *Love and Money* in "starts and lapses for a long time," and though he finally professed himself "very happy with what I had accomplished" (*WAMM*, 239), it is a patchy and coreless novel that reflects problems beyond Caldwell's unpracticed hand in the field of middle-class realism. Even the plotting seems occasionally absentminded, with assumptions made about information that the reader has not been provided with. It is tempting to believe that the struggles of the fictional Roderick Sutter to get himself to concentrate on his novel in progress must be a symbolic reflection of Caldwell's own difficulties in finding a new direction for his writing at this stage of his career, which was marked for him professionally by the end of the cyclorama and personally by the breakup of his third marriage, to his wife June. His decision to write about a writer did not promise well for future ventures into the world of more sophisticated types. However, the novel gave Caldwell a chance to rehearse, in a middle-class setting, the theme of sexual obsession and its capacity to alter and destroy the best-laid plans of its more prosperous victims just as completely as it had done among the poor whites. He had begun to test this theme in *Episode in Palmetto*, and indeed it proved to be the topic he pursued in the remaining two novels of the fifties, *Gretta* and *Claudelle Inglish*.

In the novel *Gretta* (1955), the heroine's embittered husband says of her at one point, "You might classify her as a contemporary neurotic prostitute with classical overtones" (*G*, 206), a comment whose elaboration forms the central theme of both that novel and the following one, *Claudelle Inglish* (1958). Both novels explore the peculiar psychosexual habits of a beautiful young woman who is driven to repeat certain ritual acts of prostitution by the overpowering force of a shocking event in her earlier life. Thus Caldwell would seem to have cornered and reduced here to their simplest essentials some of the most salient characteristics of his fictional world—irrepressible and somewhat unusual sexuality allied to grim determinism. Even the heroines of these two books seem formulaic; Gretta has agile breasts and pertly protruding buttocks, whereas Claudelle, in minor variation, has mobile hips and bursting breasts. Apart from their similarly kinetic bodies, both women have perfected a certain act of self-exhibition that precedes their sexual service, and both insist on being paid even though neither practices prostitution as a means of livelihood. In fact, each of them appears to find in her material payment an assurance that she has successfully pleased a man, and thus her satisfaction is emotional rather than economic. Although this may seem like a virtual blueprint for pornography, especially in the frequent necessary reiteration of sexual routines, Caldwell is surprisingly indirect in his descriptions, working most often by suggestive metaphor and innuendo. This might well be as effectively titillating as more fulsome details, but his main interest in these books appears to be in the symptomatic meaning of these women's compulsive acts.

Both women are betrayed by their fiancés before they embark on their new patterns of sexual behavior, and both ultimately provoke the suicide and death of men who become involved with them. Although the turning of abandoned women to prostitution as an act both of self-comfort and revenge may have minimal psychological validity in the real world, within Caldwell's narrowly symbolic depiction of the struggle between the sexes, it is quite feasible. All his men and women exist in a relationship of sexual barter to each other, most often with women's beauty and nurturing offered in variable proportions for men's equally variable economic support and comfort. Caldwell then simplifies these rates of exchange even further, to their most primitive tokens—a shapely body and a sweet potato pie in return for five dollars and a compliment. Thus prostitution in his world is so close to the normal relationship of the sexes (*love* being merely a term for the successful transfer of offerings between two contenders) that many of Caldwell's women come to see it as the preferred form, supplying them with constant reassurance that they are valuable and bypassing the question of loyalty, on which they have already suffered. For Gretta and Claudelle to solicit rewards and appreciation for sexual favors is thus quite consistent with Caldwell's vision of the world, and he undertakes in these two novels to explore why their behavior assumes the particular form it does, rather than merely exploiting its capacity to shock, though that, of course, is not ignored.

*Gretta* offers the most narrowly emotional theories about its heroine's fated life by moving, like *Love and Money*, outside the complex determining environment of the South, and of economic deprivation, into the anonymous northern town of Unionville, where Gretta works as a secretary for the local utility company. She was orphaned in early childhood, and the evidently crucial experience of her youth was having been paid by a man when she was ten years old to take off her stockings for his pleasure, an act she later performs ritualistically for all her clients, mimicking her first childlike performance for them. Gretta not only delights in their praise—"It's magic" (*G*, 40), "I've never seen anything like that before" (*G*, 242)—but she then is impelled to go on to perform fellatio and to ask for a "present," always a euphemism for money. Confessing this past pattern of behavior to her doctor husband, Gretta explains, in a typical metaphor, "I can't help it. It's like being thirsty and wanting a drink of water—it's like being hungry and craving something to eat" (*G*, 83). Gretta's main predicament in the novel is whether a loving marriage will be able to counter her former compulsions or whether she will be driven, against her own will and even her obvious self-interest, to return to her old ways. As might be anticipated in Caldwell, obsessions triumph over conscious effort, and

Gretta betrays her husband for the approval and dirty dollar bills of a stranger: "I can't make myself stop . . . and I really don't want to stop . . . that's the terrible thing about it!" (G, 180). Although there is some brief talk in the novel of getting psychiatric help for Gretta, this is quickly abandoned, and the novel proceeds to its inevitably destructive conclusion in her husband's suicide. Caldwell is certainly not willing to allow psychiatry to contend in the battle against fate, even in a novel that strips away most of the other forces of human determinism.

Gretta is thus both extreme and simple in its fatalism and its rejection of any way out of its character's predicament, compared with a novel like Tobacco Road, where both causes and cures are complex and incongruous. When Caldwell decided to pursue an almost exactly similar pattern of determinism, with remarkably familiar symptoms, in his next novel, Claudelle Inglish (1958), the most significant change he made in the context was a partial return to an environment close to that of his early novels. Claudelle is the daughter of a Piedmont sharecropper, who is besieged by poverty, a thankless wife, and a harsh landlord. Back among the jimsonweeds, tenant shacks, and peckerwoods, among characters with names like Lightsy Hushoure, Horace Haddbetter, and Ching Guyler, Caldwell is on perhaps too familiar territory. Nevertheless, despite the reiteration of girls with no panties, clergymen with frigid wives, and fights where people get impaled on car hood ornaments, the southern rural setting once again adds both color and complication to Claudelle's situation and redeems it slightly from the unalleviated melodrama of Gretta. At the beginning of the novel, Claudelle is rejected by her fiancé in a letter, whereupon she immediately goes on a sexual rampage, teasing and luring men by flaunting her naked body and then demanding gifts for her lovemaking. However, the "modern neurotic prostitute" element in this novel is considerably tempered by more than a few hints of a traditional pattern of prostitution. Claudelle's poverty and her desire for pretty clothes, which she is clearly unable ever to get by any other means, provide a very different motive from Gretta's for soliciting money. Gretta has first a job and then a prosperous husband, so that her payment has only symbolic value. Caldwell provides Claudelle with a broader range of causes for her promiscuity, even beyond her acquisitiveness and this single act of betrayal by her first lover. Her mother educates her continually in the financial failure of her own marriage and the need for Claudelle to avoid her mistake: "One of the things that Claudelle remembered about her parents when she was very young was hearing her mother curse her father time after time and threaten to leave him and live with any man who would give her money and clothes" (*CI*, 16). In addition, Claudelle finds in her own community not a string of anonymous men who have no function other than to provide the occasions for her misconduct, but a group of individuals who know her and each other, and come laden with their own peculiar circumstances and needs.

Claudelle is certainly not any less predetermined than Gretta, but the encumbrances of her life are less amenable to the aid of a psychiatrist, for they derive from inheritance, education, poverty, and environment. Thus Caldwell's return to a southern setting, with its emphasis on family, community and social context, and individual eccentricity, argues against the very narrow determinism of *Gretta* by depicting a more complicated web of circumstance. The characters in the novel, many of whom are members of the Stony Creek Free Will Church, are quick to deny all responsibility for their actions and to place the blame elsewhere. However, although Caldwell is willing to concede quite a number of their explanations, he is not about to vindicate them as completely as they would do themselves, and in that sense, this novel returns to the ironic mode of his earlier work in its ambiguous struggle between determinism and culpability in human behavior.

The elusive question of fatalism and individual responsibility within the realm of private, and especially sexual, relationships continued to elicit Caldwell's attention, most notably in two later works, *The Last Night of Summer* (1963) and *Annette* (1973), the latter being his last published novel. Both deal again with neurotic women, their past lives and current lovers, but both move as well into the somewhat new fictional territory of the suspense thriller, each culminating in its heroine's murder by a sinister stranger. Both novels again forsake the familiarly populated rural South for urban isolation, although Caldwell works to create a highly atmospheric setting in each, in the explosive summer heat of Grandport (in *The Last Night of Summer*) and the ominous nighttime suburbs of Zephyrfield (in *Annette*). Once again, the central characters are members of the middle class: in the earlier novel, a secretary, her boss and his wife; in the later, a kindergarten teacher and her lawyer husband. There are no concerns with food, shelter, or joblessness to mitigate the singular emphasis on emotional relationships, no racial tensions, no disorienting comedy or intrusive politics. The novels are less casually episodic than most of Caldwell's work, with their gory climaxes now clearly the focus of the narrative development. Although this nightmarish world of terrified and alienated women is very far from Caldwell's accepted métier, it was a subject that had haunted his fiction from the outset: in the criminal underworld of *The Bastard* and *Poor Fool*; in the proletarian short stories of the 1930s, dealing with girls thrown on the streets by the economic crisis; and then in the apolitical and melodramatic short stories and novels of the 1950s. In returning to the topic again in these two late novels, Caldwell shows not perhaps any deeper understanding of the issue of causality in this most mysterious and fundamental area of human behavior, but a refusal to give up on it—like the seekers in *Journeyman* who peer endlessly through the same chink in the cow-shed wall, certain that "something else" will be revealed to them each time they repeat the experiment.

In *The Last Night of Summer*, Caldwell creates a pair of victims of sexual violence, male and female, and a pair of perpetrators, female and male, so that the emphasis is not exclusively on the physical vulnerability of women, but on a world where castration is as imminent a terror for a man as rape is for a woman. Caldwell's exclusion in his writing of the finer nuances of sexual desire and destructiveness in favor of their most extreme manifestations is, despite the repetitive sensationalism, a necessary and central feature of his vision of human nature. He is intrigued by the extent to which all civilized social behavior is a mask for instincts, urges, thoughts, and wishes that are conventionally repressed and controlled into acceptably decorous actions and words, and thus he continually experiments with degrees of impropriety in the behavior and talk of his characters. His people habitually violate all conventions that might make them credible in any realistic sense, saying just what is on their minds and acting out their impulses. In Caldwell's early career, when his subjects were largely lower-class southern whites, this behavior was both defended and attacked by his critics (and the law courts) on the basis of its realism, perhaps because people were more ready to accept such indecencies from poor and debased people. However, as Caldwell gradually moved away from poor white subjects and continued to attribute such social violations to a more prosperous, educated, middle-class population, it became evident that his interest was in the irrepressible possibilities of all human conduct, not just the most obviously economically and socially determined. This necessitated a narrowing of the field of his fatalism and a more obvious disparity in his characters between the conventional external circumstances of their lives and their private behavior, which now began to seem increasingly abnormal. The gothicism of these two later novels may well have been an attempt to distance his middle-class subjects in the same way that poverty had distanced his lower-class ones—by displacing light into darkness, the known and secure into the unknown and disorienting—so that their uninhibited responses would no longer be a distraction, as they are in *Love and Money*, for example, from a more realistic mode of fiction.

Roma Anderson, the central female victim in *The Last Night of Summer*, is, by Caldwell's standards, a sexual innocent who has avoided lovemaking until, aged twenty-four, she falls in love with her boss, Brooks Ingraham. Abandoning her normal restraint, she moves almost instantaneously through a series of normal stages of intimacy, suddenly calling him by his first name, then suggesting a tryst, then embracing him. Her boss, who is older, married, and a devoted parent, tries to resist the attraction he feels for her. The entire novel is set on the night after the first disclosure of their hidden feelings, with Roma eagerly awaiting Brooks for an evening of romantic lovemaking while Brooks delays and struggles with his reservations about infidelity. In the end, what occurs in the novel is a brutal and grotesque caricature of the decisions the two have come to—both Roma's to give herself up to passion and Brooks's to refuse it. Roma, while waiting for her lover, is raped and murdered by an escaped convict, a bestial primordial creature still covered with swamp mud from his jail break, who says to her, "I bet you've been looking for somebody like me for a long time, baby" (*LNS*, 120). Brooks, having rejected his desire for Roma, is castrated by his wife with the jagged edge of a gin bottle and the remark "You'll never see another woman again" (*LNS*, 176). By these grisly parodies of the characters' own purposes, Caldwell emphasizes the connections between the gentle and civilized dreams of Roma and Brooks and the cruel and primitive instincts of the wife, Maureen, and the convict, Foxy.

Foxy and Maureen are psychopaths who play deadly and blatant versions of the games that the more normal people engage in, and the fact that the normal people are forced against their wills into the final travesties of their conscious decisions does not invalidate Caldwell's sense of their places on the same spectrum. All of the characters have limited control over their behavior, and all four are profoundly affected by random external occurrences. One of the most powerful motivating factors in the novel is the weather, the oppressive heat and humidity of the last night of summer that has accumulated with the people's tensions and finally explodes in crazy behavior—in the violence of Foxy and Maureen, but also in Roma's impulsive decision to confess her love that night and Brooks's departure from his habit of going straight home after work. The brooding, sweltering climate had long been a staple of Caldwell's naturalism, allied particularly to a low level of inhibition in his characters. It had produced bizarre and sometimes comic effects, although here it is used exclusively for suspense and horror.

In keeping with his established interest in neurotic women, Caldwell pays more attention to Roma and Maureen than to Brooks and the convict, suggesting especially for Maureen's mad fury an array of explanations ranging from an overindulged childhood to menstrual problems. Yet Caldwell also insists on a considerable element in her behavior that is erratic and largely uncalculated, so that the explanations still do not help predict the course a character's actions will take. This novel does, however, extend the boundaries of irrational violence and sexuality into ever more extreme manifestations and across social and economic categories, and suggests increasingly lurid outcomes of all relationships between men and women.

In *Annette*, his final novel, Caldwell continued his exploration of passion and its unusual and deadly variants in another intensely concentrated nighttime drama, set this time in the quiet darkness of tree-lined suburban streets. Once again, he examines both the intrinsic and extrinsic forces that affect the fate of the heroine, within the tightly circumscribed world of her relationships with family and lovers. This time, however, the determining factors in Annette's violent death are emphasized to the virtual exclusion of all exercise of will on her part. She is, much more than the neurotic Gretta or Claudelle, of questionable sanity—a condition both inherited from her mother, who is eventually institutionalized, and exacerbated by her mother's hostility toward her. As a girl, she had sought love desperately from her father and from Mr. Truelove, a life-sized teddy bear; talked to herself frequently; and fallen into the habit of sitting naked in front of a mirror, staring at herself. When fate seemed to present a solution to many of her problems in a loving marriage to her husband Wayne, he had been suddenly murdered by an unknown stranger. Annette's second marriage is undertaken in a futile attempt to have the three children she had promised her

first husband (futile, because the second has an unconfessed vasec-
tomy), and her choice of husband is guided by her friend Evelyn's
practice of astrology and casting horoscopes. Annette's naïve question "Do you believe our lives are really ruled by the influence
of the planets and the signs of the zodiac?" (A, 15) suggests, in
this educated middle-class woman, a more decadent version of
Caldwell's early characters' blind faith in a supernatural power beyond their ken.

In pursuing this question of what "our lives are really ruled by,"
Caldwell adds in this novel another to his chain of absent or unlov-
ing mothers and also the possibility of inherited mental illness,
which is certainly in danger of subsuming all other kinds of causality.
However, he also takes up again that more interesting and murky
area of men's and women's lives in which women's innate tendencies
to lure and depend upon men contend with men's responsibility for
both abusing and protecting women, so that his women seem both
seductresses and victims, while his men both idealize and mistreat
them. The alternating depiction of a woman as an acquiescent
temptress and as innocent prey shapes the central episodes of the
novel, which occur on the night when Annette has finally made an
apparently willed decision to leave her second, unloved husband.
As soon as she steps from her home into the dark, rain-soaked suburbs, she is both the victim of all manner of threatening men and a
tease toward those who would help her. Crouching in wet bushes,
embracing the bark of trees, hallucinating imaginary conversations,
Annette is at her most pathetic and vulnerable. Each effort she
makes to retreat to safety leads her into an even more ominous situation. Going to a house to use the telephone, she is harassed and
assaulted by a boy there; rescued by her best friend's husband, she
is then subjected to his sexual advances and abandoned in a park
when she rejects him. However, Annette also embraces and encourages the friend of the boy in the house who attacks her, and
although in terror of rape from one youth, fantasizes sex with the
other. If this seems somewhat disconcerting in a woman at that very
moment in terror of rape, no less so is the way Annette acts toward
her friend's husband, alternately embracing him passionately and
then repelling his advances. There is certainly no hint on Caldwell's
part that she invites either rape or her ultimate murder, but she
displays ambivalent and confusing ways of discouraging her assailants. She is trapped in a tangle of circumstances, and yet once again
does not seem wholly innocent in her own fate, a statement that

might be made about the vast majority of Caldwell's characters from his first novel to his last one.

Stripped of all economic and social pressures, remote from any deity on whom they can foist their fatalism, Caldwell's characters at the end are no more in control of their destinies than they were at the beginning. His female characters, though now more frequently equipped with careers and some measure of fictional independence, are just as vulnerable to men's violence and mistreatment as ever; and yet as one of them says bluntly, "We need a man. And that's why there are two kinds of us—loving wives . . . and wide-legged prostitutes" (A, 5). In this last lurid novel, there is no escape from terror for women except in sex, and that only leads back again into mortal danger. There is no suggestion of hope, in the form of a change in the circumstances of the world that these characters inhabit, or of levity, in any comic or whimsical presentation of their behavior, or even of distraction or consolation, in the guise of any transcendent dream or obsession to which they can adhere. Unlike the early cyclorama novels, there is no division here between correctable social wrongs and people's incorrigible nature; Caldwell's formerly complicated vision of social conscience and private consciousness that was responsible for the grotesque nature of that early work is reduced to the more single-minded pursuit of a psychological thriller. His female characters turn out to be his ultimate victims, more even than the desperate poor or persecuted blacks, for Caldwell seems to suggest that the seeds of their own destruction are more permanently sown in their own natures than in those of the others. As early as 1934, Caldwell had written, in an introduction to *God's Little Acre*, the curious and at that time somewhat inexplicable comment "No man as yet has reached the depths to which a woman can sink"—apparently a comment on both her economic and moral degradation and their inevitable interaction.[4] From that point on, much of his fiction had charted these lower depths of women's lives, with moral outrage for their abuse and fascination with the forms of their degeneracy. Unfortunately, the range of illustrative examples tends to be narrow and repetitive. The recurrent symbol of the wronged woman who turns to variations of prostitution and deviant sexuality is required to bear a heavy burden of meaning for its limited depth, especially since Caldwell

4. Erskine Caldwell, Introduction to *God's Little Acre* (1933; rpr. New York, 1934), ix.

is not an expert in nuances of psychological conduct. The castrating abortionist Mrs. Boxx, in the 1930 novel *Poor Fool*, is a more vital character, despite her incredibility, than the neurotic and wealthy Maureen in *The Last Night of Summer*, who repeats the same castration ritual thirty-three years later in a much less stylized milieu. Mrs. Boxx is loathsome, outrageous, comic, and richly allusive, whereas Maureen is merely the vicious embodiment of a complex. The lust of Sister Bessie and Ellie May in *Tobacco Road* equally transcends all the later reductivist theories about victimized nymphomaniacs. The combination of sympathy and farce in the early books about women is slowly replaced by a concerted effort to dissect and analyze them that succeeds only insofar as the later female characters become mere objects for study. Ironically, they finally seem more alien as characters than the freakish Ada Lesters and enigmatic Griseldas, who retain a spontaneity missing from the more doctrinaire analyses.

Caldwell's pessimistic and fragmentary view of women is not by any means the exclusive emphasis of the novels of his later years, for during the 1960s and early 1970s, he returned with renewed interest to one of the major social and ethical concerns of his early work—the treatment of black people and the dramatic change it was undergoing during this period. Thus, while he was writing novels about women that focused more and more exclusively on their private neuroses, he was also writing novels about blacks that once more took up public and political issues, in addition to blacks' personal relationships by both friendship and kinship with whites. Before the appearance of *Jenny by Nature* in 1961, the last novel that Caldwell had written to explore black issues, or even to give the most minimal attention to them, had been *Place Called Estherville* in 1949. In the intervening years, he had published five novels (*Episode in Palmetto, A Lamp for Nightfall, Love and Money, Gretta,* and *Claudelle Inglish*), three of which moved completely away not only from the South as a setting but also from the public world of social and political relationships. His two short story collections of the 1950s, *Gulf Coast Stories* and *Certain Women*, had equally turned aside from social to personal issues and again particularly to the concerns of women. After more than a decade of neglect of all topics related to race, his return to black characters and concerns during the 1960s was inevitably a result of his renewed interest in southern material, first indicated in *Claudelle Inglish* in 1958, and of the impact of the civil rights movement. This movement provided a public forum for new ideas and dramatic action somewhat akin for Caldwell to the ideological debate stirred by the depression of the 1930s; and though he repeatedly denied the role of social reformer for himself, his best fiction and nonfiction works were generally done in periods that were informed by profound public conflicts over national social policy. The emphasis on racial tension and injustice that had surfaced irregularly throughout Caldwell's early works became a concerted focus in the 1960s, with four novels, *Jenny by Nature* (1961), *Close to Home* (1962), *Summertime Island* (1968), and *The Weather Shelter* (1969), and two works of nonfiction, *In Search of Bisco* (1965) and *Deep South* (1968), devoted almost exclusively to those topics, and two more novels, *Miss Mamma Aimee* (1967) and *The Earnshaw Neighborhood* (1971), revealing a keen consciousness of them. Although these works continue to explore many of Caldwell's earlier racial themes, they also move on to newer concerns; however, as might be expected of Caldwell, these are frequently not congruent with the particular issues and symbols on which the actual contemporary debate was concentrating.

Caldwell's earlier depiction of the situation of blacks in the South had been marked by a penchant for the most sensational symbols of their abuse—of rapes, chain gangs, and lynchings—and also by a tendency to turn his black characters into what one critic has called "neutered paragons," devoid of all the varieties of unregenerateness that distinguish his poor whites.[5] He had shown innocent blacks trapped into dissimulation; victimized blacks forced to acquiesce in their own humiliation; blacks offered casual friendships and charity by whites, but never commitments of principle; and blacks as the objects of white lust but almost never of love. On the rare occasions when black men resisted white authority, as did Candy-Man Beechum, Clem in "Kneel to the Rising Sun," and Hardy in *Journeyman*, they were murdered or maimed; black women, doubly powerless, found their only advantage in exploiting themselves and their allure for white men, as they did in "The Picture," "Yellow Girl," and *A House in the Uplands*. Those few who spoke out, ironically sometimes in defense of white children, as in *Journeyman*, were simply ignored. When Caldwell returned to the subject of black people in the 1960s after his long break, none of these earlier symbols or attitudes was relinquished, despite the fact that many of them seemed to look back to a time of more explicit and uninhibited

---

5. Devlin, *Erskine Caldwell*, 96.

Erskine Caldwell and the Fiction of Poverty

antagonisms than those of his contemporary world. Black women are threatened with rape or are raped by white men in *Jenny by Nature* and *Summertime Island;* black men are threatened by lynch mobs or murdered by whites in *Close to Home, Summertime Island,* and *The Weather Shelter;* a black woman is burned to death in *Jenny by Nature;* and a black man is deliberately run down by a truck in *Summertime Island;* yet the black characters remain themselves uninfected by the vices they are often uniquely privy to in the whites. Caldwell appears in many ways to be working within a vision of race relations that impressed itself on him early in his life— that is, early in the twentieth century—and that he was re-creating at this time in his two nonfiction books of reminiscence, *In Search of Bisco* and *Deep South.* His simple partisanship is curious in the light of the complex mixture of sympathy, crusading zeal, contempt, and shock that his poor white subjects had elicited; but as a white Southerner he undoubtedly felt that he had considerably more latitude in ridiculing the quirks and flaws of his own ethnic group than in exposing the underside of its victims. Nevertheless, the fictional vitality of his black characters suffers a good deal from their insistent virtue.

In addition, however, to repeating his earlier range of racial themes, Caldwell added a variety of new issues and developed both his characters and his concerns in new directions. Most significant was the movement from passivity or quiet adjustment on the part of his blacks to a much more active role in attempting to design their lives and articulate their discontent. Given the pervasive determinism of Caldwell's view of people's control over their own fates, this effort has limited success for his characters, but the likelihood of success never qualifies Caldwell's endorsement of the need for change. His black characters now can claim some legal protection when they insist on fair wages, the right to live outside ghettoes, and the right to pursue careers outside domestic service. They turn from nurturing white children to a concern for raising their own families and from being the unwilling parents of mixed-blood children to becoming seekers after rightful recognition from their kin of both races. They become more obdurate, more outspoken, and more ambitious, and though they are still shown to be vulnerable to all manner of manipulation and brutality, they begin to find a few reciprocal responses in whites. Many of these are the instinctive responses of affection, loyalty, and dependency, but there are also the beginnings of stirrings of conscience and acts of principle.

Caldwell pursues his longtime fascination with mulatto women, quadroons, and high yellows, and their attraction for white men; but now darker-skinned blacks begin to assert a new sense of pride in their color and racial heritage. His former attention to illicit sexual unions between black and white now shifts to a concern with the relationships between the children of these unions and their parents, and the tragedies of divided families. Caldwell continued to suggest in public interviews that the only solution to racism in the United States was "amalgamation," with Brazil his favorite example of a society where gradations of skin color had little significance.[6] His novels still suggest that such a solution is far from imminent and is fraught with great pain for those who take the first steps, yet they show relatively little interest in the political efforts of the civil rights movement to seek improvements through legislation. This is not wholly surprising, because Caldwell's fiction had rarely set out political reform programs; but as a consequence of the diminution of any comic or grotesque vision and the prevalence of uncomplicated and conventional black characters, the main interest of the novels must now be borne by incident and plot, not usually the strongest feature of Caldwell's writing. However, since Caldwell tends in these works to assume that racial conflict emanates entirely from his own region, these novels have at least the advantage of taking him back to his native southern ground again and thus restoring much of the interest in setting, community, and local custom that was lost in the anonymous and rootless urban novels of his studies of neurotic females.

Caldwell's novel *Jenny by Nature* has so many of the features of his earlier southern comedies that its ideological issues rarely risk didacticism, as do some of the later novels on racial conflict. The familiar cast of the book has a fat, middle-aged woman of easy virtue, a boarding house of assorted misfits, a fanatical and prurient clergyman who becomes involved with a prostitute, and various representatives of the law who all place their own priorities above justice. Yet beneath this hackneyed surface comedy, there is a virtual moral allegory of integrity struggling with compromise, disruption with inertia, and principle with timeworn practice. The representative of honor is an aging, ill-educated former madam, Jenny Royster; her antagonist is also her longtime suitor and legal mentor, Judge Milo Rainey. The conflict between Jenny and the Judge over

---

6. Tharpe, "Interview with Erskine Caldwell," 65.

the right of a woman who may be black to live in Jenny's white neighborhood is not based on the personal racial loyalties of either contender, because Lawanna Neleigh, the dark-skinned woman, is unknown to Jenny when she takes her into her household, while the Judge maintains an intimate companionship with his lifelong black manservant but opposes Jenny's actions, in concert with all the main powers of their Piedmont community.

Although Jenny is good-natured and an easy touch for all the outcasts of society—witness her sheltering of Betty Woodruff, a call girl, and Veasey Goodwillie, a circus midget, in her home—this is not ultimately the symbolic meaning Caldwell attaches to the "nature" of the book's title. Early in the novel, Jenny identifies herself as "Jenny by name and Jenny by nature" (JN, 6), implying at that point a softhearted generosity and tolerance, especially where men are concerned. However, by the end, when Jenny has affirmed her decision to take a stand on principle for Lawanna's rights, she reiterates the phrase, this time suggesting that her nature, unlike the Judge's, insists on public commitment as well as private virtue. The Judge—like Caldwell's previous sympathetic but weak guardian of the law, Sheriff Jeff McCurtain in Trouble in July—is incapable of extending the bonds of private decency into public action, especially when it will mean the disruption of his comfortable and settled ways. Though he tries to make his inertia into a code of conduct—"In the private domain of our lives, we live by truth alone, Jenny. For the eyes of the world, all else is sham and deceit" (JN, 23)—the flaws in such a stance are quickly revealed. The Judge revives a troubled character who had haunted much of Caldwell's 1930s fiction—the decent, compassionate individual who perceived the ills of his society quite clearly but remained a bystander and observer of them, either from passivity, cowardice, or skepticism of improvement. Only the gang murder of Lawanna jolts Judge Rainey into the recognition that he can no longer drift with the current and try to exonerate himself by private disavowals and acts of kindness. His final vow to prosecute the murderers forms part of a tendentious conclusion to his awakening to the lessons he can learn from the disreputable Jenny.

The racial and ethical allegory of the novel is, however, for the most part concealed beneath a good deal of vulgar sexual comedy and triviality on the part of the other main white characters. When Jenny's house is burned down, her first thought is for her houseplants rather than Lawanna; and in the aftermath of this disaster, she enters into a fight with her neighbor, Clara Crockmore, over which of them will woo and win the affections of the circus midget. As the moral heroine of the novel, Jenny is crude, foolish, sentimental, and self-indulgent. She lives in a purely comic world that tends to absorb and subsume the tragedies of others, including that of the black woman, Lawanna Neleigh. As usual, Caldwell's main black character is both unsullied by comic flaws and somewhat uninteresting in her formal role as sacrificial victim to racism. Her actual ethnic roots are significantly unclear. She may have black or Indian ancestors, or perhaps neither, so that Dade Womack can comment: "Part African Negro or part American Indian—it's all the same. What difference does that kind of quibbling make, anyhow? The color is there no matter what you call it" (*JN*, 181). Lawanna faces with dignity the usual litany of assaults on black women. Though trained in business school, she is offered only positions in domestic work; though refused service in the Johnny Reb Café, the owner assures her salaciously, "I've got a big weakness for girls with your kind of color" (*JN*, 149); challenged by a white man, "You think you're too good for me," she is trapped into the dissimulating reply, "I don't know" (*JN*, 145). She assures Jenny, "I'm proud of what I am" (*JN*, 111); but despite Caldwell's insistence on her integrity as an individual apart from any racial labels, she is finally a character defined entirely by her external predicament, a nonwhite woman in a white racist town. Her death is an abstract symbol rather than a tragedy. Jenny's houseplants do indeed cause more lively concern, and the pugnacious midget, who is a dues-paying member of the Little People of the United States, comes equipped with a much livelier personality and individual history. The white comedy and the black morality play are not so completely fused in *Jenny by Nature* as to create the grotesque vision of *Tobacco Road* or *God's Little Acre*, but the novel does move closer once more to moral satire after the private emotional concerns of Caldwell's work in the 1950s, and in that sense heralds the return of more social subjects.

In his next novel, *Close to Home* (1962), Caldwell once again created a black tragedy in the midst of a white comedy, but in this novel he fuses the two more closely than in *Jenny by Nature*. He removes the sympathetic and progressive white characters entirely and concentrates on those whites who have the most intimate acquaintance with blacks, through sex and violence, and who are the carriers of the most traditional attitudes toward them. At the core of this novel is the relationship between the white Native Hunnicutt and his octoroon lover, Josene Maddox, and all the complications arising from such affairs in small southern towns. The novel is one of Caldwell's most shocking in its free mixture of crude humor and extreme horror, and one of his most disorienting in its alternations between heavy didacticism and disinterested, albeit exaggerated, naturalism in the treatment of black victims and white villains. It continually raises questions about the nature of Caldwell's irony because of the ambiguous attitudes he displays and evokes toward his characters, attitudes that never resolve themselves into a clear authorial point of view. It is in this novel that he introduces, for the first time, a variety of authorial voices that enter the text and elaborate or comment on the action. This might have served as a kind of editorial device to emphasize a larger vision of all the disparate elements in a small-town conflict, but Caldwell uses it randomly and rather casually, sometimes to expand on a character's opinions, sometimes to insert a more omniscient point of view. The result is not a more comprehensive perspective for the reader, but rather some discomforting narrative inconsistencies.

Certainly, the chief enigma in this seemingly raw mixture of formulaic farce and brutal suffering is Caldwell's central character, the white Native Hunnicutt. Native is a quintessentially comic type, a happy-go-lucky, lazy tinkerer who is as casual about exacting obligations from others as he is about performing his own. His lifelong good fortune manifests itself in everything from his success in pitching pennies at a crack in the post-office floor to winning a double lot in the church cemetery in a raffle. Native's achievements and obsessions are on an equally modest comic scale; he is an ace on the tavern pinball machine, "Beach Girls at Play," and his greatest pleasures are possum hunting and sweet potato pie. Native's motto, "Being satisfied is the best part of living" (*CH*, 202), is a manifestation of his easy nature, low horizons, and inert resistance to change. He has a long-standing affair with the light-skinned Josene, and fate appears to crown his fortunes by offering him, in addition, the chance to marry a wealthy white widow. However, Native's luck turns at this point, for his new wife, Maebelle, although willing to play second fiddle to possum and pie, will not tolerate a nonwhite rival. Thus the classic material of a bedroom comedy suddenly becomes a threat to an entire community's way of life when Maebelle insists that its miscegenation laws be enforced against Native and Josene. When Josene suggests that they go away together and live publicly elsewhere as man and wife, Caldwell now has the affable and trivial Native in a dilemma of some significance. Native, like almost every other white male in the town of Palmyra, cannot see any reason why such comfortable illicit relationships between white men and black women should not continue as they have always done, and he becomes a symbol of this cause. However, to pursue Josene's proposal would necessitate a disruption in his life, and so he rejects it and leaves her to make a new life alone elsewhere. Native thus is a defender both of miscegenation and the status quo, whereas Caldwell wishes to defend "amalgamation" as a natural act, condemn the status quo as intolerable for blacks, and preserve Native as a source of genial humor.

Caldwell puts into the mouths of Native and the other white men arguments that seem very close indeed to what he himself contended repeatedly, both in personal interviews and in the larger import of much of his fiction: "There's nothing much you can say against a white man mixing with a Negro girl. . . . [I]t seems like a natural thing for a white man to do. That's why you can't say it's right or wrong" (CH, 44–45). However, his rather tolerant humor toward the "race-mixing" sexual misbehavior of the good ole boys of Palmyra and his ridicule of the offended white women induce or reflect a certain amused attitude toward the old ways, which he elsewhere undermines completely by exposing to the reader the tragic black side of this traditional white comedy. From this other perspective, Native Hunnicutt is not only cowardly and irresponsible, but his luck is obtained at the expense of a black suitor of Josene's who is murdered and castrated in an incident as random and casual as Native's success in the lottery. Caldwell's satire on white male self-indulgence and double-talk gets confused in this novel with his satire on prudery, repression, and the artificial separation of the races, partly because in the world of Palmyra, racial amalgamation can only mean the exploitation of black women by white men or, at best, some willing but clandestine relationships between the two groups.

For the black characters in the novel, Caldwell allows neither comic immunity from harm nor any comfortable compromises. Josene, who has all the strength of character lacking in Native, sees her predicament lucidly and takes active steps to combat it. Realizing she cannot depend on Native for a home for herself and her daughter, she determines to marry a black man; when he is killed, she plans to begin a new life elsewhere. All of the black characters in the novel form a chorus of protest to the more insignificant masquerade of the whites' activities. Josene's great-grandmother pleads, "When I'm dead and put in the ground, I want all you folks to get happy and stomp your feet, because that's when I'll have all my misery left behind me up here on the top side of the ground" (*CH*, 143). A black prisoner sings a "sorrowful work camp ballad": "I've looked for the good and got the bad. . . . That's all us black folks ever had." (*CH*, 92). The white response to this suffering is to request that the singing be stopped because "it sounds too mournful" (*CH*, 93) or, in a burst of revulsion at the atrocities performed on the innocent black man, Harvey Brown, to work up an objection to the methods used on him, though not the intent behind them: "Nobody can go around these days butchering a Negro boy like that one was last night and not suffer for it. I don't believe in things like that. Shoot him if you have to, but let it go at that" (*CH*, 146). In fact, vigilante revenge is ultimately done in the novel on the perpetrator of the crime, and the white population consoles itself that "that's the best way for it to be, anyhow" (*CH*, 200). Thus they assuage their consciences by a measure as temporary and futile as the silencing of the mournful black song.

The black characters curiously display neither resentment nor antagonism toward the whites, despite the fact that Caldwell allows them to show a new degree of racial pride in this novel. Like Lawanna in *Jenny by Nature*, Josene asserts that she is just as good as Native's white wife, and Harvey attempts to stand up for his rights to the white deputy who kills him. Such restraint is consistent with Caldwell's blameless victims; but in this novel, such virtual neutrality in what might otherwise be a war is shown to stem from the ambivalent situation of these small-town blacks, many of whom are of mixed racial ancestry and bear striking physical resemblances to the town's white families. Josene herself is a prime example: a light-skinned octoroon, she is the daughter of one of Palmyra's leading lawyers who is so embarrassed by her obvious similarity to him that he bribes her to leave town to avoid scandal in an upcoming election. Josene's response, for all the betrayal this demonstrates, is pride in having so successful a father and confidence in the beneficial effects on her daughter of such ancestry. This child, who seems likely to be Native's, is, like her mother, about to grow up unacknowledged by her white father. Despite Caldwell's endorsement of amalgamation as the solution to racial conflict, he indicates not only the emotional pain for the products of "amalgamation" in their neglect by their fathers, but also the loss for these fathers of any normal bond of affection with their unrecognized children. Josene's white father, Dalton Burrows, must force himself not to comfort her or speak kindly to her; Miller Hyatt, a white lawyer, is depressed every time he sees his tan-skinned son because he does not even know the boy's name; and even Native is preoccupied with wondering if he is the father of Josene's child, but is afraid to ask for the truth.

Caldwell's indictment of passive whites who are uncomfortable with the consequences of racism, either in their unacknowledged lovers and children or in violent brutality and economic exploitation, is in many ways a more effective protest than his villainous portraits of the pathological white racists who perpetrate the most sensational atrocities. Caldwell is often willing to explain, though never to justify, the actions of these extreme racists by depicting their intellectual and social inferiority, their lack of education, and their resentment of more obviously competent blacks. What he contemplates with bewilderment and no effort at explanation is the inertia of whites whose consciences are troubled, who are personally fairly benevolent, and who dissociate themselves utterly from the horrors and excesses that are performed by others. This covert acquiescence is always depicted by Caldwell as one of the most sinister aspects of social misconduct. In *Close to Home*, the castrating and murderous Clyde Hefflin is a monstrous and incredible character in the excesses of his vicious racism. He randomly punches and even kills blacks in the course of the arrests he makes as sheriff's deputy and regularly rapes black women in the jail. However, the blatant exaggerations of Clyde's character serve as a measure of the tolerance of more normal whites in the novel of such evil; it is their collaboration, no matter how critical and uneasy, that permits his behavior.

Caldwell's novel *Summertime Island* (1968) takes up this theme again with yet another larger-than-life white racist, Troy Pickett. Unlike those passive whites who may profit from racism but are troubled by it, and unlike the exploitive whites who deliberately engineer prejudice and segregation so they can reap financial rewards, Troy, like Clyde, is animated purely by a burning hatred of black people. He is a lower-class, almost wholly uneducated man whose main pleasure in life derives from the exertion of power over those who have no authority to protect them. Because Troy has no political or business connections to manipulate, the power he enjoys is brute physical sadism, escalating from kicks and punches to raping a girl and deliberately running a man down with his truck. This novel examines once again the reactions of more moderate and ordinary whites to the extraordinarily repulsive conduct of one of their kind. Troy is a grotesque caricature of the attitudes that all normal people self-righteously disavow. In the novel, he goes on a fishing trip with a middle-aged, tolerant white man, his adolescent nephew whom the older man is trying to educate in similar ways, and a young black schoolteacher. When Troy arbitrarily leaves this group at a picnic lunch to rush into a neighboring field and seize a young black girl, the situation clearly defies credulity as a piece of realistic fiction. Even more amazing is Troy's rape of this girl while a dozen black women stand around wailing at his actions, while on the other side of the saplings that separate them, the two white men and the black schoolteacher listen "helplessly" (*SI*, 159) to what is taking place. Such an episode is feasible only if it is read allegorically (despite Caldwell's assertion that there was "not a bit" of symbolism in his books) as a reflection of both black and white passivity in the face of obvious wrongdoing.[7] Troy is unarmed and the black women have hoes, but their only actions are begging, wailing, and chanting. The three men stand sweating in the sun as they eavesdrop, yet the uncle asks unhappily, "What can anybody do?" (*SI*, 159), while the black man fears the consequences of intervening and incurring Troy's wrath, something he has clearly done already merely by being black. Later, Troy runs him down with his truck, breaking both his legs and some of his ribs, so his inaction does not in fact purchase him any immunity.

Although *Summertime Island* is didactic in its treatment of racism and inaction, the novel evokes Mark Twain's America more than any topical situation. As late as 1982, Caldwell remarked in an interview that he was still unfamiliar with Twain and looked forward someday to reading *Huckleberry Finn*, for he had heard so much about it.[8] In fact, this novel, for all its lack of comedy, comes very close indeed to the central concerns and themes of Twain's novel. Narrated by a passive but observant adolescent boy, *Summertime Island* deals with a friendship between a white youth and a slightly older black man, which flourishes briefly on the Mississippi River but is recognized by both of them as an idyllic interlude away from the society in which they lead their normal lives. The symbolic sug-

7. Broadwell and Hoag, "The Art of Fiction LXII," 134.
8. *Ibid.*, 154.

gestions are identical to Twain's. On the river, artificial distinctions between people wither and a more natural order of precedence based on skill is established; back in society, even the few hundred yards from the island to the shore, youth and poverty, skin color and sex again become the basis of prejudice and abuse. The party that goes to fish on Summertime Island, which is in "Tennessee, Kentucky or Missouri" (*SI*, 6), consists of the boy narrator, Steve; his uncle Guthry; Troy Pickett, who is necessary only for the use of his truck; and Duke Hopkins, the "colored fellow to help out around the camp" (*SI*, 8), brought at the insistence of Troy. Troy mistreats Duke, with Guthry's uncomfortable assent and Steve's silence, all the way to the Mississippi River. Troy rails in outrage, like Huck Finn's Pap, when he discovers evidence of the black man's superior learning: "An educated nigger! Now ain't that something! You stand still and don't move so I can get a good look at you" (*SI*, 29). However, as soon as the mainland is left behind, Troy is forced by his selfishness and ineptitude to rely more and more on Duke. Duke rows him, semiconscious, across treacherous river currents, and Duke saves his life when their boat capsizes. Duke eventually defends himself against Troy's aggression on the island and uses the opportunity to force from Troy a symbolic concession of equality. As long as they are on Summertime Island, Duke will no longer call Troy "Mr." but will be on a first-name basis with him. Between Duke and the boy Steve a steady companionship grows on the island. Like Huck and Jim, they swim naked together in the river, life is "easy and natural" (*SI*, 154), and the boy learns a great deal from the man. Like Huck and Jim, too, their river isolation is constantly invaded, not just by the presence of Guthry and Troy, but by the arrival of another fishing group that has brought along a tantalizing young woman. For Caldwell's boy narrator, the sexual initiation that this Bonnie brings is, not surprisingly, a great deal more explicit and physical than Huck's awakening to the charms of Mary Jane; but it brings a similar sense of complication to the simple codes of the male world. At the end of the novel, Duke, like Jim, is injured, not as the result of the thoughtless child's play of a Tom Sawyer, but by Troy Pickett's vindictiveness. However, as with Jim, there will be some reward for the suffering, in that Guthry determines that the next trip to the island will exclude Troy altogether.

One very significant difference between Caldwell's river novel and Twain's is that, although Caldwell acquires the moral serious-

ness of *The Adventures of Huckleberry Finn*, he sacrifices almost all
of his humor. That he seems aware of this loss is hinted in an anecdote told by Guthry late at night to the fishermen. Guthry's tale is
a sad and unresolved one of a farmer's wife who attempts to run
away from her suffering and is finally dragged back to it. Apart from
the suggested parallel between the woman in the tale and the black
man in the novel, Caldwell has the repellant Troy object to the story
because it is neither salacious nor funny, but serious. However,
Caldwell had managed the combination of all three successfully in
the past, and this device does not compensate for the heavy didacticism of the novel, which might elsewhere have been qualified and
complicated by Caldwell's comic eye for the incongruous and irrational in people's behavior. However, Duke, unlike Twain's Jim, is
never foolish or less than noble; Troy, unlike Huck's Pap, draws
more vituperation than satire. Caldwell is able to justify the extreme
characterizations and the simplicity of the depiction of racism partly
by setting the novel some distance in the past, in an ambiguous time
of unpaved roads and ankle-length dresses for women, when trucks
are relatively rare and white men could go unprosecuted and even
unreported for the rape and maiming of blacks. Although this perhaps vindicates the extremism of the novel, it evades political, legal,
and social questions about the situation of blacks in Caldwell's contemporary world. The same might be said of Twain's novel, written
about slavery long after its end, but there the subtlety of the characters and the humor supplement the simple moral framework. In
Caldwell's novel, unlike Twain's, one has the feeling that anyone
failing to find a moral in the book might well incur the fatal displea-
sure of the author, for he has worked to eliminate almost any other
response to it.

In the year following *Summertime Island*, 1969, Caldwell published *The Weather Shelter*, a novel focusing exclusively on miscegenation and its consequences for the new family groups that result
from it. Like *Summertime Island*, it is almost wholly devoid of humor, and what there is involves lower-class whites but never blacks.
Unlike the previous novel, however, there is no intervention between the reader and the serious nature of the subject by an impas-
sive adolescent narrator and thence no irony or distancing from the
main point. *The Weather Shelter* distills almost everything Caldwell
has to say on racial amalgamation, but whereas he had previously
intended to endorse the practice broadly while revealing the tragic
results in particular situations, in this novel he tries to provide not

only more precise justification for his endorsement, but also evidence of new attitudes that are gaining strength, albeit slowly, toward marriage and family relationships between the races.

The novel is set on the Tennessee pony-breeding farm of Grover Danford, the only livestock farm of its kind amid the surrounding dairy land and a model of an intelligent and well-operated business. Although the farm has traditionally bred Shetland ponies, Grover and his chief stableman have agreed that now "it's time to introduce some strong new bloodlines and improve the breed of Danford ponies," because they "don't want to live to see Danford ponies get inbred and peter out to nothing but common third-rate scrub stock" (WS, 35–36). This notion that crossbreeding injects vitality into a decadent line was, of course, first explicitly stated in Caldwell's *A Lamp for Nightfall*, written in the early 1930s, when the lines to be mixed were French Canadian and Maine Yankee, and pursued further in the portrait of southern white inbreeding in *Miss Mamma Aimee* (1967). It is implicit in all Caldwell's depictions of mixed blood people as handsome, intelligent, and morally upright, from Hardy in *Journeyman* to Ganus and Kathy Bazemore in *Place Called Estherville*, Lawanna Neleigh in *Jenny by Nature*, Josene Maddox in *Close to Home*, and Duke Hopkins in *Summertime Island*. In *The Weather Shelter*, the animal breeding analogy is applied specifically to the affair Grover Danford has had in his young manhood with the mulatto woman Kathlee, and to the light-skinned son of that union, Jeff. Because Grover's current white wife in the novel proves to be a shrewish and recalcitrant lesbian, Jeff is not only the inheritor of the best qualities of his black mother and white father, but clearly the only son Grover will ever have to carry on the family business. This motif of the solitary mixed-race child at the end of a white family line is common enough in the novels of Faulkner and Stribling, but is distinguished in Caldwell by the zeal with which he advocates and approves the begetting of such children.

However, Caldwell explores in this novel the burden that such children of mixed race bear both in their rejection by their white families and white society and in their resentment and denial by dark-skinned blacks, who are beginning to develop a militant pride in their own race. When Jeff is a boy, black children sing taunting rhymes at him on the street:

> I have a little brother
> With shiny brownish hair.

My mama says she got him
Out behind the county fair. (WS, 31)

When he is an adolescent, his black grandfather refuses to take him
in: "I don't want nobody in this town seeing a white-nigger hanging
around my house. I'm a black man and I stay proud of it" (WS, 152).
When Jeff drives around with his white father, they are challenged
for sitting together in the front seat of the car and can find no restaurant to serve food to them jointly. Thus Jeff, for whatever advantages he gains in his breeding, is condemned to loneliness and os-
tracism. He is also exposed to a much greater danger when a white
woman forces herself on him and bears his child, for her infertile
husband rounds up a lynch mob to go after Jeff. The theme is reiterated in this relationship that only crossbreeding will produce a
continuation of the white line, but the resulting baby will surely
suffer for it in a still largely benighted society.

The community in *The Weather Shelter* remains far from progressive, but Caldwell appears to hold out more hope for change in
this novel than in any other—in individuals if not yet in the attitudes of the larger group. Grover Danford himself is willing to abandon his beloved farm in order to go away with Kathlee to a place
where their marriage will be permitted, and is prevented only by
her sudden death. He rescues his son from the lynch mob many
years later and tastes the pleasure of feeling the boy's arms around
his neck—the commonest of caresses denied to so many of Caldwell's white men. In the end, he is determined to raise Jeff openly
as his son and prepare him to inherit the family estate. This is certainly not a political triumph for the large black and mixed-race population of the novel that inhabits the run-down neighborhoods and
performs the menial work of the small town that the Danford estate
overlooks. Grover's motives, like those of most Caldwell characters
outside the novels of the 1930s, are wholly personal. His concern is
for *his* lover, *his* son, and *his* family business, but he at least goes
through the awakening of experiencing for himself the cruelty of the
laws and customs that distinguish between black and white.

At least as significant as Grover's awakening is the change in attitude that occurs in his head stableman, Jim Whittaker, a decent
and kindly man who, nevertheless, has what he calls "white man's
principles" (WS, 34). He initially resists Grover's request that Jeff
be trained and taught the business, fearing that he may ultimately
be replaced in his job. By the end of the novel, Jim has not only

aided in Jeff's escape from the lynchers, but he also encourages Grover to bring him back to the farm when the threat is gone and supports Grover's newly acknowledged relationship with the boy and his intention to leave him the farm. Even the violent racist group in this novel is small and eccentric, though significantly accompanied by a minister of the Unity Brotherhood Church. They are inept villains, drinking and quarreling with each other, too stupid to track down their victim, and in the end killing one of their own instead. Nevertheless, *The Weather Shelter* does not suggest that the community at large has had any change of heart over the inequities and evils of segregation and bigotry. The Tupelo police harass Grover on the suspicion that he is a civil rights activist; black children on the street take aim at his car with imaginary rifles; his lawyer's response to his inquiry about marrying Kathlee is "You damn fool! You Yankee! You foreigner! You Communist!" (*WS*, 75).

Even Grover, though capable of transcending or ignoring race when it is a matter of his lover or his child, demonstrates some profound prejudice in his fears for Kathlee: "His only worry . . . was that she would be raped by a white man and now he was even more upset and worried knowing that a Negro man wanted her" (*WS*, 62). That Grover is driven to increasingly radical action in favor of his son is as much a result of his wife Madge's cruelty and sexual rejection as of his goodwill toward the boy. Thus this vicious wife, as much as or more than any noble principle, proves to be the agent of solidarity between the white man and his black son, and the seemingly triumphant moral drama of the book emerges in fact from painful sexual conflicts as well as instinctive paternal affection. The book forms a companion piece of a kind to *Close to Home*, which culminated in the breakup of a similar interracial family and the return of the white husband to his sexually unappealing wife; but the difference between Grover Danford and Native Hunnicutt is not one of social and political ideals of equity and justice, but of Grover's greater depth of feeling and the accompanying energy to break new ground. Thus Caldwell seems to suggest that though the instinct for racial amalgamation is a strong and enduring one, its fortunate outcome in the advent of legal marriages, improved family relationships, and a consequent sharing of wealth and property between black and white depends on the accident of character and fortuitous circumstances (such as a lesbian wife or a craving for sweet potato pie) as much as it does on the achievement of major social reforms. Though the civil rights movement, with its appeal to legal and political action, is briefly indicated in the background of the novel, Caldwell goes his own private fictional way in the handling of racism, much as he had done several decades earlier in the treatment of poverty in the shadow of an equally powerful public debate on communism and class revolution.

Only in the two late comic novels, *Miss Mamma Aimee* (1967) and *The Earnshaw Neighborhood* (1971)—both books in which blacks play lively but minor roles—are the real political, legal, and social changes of this era acknowledged. In *Miss Mamma Aimee*, Caldwell reports the rape of a black child by Graham Mangrum ten years previously, which had gone unprosecuted but could no longer do so because "times have changed too much" (*MMA*, 5); Gene Infinger, a garage owner, complains that the government forces him to pay a black employee the same minimum wage as a white; and the Mangrums' black maid, Martha Washington, quotes Martin Luther King in defense of her claims for better treatment. The recognition of these changes, and the comic method of the novels, allow for something of a transformation in the black characters, permitting them to be more assertive and outspoken in criticism of their white employers. When accused of removing a piece of furniture, Martha Washington replies, "I don't get paid much for cooking and nothing at all for taking blame" (*MMA*, 23), and later she quits the Mangrums to work for some "yankee Jews" who offer her better conditions. When questioned about her loyalty to the "good families" of the South, she says, "I don't care who it is who pays me right and makes it a better job" (*MMA*, 127). Similarly, the black maid Zerena White in *The Earnshaw Neighborhood* finally rejects a distinction that had been rigidly adhered to and used symbolically throughout Caldwell's work, insisting that her employer call her "Mrs. White" (*EN*, 8). She refuses to let her daughter model before a group that is not integrated and attacks her daughter's attempted white seducer with a breadboard. There is talk in this novel, too, of Martin Luther King, George Wallace, and school integration, although these are all tangential to the main concerns of the white characters of this book, who are certainly among Caldwell's most vacuous and dissolute. In neither of these novels do the black women have any sexual liaison with white men in the households, so there is no disguised motive or dissimulation in their newfound boldness. Both Martha and Zerena have a touch of sharpness in their characters, but this is as far as Caldwell goes in moving these black women from their habitual virtuous martyrdom; otherwise, their integrity and sense of purpose continue to contrast with the aimless degeneracy of the whites. Against the background of the civil rights movement, Caldwell continued to develop a vision of blacks that he had first articulated in the early thirties when he wrote, "The Negro has yet to sink as low, economically and morally, as the white man. . . . I doubt very much if the Negro will ever fall to the lowest depths of the white race."[9] Although it is unfair to hold all of Caldwell's later work hostage to this remark, it certainly suggests severe qualifications on any naturalistic presentation of blacks and, consequently, given Caldwell's strong deterministic bent, the narrow limits of their viability as characters. The newly awakened public concerns with race, prejudice, and inequity in the 1960s, though rarely made explicit in his fiction, permitted Caldwell to explore his private and perhaps eccentric vision in the context of this larger arena of ideas. Thus, despite the constrictions of wholesomeness and good sense on his blacks, there was in the works of this decade a rejuvenation of purpose and moral concern in contrast to the abject fatalism of many of the other novels that followed his southern cyclorama.

Throughout his fictional career, Caldwell's success with his narrow and exaggerated vision of people's "antics and motivations" depended to a considerable extent on the currency of a larger, more varied, and empirical public debate on the moral questions at the heart of his novels. Though his characters seem to dwell on the distant periphery of the social and political movements of their time, and certainly do not choose the terms of their own conflicts, nevertheless the connection between their fictional terms and the actual historical ones is vital if Caldwell's work is not to be read as mere sensationalism. This connection is most apparent in the novels of the thirties and, to a lesser extent, the sixties; it is least so in the novels about private female neuroses in the fifties, although eventually the women's movement and changing sexual attitudes might have provided a wider public arena for this debate as well. Without the connection, Caldwell's paradoxical vision of human affairs, which had so provoked and puzzled his early readers, dissipated into its rather banal elements. Instead of the tension between the incorrigible and the remediable aspects of the world, Caldwell offered, in separate strands, grim fatalism, antic foolishness, and heavy didacticism. Despite his early studies in the social sciences,

9. Caldwell, Introduction to *God's Little Acre*, viii-ix.

Caldwell was neither an astute psychologist, economist, nor sociologist in his fiction. He needed the ongoing dialogue between his fabrications and social reality more than such naturalists as Steinbeck and Dos Passos because, unlike them, he rarely attempted to incorporate broader documentary material into his novels. He refused the mantle of social reformer in order to probe the more primitive and irrational areas of human conduct, but his fiction profited greatly from its relationship to social and political activism and debate. His best talents lay in creating grotesque and self-contained worlds that had enough divergences from recognizable reality to preempt their reading as simple moral allegories, or worse, misguided failures in social realism, and enough correspondences to it to keep them provocatively linked to the central social and ethical concerns of his time.

# 6

# Caldwell's Nonfiction

*Journalism had given me my first schooling in writing and it never failed to renew my spirits.*

—*Erskine Caldwell*

*This is the best thing in Caldwell's reportage: the struggle of his fellow feeling against his ideology.*

—*William Stott*

Although Caldwell's literary reputation rests almost exclusively on his fiction, he was also the author of a large number of nonfiction works, some of which helped to establish a new genre of American documentary writing in the 1930s. Not only are his nonfiction works a significant and original contribution to that mode, but they also reveal a great deal about the choices Caldwell was making in his fiction writing and the extent to which those choices were consciously determined by different artistic and ideological purposes. Like many other American fiction writers both before and after him, Caldwell began his literary career in the newspaper business, though with no intention of pursuing journalism beyond its immediate pragmatic value to him as a source of income and an apprenticeship to one kind of professional writing. From a high school summer job turning the handpress of the local Jefferson *Reporter*, he progressed gradually to writing baseball columns as a string correspondent for the Augusta *Chronicle*. Later, having gleaned what was useful to him from his English and sociology courses at the University of Virginia, he went on to write obituaries and local news for the Atlanta *Journal*, now as a full-time reporter. At the *Journal* he learned to eliminate verbosity and cultivate detachment. When he attempted to write a lengthy and empathetic account of a suicide that he was sent to cover, Hunter Bell, the city editor, threw it into the wastebasket and told him harshly, "When I want a sob story, I'll send Peggy Mitchell" (*CE*, 40). He learned from Margaret Mitchell of the trust in one's writing required to give up a steady job for the risky life of a fiction writer, and after a year at the *Journal*, he abandoned newspaper work in order to devote himself full-time to stories and novels. Although journalism clearly was for Caldwell a deliberately used stepping-stone to a career in fiction, it provided an immediacy of contact with the raw material of his imagination, and he found himself returning to reportorial and nonfiction writing at regular intervals throughout his career as a way of vindicating his own remembered sense of reality and of refreshing his spirits with a change of mode (*CE*, 163, 161–62). Eleven books resulted from these excursions out of fiction: *Some American People* (1935); *You Have Seen Their Faces*, with Margaret Bourke-White (1937); *North of the Danube*, with Bourke-White (1939); *Say, Is This the U.S.A.*, with Bourke-White (1941); *Russia at War*, with Bourke-White (1942); *All-Out on the Road to Smolensk* (1942); *Moscow Under Fire* (1942); *Around About America* (1964); *In Search of Bisco* (1965); *Deep South* (1968); and *Afternoons in Mid-America* (1976). The interest and vitality of these books varies markedly, the best tending to coincide with the best of Caldwell's fiction in the 1930s and again in the 1960s, when he was most ideologically, as well as artistically, engaged with his material. However, almost all of them give valuable insights into the vision of human nature and the techniques that inform his fiction and, as well, display a style of documentary reporting that is unique, highly innovative, and of considerable literary interest in its own right.

Caldwell's first book of nonfiction, *Some American People*, was the fruit of a six-week cross-country tour from California to Maine that he took in the late summer of 1934, and of a trip to Georgia that same year to gather material for his pamphlet *Tenant Farmer*, which was then included in the larger book. It was published in the heart of the Great Depression, relatively early in a decade that would later produce the great flowering of the documentary genre in literature, photograph, and film. Caldwell's account of his highly personal journey through the agricultural and industrial states of mid-America, with a long incursion into his native South, appeared in the same year as Sherwood Anderson's journalistic picaresque book *Puzzled America*, with which it has many affinities. Not least of these are the simple and colloquial prose style, the easy empathy for ordinary people, and the sense that the South epitomizes the most startling and extreme section of a devastated nation. There are striking similarities of interest, too, to Anderson's 1932 nonfiction account of a tour of southern cotton mills, *Perhaps Women*, in Caldwell's fascination with the machines of an industrialized society and their impact on the workers whose lives are given over to attending their functions. Though Caldwell often acknowledged an admiration for Anderson, this similarity seems as much a coincidence of interests and sympathies as it is a matter of influence, much as many other writers were to display in the reiterated element of national discovery in their documentary journeys. After Anderson's *Puzzled America* and Caldwell's *Some American People* came James Rorty's *Where Life Is Better: An Unsentimental American Journey* (1936), Nathan Asch's *The Road: In Search of America* (1937), Louis Adamic's *My America* (1938), Archibald MacLeish's *Land of the Free* (1938), and Paul Taylor and Dorothea Lange's *An American Exodus* (1939).

Like Anderson and Caldwell, many other writers, best known for their fiction, turned to reportorial and documentary meditations on their country—among them Steinbeck, Hemingway, Dreiser, Lewis, and Dos Passos. Such a large-scale movement in the thirties, from the more studied art of fiction to the immediacy of journalism, has been variously explained by scholars of the period. One theory has suggested that writers were rejecting the seeming frivolity of the imagined world in light of the horrors of the real one; another, that the movement was a consequence of the failure of the traditional news and communications organs to provide adequate information about the national crisis. Still another has argued that this turn to journalism and documentaries was an admission on the part of many leftward-leaning artists and intellectuals that no form of imaginative art could make sense of the collapsing and bewildering world they saw around them.[1] In Caldwell's case, there is a measure of truth in all these explanations. By 1935, he had already achieved remarkable success with *Tobacco Road* and *God's Little Acre*, but the novels had been criticized as distortions of the real conditions of poverty in the nation and also as inappropriately didactic in their intrusion of sociological commentary and economic proposals into the fictional text. By turning to nonfiction, Caldwell could vindicate the accuracy of his social vision, take a stand on issues that were necessarily ambivalent or subordinate in his fiction, and extend his

1. Daniel Aaron, *Writers on the Left: Episodes in American Literary Communism* (New York, 1961), 393; William Stott, *Documentary Expression and Thirties America* (New York, 1973), 67–73; Richard H. Pells, *Radical Visions and American Dreams: Culture and Social Thought in the Depression Years* (New York, 1973), 195.

own contact with the current state of his fellow citizens. He could justify his fiction, but he could also discover many aspects of American life that were new and fascinating to him; and throughout his life, from his earliest days of wandering to his latest celebrity journeys, Caldwell proved an avid and curious traveler.

In the preface to *Some American People*, Caldwell gave one of the most important clues to his attitude toward his reporting, namely, that it might alter him as much as and more than he might affect the world he reported on: "There is nothing to be gained in travel," he wrote, "if the traveler is not prepared to accept, or capable of experiencing, a change of habits, thought, and diet" (*SAP*, 5). He was intrigued by people and their oddities and vagaries of habit and conduct, but wary of any intrusion into their private worlds. When Margaret Bourke-White went south with him in 1936 to gather material for *You Have Seen Their Faces*, she acknowledged that Caldwell introduced her to "a whole new way of working. He had a very quiet, completely receptive approach. . . . He would wait patiently until the subject had revealed his personality, rather than impose his own personality on the subject." She recalled that he spoke severely to her on one occasion when she had rearranged the possessions of a black woman's cabin she wished to photograph. Caldwell observed to Bourke-White: "How neat her bureau had been. How she must have valued all her little possessions and how she had them tidily arranged *her* way, which was not my way. This was a new point of view to me. I felt I had done violence." This respect for the paltry possessions of poor people never became in Caldwell's hands an attempt, like that of James Agee in *Let Us Now Praise Famous Men*, to imbue them with a reverential quality. He was too aware of their foolishness and absurdity as well as their individual integrity to do that; but he was aware, like Agee, that the lives of the poor and ordinary people he observed had an intrinsic interest and value apart from any social, political, or economic theory for which they might serve as convincing evidence. One critic found what he called this "struggle of his fellow feeling against his ideology" to be the best thing about Caldwell's reportage, a tribute to genuine curiosity in the midst of keen partisanship.[2] Caldwell's nonfiction is in that sense like his fiction, ever open to the possibilities of individual eccentricity and

2. Bourke-White, *Portrait of Myself*, 125–27; Stott, *Documentary Expression*, 243.

social incongruity, and ready to embody them in structured anecdotes and powerful images. Yet Caldwell's nonfiction, for all the imaginative techniques he uses in it, is distinctly different from his fiction in the kind of latitude he permitted himself, as author, to shake off the naïve, unfeeling detachment of his fictional persona and to become instead authoritative, informed, sympathetic, and sophisticated. Because he guarded this personality even in his interviews and autobiographical writings, the nonfiction works offer an interesting and complementary view to that (perhaps cultivated) ingenuousness.

The subject matter of *Some American People*—western and midwestern farmers, the Ford assembly lines in Detroit, and southern tenant farmers—took Caldwell back into contact with the deepest sources of his imagination and sympathy, the lives of poor people. It permitted him to verify for himself and a skeptical public the extremities of degradation and the ironies of public policy that might be uncovered anywhere in depression America, and to make constructive suggestions about improving conditions without being accused of tendentiousness or disguised propaganda. The method of the book is perfectly in accord with his account in *Writing in America* of the main intellectual interest of his literary life, that is, pondering and recording the "antics and motivations" of human behavior. In *Some American People*, however, the comedy and the naturalism are largely separated and taken out of conflict in contrast to his fiction. On the western and midwestern portions of his journey, Caldwell meets a variety of people who are recorded in amusing personal anecdotes. Although most are victims of the Great Depression or of Dust Bowl storms, they are not presented as scientifically determined products of their environment but as quaint and quirky individuals. By contrast, in the sections on the Detroit automobile plants and the southern farms, there is neither comedy nor individualism, but a somber and angry exposé of conditions that virtually deprive people of any human capacity to be their eccentric selves. The greater the poverty and exploitation, the further Caldwell moves from his comic vision, a situation directly contrary to the novels, where his imagination yokes and fuses the two. *Some American People* thus sacrifices the complexity of the fiction but makes a clearer ideological point: what is most appealing and sympathetic in human nature is also what is most directly threatened by material deprivation.

The most innovative reportorial techniques occur in the "Cross-

Country" section of *Some American People*, which describes Caldwell's encounters traveling eastward from Washington and Oregon
to Maine. One sketch, "The Barber of the Northwest," is a good
introductory sample of what is typical and best in his early documentary writing. The narrator is in Bismarck, North Dakota, watching a baseball game between the local team and some visiting,
bearded House of David players when a Northern Pacific freight
train disgorges a group of tramps onto the embankment above the
ball park. One of them, after registering the score and the bewhisk-
ered players, begins to unpack a rather elaborate set of shaving
equipment. He is a freight train barber who recounts his story
against the chorus of advancing scores from the ball game. For a
nickel or a dime, any tramp between "the Lakes and the Rockies"
(*SAP*, 41) can have an in-transit shave or haircut by a graduate of
the Kansas City Barber College who has abandoned wife and children in favor of the traveling life. The sketch combines many of
Caldwell's most effective techniques: the laconic humor of the narrator; the absurdity of the tramp laying out an orderly collection
of pearl-handled razors and whetstones on a railway embankment;
the choral effect of the baseball game in the background as the lather
is mixed and the instruments sharpened; the imagist emphasis on
the bearded (and winning) House of David players, while the barber finds no takers for his business; the mixture of whimsy and cruelty in Flynn, the barber, that leads him to speak flippantly of the
family he abandoned; and, underlying all, the evidence of the depression that has helped drive him from his usual business into this
ever-burgeoning nomadic world. Flynn has a trick of concluding
each of his remarks with a challenging "O.K.?"; the tale ends on
the same word, dangling ironically at the end of a sketch of this mixture of normalcy and ominous hints of disruption in contemporary
America.

If there is a thesis in this first part of *Some American People*, it
is clouded and modified by the variety of topics, characters, and
approaches in Caldwell's repertory. He ranges from extravagant
tall tales of delusion in the Badlands to tragicomic accounts of paupers picking the Omaha dump and complacent Iowa farmers who
subscribe to the *New Yorker* and educate their children at Harvard. The narrative voice shows a comparable range. At times,
Caldwell is the impersonal researcher, master of facts and figures:
"Ranchers who had been buying hay at eighteen dollars a ton had
reached the end of their rope; banks had long since stopped lending

money to feed stock on a declining market; and the Federal Government had laid down a policy of not making feed loans on anything except breeding stock" (*SAP*, 32–33). At times, he depicts himself in the third person as "the visitor"; at times in the first person, as "I" and "we"; and at times in the second person of the colloquial "he says—you say" exchange. Underlying this diversity, however, certain constant elements emerge that reveal both Caldwell's understanding of personality and his ideological and political preoccupations at this time. The depiction of individual perversity is pervasive; it is most aptly illustrated in the mystery of the derelict old panhandler in Fargo who stubbornly continues to beg for an insulting and loathsome subsistence when he might obtain both food and accommodation from the Transient Relief Agency. Habit and inertia prolong his degradation as much as any external circumstances and are unlikely to yield easily to optimistic public welfare schemes. Indeed, for all Caldwell's distress at the suffering he observes in the midst of the Great Depression, he seems even more concerned at the damage that may be done in trying to alleviate it. Even at the height of Caldwell's public commitment to a radical left-wing ideology, there is a conservative countercurrent in his writing that fears the takeover of individuals by the government just as strongly as it promotes the ideals of union, power, and fraternity. This conservatism is, in considerable measure, a nostalgia (frequently encountered in the works of Faulkner and Steinbeck as well) for a rural American epoch that has died, partly because of the treachery of nature itself against the farmers who believed its bounty was endless, partly because of the greedy, exploitative, and foolish kind of farming they practiced. This double emphasis, on human quirkiness and intransigence, and on the failure of Americans to conserve the land that brought them prosperity, runs throughout the first section of *Some American People*, but the mode of its presentation is sardonic and folksy rather than didactic. By contrast, the two remaining sections of the book display a rage and anguish that is unmitigated by any frivolity.

In the "Detroit" section, the vein is still ironic, but now it is savage satire of Henry Ford's insulated industrial kingdom, where flower gardens cover the place where Ford's police gunned down his workers, and employees, mutilated by unsafe machinery, are turned out onto the streets to scavenge for what they can get. Once again, a startling image is used to focus the reader's emotion: "Once you become eight-fingered, you are a marked man in Detroit. Hotels will not hire Negro porters if so much as one finger is missing. Transportation companies inspect the hands of applicants even before handing out application blanks. Store owners shake their heads at job seekers whose fingers are not all there. . . . Eighteen or forty, it does not matter what the age may be; if you are eight-fingered, you are done for in Detroit" (*SAP*, 172). This passage exemplifies a familiar technique from Caldwell's fiction. A great intensity of meaning is coalesced into one grisly image, here the eight fingers with their freakish suggestion; then the phrase is used repeatedly, cumulatively, and finally, obsessively. However, unlike the fiction, its purpose here is directly propagandistic. The reader is shocked and frustrated but confronted at once with the correct response to take to this atrocity: "The mangling of hands and the crushing of life will only stop when workers succeed in forming their own rank-and-file union. There are no other means of forcing automobile manufacturers to reduce the speed-up and to install, and operate, safety devices that cannot be disconnected by the foremen" (*SAP*, 172–73).

The final section of *Some American People*, "Southern Tenant Farmers," takes Caldwell to his homeland and the familiar fictional territory of poor white tenants and sharecroppers. Like the people in *Tobacco Road*, these tenants and croppers are physically malformed and given to strange habits like dung and clay eating; unlike the people of *Tobacco Road*, the people of "Southern Tenant Farmers" are neither mysterious nor amusing. Caldwell admits candidly that the horrific cases he cites are not typical of the South but are nevertheless representative of how thousands of families live. They are victims of a corrupt and wasteful agricultural system, who must put their babies to suck at the teats of a dog because they have no other resources to offer. Again the shocking image is explored and reiterated; again it is a peculiarly appropriate horror in its unnaturalness, like Steinbeck's more famous use of a similar perversion of the act of nursing at the conclusion of *The Grapes of Wrath*. Again Caldwell advocates a union of sharecroppers as the first step toward a solution for these people. However, in contrast to the simple assurance in *Tobacco Road* that "co-operative and corporate farming would have saved them all," Caldwell now finds the design of a new system of agricultural labor "problematical" (*SAP*, 265) and hesitates between collective farming and a more Jeffersonian model of agrarian independence.

*Some American People* thus proves finally almost as complex as, but less desperate in its political ideology than, the fiction that pre-

ceded it, and it benefits immensely from the proven imagist and repetitive methods and the inventive skill of the storyteller. The book
was generally well received by the reviewers, although Albert Halper
in the *New Masses* wished for more facts and statistics, asking of
Caldwell's account of the drought in the western states "how much
top soil was blown away, how far it blew, how the cattle stood it, the
reaction of the farmers' families etc." Halper argued that Caldwell
could easily have found a "farm-school graduate along the road who,
in an hour's time, could have given him all kinds of information
and data," but such academic documenting plays a very small part
in Caldwell's eclectic and often impressionistic method of reporting. Instead of answering Halper's questions directly, he suggests
in vivid and colloquial images the impact of the drought on the
ecology: "In Central Oregon, on the eastern slope of the Cascade
Mountains, the shriveled grass is lying on the range like scraps of
steel shavings. A gust of hot wind sweeps down to earth, and with
your ear to the ground you hear a sound like somebody kicking rusty
springs through the wiry brown grass" (*SAP*, 13). This prose is often
more figurative and less impersonal than that of Caldwell's fiction,
suggesting the extreme control he exercised in the fiction. The New
York *Times* critic Robert Van Gelder objected to the frequency of
what he called Caldwell's "lapses into fiction" in a purportedly documentary book, but such writing can scarcely be considered "lapses"
so much as conscious and deliberate use of the imaginative and traditionally fictive methods for an end quite distinct from that of the
apparently more detached novels and stories.[3]

Between 1935 and 1937, the year of the publication of Caldwell's
next nonfiction book, *You Have Seen Their Faces*, the desire of
American artists to witness and record the lives of ordinary Americans during the crisis of the Great Depression was blossoming into
the relatively new genre of the documentary, realized in the medium of Pare Lorentz's films, the oral history programs of the Federal Writers Project, the photography project of the Farm Security
Administration created by Roy Stryker, and the mixing of written
word and picture in dozens of documentary books.[4] Although the
genre of documentary was not wholly original to the 1930s, it came
into its own in that decade, especially in the picture-text combina-

3. Albert Halper, "Caldwell Sees America," in *Critical Essays*, ed. MacDonald,
42; Robert Van Gelder, Review of Erskine Caldwell's *Some American People*, New
York *Times*, December 15, 1935, p. 9.
4. Stott, *Documentary Expression*, Chap. 4 *passim*.

tion, often the product of an artistic collaboration, such as that of Muriel Stoddard and Bayard Wootton in *Cabins in the Laurel* (1935), Dorothea Lange and Paul Taylor in *American Exodus* (1939), and James Agee and Walker Evans in *Let Us Now Praise Famous Men* (1941). Caldwell and Bourke-White's picture-text was thus not the first in the tradition, but it was, like *Some American People,* highly innovative in its insistence on mixing obviously imaginative material with the results of more objective kinds of observation.

*You Have Seen Their Faces* is an exploration of the lives of rural poor people in the South, with blacks and whites sharing approximately equal attention. Caldwell later said that his purpose was "to show that the fiction I was writing was authentically based on contemporary life in the South," and that the decision to document the verbal reporting with photographs was his (*CE,* 163). Margaret Bourke-White believed of her assignment that "he wanted to take the camera to Tobacco Road," suggesting that the book would be in some measure an effort to vindicate the accuracy of the fiction. As she was a complete newcomer to both the South and the particular subject, she found herself initially waiting to be told what Caldwell's vision for the book might be and was greatly surprised by his patient and passive receptivity to the people they encountered. In the end, she found herself responding to and sharing his naturalistic views, not as a means of documenting his vision but of enlarging her own. Of her time among these southern sharecroppers, she later wrote: "I was learning that to understand another human being you must gain some insight into the conditions which made him what he is. The people and the forces which shape them: each holds the key to the other. . . . I began watching for the effect of events on human beings. I was awakening to the need of probing and learning, discovering and interpreting."[5] These comments seem to qualify the notion that Caldwell was merely out to justify a particular piece of his fiction and suggest that he was again attempting, in a different medium, to explore those aspects of the South that most moved and enraged him.

He and Margaret Bourke-White spent the summer of 1936 touring the South and collecting their material, although the writing was not done until later in the fall of that year, when the two authors selected the photographs and wrote the captions together. She later wrote of this task: "Ours was a real collaboration. We did not want

5. Bourke-White, *Portrait of Myself,* 113, 134–36.

the matter of whether the pictures 'illustrated' the text, or the words explained the pictures, to have any importance."[6] The form of the book is, on first appearance, a fairly simple alternation between sets of photographs (often with some thematic link) and sociological essays discussing the origins, development, and decay of agricultural life and society in the region. However, although each photograph is given a "quoted" caption in the dialect and accent of its subject, Caldwell is careful to point out at the beginning that these are imagined, as are the monologues at the opening and closing of many of the essays, which also speak in the tones and accents of the people themselves. Such documentary writing clearly makes no pretense of scientific objectivity, although contending all the while for the essential truthfulness of the material. It is an interesting and typical piece of ingenuousness on Caldwell's part that he can simultaneously insist that "no person, place or episode in this book is fictitious," while admitting that the quoted passages "do not pretend to reproduce the actual sentiments of these persons" (*YHSTF*, "Preface"). This distinction between the actuality and the authenticity of the sentiments recorded is crucial to any consideration of the documentary medium, especially as expressed in the 1930s. When James Agee and Walker Evans first tried to capture the "unimagined existence" of the Alabama tenant families in *Let Us Now Praise Famous Men*, Agee felt that he must try to avoid not only the shaping imagination but, consequently, words themselves, because of their distorting intervention between the fact and the record of it. Unable to avoid words, part of Agee's solution was to project himself fully into his text so that the reader might be as acutely aware as possible of all the eccentricities and prejudices of the author, who purported to tell the truth, and could presumably then subtract that bias from the text. Caldwell, equally skeptical of reproducing pure documentary evidence, turns to a playful subversion of a pretense of objectivity by providing real people with invented dialogue and making the whole report bear witness to a personal and particular vision rather than an impersonal and general set of facts.

The result of this mixture of subjective and objective methods, and of the exclusive concentration on Caldwell's home region, is a complicated and paradoxical work about the South, a work in which love struggles with hate, anger with sympathy, and hope with despair. Speaking of the South, Caldwell writes: "This is the place

6. *Ibid.*, 137.

where anybody may come without an invitation and, before the day is over, be made to feel like one of the home-folks. . . . Mark against the South its failure to preserve its own culture and its refusal to accept the culture of the East and West. Mark against it the refusal to assimilate the blood of an alien race of another color or to tolerate its presence. Mark against it most of, if not all, the ills of a retarded and thwarted civilization" (*YHSTF*, 26). Once again Caldwell focuses strongly on the destructive effects of neglect of the land through ignorance and inertia. The people can neither conserve nor adapt; the land suffers; and because it does, the people suffer too, becoming "god-forsaken, man-forsaken" (*SAP*, 222). The essays in *You Have Seen Their Faces* continue the use of the repetitive techniques of the fiction to re-create the vicious cycle of despair that traps every generation of southern agricultural workers. Their degradation is so extreme as a consequence of their "back-breaking, spiritcrushing" existence that Caldwell feels obliged to assure us at one point that "they are still people, they are human beings. They have life" (*YHSTF*, 168). This statement reiterates the essence of Caldwell's fiction; but whereas in the fiction "having life" and "being human" are most frequently exemplified by freakish behavior and preposterous attitudes, in the nonfiction, such basic humanity demands a practical solution for its predicament rather than a pessimistic shudder. At the end of *Tobacco Road*, there is a marked dichotomy between Caldwell's desperate proposals for a revolutionary turn to collective farming and the actual world he depicts in the novel, where each generation is sinking to new depths of incompetence and degeneracy and there is no person or agency to further any change or improvement. At the end of *You Have Seen Their Faces*, Caldwell resolves the conflict of *Tobacco Road* and the uncertainty of *Some American People* into the determination that the young people of the South, "with hope and a dream before them . . . can change a hell into a living paradise" (*YHSTF*, 169). This now demands a reversal of the tendency of the generations to deteriorate, which Caldwell had illustrated in *Tobacco Road*, and insists, by a sheer act of will, on action coming from these enervated people: "The older ones can be helped by charity and relief, and the remaining days they live can be made easier for them. . . . The young people still have strong bodies and the will to succeed. They can change the agricultural system that broke the bodies and wills of their parents. They can stand up without fear and demand that they be paid adequately for their labor" (*YHSTF*, 168). There is no mention now of specific plans for change, although Caldwell's support of unions remains strong. One does not doubt for a moment the strength of the desire for improvement that lies behind this statement of Caldwell's convictions; yet at the point of their most forceful assertion, his imagination enters the text to undermine the moral simplicity of the essays. The legends invented to match the last series of photographs in the book depict an old woman saying, "I've done the best I knew how all my life, but it didn't amount to much in the end," while a young man admits, "It ain't hardly worth the trouble to go on living" (*YHSTF*, 183, 185). This occurs in immediate juxtaposition to the last sentence of the nonfiction, or "unimagined," text: "When fear has been banished, and self-respect restored, America will wake up to find that it has a new region to take pride in" (*YHSTF*, 169). Such obstinate optimism from the author, allied to the fictional despair of his subjects, effectively suggests the complex documentary medium that Caldwell creates in this book.

Margaret Bourke-White's photographs play an essential and equal role in *You Have Seen Their Faces*. Of the three books she did with Caldwell, it is in this one that image and word seem most perfectly integrated. An early photograph in the volume shows, silhouetted against an overcast sky, a man with a two-horse plow moving across a sloping hillside. The image suggests a primal, almost mythical, relationship between the farmer and his land, and Caldwell's legend captures this sense of harmony in the simple terms of the farmer: "There's lots of things easier to do, and pay more money, but plowing the land and harvesting the crops gives a man something that satisfies him as long as he lives" (*YHSTF*, 59). In the final section of the book, a photograph of ravaged land undulating in gullies of dust is captioned: "It looks like God can't trust people to take care of the earth any more" (*YHSTF*, 175). The photographs show the strength and beauty of poor people in the South as well as the many ways they may be distorted; they illustrate Caldwell's central thematic concerns in the essays with race, religion, and land; their tone is both elegiac and angry, like the text. However, it must be noted that some elements of caprice enter into Caldwell's imagined monologues for the photographic subjects. A black woman looking mournfully from behind prison bars says, "I've only been misbehaving" (*YHSTF*, 97), and a white man living in a dilapidated, three-sided shack insists lazily that he likes his open-ended house better than when it had four walls. Some of the people express satisfaction, some humor, some mischief; the abstract truth of their victimization as a group is dispelled a little by the presence of their individual personalities. The captioned photographs replace the anecdotes of *Some American People*, but fulfill a similar purpose by appearing to modify a didactic thesis while at the same time justifying the humane ends of such propaganda.

Much of the critical response to *You Have Seen Their Faces* was, understandably, determined by the political sympathies of the critic, from Malcolm Cowley's enthusiasm, "These quotations printed beneath the photographs are exactly right; the photographs themselves are almost beyond praise," to Donald Davidson's objection that this piece of photographic journalism was "punily, sickeningly incomplete" because it failed to show either urban squalor or northern absentee landlords or indeed anything else on the agenda of the Southern Agrarians in its presentation of rural poverty.[7] That most of Caldwell's nonfiction of the 1930s was propaganda of a kind seems beyond dispute—the genre is almost inseparably linked to it; but it is propaganda of high artistic quality, with subtlety, humanity, and complexity. His rage against the human condition is always tempered by his relish for discovering and appreciating how people live their lives, and this curiosity remains constant, whether or not he is simultaneously calling for major shifts in the social order.

One manifestation of this curiosity was Caldwell's enthusiasm, in 1938, for assuming the editorship of a projected series of regional books, American Folkways, to be written by skilled writers from various parts of the country about their own regions. Their purpose, according to Caldwell, would be to describe "the cultural influences implanted by the original settlers and their descendants and . . . explain the manner in which life in one region of the country differed from the way of life in another region" (*CE*, 183). The series, under Caldwell's direction, eventually comprised twenty-five volumes, generally highly regarded. Caldwell hoped the series would "reveal the ingrained character of America" (*CE*, 183); but this character was clearly anticipated to be pluralist and strongly shaped by the individual writers who created the books, since Caldwell promised them that his only role as editor would be to offer suggestions when asked. The series shows an emphasis on the shaping environment that is now as much ethnic, cultural, and historical as it

7. Malcolm Cowley, "Fall Catalogue," in *Critical Essays*, ed. MacDonald, 56; Davidson, "Erskine Caldwell's Picture Book," 61.

was sociological and economic in Caldwell's own earlier nonfiction books. Interestingly, the decision to embark on the American Folkways series was made by Caldwell after his return in 1938 from a trip to Czechoslovakia with Margaret Bourke-White. This was Caldwell's first travel outside the United States, into another kind of pluralistic society that survived precariously in the midst of powerful totalitarian threats. The book that emerged in 1939 from this second collaboration was *North of the Danube*, a work that shows a newfound respect for democratic pluralism, both at home and abroad, as well as Caldwell's typical fascination and sympathy with the lives of ordinary people.

*North of the Danube* is, once again, a merging of photography and text, structured similarly to *You Have Seen Their Faces*. It contains eight essays, each set in a different region of Czechoslovakia, that are individually followed by a set of six to eight plates, illustrating and complementing them. However, the photographs are factually, rather than imaginatively, captioned. This is a small symbol of a major difference between the two books, for in *North of the Danube*, Caldwell was working for the first time in a completely alien environment. He knew little of the customs and longer history of the country, and he spoke neither of its major languages, getting by with German and English in the major cities and western regions, having immense difficulties in the eastern part of the country. As a consequence, relatively few interviews were conducted with the subjects of the book. A further measure of Caldwell's distance from the people is its relative dearth of humor. Caldwell's normal mode of grotesque humor, for all its seeming detachment on the part of the author, depends on a considerable degree of intimacy with the lives of the people he observes and on an understanding of the traditional stereotypes attached to them. In Czechoslovakia, where both the author and his eventual audience were unfamiliar with the types and customs of the people, such comedy might appear merely cruel and ineffectual. Thus Caldwell restricts his humor in *North of the Danube* to situations where he himself, as the ignorant outsider, or the prosperous and successful people within the society bear the brunt of it. The peasants in the photographs, unlike their southern counterparts, do not speak directly, and very few look straight at the camera; indeed, the details that echo through the visual images are as foreign as the language and customs with which the writer has to deal. The people's lives do not seem to be invaded, either by Bourke-White's camera or by Caldwell's reporting, a reticence that is only partly due to their distance from the culture. There appears also to be a philosophical motive behind it, because invasion is the main political fact of the book. Czechoslovakia is seen as a fragile democratic union of national and ethnic groups that is being violated and dismembered for the aggrandizement of the power-hungry surrounding countries. A democratic culture sprung from diversity is being dismantled in favor of varieties of totalitarianism and greed.

However, *North of the Danube* is much more than a requiem for Czechoslovakia. It is both a celebration of human variety and cultural pluralism and a grim reminder of the exploitation and persecution that people are prone to in societies where such differences exist. In the early morning markets of the town of Uzhorod, Caldwell notes with some pleasure that "the wives of Czech railway workers and the wives of German bankers stood side by side with the wives of Jewish merchants and the wives of Gypsy traders. German and Jew, Czech and Gypsy, each in her own language, talked excitedly to the Ruthenian peasants, who understood nothing except the desire to sell their food and flowers" (*ND*, 11). When the day's business is ended, the Ruthenians, Czechs, and Germans leave on bicycles; the Jews and Gypsies walk. On the land, a Czech vineyard owner notes the pattern of "Slovak workers, Hungarian overseers, and Czech landlords." Then he adds more grimly, "And over us all, the German God Almighty" (*ND*, 62). The ominous signs of impending war are everywhere in the book, from an ugly train incident in which a compartment of Czechs, Slovaks, Ruthenians, and Hungarians stand passively by while a Jewish woman is attacked by a German, to an even more explicit encounter in Prague with German propaganda agents who are determined to eradicate all that does not conform to their own monolithic dictates.

Lest one have any doubt of Caldwell's implicit political sympathies, he attaches to the end of each chapter quotations from politicians, historians, and artists to make explicit his own more subtle emphasis. For example, the chairman of a refugee commission says that these people have "found a haven in democratic Czechoslovakia," while Hitler describes the country as "a tumor which is poisoning the whole European organism" (*ND*, 79, 112).

As with *You Have Seen Their Faces*, *North of the Danube* is undisguisedly partisan in its response to prejudice and poverty. However, it is also a travelogue of a new world for Caldwell, and he responds to that novelty in the same way as to the whimsical interest of the people he encountered in *Some American People*, although in Czechoslovakia it is more to custom and incident than to individual personality. Two chapters, "Bread in Uzok" and "The Dogs of Ceske Budejovice," illustrate once more the laconic narrative method whereby Caldwell finds an image around which to crystallize an experience and then develops and reiterates the image to the edge of absurdity. The motif in Uzok is the frenzy of people who have not even seen bread in six or eight years. When Caldwell and Bourke-White are chauffeured to visit them, they fill their trunk with loaves of bread and then discover they must fight off the peasants with knives and sticks in order to distribute it. The chapter is a polemical statement on the shame of such hunger, illustrated through the most literal application of its common metaphor, bread. Caldwell is both appalled and intrigued by the familiar sight of poverty and its unfamiliar manifestations, such as the urban dog owners who sit hopefully all day on their doorsteps in Ceske Budejovice, awaiting a summons to use their dogs and carts to transport small loads around the town. He discovers there are rituals and codes of conduct to be observed and conveys nicely the sense that what is exotic to him is merely part of a daily monotony of endurance for the people he describes. While a Czech farmer entertains Caldwell to a feast of wine and asparagus, he notes that the farmer's overseer is beating with a stick the knuckles of a Slovak peasant woman who has fallen behind in her hoeing. Ever alert to the signs of peonage, Caldwell is conscious in *North of the Danube* of a more comprehensive and complicated context for them than in preceding documentaries. For the first time, he has neither solutions nor suggestions to offer; that would only mean assuming the arrogance of the other outsiders who think they know what is best while destroying Czech culture. Instead, he concentrates on creating very personal images of a bewildering society that are richly supplemented by Margaret Bourke-White's photographs. She provides pictures of architecture, industry, and urban life that modify Caldwell's rather agrarian and individual bias. The book is in some ways the most interesting of their three collaborations, because the camera provides what James Agee called in *Let Us Now Praise Famous Men* a "coequal" study to the text, rather than an illustration of it, as in *You Have Seen Their Faces*, or a counterpoint to it, as in their next work together, *Say, Is This the U.S.A.*, which the two had embarked on in 1940 following their marriage in 1939.[8]

Published in 1941 on the edge of a new era of patriotism and

8. Agee and Evans, *Let Us Now Praise Famous Men*, xv.

imminent war, *Say, Is This the U.S.A.* is a lively social history of the time, but also a portent of the end of Caldwell and Bourke-White's collaboration in word and photograph. Caldwell's first legend in the book suggests that the vision of the United States that it will embody is one of tensions, oppositions, and variety: "This America is a jungle of men living in the extremes of good and bad, heat and cold, wealth and poverty. You are born here and you die here, and in the intervening years you take out more than you put back" (*SUSA*, 4). Curiously, the photograph opposite this caption is of a steam engine silhouetted between a row of telegraph poles on one side and a row of gigantic grain elevators on the other, with one small human figure dwarfed by these symbols of human enterprise. The photograph, in isolation, suggests the heroic, and perhaps the inhuman, aspects of agricultural production, commerce, and communication, but there is no obvious way in which it is matched by the caption. This discreteness of word and image anticipates much that is to come in the rest of this somewhat contentious book. In discussing this particular collaboration with Caldwell in an afterword to the book, Margaret Bourke-White wrote: "Working together with the same purpose in mind is essential, because even though one half of the team uses a typewriter and the other a lens, the two mediums must function congenially so they will come together and weld. Together they produce something quite different from the activities of either and build together something they could not construct separately" (*SUSA*, 176). This rationale might help explain the seeming incompatibility of word and picture in the book, which recurs frequently, as a deliberately engineered ironic play between the two media, but it is not quite consistent enough to suggest this artistic tension. One of Caldwell's anecdotes in the book seems to hint that it was perhaps the genre itself that was becoming overworked and in need of some novelty by the end of the 1930s and the glut of documentaries that the decade had produced. Caldwell attempts to interview an attendant at a Missouri filling station and is met with the following response:

> With a business-like gesture the attendant handed me a neatly printed card. It read as follows:
> "I am 36 years old. I smoke about a pack of cigarettes a day, sometimes more and sometimes less, but it evens up. I take an occasional drink of beer. I am a Baptist, an Elk, and a Rotarian. I live with my own wife, send my children to school, and visit my in-laws once a year on

Christmas Day. I wear No. 9½ shoes, No. 15½ collar, and No. 7¼ hat.
I shoot a 12-gauge shotgun and have a 27-inch crotch. I like rice, sweet
potatoes, and pork sausage. I vote for F.D.R., pull for Joe Louis, and
boo Diz Dean. I wouldn't have anything against Hitler if he stayed in
his own backyard. I don't know any Japs, but I've made up my mind to
argue with the next one I see about leaving the Chinese alone. . . . If I
have left anything out, it's an oversight. . . . If you want your tank
filled, just nod your head. If you don't want anything, please move
along and give the next fellow a chance. I thank you. Hurry back."
(*SUSA*, 10, 12)

William Stott has called this the epitaph for the "I've seen America"
book of the thirties. Whether Caldwell's anecdote is real or imaginary, it effectively conveys a sense of the embarrassing surfeit of this
approach to documentary.[9]

Perhaps part of the problem for Caldwell and Bourke-White lay
in the breadth of the endeavor itself; she wrote of it, "Our object
was to give the impression and feel of America" (*SUSA*, 176). Ironically, such an effort seems more feasible in the case of Czechoslovakia, when the country was an alien one to both artists, because
they could discuss and synthesize newfound attitudes and fresh
impressions. In the case of their earlier collaboration, *You Have
Seen Their Faces*, Bourke-White was more obviously documenting
Caldwell's vision of agricultural poverty in the South, a narrowly
defined topic on which she expected to defer to his greater expertise. However, when the two came to create a mutual vision of
America on the edge of war, they seemed to start from premises
about American society that were distinctly at variance; therefore,
the result, though interesting, is hardly so much a collaboration as
an ongoing debate.

Bourke-White's photographs in this volume are most clearly cele-
bratory; a large number of them are angled from below the subjects,
silhouetting them against landscape and sky, anticipating the final
heroic shot of the Statue of Liberty. Her topics shift between farm
and industry, work and play, and the variety of ethnic groups that
constitute America, suggesting the diversity and democratic range
of American life. The visual images of this book thus seem to bear
out Stott's theory about documentary books in the thirties—that
they began by exposing what was wrong with America and ended

9. Stott, *Documentary Expression*, 256.

by exhibiting what was right with it.[10] However, Caldwell appears to have been less attuned to this affirmative note than Bourke-White. Where she sees ethnic variety, Caldwell still calls attention to racism; where she depicts industrial progress, he points to exploitation; her photographs show a rich and fertile land, his text turns once again to the decline of agrarian ideals. It must be noted that Caldwell's text is also at times intensely nationalistic and patriotic. This doubleness is present in much of his pedestrian text, whereas Bourke-White's photographs show both brilliance and a less ambivalent vision. Caldwell had already proved a master of incongruity and doubleness in his fiction, but the dichotomies in *Say, Is This the U.S.A.* appear not to be fully under his direction. Opposite Bourke-White's titanic image of the Statue of Liberty, Caldwell's caption reads: "Car hops and bobbin boys, auto courts and night shifts, hitch hikers and hotel greeters, beauty queens and bank nights, prayer services and union meetings, personal appearances and gossip columns, all-night movies and bunion derbies" (*SUSA*, 174). This is certainly an amused and appreciative and gently ironic description of the diverse life of New York City, but it seems a somewhat embarrassing contrast to the heroic overtones of the photograph—almost as though Caldwell were developing a kind of unconsciously dialectical argument with Bourke-White's imagery. Earlier in the book, in response to a photograph of schoolchildren seated around a piano, an American flag in the background, and a pretty teacher playing to them, Caldwell writes as the legend: "They like to tell their teacher when their fathers have jobs and are working, but they do not like to talk about it when their fathers cannot find any work to do" (*SUSA*, 102). Opposite a picture of the bountiful wheat fields of Kansas, the caption tells us: "In Kansas City a man is arrested on a charge of vagrancy because he begged for something to eat" (*SUSA*, 12).

Not all of Caldwell's captions, by any means, are of this rather contentious nature. Many of them are Whitmanesque catalogs of local activities, produce, or unique regional qualities associated with the photo images; they show a fascination with language and a mastery of colloquialism and slang that is much less in evidence in Caldwell's fiction, where the vocabulary is often pruned to the barest minimum. For perhaps the first time in Caldwell's writing, one sees the author's sheer delight in the resources of language rather

10. *Ibid.*, 237.

than its willful limitations. A freight train entering Dodge City is captioned "Skippers, rail benders, rear stacks, hog heads, tallow pots, smoke artists, snakes, bull snakes, goats, pig snouts, and Mae Wests" (*SUSA*, 20); a Texarkana stock market bears the description "Foals, colts, yearlings, fillies, mares, dams, geldings, stallions, mustangs, pintos, palominos, bronchos, cayuses, plugs, jackasses" (*SUSA*, 128); and Elko, Nevada, evokes the legend "Dashboard fronts and boot hills, pay streaks and ghost towns, floaters and fancy women, bindlestiffs and divorcees, sagebrush and salt flats, range horses and pipestones" (*SUSA*, 80).

The text itself is not arranged, as in the earlier books, into sections of essays and blocks of photographs, but instead has a continuous series of photographs on each right-hand page, opposite a running text on the left, in addition to a caption for each picture. Sometimes the text and photographs happen coincidentally to be about the same place, person, or incident, but often there is only an oblique connection. Caldwell continues his method from *Some American People* of relating personal anecdotes built around an image that is used for a choral effect, such as his tale of the Washington, D.C., cabdriver who is too engrossed in his income tax returns to take any customers; opposite his story are industrial workers in Chicago and Cedar Rapids and the still unemployed in New York City. The juxtaposition suggests that whereas the taxi driver may be enjoying the burden of his flourishing business, the depression is far from over for many other Americans. Caldwell's account of the weary B girl who is sick of drinking champagne for a living, concludes with the remark "What the hell kind of a country is this, when the girls have to make a living that way" (*SUSA*, 126), a comment that has neither equivalent nor counterpoint in the opposing photograph of a Texas horse auction. Occasionally, Caldwell turns up a story with the powerful primal imagery of his early novels. Such was his anecdote of "Bread in Uzok" in *North of the Danube*, and such again is his account in this book of a black coffin maker, whom Caldwell bumps into one dark night on a deserted city street. He is most literally an underground man. Three years on a Georgia chain gang have driven him out of this world to take up permanent residence in a dark basement where daylight never penetrates. There he plies his trade, making boxes for the underground burial of his fellow blacks. Caldwell presents the encounter in his most restrained and prosaic language, but the image of America in it has no possible parallel in the photographs. Indeed, it is difficult to imagine that any medium other than words could convey the subterranean gloom of its suggestions.

After they had completed *Say, Is This the U.S.A.*, Caldwell and Bourke-White decided to embark on one further collaboration— this time in Russia, where she was the seasoned traveler and he the novice. In May, 1941, they arrived in Moscow after an arduous journey and were rapidly engulfed in the course of world history there. When the Russian-German war began in June, Caldwell found himself in great demand as a war correspondent, and Bourke-White began taking photographs for *Life*. Whatever plans they had for a more leisurely and considered book were abandoned; and their last joint book, *Russia at War*, though conveying the immediacy of the crisis situation in word and picture, seems less a collaboration than the expedient and rather perfunctory coincidence of a writer and photographer who happened to be in the right spot at the same time. With seventy-eight photographs, an eight-page introduction by Bourke-White, and a sixteen-page essay by Caldwell, his writing in this book is not only subordinate but, once again, only occasionally congruent with her interests. Bourke-White is intrigued, both in her prose and pictures, by the various forms of religion and irreligion in the Soviet Union, whereas Caldwell, curiously, ignores the subject absolutely, perhaps because it does not lend itself to his interest in either orgiastic manifestations or transcendent goals. Caldwell, on the other hand, is fascinated, true to his fictional concerns, with the place of women in this society, with their jobs, status, appearance, and even their clothing, whereas Bourke-White oddly bypasses this subject except for some passing references to women's role in the war effort. Both of them produce a clearly partisan document emphasizing the loyalty, stoicism, and courage of the Russian people and depicting the Germans as halfhearted and cowardly. Bourke-White photographs Stalin to bear out her comment "I thought he had the strongest face I had ever seen" (*RW*, 14). Caldwell has no part in this episode whatsoever, but instead interviews some captured German soldiers, who make such unlikely but useful remarks as "We thought the Russians would be easy, but the Russians were not as weak as we thought" (*RW*, 22). He reports solemnly but uncharacteristically on military maneuvers and strategy and appears utterly isolated from the kind of anecdotal connection with the people that is elsewhere the mainstay of his nonfiction writing.

Besides *Russia at War*, Caldwell produced by himself two further works of nonfiction from this period in the Soviet Union, *Moscow Under Fire* and *All-Out on the Road to Smolensk*. In addition, he made twice-daily broadcasts to New York City for CBS, sent a daily radiogram report for North American Newspaper Alliance, and wrote articles for *Life* and the newspaper *PM*, so it is not surprising that these books should sound both exhausted and repetitive. Published in 1942, *Moscow Under Fire* is in the form of a wartime diary, kept from June 26 to October 1 of 1941. Caldwell has slightly more opportunity in this work to use his whimsical style, although it is clearly not often appropriate in a book in which he has to be a mouthpiece, much of the time, for those facts that the Soviet Union and the Red Army choose to disseminate. Although Caldwell has some occasional criticisms of censorship and regimentation, he writes sympathetically about a future ally in a critical period of history and clearly does his part to further harmony in Soviet-American relations. He describes the Moscow Agricultural Exhibition as "like a day last summer at the New York World's Fair" (*MF*, 6) and notes that "Russians admire the efficiency and spirit of the American people" (*MF*, 7). He relays anecdotes about the superiority of Russian soldiers over base Germans and about the stoicism of the Muscovites: "It would be natural to expect people to grumble because they had to sleep on a hard bench or to sit on a hard floor, but there is nothing like that in Moscow now" (*MF*, 33).

The book is, of necessity, a reiterated daily account of the bombing of Moscow, written from a direct, personal perspective, interspersed with third-person narratives passed on from Russian officers at the front line. Occasionally, Caldwell relieves the solemn, obligatory tone of his reports by making himself the butt of a comic tale—telling about being lost in a Moscow blackout and trying to determine his whereabouts by climbing and identifying statues or depicting himself as an aimless American looking for a good time amid the more high-minded Russian citizens. Once, in a candid moment, he provides a telling clue to his attitude toward the whole endeavor: "There is much to admire in the Soviet Union, but it is rather difficult to maintain a Pollyanish attitude day after day, week after week, when a pinch of salt would liven everyone's existence" (*MF*, 90). Clearly, none of the nonfiction produced from this trip to the Soviet Union was of the kind Caldwell's talent was best suited for, but, always a pragmatist in his approach to writing, he came up with what the times seemed to demand. Indeed, his second solo book on his Russian experiences, *All-Out on the Road to Smolensk*, is a minimal reworking of much of the same material as *Moscow Under Fire*, so that Caldwell had essentially produced three books from the same experience, although not without expressing a considerable sense of relief when he and Bourke-White finally departed from Arkhangelsk in October of 1941. The three books were, according to Caldwell's account in *Call It Experience*, put together from notes, journals, and broadcast records made during the five-month Russian stay, two of them in England before returning home, and *All-Out on the Road to Smolensk* at a slightly more leisurely pace back in the United States. In 1942, Caldwell wrote the novel *All Night Long*, about guerrilla warfare in the Soviet Union, and, in light of his experience, was quickly invited to Hollywood to work on the screenplay of the controversial film *Mission to Moscow*. The year marked Caldwell's divorce from Margaret Bourke-White, whom he had married in 1939 and with whom he had worked so productively, and it also marked the end of Caldwell's engagement with nonfiction writing for over twenty years. When he returned to it again in the 1960s, it was at his own leisurely pace, rather than under the pressure of events and deadlines, although once again it was a crisis in public life that engaged his sympathies, in the same way as did the poverty of the Great Depression. This was the emerging civil rights movement.

Caldwell's nonfiction, like his fiction, flourished best when his ideological commitment was strong and he was free to pursue his interests in his own idiosyncratic way. His two major works of reportage in the 1960s, *In Search of Bisco* (1965) and *Deep South* (1968), took him back once again to the concerns of poverty and racial injustice on his native grounds, after a minor collection of more general travel essays, *Around About America*, which he published in 1964. In attempting to catch the incongruity and variety of American life in the early sixties, Caldwell modeled this book, though without the photographs, on *Say, Is This the U.S.A.*, even to a parallel opening suggestion of the nation's contradictions: "Dynamic. Depressing. Open-all-night. Closed-for-the-season. Everybody welcome. White only. Colored entrance. Bloated with wealth and despairing in poverty. Aggressive and reactionary. Devoutly religious and amorally uninhibited" (*AA*, 11). However, despite these hints of drama to come, the book is a very low-key version of Caldwell's earlier nonfiction journeys, whimsical in tone and relatively mild in indignation. Though Caldwell is still highly partisan in behalf of miners in West Virginia and blacks in the South,

the dominant mood is bemusement at small-town America, interspersed with the minor irritations and mishaps of traveling—from
rented cars and road food to worries about what is happening to the
lawn back home. This domesticated Caldwell reveals his concerns
about teenagers and alcohol, praises a college because it has no
"jock" courses, and heartily endorses the Salvation Army as a pana-
cea until "the time comes when the welfare state provides for all in
need" (AA, 210). This is pretty tame stuff from the author of *The
Sacrilege of Alan Kent* and the former correspondent of the *New
Masses*. The only issue that arouses much fire is racism. Caldwell
tells two tales of extraordinary bigotry toward blacks and devotes
the entire section titled "Birmingham, Alabama" to a self-interview
on the subject of integration. In this exchange, Caldwell not only
repeats his belief that intermarriage will prove the best form of integration, but argues that the current demands of blacks are in the
tradition of the great revolutionary movements of history, like the
American Revolution and the revolt of the Warsaw Jews against the
Nazis. Although Caldwell notes other instances of inequity and
prejudice within American society, it is to the predicament of black
people that he returns most often in *Around About America*. This
book thus proves an appropriate harbinger of his complete return in
his next nonfiction book, *In Search of Bisco*, to the world of his
childhood in the South and the specific topic of race relations.

In Search of Bisco is much more directly autobiographical than
any of Caldwell's earlier nonfiction works, not because it contains a
great deal of his own history, but rather because it conveys a powerful sense of the background of his early life and, most particularly,
of his sense of place in the South. All of his nonfiction is dominated
by its locale, and all of it is to a considerable degree travelogue, but
it is travelogue that moves from exploring a place into an immediate
concern with the shaping effect of that environment on every aspect
of the lives of its inhabitants. In this it is very close to Caldwell's
fiction, and indeed, *In Search of Bisco* often reveals the genesis of
many of Caldwell's characters and plots, assuming, of course, that
the fiction has its origins in the material of the nonfiction, and not
vice versa. There are many familiar incidents in this book that are
presented in slightly different versions in *Trouble in July, Georgia
Boy*, and a number of the later novels. In fact, so fictive is their
manner of presentation that it is impossible to know whether these
are the facts from which Caldwell created his fiction or whether this
documentary account contains many of the fabrications of the story-

teller. The form of the book is a series of chapters, each set in a different southern town where the author is searching for news of Bisco, his black childhood companion with whom he has lost touch. Caldwell suggests that he himself discovered racism at an early age through his friendship with Bisco, when his own mother had refused to let the children spend the night together, offering her son as the only explanation, "It was because I was white and he was Negro" (*ISB*, 7). The narrative motif of the older Caldwell's search for Bisco is a device to explore southern attitudes, black and white, toward race; it results in his realization that every black man may be Bisco, his lost and betrayed friend.

Each chapter is in the form of a monologue by a person from one of the regions visited, who expresses his or her opinions, tells anecdotes, and reveals attitudes in a manner that makes little pretense of simulating an actual interview. These characters dwell in a realm somewhere between the real and the imaginary; they are often larger than life, their comments are presented in an ironic manner, and their stories make perhaps too neatly orchestrated an indictment for a work of pure reportage. Although the search for Bisco is supposedly taking place in the near present, some of the interviewees or characters speak out of the distant past, and the book shows how many of Caldwell's own attitudes are grounded in a historical consciousness that rarely intrudes into his fiction. Though the book was clearly spurred by the civil rights movement and Caldwell's support for it, its examples and details deal as much with former as with contemporary aspects of racial conflict. Caldwell is still more at home aesthetically (as in his novels) with accounts of chain gangs, lynchings, and rapes, than with desegregating schools and lunch counters and analyzing the significance of black voting strength. The book cannot be said to add any profound insights into the origins of the civil rights movement, but it suggests the human consequences of segregation and exploitation in the South, and explores candidly the normally unarticulated prejudices of the white population. Caldwell's talent for uncovering the incongruous situation and the absurd character is focused here exclusively on the mechanism of bigotry: "What they don't understand up North is that niggers—or Negroes, as they say it—haven't gone through evolution as far as white people. They're still primitive—just like wild Indians used to be. They just don't have the intelligence we've got and it's going to take time for their brains to grow bigger so they can go through their cycle of evolution like we've already done" (*ISB*,

86–87). As in his novels, these people express in vulgar and blatant language all the prejudices, folk beliefs, and unconscious attitudes that would normally remain unarticulated and repressed. One reviewer of *In Search of Bisco* felt that, because of attitudes like these, the book rang "disturbingly of fiction," although its major impact was, somewhat paradoxically, its tone of "piercing reality and immediacy." [11] In fact, Caldwell had made use of fictional methods in his early works of reportage, and his two books on race in the sixties merely increase this tendency. Because they simultaneously eliminate the degree of actuality lent by the photographs to the earlier works, it becomes impossible to draw a line between fact and fantasy. Their authenticity becomes a matter of taste and aesthetic judgment rather than something capable of objective verification.

Caldwell's next nonfiction work, *Deep South* (1968), takes him into the investigation of a subject that pervades his fiction—the impact of southern Protestantism, in all its manifestations, on the lives and conduct of its adherents. Caldwell had already been intrigued with this topic as early as 1926, when he wrote the essay "The Georgia Cracker," a rather Menckenesque description of Snake Charmers, Holy Rollers, and the rituals of coming through. He had pursued it in *Some American People*, where he suggested that religion for the poorest of people "served to take the place of normal entertainment" (*SAP*, 261) and illustrated it through Bourke-White's photographs of both black and white religious ceremonies in *You Have Seen Their Faces*. In his fiction, he had explored both the yearnings for escape and transcendence and the struggles and manipulations of numerous preachers to accommodate spiritual and sexual ecstasy to conventional moral precepts. The ethical poverty of southern Protestantism, whereby it could be made a tool of boosterism for the prosperous or fanaticism for the poor is implicit in much of Caldwell's fiction, but is explicit for the first time in *Deep South*, which is a retrospective look, like *In Search of Bisco*, at the same source material as the fiction.

The book is built around Caldwell's memories of his clergyman father, Ira Sylvester Caldwell, who had encouraged his son to observe and debate candidly every variety of southern religious experience, so that his novelist son could later write, "Being a minister's son in the Deep South in the early years of the twentieth century

11. C. L. Cooper, Review of Erskine Caldwell's *In Search of Bisco, Saturday Review*, May 1, 1965, p. 39.

and growing up in a predominantly religious environment was my good fortune in life" (DS, 1). From his first childhood memories, Caldwell moves into a larger consideration of southern religion, comparing his recollection of the 1920s to the current situation in the 1960s, examining the differences between the conservative middle-class churches and the poorer fundamentalist ones, considering the development of the black churches in the twentieth century and the relationship of all the churches to ethics, politics, the civil rights movement, and the whole issue of race relations in southern society. It is a tall order for any one book, especially when allied to affectionate reminiscences of his father and a host of anecdotes and tall tales that are frequently marginal in their relevance to the main concerns. However, the book is given coherence not merely by Caldwell's reiterative style but equally by a sense of the moral quest for values that the older and younger Caldwell each pursue in their separate professions.

The Reverend I. S. Caldwell's job, as a kind of roving troubleshooter in the various congregations of the Associated Reformed Presbyterian Church, gives Caldwell an excellent opportunity to use the methods of documentary writing that had succeeded well for him during the 1930s—a mixture of storytelling, first-person monologues by characters, and more general analysis in Caldwell's more "educated" voice. This leads to an easy balance between tales of humor and horror and partisan theorizing that also evokes many of the qualities of Caldwell's fiction, though with the significant difference here of the intrusions of a highly opinionated author. Once again, Caldwell shows his taste for people in outlandish situations. The Reverend I. S. Caldwell officiates at literal shotgun weddings, refuses to pray for the victory of the local baseball team in order to save the bets of church members, becomes the innocent accessory of a bootlegger, and tries to arbitrate between the factions of a congregation that has split over the issue of whether or not to carpet the church floor. In this latter confrontation, "the bare-floor and the carpet-floor advocates had stopped speaking to one another, two divorces had occurred in intermarried families, and there had been a shooting affray in which one member was killed and another paralysed for life" (DS, 18). This is clearly the raw material of fiction, and pretty tall tales at that, but it captures the combination of pettiness and fanaticism that Caldwell finds everywhere in the churches.

He notices that "money becomes more scarce and religion becomes increasingly plentiful" and that the frenzies induced by the "frequent priming of emotional glands" (*DS*, 25) act as a narcotic or distraction from the pain of everyday life. On a trip through a poverty-stricken region, father and son are accosted by an excited farmer searching desperately for a preacher for his dying wife. When the Reverend I. S. obliges, he and his son find a scene of suffering and deprivation equal to that depicted in any of Caldwell's novels. However, the emaciated and feeble patient has apparently been expecting a faith healer, and when I. S. fails to oblige, she turns into a spitting, swearing shrew who collapses only after she has exhausted her venom. For the clergyman father, such departures into irrational and hysterical behavior constitute a betrayal of his conception of Christianity; but for his son, these are an inevitable and intrinsic part of the religion's appeal to the poor, because it compensates in good measure for the physical and spiritual deprivation of their lives.

The more serious indictment from Erskine Caldwell against these southern churches is that they nourish a rabid anti-intellectualism that denies all independent, speculative thinking in their members on matters of public morality, social action, and political change. The congregations are deliberately aided by the institutions of the church in becoming superstitious, bigoted, reactionary, unethical, and prey to their emotional manipulation. Encouraged in the belief that they are chosen and sanctified, their zeal is also channeled into racist organizations, where ideology and self-interest become hopelessly entangled. The owner of a general merchandise store makes Caldwell's point for him: "I'm a good Christian and I'd get down on my knees and wash the feet of Jesus Christ if I had the chance. But you'll never see me getting down like that in front of a black nigger and tying his shoe laces for him. But the Jews will do it, because they're Jews" (*DS*, 149). Caldwell makes the transition so frequently in his text from religious fervor to racism that it eventually becomes a tacit association, and he writes freely of racism without even mentioning the connection. Amid the wealthier urban churches of the conservative Protestant denominations, Caldwell finds not so much a perversion of ethics (as in the fundamentalists) as a bland evasion of all moral questions in favor of good fellowship, good business, and complacency. Such churches assess their mission wholly in numbers—membership, seating capacity, attendance, "four complete sets of choir robes so that the twenty-four members of our choir would have a complete change of costume in a different colour for each Sunday of the month" (*DS*, 81–82). Financially, these churches make their most successful investments in low-income rental housing to blacks and poor whites, and enjoy large bequests from benefactors who have been wooed away from their families by assiduous church committees. Although the mode of the book is comic and anecdotal, it is a bitter satire on the practices of southern Protestantism and, curiously, a loving tribute to a father who represented to Caldwell the best that could come out of that tradition.

Caldwell devotes the larger part of *Deep South* to white churches and a second, smaller part to black churches. He explores the latter's history and customs in a much more sympathetic fashion, finding their religion both more congenial and more attuned to society and political action. However, it is apparent from the lengths of the two sections of the book that it is the orgies and hypocrisies of the white churches, of the Hammer Heads, speakers in tongues, and blood drinkers, and the machinations of the con men, revivalists, boosters, and show business promoters that fascinate him. The book gives a biased and highly personal view, though not seemingly without considerable empirical basis, of southern religion and ethics. It does not perhaps offer a complete explanation for Caldwell's fictional bigots and zealots, but it shows once again the extent to which Caldwell's seemingly naïve material and technique is the result of a conscious and more sophisticated perspective.

In 1976, when Caldwell was in his seventies, he produced his last work of nonfiction (apart from his posthumously published autobiography, *With All My Might*), the travelogue *Afternoons in Mid-America*. The tendency in Caldwell's later nonfiction to drop the guise of simplicity and permit himself a broader range of omniscient speculation is furthered here. Caldwell's perspective on Middle America is now that of the urbane world traveler who has visited spas in Czechoslovakia, dined with Picasso, and met European monarchs. His vocabulary is also markedly different in range from the novels; in fact, it is only by reading Caldwell's nonfiction that one becomes aware of the extent to which the fictional voice and tone are consciously, rather than genuinely, naïve. However, the middle western states in the seventies do not provide Caldwell with the kind of stimulus necessary for his best work. Although he returns again to some of his enduring concerns, such as the preservation of the land and the relations between various races and ethnic groups, what he sees provokes neither outraged laughter nor concerned pity. Farmers are now aware of the need for conservation:

"The good rich soil we're blessed with here in the valley is a precious thing, and every inch of it ought to be protected against erosion and abuse" (*AM*, 142); and although racial divisions are still keen, Caldwell protests in this book not against lynching and chain gangs but against "sick jokes and ethnic anecdotes" (*AM*, 121). He is still moved by poverty and injustice, but his perceptions of them are less harsh, and a mellow Erskine Caldwell is not much Caldwell at all. Almost without exception, the liveliest parts of *Afternoons in Mid-America* are reminiscences of Caldwell's childhood and his southern background that evoke the familiar blend of cruelty, titillation, and compassion, although such stories can scarcely be justified as relevant to the main material of the book. Caldwell's imagination and his conscience, the two key elements of his nonfiction, had always functioned best in an extreme environment. With neither crisis nor chronic perversion of normality to encourage him, he resorts to the memory of these in the Great Depression and in the South in order to recapture his personal tone.

Any final assessment of Caldwell's contribution to the documentary genre in America must rest on the work he did in the 1930s, when he developed the techniques that served him throughout his literary career. He recognized from the outset that documentary truth has more kinship with the authenticity of fiction than with scientific poll taking; therefore, he never assumed a factitious air of disinterestedness about the material he recorded. Documentary and nonfiction writing was always for Caldwell partisan, personal, and highly selective; his imagination played as vital a part in it as his conscience and observation. Yet there are clear stylistic and ideological distinctions between Caldwell's fiction and nonfiction. Despite the obvious inventive quality of much of his reporting, which led several of his critics to label it fiction, Caldwell maintains a separate persona, vocabulary, and technique, and even point of view in his nonfiction. Although the fiction is almost consistently notable for the author's disengaged stance from the "antics and motivations" of his characters, the nonfiction permits an intrusive author, calling attention to his presence, his awkwardness, his anger, and his sympathy. The more educated vocabulary of the nonfiction reveals to what extent the ingenuous style of the fiction is a consciously contrived technique, while the tendency to separate comedy from degradation in the nonfiction suggests a very different ideological purpose—reform rather than despair for the victims of economic and racial exploitation. And while the underlying vision of human nature and society, especially as symbolically manifested in the South, is consistent in all his work, it is in the nonfiction that the intensity of Caldwell's moral purpose is most evident. By developing a carefully wrought, inventive literary method for his documentary reporting, he succeeded, in his best works, in negating the conventional distinction between effective propaganda and genuine and worthy art.

# 7

## Caldwell and the Critics

*The poor South! The genteel novelists of the 1900s sentimentalized it beyond recognition; Caldwell has vulgarized it in a version which France, Russia, and Japan accept as sober (and welcome) truth.*
—Willard Thorp

*Doubts concerning the universality of aesthetic values can be particularly reinforced by the acuteness of the differences between one nation and another in their respective estimations of artistic achievement.*
—Levin Schücking

If Erskine Caldwell's nonfiction and documentary writing demonstrate the skillful application of the techniques of fiction to the revelation of observed fact, no less creative are the various autobiographies, interviews, and public addresses through which he depicted his own career and aspirations as a writer. From the early 1929 broadside *In Defense of Myself*, through his three literary autobiographies—*Call It Experience* (1951), *Writing in America* (1967), and *With All My Might* (1987)—as well as in numerous lectures, letters to newspapers, and interviews given as late as his eighty-first birthday, Caldwell was consistent and masterful in selecting, omitting, emphasizing, and indeed inventing the elements of his own literary image. Throughout his long career, these carefully manufactured attitudes and self-portraits formed one side of a species of absentee dialogue between Caldwell and his critics, whom he otherwise ridiculed, berated, and purported to ignore completely. His critic baiting ranged in mood from caustic humor to charged indictments. The critic, he wrote, is a "literary eunuch or procurer" (WA, 11); he is "the person who kicks the author's shins and flails the reader's spirits whenever consummation between them takes place without his active procurement" (WA, 11); he is "the lazy sparrow who moved into a ready-made crow's nest in the top of a tall tree" (WA, 31); and, most damningly, "The poverty of contemporary fiction has been caused by the inept, inert, and inadequate knowledge and experience of the American literary critic" (*WA*, 59). The frequency and intensity of Caldwell's disparagement of critics and reviewers suggest some keen disappointment in their reaction to him, and yet the image of himself that he nurtured was not one that was likely to encourage more profound and serious readings of his work. His pose as a literary innocent, a *mere* storyteller, continually evaded and denied many of the most salient artistic and ideological qualities of his fiction, and asserted his defiance of any judgments on his achievements other than his own and those of his vast popular audience. He resolutely avoided discussing the grotesque and dissonant nature of his writing, and though he appeared to speak freely and frequently on his methods and intentions, he proved ultimately to be as cagey and contradictory as the fiction itself.

The complement to Caldwell's perplexing side of this dialogue was the variety of judgments made on him by a remarkable range of literary and political partisans and antagonists, by an international array of scholars and artists, and, implicitly, by his enormous reading public. Though Caldwell's carefully molded image proved in the end to be quite distinct from the vagaries of his literary reputation, the two shed an oblique light on each other. They show that Caldwell's startling simplicity and originality were the potential source of lively intellectual debates that never came to full fruition, partly because of the author's own recalcitrance in cultivating his literary innocence and critical isolation, and partly because of the attenuated quality of his lengthy professional career. However, Caldwell's critics too often resisted what was most novel and disturbing in his work during the major formative years of his reputation. Especially in his own country, critics looked for ideological impurities and base motives that demonstrated the perversion of a genuine talent; and, in their desire to classify and define a writer who confounded traditional categories, they tried to advise and guide him into more recognizably acceptable genres and modes. Critics in other countries, for different reasons, responded much more enthusiastically to Caldwell, and their reactions too form a very significant part of that incipient dialogue that helps to reveal both the forceful and unsettling nature of his writing.

Caldwell's earliest contribution to the critical debate on his work began before he had published any fiction, and even in advance of his first literary self-portrait, *In Defense of Myself* (1929). He set the pattern with what was later to prove a typically incongruous essay, "The Georgia Cracker," which appeared in 1926. In ridiculing his native state's boosterism, religious fanaticism, and racism, Caldwell revealed for the first time a satirical impulse that veered between bitter vituperation and slapstick farce, between an intense commitment to ethical and ideological concerns and a disconcerting glee in the vulgar idiocies of human nature. These conflicting tendencies to sermonize, shudder, gape, and giggle were precisely those qualities that informed so much of Caldwell's later fiction; yet in all of his discussions of his writing, he never dealt with the contradictory emotions and paradoxical attitudes evoked by it. He did concede the truism that "there is comedy in tragedy and tragedy in comedy," but quickly retreated from even this admission into his usual ingenuousness about his own procedures: "By the time I got halfway through the chapter [I was writing] I still wouldn't know whether the effect was going to be funny or sad." Rather than trying to articulate his sense of incongruity, Caldwell tended to dwell instead on his minor stylistic devices and isolated tags of theory, and to insist on what he was *not* doing in his writing. He was not, he said, a social critic; he was not a humorist; he was unread; he rejected symbolism, excluded dialect, had no preconceived notions about his work, and, finally, it didn't "mean a thing."[1] Not all of Caldwell's pronouncements were so nihilistic or even so modest, but they were all essentially reductive in nature. They tended to acknowledge opposing possibilities in his work only in isolation from each other, elsewhere reversing the emphasis, but never offering a theory commensurate with the complexity of the fiction. From this first minor essay through all his later commentaries, he revealed a similar waywardness with many of the central areas of critical concern, from questions about the accuracy and authenticity of his fictional world to challenges to his ideological intentions, popular success, and even his own durability as a significant voice in American literature.

Perhaps the most extreme example of Caldwell's capacity to engender confusion over an issue particularly relevant to the critical debate that arose over his work in the 1930s was his handling of the vexed question of the fictiveness of his fiction and the realism with which he depicted the people and circumstances of his novels and stories. Although the two fictional perspectives of the imaginary and

1. Erskine Caldwell, "The Georgia Cracker," *Haldeman-Julius Monthly* (November, 1926), reprinted in Sutton, *Black Like It Is/Was*, 123–27; Tharpe, "Interview with Erskine Caldwell," 74; Collins, "Erskine Caldwell at Work," 22.

the mimetic need not necessarily be antithetical or mutually exclusive, they certainly became so in the politically and socially charged atmosphere of the 1930s, when Caldwell wrote his major fiction—especially when the subjects of that fiction were people existing in peripheral regions of extreme poverty and isolation. In *Writing in America*, Caldwell took a stand on a position he frequently reiterated elsewhere on the transcendence of fiction over external fact: "Fiction . . . is not reality, but the illusion of reality is real and genuine. Even the label of realism or realistic or naturalistic placed upon a novel signifies only that it is a modification of the real for the purpose of fiction. . . . At its best . . . fiction is a deft and magic projection of the imagination beyond all existing limits of reality" (*WA*, 76). He discussed the transformation of fictional characters from names on paper to something "even more real and lifelike than life itself" (*WA*, 14), argued for the need for the imagination "to invent something better than life because life itself is dull and prosaic," and reflected on the greatness of Faulkner's writing because "it was not a reproduction of life. It was a creation of life, and therefore it was much sharper, much more true than the reality of it would have been." He seemed to enjoy reminding his readers that fiction was a form of "crafty dishonesty," that in his tale "It Happened Like This," "none of the events in the story ever took place," and that "there is nothing so dispiriting as adventure, nothing so exciting as imagination." He even warned: "It is to the credit of fiction as a form of art that readers are moved to ask for proof, but it also shows a lack of discrimination on the part of readers when they are unable to distinguish between fantasy and reality."[2] Such rejections of the social veracity and actuality of fiction were accompanied by frequent disavowals from Caldwell that his own fictional world was created with any intentions to use his imagination to redress or reform the problems of his society, again a particularly tricky contention, given his subjects and the milieu of the Great Depression. A chorus of denials runs through his many interviews: "I'm a writer, not a crusader. I leave the crusading to others"; "I've never had the ability to be a social critic. . . . I have not consciously and knowingly set out to be a social critic"; "I get the feeling that people think I'm trying to reform something"; "I've always consid-

2. Broadwell and Hoag, "The Art of Fiction LXII," 131; Tharpe, "Interview with Erskine Caldwell," 68; Caldwell, Introduction to *Tobacco Road*, in *Critical Essays*, ed. MacDonald, 223; Erskine Caldwell, *Jackpot: The Short Stories of Erskine Caldwell* (New York: 1940), 165, 111, 29.

ered myself essentially an observer, a bystander"; "I'm a writer, not
a reformer."[3]

Although Caldwell appeared to endorse, on general principle,
these theories of purely imaginary, nonreformist fiction, he did in
fact concede in many specific instances that his stories and novels
had originated in his observations of social and economic inequities,
that his sympathies were partisan, and that he believed that literature had certain clear social responsibilities. He agreed that "Kneel
to the Rising Sun" was "a story about the injustice of a Southern
landowner in dealing with one of his white tenants" (CE, 154);
"Blue Boy" was written "to give expression to my feelings after having seen a person of inferior position being mistreated by one of
superior force" (J, 219); God's Little Acre, he acknowledged, was
based in part on the strike of southern textile workers at Gastonia;
Tobacco Road was an attempt to show that the South had "produced
a coolie serfdom" and had been written out of love for the South
and "as a means of exposing the shame of its civilization." His most
general and emphatic statement of these attitudes came in response
to what he believed was a typical criticism of his work: "You write
too much about poor people. Why don't you write about the pleasant things in life?" Caldwell replied: "Those enjoying the pleasant
things in life are fewer than those enduring the unpleasant. When
this social condition no longer exists, I'll feel there is no longer any
purpose in writing about the effects of poverty on the human spirit"
(CE, 235). Although none of these examples of explicit social concern undermines the notion of Caldwell's fictional world as an invented rather than an imitated one, he also freely admitted on various occasions the extent to which he was motivated by the desire
not just to create but to record the buried lives of people outside
the American mainstream. When his first novel, The Bastard, was
banned in 1929, he immediately issued a broadside defending the
work and its subject, which he said "was conceived and written as
an important and untouched phase of American mores," and he repeatedly endorsed the value of regional and local fiction by noting
(in language that might be as apt for sociology as for literature) that
"it keeps the records for, and makes the interpretation of, the social
and racial structure of the nation. It is the vivid history of the folkways of the country; it is the personal diary of the people" (WA,

3. Broadwell and Hoag, "A Writer First," 92; Tharpe, "Interview with Erskine
Caldwell," 64; Collins, "Erskine Caldwell at Work," 22; Broadwell and Hoag, "A
Writer First," 95.

119).[4] He placed his hopes for an enduring American fiction in works that would be "a record and a revelation of the social, moral, political, and economic history of America" (*WA*, 122), and he challenged young writers "to dramatize and interpret and give meaningful direction to the unresolved economic and racial inequalities" of their country (*WA*, 117).

On some occasions, Caldwell even took the final leap from this "fiction as social history" position to a complete merging and identification of imaginary characters and episodes and their actual historical and sociological sources, in both the fiction of others and himself. Of the lower-class characters in Ben Field's *The Cock's Funeral*, he wrote, "If their language and habits offend, it is not their shame, but America's." His most inextricable association between his own fiction and social reality came in a heated response to the banning of *Tobacco Road* and *God's Little Acre* by the Teachers' College of Columbia University, when he wrote: "These future teachers go to all parts of the nation; they will now go with prejudiced minds to your community and mine, to teach our children that the people of Tobacco Road in Georgia are not worthy of thought or notice. . . . Teachers' College of Columbia University . . . has beheaded the teeming thousands of Tobacco Road by the simple method of refusing to admit their existence." This rather remarkable demand for the recognition of a supposedly imaginary world (from one who had warned of the danger of confusing fiction and reality) was followed by advice from Caldwell to politicians about how Tobacco Road might eventually, "with the help of science, economics, sociology, and common humanity . . . be wiped completely off the map."[5] If a writer as concerned as Caldwell about discriminating between fantasy and fact could, in the heat of the economic and literary class wars of the Great Depression, so completely conflate *Tobacco Road* with the actual tobacco roads of Georgia, it is hardly surprising that reviewers, critics, journalists, politicians, and the general public followed suit in applying to Caldwell's fiction standards distinctly beyond normal literary conventions.

4. Ronald Wesley Hoag and Elizabeth Pell Broadwell, "Erskine Caldwell on Southern Realism," *Mississippi Quarterly*, XXXVI (1983), 580; Erskine Caldwell, "Tobacco Roads in the South," in *Critical Essays*, ed. MacDonald, 52, 51; Caldwell, *In Defense of Myself.*
5. Erskine Caldwell, Introduction to Ben Field, *The Cock's Funeral* (New York, 1937), 9; Erskine Caldwell, "Mr. Caldwell Protests," in *Critical Essays*, ed. MacDonald, 33; Caldwell, "Tobacco Roads in the South," 53.

The resulting scrutiny of the accuracy of Caldwell's fiction led to judgments on the economic viability of his analyses, the political orthodoxy of his imaginary characters, and the motives for which he was re-creating the lower depths of American life. Newspapers sent investigative reporters to check "the statements in 'Tobacco Road,'" courts of law considered "the truth and honesty" of *God's Little Acre*, and Georgia Representative Braswell Deen argued in Congress that, though he believed *Tobacco Road* to be set in his district, it was nevertheless "predicated on conditions which are as far from the truth . . . as the East from the West," or, indeed, he might have added, as fact from fiction.[6] Literary critics and reviewers were no more immune to ideological and political responses to Caldwell's work than were reporters and politicians, although they were considerably more skillful in making their partisan judgments appear to derive from impersonal and unbiased criteria. Among the critics who had the greatest vested interest in Caldwell's particular literary universe in the 1930s and early 1940s were the Southern Agrarians and their sympathizers and the Marxists and other leftward-leaning writers. Each group had a social as well as a literary program for the South, and for a number of years, Caldwell's work was closely read by both for evidence of orthodoxy or the taints of heresy. Together they gave Caldwell some of his liveliest and most doctrinaire responses, all in the service of a purportedly more ideal and objective vision of contemporary southern poverty.

For the Agrarians, Caldwell's poor white subjects, who fell economically and morally well below the rank of yeomen farmers or even good plain folk, were innately uncongenial to their pastoral, Jeffersonian ideology. When Donald Davidson contributed his survey "The Trend of Literature" to the 1935 anthology *Culture in the South*, he decided to pass over all books dealing with poor whites, because he believed them to be the result of a state of mind that was "not quite healthy." He suggested that writers who focused on this subject or on "Negro life" displayed a manifestation of blocked creative powers that turned them away from "southern life in its broader aspects." Davidson envisioned the contemporary southern writer in a dilemma that was in fact largely of the Agrarians' own creation, trapped between the pressures of an alien urban call to literary arms from "the little Russians of *The New Republic*" and a native preoccupation with time-honored regional concerns. He

6. "What Will Good People of Jefferson County Say of This?" in *Critical Essays*, ed. MacDonald, 107; "*People* v. *Viking Press, Inc.*," 30; "'Tobacco Road' Winds Its Way into Congress," in *Critical Essays*, ed. MacDonald, 49.

wrote: "The southern writer finds himself inhibited at the very moment when the greatest opportunities seem to open before him. The social programs that emanate from the metropolis, bearing in their train a host of powerful aesthetic ideas and literary modes, urge him in one direction. His sense of loyalty to his own tradition, indeed his fidelity as an artist to his subject-matter, pulls him in an opposite direction." Davidson's assumption that fidelity to one's subject matter excluded Negro and poor white life was not so overtly endorsed by other Agrarians, but Robert Penn Warren agreed in some measure with his sense of the "tragic contradiction" that faced the modern southern writer who sought to embrace both regional and contemporary political concerns in his work. Warren defined regional literature and proletarian literature as antithetical pursuits: the former was interested in the past, in a special place, almost inevitably rural, and in a way of life markedly individual; the latter focused on the future and on the industrial life of a particular social class. Warren defined his regional writer as apolitical, whereas his proletarian was likely to be a propagandist. However, for both he saw the danger of literary faddism. Such prescriptive definitions effectively excluded Caldwell from either category precisely because he shared so many concerns of each camp but conformed to neither. Rather than seeing Caldwell as an interesting embodiment of the literary possibilities of "tragic contradiction," those Agrarians who looked closely at his work tended to measure him against their own standards. John Donald Wade, for example, an ardent Agrarian, found Caldwell's sexual mysticism ludicrously unconvincing, whereas his agricultural mysticism was both "agreeable" and "substantial" because it laid the predicament of the southern farmer "distressingly close to Wall Street's own front doorstep." Wade declared that Caldwell's depiction of his own region's degeneracy was a means of pandering to New Yorkers' ("detached, nervous, thrill-goaded metro-cosmopolitans") literary taste for southern freaks, but curiously, he found the Maine story "Country Full of Swedes" to be "an uproarious account of the bewildered stupidity of native Down-Easters." Like many of the Agrarians, Wade disputed Caldwell's sociology under the guise of criticizing his aesthetic objectivity: *Tobacco Road* was, he insisted, "an individual case-study," "a particular" rather than a "universal," as though the subject itself was the arbiter of universality. W. T. Couch, in responding to the nonfiction book *You Have Seen Their Faces*, perhaps more reasonably raised the question of the narrowness of

Caldwell's indictment, but he showed the same readiness to confound and condemn Caldwell's political and imaginative responses to the South: "If Southern tenant farmers are at all like the Jeeter Lesters and Ty Ty Waldens with whom Mr. Caldwell has peopled his South, I cannot help wondering what good could come out of their collective action." Like Warren and Wade, Couch suggested that the tastes of the times were largely responsible for Caldwell's "merriment over psychopaths" on one hand and "sentimental slush" and "undiscriminating sympathy" on the other. Donald Davidson, writing on the same book, once again assumed regional treachery on Caldwell's part, asking, "What is the matter with any Southerner who turns state's evidence under circumstances like these?" Davidson found Caldwell's ideology at the core of his artistic treason, commenting that "as a student of farm tenancy in the South Mr. Caldwell would make a splendid Curator of a Soviet Park of Recreation and Culture."[7]

In the aftermath of such partisanship, Cleanth Brooks, attempting a calmer reassessment in "What Deep South Literature Needs" (1942), objected strenuously to readings of southern literature that assumed it must either be "whitewashing the magnolia blossom or urging us to some particular reform." Brooks seemed thus to stand above the fray; but when he turned to his study of individual writers, he asserted that Caldwell had "frequently been pushed into propaganda for various causes with a resulting confusion of his attitude toward his material" and, indeed, that "Mr. Caldwell frequently misunderstands his own purpose." Brooks rejected what he presumed to be Caldwell's "gleeful exultation at the collapse of a way of life" and his "propagandizing for a particular program which will make all shiny, sanitary, and aseptic," whereas he praised by contrast Faulkner's tragic vision, which did not indulge "in a sardonic and cynical description of decay."[8] Thus, despite his initial reservations about narrowly ideological readings of southern literature, Brooks joined his Agrarian compatriots in rejecting Caldwell's

7. Donald Davidson, "The Trend of Literature: A Partisan View," in *Culture in the South*, ed. W. T. Couch (Chapel Hill, 1935), 204, 185, 199; Robert Penn Warren, "Some Recent Novels," *Southern Review*, I (1935–36), 624–33 *passim;* John Donald Wade, "Sweet Are the Uses of Degeneracy," *Southern Review*, I (1935–36), 457, 466, 459, 455; W. T. Couch, "Landlord and Tenant," in *Critical Essays*, ed. MacDonald, 58, 59; Davidson, "Erskine Caldwell's Picture Book," 67, 62.

8. Cleanth Brooks, "What Deep South Literature Needs," *Saturday Review of Literature*, September 19, 1942, pp. 8–9.

art because of a revulsion from his politics. Though Caldwell was not read very sympathetically by the Agrarians, Brooks found in his writing a vitality and earthiness, encouraged him to write more folk comedy, and perceived the power of his grotesque vision. The others, though dismayed by what they viewed as his treachery and capitulation to northern, urban values, often seemed to be concerned in their own ways with exactly those questions and conflicts over region, poverty, rural life, decay, loyalty, and local custom that most preoccupied Caldwell, and all of them seemed at least tacitly to recognize this by paying him the compliment of taking his work very seriously indeed.

The other group of literary critics who approached Caldwell with committed fervor were those on the left wing. Once again he presented a frustrating paradox to them, both in his conception of the character of poor people and in his descriptive mode for their lives. Marxist reviewers like Norman Macleod and Jack Conroy, although professing pleasure (unlike the Agrarians) that Caldwell had "penetrated the lower crust of the south" and had produced in his novels "social document[s] of no small importance," nonetheless found his ideological sympathies insufficiently informed by correct political understanding. He needed to "go left," improve his sociology, go into "the higher sphere of dialectical development," and, above all, resist the weird and fantastic elements in his fiction that were in danger of neutralizing any advances he made in "social awareness."[9]

Caldwell's simple and unaffected prose style was uniformly applauded by these critics in appropriately hard-boiled terms. It was "a mighty wallop aimed flush at the jaw of industrial and agrarian exploitation"; it was "swell all the way through"; and one reviewer at least confessed that he had "never read anything to beat it." However, even the brashest of these proletarian sympathizers quailed before the sexual antics of Caldwell's characters and his mixture of concern for and detachment from them. The Marxists were no less distressed than the Agrarians by what they labeled the "decadent possibilities" of his interests, though the danger of pandering to the urban North with southern freaks was replaced for them by the danger of amusing the bourgeoisie with tales of lower-class lust and degeneracy. On the vexed question of the authenticity of Caldwell's fiction, Edward Dahlberg, while in his Marxist phase, wrote ap-

9. Macleod, "A Hardboiled Idealist," 6; Conroy, "Passion and Pellagra," 18; Macleod, "A Hardboiled Idealist," 7; Rolfe, "God's Little Acre," 25, 24.

provingly of *Tobacco Road:* "Not until Mr. Caldwell has learned to make poverty, hunger and sex something that can be nostalgically mistaken for art rather than truth will his writings be widely praised." However, just a year later and in a more politically disaffected mood, Dahlberg found the characters in *God's Little Acre* to be moving in "a quasi-Marxian haze ten thousand feet above Georgia and Carolina," their vitality sapped by the demands of "left band-wagonists." Oscar Cargill found Caldwell's fiction so convincing that he wondered how any Southerner could avoid recognizing the "shameful truths . . . told by a native son," or any future historian of southern literature deny the "patent authenticity" of such volumes as *Kneel to the Rising Sun.* The British Marxist critic Philip Henderson both anticipated and reversed Cleanth Brooks's judgment for Faulkner's tragic vision and against Caldwell's descent into propaganda. Henderson praised instead the convincing social reality of Caldwell's world and his proposed remedies for it, beside which he found Faulkner's creations to be "but the twisted shapes of his own despair."[10]

The one issue on which Agrarians and Marxists largely agreed on Caldwell—besides his irritating fascination for both groups—was his inability to put what they both agreed were his considerable talents to what they each considered to be their best use. For the Agrarians, this use was to employ his comic skill on regional folk material; for the literary left wing, it was to acquire that "social understanding which is the life of revolutionary prose." Given Caldwell's already cynical disappointment at the reception of his earliest books, it is hardly surprising that he began his response to a 1934 Symposium on Marxist Criticism in the *New Masses* by announcing: "In so many words, my complaint against criticism, both revolutionary and static, is that it is about 90 percent soap-suds. . . . A Marxist critic can work up just as much lather from a cake of soap as a capitalist reviewer." The doctrinaire readings of his fiction, interspersed with prescriptions and Olympian admonitions about how Caldwell might best discover his own true purpose, obviously soured the author on the value of critical exchange. This may well

10. Halper, "Caldwell Sees America," 41; Ferguson, "Caldwell's Stories," 70; Halper, "Caldwell Sees America," 42; Rolfe, "God's Little Acre," 24; Edward Dahlberg, "Raw Leaf," in *Critical Essays,* ed. MacDonald, 17; Edward Dahlberg, "Erskine Caldwell and Other 'Proletarian' Novelists," *Nation,* March 8, 1933, p. 265; Cargill, *Intellectual America,* 393; Philip Henderson, *The Novel Today: Studies in Contemporary Attitudes* (London, 1936), 150.

have had ultimately unhappy consequences for Caldwell's work and reputation; for despite their notable lack of disinterestedness, Caldwell's partisan critics offered him not merely lively ideological exchange but useful, if sometimes unpalatable, responses to his grotesque humor, his vulgarity, and his vision of pervasive irrationality and suffering. That his humor was so frequently perceived as cruelty, his vulgarity as titillation, and his incorrigible human beings as freaks beyond the pale of the civilized world might understandably have annoyed Caldwell, but his future works might also have benefited from a recognition of what was most provocative and challenging in them to such different groups of concerned readers. Instead of moving to polarize his later work toward sensationalism on the one hand and didacticism on the other, Caldwell might have discovered that these critiques reinforced his own innate sense of the power of incongruity to intrigue and confuse and finally to lead his readers into debates, albeit unresolved and fractious, about the very issues that most concerned him—how best to convey the treacherous relationships between the "antics and motivations" of a depraved and deprived human nature. Malcolm Cowley, in a retrospective essay on Caldwell's career, claimed that Caldwell lost valuable stimulation in the formative years of his career by his willful isolation from other writers and their ideas; the same point may well be made about Caldwell's absolute rejection of the criticism and reviews of his major work.[11] Far from being the hacks, parasites, and procurers of his characterizations, the authors of this criticism included some of the best literary minds of the day, from all parts of the political spectrum, from Cowley himself, Kenneth Burke, Edward Dahlberg, James T. Farrell, and Richard Wright to Randall Jarrell, Donald Davidson, Robert Penn Warren, and Cleanth Brooks. Almost all were partisan; many were intemperate, high-handed, and sometimes obtuse; but they were passionately engaged with his work as an element in their own involvement in modern literature and ideology, and his rejection of them removed a vital intellectual context for his own thinking.

Caldwell's determination to be his own solitary taskmaster was not particularly different from the independence from any external authority or influence claimed by many other American writers; but in his case, the resistance to his fellow writers and literary profes-

---

11. Conroy, "Passion and Pellagra," 18; "Authors' Field Day: A Symposium on Marxist Criticism," *New Masses*, July 3, 1934, p. 27; Cowley, "Georgia Boy," 324.

sionals seemed to many of them to be accompanied by a growing popular success that was not entirely fortuitous, and on which few of them looked kindly. As early as November, 1931, Ezra Pound had written to the editor of *Pagany*, where a few of his first stories had appeared, "Wdnt. it be better for people like Caldwell . . . to be able to afford to stay in a li'erary mag. instead of its being one's human duty to bid 'em god speed for the gate receipts?" This assumption that the rarefied experimental air of the little magazines and the company of other aspiring and serious writers would be good for Caldwell was not one that seemed likely to be challenged in 1931, when he had no alternative channels for publishing his work and a very select audience indeed. In fact, Pound himself had conceded, "I admit the case dont immediately rise." However, the case did rise very rapidly with the publication of *Tobacco Road* in 1932 and, more significantly, with Jack Kirkland's dramatization of the novel, which began its Broadway run on December 4, 1933, and continued for seven and a half years, then a record for the New York theater. The production continued virtually uninterrupted in the United States or abroad for the next seventeen years. Caldwell candidly attributed its success to a series of enthusiastic editorials in the *Daily News*, to the talents of the actors playing Jeeter and Dude, and to Jack Kirkland's determination to keep it going (*CE*, 151). However, Ralph Ellison much more recently suggested that the Caldwellian manic comedy of the play evoked a "shock of recognition" from the audience at the play's vision of extreme irrationality both in individuals and their dislocated society, a shock Ellison compared in impact to the contemporaneous Dadaist exhibition at the Museum of Modern Art, which likewise proved widely successful.[12] Whatever the cause of its popularity, the play brought the unknown young novelist a notoriety that was aided by the 1933 pornography trial of *God's Little Acre* and a number of subsequent efforts to ban and censor his work. It also gave him the beginning of the "gate receipts" that eventually enabled him to live comfortably as a professional writer. By his own account, he progressed from bare subsistence on rat-trap cheese and a daily bowl of soup in 1931 to weekly royalties of $2,000 in 1937 from the play alone and additional monthly royalties of $1,000 from his books (*CE*, 112, 113, 172).

Caldwell became an astute businessman (despite his professed

12. Ezra Pound, as quoted in Halpert, *A Return to "Pagany,"* 327–28; see Ellison, *Going to the Territory*, 181–86.

early naïveté about money), signing 25-cent paperbacks in drugstore receptions and cooperating with his publishers in every aspect of the promotion and sales of his work. His financial success and his enjoyment of it brought innuendoes and more overt attacks from critics who did not hesitate to impugn his literary motives, although Caldwell never pretended to consider writing anything other than a paying profession. John Donald Wade's accusation that Caldwell was pandering to decadent metropolitan tastes, Jonathan Daniels' suggestion that he had found "pay dirt" in ridiculing half-wits, and Harrison Smith's description of Caldwell's readers as "customers" looking for eroticism and bawdy humor suggest that Caldwell's intentions were frequently scrutinized and found wanting. Victor Weybright, Caldwell's publisher for many years at New American Library, retaliated by challenging the critics' integrity, arguing that "the massive multi-million sales of Caldwell's books . . . gave fastidious critics . . . [a] hypocritical reason to aver that Caldwell was too successful to be really good," and noted that Caldwell had snubbed the critics by being interested only in "three points of view: his own, that of his publishers and that of his readers."[13]

The question of whether Caldwell's popularity involved a diminishment of his artistic integrity or was merely the occasion for what Weybright termed the "reverse snobbism of literary critics" has been interestingly discussed by one of his modern critics, James Devlin, who concludes, after a careful study of Caldwell's attitudes and of the formulas common to best-selling fiction, that he both accedes to and departs radically from its standards. Devlin argues that his simple prose style, his emphasis on humor and sexuality, his topicality, his "exotic" southern settings, and his sometimes "protean" characters who bend to the needs of the novel are indeed in accord with best-seller patterns, but his more general concern for character over plot and the inability of most of his characters to come to self-knowledge or to change their ways are less typical. Devlin concludes that Caldwell "seeks not just to win an audience . . . but to change one," and thus he uses certain "popular 'ingredients'" that are made to serve an other than best-selling intention, although he openly enjoys the fruits of his hard work and success.[14]

13. Edward E. Lewis, "Letter to Victor Dalmas," *Pembroke Magazine* XI (1979), 121; Victor Weybright, "Georgia Boy—A Recollection from the Inner Sanctum," *Pembroke Magazine*, XI (1979), 118–20; Smith, "Comic Citizens of the South," 89; Weybright, "Georgia Boy," 115, 118.

14. Weybright, "Georgia Boy," 118; Devlin, *Erskine Caldwell*, 133–38.

A certain irony in this whole issue of Caldwell's popularity and artistic integrity is the fact that Caldwell's very best-selling novels, *God's Little Acre, Tobacco Road, Tragic Ground,* and *Trouble in July,* are in fact also those that have been accorded the most critical acclaim, whereas many of the later and weaker novels, by reviewers' standards, do not appear to have sold so well. Further complicating any simple correlation between the pursuit of "gate receipts" and artistic decline is the fact that both *Tobacco Road* and *God's Little Acre* initially sold quite poorly—five thousand copies of *Tobacco Road* in its first year, ten thousand of *God's Little Acre*. Only after the successful staging of the Kirkland play did the sales really begin to escalate, without, obviously, any change in the texts themselves. In addition, Caldwell's short stories seem to be an exception to any conclusions that may be drawn about his novels, for 65 percent of them were written before 1940. They were generally of very high quality indeed, yet they have been generally neglected by both publishers and critics alike. Caldwell himself, as usual, contributed to these ironies and inconsistencies by his public pronouncements on the issue: "I never wanted to have a bestseller"; "I've never pushed my books at the reader"; and, in some measure of contradiction, "I like to take part in the distribution of what I do. I'll go to a sales convention with a publisher, for example, and spend a week there talking to people in the business, make a little speech to salespeople." On the effect of the potential reader on his work, Caldwell allowed similar discrepancies: "Whatever I accomplish as a writer I accomplish for myself, not for the reader"; "I don't know what a reader is, you know. He's somebody I don't visualize at all"; but when asked about his audiences abroad, "I don't write anything now that has dialect in it. . . . I have nothing against it, it's fine and all right and a writer should do it if he wants to; but I don't think you can translate dialect."[15] However, because Caldwell had eschewed dialect virtually from the start of his career and for other, more artistic reasons, it is difficult to make a case that even this seeming acquiescence to the demands of a mass market actually altered the nature of his fiction.

Besides the critical accusation that Caldwell was too popular, he was also reprimanded for having written too much. This further taint did not so much blur Caldwell's reputation as help put him

15. Noble, "Erskine Caldwell," 171; Tharpe, "Interview with Erskine Caldwell," 73; Hoag and Broadwell, "Erskine Caldwell on Southern Realism," 583; Tharpe, "Interview with Erskine Caldwell," 65; Hoag and Broadwell, "Erskine Caldwell on Southern Realism," 583; Collins, "Erskine Caldwell at Work," 23, 26.

outside the realm where reputations are assessed. After the mid-1940s, Caldwell's new writings failed to be taken seriously by critics and reviewers in the United States; and, by a cruel reaction, this caused his considerable body of already accomplished writing to be similarly neglected, so that the weaker works appeared to qualify and in some measure actually negate the stronger. Scott MacDonald characterized this response as a feeling that "if Caldwell could write books *this* bad . . . those famous earlier novels must be less significant than we've realized." Clearly, it never occurred to Caldwell to stop writing and rest on his achievements or even to alter his pace significantly. He viewed writing as his life's ongoing business rather than as a series of accomplishments, and in a telling response in 1982 to an interviewer's question as to whether he had ever had long dry spells, he replied, "No. You can always write something." Yet, in the late 1930s, Margaret Bourke-White reported one of Caldwell's favorite sayings to be "The life of a writer is just ten years"—apparently a fear that he was already coming close to the end of his innovative period.[16]

Certainly, the critical response to him tended to vindicate his own ten-year theory. Although he retained a certain notoriety as America's best-selling writer that brought him interviews in *Esquire* and *Life* and features on his Arizona home in *House Beautiful*, in the years after 1943, in terms of his treatment by academic critics, Caldwell went from controversy to neglect. In studies and histories of American literature, Caldwell shrank from equal treatment with Hemingway, Fitzgerald, Faulkner, and Anderson in such works as Oscar Cargill's *Intellectual America* and Joseph Warren Beach's *American Fiction, 1920–1940*, both published in 1941, to Willard Thorp's irritable aside in his 1960 survey *American Writing in the Twentieth Century:* "For every American who has read a novel by Elizabeth Roberts or Eudora Welty there are 10,000 who read Erskine Caldwell." Caldwell continued to be taken seriously in a number of thematic studies of American literature that examined his role as a grotesque, proletarian, or southern writer, but in his own country at least, he was certainly no longer in the league of what the French had named "Les Cinq Grands"—Caldwell, Faulkner, Hemingway, Dos Passos, and Steinbeck. Contributing as much to Caldwell's disappearance from the American literary canon as the in-

16. MacDonald, Introduction to *Critical Essays*, xv; Broadwell and Hoag, "The Art of Fiction LXII," 140; Bourke-White, *Portrait of Myself*, 196.

difference of the critics was his virtual exclusion from anthologies and textbook series designed for classroom use, a telling omission for an author of so many fine and brief short stories. In 1940, Richard Wright had noted in his review of *Trouble in July* that Caldwell's depiction of the white sheriff had made us "understand why lynchings are possible"; but in 1984, James Baldwin and Julius Lester agreed in a New York *Times* interview that no white writer had attempted to write about lynching from the point of view of the lyncher, and that the "effort to avoid the presence of black people" as a subject was constricting American literature.[17]

Though such comments must have been galling to him, Caldwell remained sanguine about the vicissitudes of his reputation—in keeping with his insistence that his accomplishments were for himself and not for his readers or critics. He reflected several times on his sense that works of literature, including his own, were intimately tied to the contexts in which they appeared. This seemed to him to be especially true of that new American literature that began in the 1930s in an era of "despair and despondency" when a "new generation of native writers" allowed Americans to see "their lives in true perspective" (*WA*, 116). He insisted that "fiction in America changes almost from one day to the next. We are still a very volatile civilization. . . . In America, fiction reflects current lifestyles, economic conditions, wars, lots of things. The interests of American readers change with the times. Especially here, writing has to be contemporary." Acknowledging that his own work would never be contemporary again, he suggested rather modestly near the end of his life that any revival of interest in it would no longer be for the "content" but perhaps for the style or "maybe for some historical appeal." There seems certainly to be a tacit recognition in this that his central concerns (the "content" that is no longer of interest) must have fallen away in significance from the vivid relevance of the depression years, although in fact his focus on poverty, racism, sexual combat, and irrationality seems in no real danger of obsolescence. In discussing the evolution of his writing and his literary material, Caldwell never on any occasion mentioned what appears to be in the early 1940s a gradual abandonment of the most salient icon in his fiction—the grotesque southern poor white—for more conventional subjects and modes. Whether this was an effort to take a new

17. Willard Thorp, *American Writing in the Twentieth Century* (Cambridge, Mass., 1960), 261; Wright, "Lynching Bee," 72; Lester, "James Baldwin," 23.

direction in writing after his first ten-year "life," or an attempt to keep up with what he perceived to be the changing interests of a kinetic civilization, or simply a need to keep on writing something else because that was his self-defined purpose in life, it is clear that the decline of his reputation coincided much less with a turn to popularizing than with the turn away from the central source of his originality of vision. Even the best of Caldwell's later works drew scant attention, and in conjunction with this neglect, his former achievements were rarely discussed in his own country. When Faulkner commented on Caldwell's checkered career, he noted in praising him, "I think that the first books, *God's Little Acre* and the short stories, that's enough for any man," but in the end it seemed not enough to redeem his former controversial esteem from the shadow of his later work and his popular success.[18]

One curious fact about the dramatic decline of Caldwell's reputation is that it occurred almost exclusively in his own country. In 1982, when Gabriel García Marquez won the Nobel Prize for Literature, he said of his literary masters, "I learned a lot from James Joyce and Erskine Caldwell," with no hint of the irony such a juxtaposition might provoke in Caldwell's homeland. Caldwell's eightieth birthday in 1983 was the occasion of a substantial article on him in a Tokyo newspaper by Fugisato Kitajima, who had the previous year published in Japanese a bibliography of Caldwell. None exists yet in English. Caldwell is the subject of ongoing critical and academic interest in France, Italy, Germany, the Soviet Union, and Japan, and retains the status in those countries, which he perhaps enjoyed almost from the beginning, of a major American artist. Among eminent artists in other countries, Albert Camus staged *Tobacco Road* in 1938, Cesare Pavese applied to translate *God's Little Acre* because Caldwell "fascinated him," Picasso planned to collaborate with Caldwell to illustrate *The Sacrilege of Alan Kent*, and Alberto Moravia, André Maurois, André Gide, and Jean-Paul Sartre all expressed their admiration for him. In France, where Caldwell's standing was always high, there was at one point even an odd reversal of his American predicament, with Caldwell in high critical esteem but not at all among the best sellers.[19]

18. Broadwell and Hoag, "The Art of Fiction LXII," 152; Hoag and Broadwell, "Erskine Caldwell on Southern Realism," 583; Frederick L. Gwynn and Joseph L. Blotner, eds., *Faulkner in the University: Class Conference at the University of Virginia, 1957–1958* (Charlottesville, 1959), 143.

19. Marlese Simons, "A Talk with Gabriel García Marquez," *New York Times*

The reasons for a writer's being dismissed at home and admired abroad are legion and often incidental on both sides to anything so elusive as a sense of intrinsic merit in the literature. In France, Caldwell enjoyed a reputation as, among other things, "one of the prides and joys of the French avant-garde," as *the* archetypically American writer, and as the inheritor of the celebrated Gothicism of Edgar Allan Poe. The comparison with Poe, whom Caldwell naturally claimed never to have read, is an interesting one more for the process of the making of a literary reputation than for the supposedly similar necrophilic tendencies. Certainly, Poe's aristocratic and revivified Madelines and Ligeias are hardly in the same literary realm as Jeeter Lester's rat-eaten father or the copulating corpses of *Poor Fool.* However, Caldwell, like Poe, had the good fortune to have an extremely talented translator of his works into French, and not merely a translator but a man of considerable literary sensibility and authority who prepared the way for the advent of Caldwell's books in France with articles on him and introductions to his work. Maurice Edgar Coindreau, who also translated the other members of the "big five" as well as William Styron, Truman Capote, and Flannery O'Connor, published his translation of *God's Little Acre* with a preface by André Maurois in 1936. In 1934, he had reviewed the American edition of *Tobacco Road* in *Nouvelle Revue Française,* and in a 1936 article in the same journal, he introduced Caldwell generally to the French reading public as "among the best short story writers in the United States."[20] He translated *Tobacco Road* in 1937 and wrote the preface for a translation of *We Are the Living* in the same year; he later translated *Poor Fool* and *Tragic Ground.*

As Poe's reputation in France in the nineteenth century was stimulated and shaped by the translation and criticism of Baudelaire and Mallarmé, so in a more modest way was Caldwell's in the twen-

*Book Review,* December 5, 1982, p. 60. For Caldwell's high standing among foreign artists and intellectuals, see also, Ioan Comsa, "Caldwell's Stories: Common Reader Response, Analysis and Appreciation at Home and Abroad," *Pembroke Magazine,* XI (1979), 51–58; Edward P. Schwartz, "Caldwell 'On-the-Road' and Censorship Interlude," *Pembroke Magazine,* XI (1979), 85–87; Giordano De Biasio, "Who Is Afraid of the Jeeter Lesters?" *Pembroke Magazine,* XI (1979), 99 n. 16; Stewart H. Benedict, "Gallic Light on Erskine Caldwell," in *Critical Essays,* ed. MacDonald, 257–59; Sidney D. Braun and Seymour Lainoff, eds., *Transatlantic Mirrors: Essays in Franco-American Literary Relations* (Boston, 1978), 242.

20. Smith and Miner, *Transatlantic Migration,* 32, 155; Maurice Coindreau, as quoted in Benedict, "Gallic Light on Erskine Caldwell," 256.

tieth century by Coindreau. He introduced Caldwell by placing him
in a new generation of American writers, men like Robert Cantwell
and Edward Dahlberg, who had moved beyond what Coindreau
considered the romanticism of the postwar generation, into impas-
sive contemplation of people's cruel and degraded lives. He did not
dwell at all on the didactic or propaganda elements in Caldwell's
fiction that had bothered American critics, but emphasized instead
his pleasure in a grotesque mode of fiction at which he hardly knew
whether to laugh or cry, but was compelled to admire. He invoked
Rabelais, Swift, Twain, Goya, Walt Disney, and Charlie Chaplin to
suggest the qualities of Caldwell's vision, and found in his candid
treatment of instinctual behavior a sign of his maturity rather than
of a desire to shock or titillate. Caldwell's later French critics followed Coindreau in endorsing his "grotesque," "macabre," "burlesque" vision, and in admiring his "naïveté"; the vocabulary alone
suggests the French affinity for him. In his brutal and hard-boiled
pessimism, he was declared "particularly American" ("No one is
more American than Erskine Caldwell"). In his vulgar humor, he
was "proof of the health and youth of America," and his vigorous
writing was contrasted by French critics to their own morbid novels
of psychological analysis. So partisan were Caldwell's French critics
that they scolded and ridiculed his American detractors. Camus
boasted that Caldwell's books sold ten times as well in Paris as in
New York, and Sartre satirized the puritanism of Americans who
said to the French, "Can't you ever like anything but filth?"[21]

These were apt responses to critics like Willard Thorp, who was
distressed at the number of Americans who preferred to read Caldwell to Elizabeth Madox Roberts or Eudora Welty, and to Carl
Bode, whose explanation for Caldwell's success at home and popularity abroad was simply, "Sex did the job." There was another suspicion, too, often voiced by American critics, about the nature of
the French enthusiasm for Caldwell, namely, that it was based on
an unseemly delight in seeing the poverty, violence, and failure
of American society harshly exposed to the world. Faulkner and
Steinbeck were most frequently included with Caldwell in this accusation, a more sweeping national version of Donald Davidson's

21. Maurice Coindreau, "Lettres Étrangères," *Nouvelle Revue Française*, July
1, 1934, p. 127; Maurice Coindreau, "Lettres Étrangères," *Nouvelle Revue Française*, November 1, 1936, pp. 909–11; see Smith and Miner, *Transatlantic Migration*, 157, 154, 151, 79, 48; Jean-Paul Sartre, as quoted in Braun and Lainoff, *Transatlantic Mirrors*, 245.

indictment that Caldwell had betrayed his region by turning state's evidence. Sartre responded to this theory, too, by arguing that the French admired these writers not because they attacked America but because the fictions they created were "a sign of the imperfections of our time. . . . [W]e took the lesson to ourselves." A number of other American critics tried, in broader cultural terms, to explain the peculiar attraction of American literature, especially in the 1930s, for French audiences. Alfred Kazin, in *On Native Grounds*, looked to the political situation in Europe and noted: "While American writers had been trying to come of age longer than it seemed decent to remember and to meet the standards of Europe, Europe was trying desperately to stay alive. . . . In a moribund world [they] seemed a phenomenon of energy—reckless, aggressive, inventive, the symbol of a world . . . that . . . would remain vigorous and new." F. O. Matthiessen similarly argued: "It is a paradox that America, spared so far the worst violences of Fascism and war, has yet projected imaginative violence in a way that seems authentic to Europeans." Caldwell himself believed that the work of these naturalistic novelists in America in the 1930s was "the first enduring native tradition in fiction" (*WA*, 116) to come out of his country, and thus was for the first time something authentically American. Caldwell spoke of this new literature in *Writing in America* in terms very close to those of the French critics, and to Kazin's and Matthiessen's sense of the appeal of the brash force and fearless risk taking of this writing: "Novelists were writing in a language that everybody could understand—the American language—and they were able to reveal and interpret the true character of the American people for the first time. These books were hard and tough and relentless in wording and content; some were clumsy and awkward and misshapen; but all of them were revealing and unrestrained" (*WA*, 116). Caldwell here, as elsewhere, displays what Kazin noted as one of the most appealing features to Europeans about American writers—that the most interesting of them "gave the impression that no one had written before them."[22]

French critics, more than all others, seemed attuned to the sheer novelty of Caldwell's work and embraced the central incongruities

22. Bode, "Erskine Caldwell," 246; Jean-Paul Sartre, as quoted in Braun and Lainoff, *Transatlantic Mirrors*, 247; Alfred Kazin, *On Native Grounds: An Interpretation of Modern American Prose Literature* (New York, 1942), 370; F. O. Matthiessen, *From the Heart of Europe* (New York, 1948), 55; Alfred Kazin, Postscript to *On Native Grounds* (abr. ed.; Garden City, N.Y., 1955), 408.

Erskine Caldwell and the Fiction of Poverty

of gothic comedy and social exposé that had seemed so to confound his native commentators. Sartre also took pleasure in what was another stumbling block for some American critics; he approved of characters who were presented synthetically and whose acts defied analysis: "The heroes of Hemingway and Caldwell never explain themselves—do not allow themselves to be dissected." American critics of Caldwell, focusing on precisely the same quality, found his characters "unsuccessfully motivated" and merely "simplified response-systems," and seemed to be demanding the very psychological analysis that the French were rejecting in their own literature. The French, likewise, saw only virtue in Caldwell's authorial detachment, which Jack Conroy had compared negatively to that of "a bored and bilious God," and in his naïve and spontaneous style, which was described at home as "a hit-or-miss manner."[23]

Stuart Benedict, a scholar who undertook an analysis of the Franco-American debate on Caldwell, concluded from it that, because the French are "neither blind nor obtuse, [their] views make it seem that American critics might find it worthwhile to undertake a reappraisal of the work of Erskine Caldwell." Curiously enough, despite the contrasting judgments they made on Caldwell, critics on both sides of the Atlantic tended to note exactly the same elements in his writing; the differences in their reactions lay in tastes and values and in their changing social and political circumstances. A reappraisal of Caldwell by the same critics might well lead to a higher estimate at home, now that his patriotism is no longer likely to be impugned for exposing the failures of American society, nor his characters' sexual antics considered to be so lubricious. The French critics' high opinion may never be matched; indeed, they, too, eventually began to tire of the "hard-boiled formula" and to feel that they had been "enchanted by the platitudes of an easy naturalism." Camus attempted to arrest excessive enthusiasm by insisting that "the French must see the greatness of Melville and Hawthorne over Steinbeck and Caldwell; they must remain calm." Nevertheless, the French critics responded to the totality of Caldwell's vision, as T. S. Eliot noted that an earlier generation of them had responded to the totality of Poe's. Rather than making a series of separate judgments on variously flawed works by Poe, the French, Eliot

23. Jean-Paul Sartre, as quoted in Braun and Lainoff, *Transatlantic Mirrors*, 248; James T. Farrell, "The Author of 'Tobacco Road' Takes Us Again to Georgia," in *Critical Essays*, ed. MacDonald, 27; Randall Jarrell, "Ten Books," in *Critical Essays*, ed. MacDonald, 37; Farrell, "Heavenly Visitation," 39.

noted, took seriously the larger vision in these works. The consequence was Eliot's own reappraisal of Poe and his willingness to turn
away from emphasizing his "slipshod writing, puerile thinking un-
supported by wide reading or profound scholarship, haphazard experiments in various types of writing," to becoming "more thoroughly convinced of his importance, of the importance of his *work*
as a whole."[24] Caldwell's French critics likewise paid him the tribute
of not assuming either base motives or an inability to write what he
really meant; they were thus more open to a sense of his complete
vision and originality than those who chided and chivied him into
ideological or aesthetic pigeonholes rather than acknowledging his
capacity to elude them.

As Caldwell's positive reception in France was attributed at home
to a taste for the bizarre and a certain *schadenfreude* about American social conditions, his high reputation in the Soviet Union might
logically be expected to be laid to his left-wing political sympathies
and the "propaganda" element in his writing. It is certainly true that
Caldwell's fiction in the 1930s was translated into Russian because
he was initially perceived as a leftist who denounced the stagnation,
greed, and emptiness of bourgeois existence. However, Soviet critics proved closer than those of any other nation to their American
counterparts in opposing certain central elements of Caldwell's writing, which have been characterized as "pathological characters that
border on the ridiculous, bizarre social situations that give way to
burlesque, and an extravagance in treating sexual themes that vio-
lates the canons of plausibility and good taste." The Soviet critics
disapproved of his "biologism" and his emphasis on the irrational as
a motive for human behavior, though they went far beyond their
American colleagues by rejecting any Freudian or symbolic tendencies. In the Soviet Union, Caldwell was not considered one of the
American proletarian writers, who were criticized for their "sche-
matism" and parading of social messages, but was appreciated instead for his interest in folk culture, his humor, and his wide range
of social concerns. Soviet critics, like those elsewhere, found the
term *grotesque* a most useful one in discussing Caldwell, although
they likewise found it a conception capable of many different interpretations. Nevertheless, the presence of incongruity, contradiction, and disorientation was seen by them as a deliberate aesthetic

24. Benedict, "Gallic Light on Erskine Caldwell," 259; Smith and Miner, *Transatlantic Migration*, 53, 50, 49; T. S. Eliot, "From Poe to Valéry," in Eliot, *To Criticize the Critic and Other Writings* (New York, 1965), 27, 42.

choice on Caldwell's part that was a means of uncovering, understanding, and criticizing his world. Mikhail Landor, in comparing Caldwell to Gogol, noted that "our critics have always warned readers of the fallacy of a literal understanding of Caldwell," and Landor defended Caldwell's eccentricity as a mode of revelation of what lies in the common world. Anatoly Kaduk noted with some pride that the first two monographs completely devoted to Caldwell were in Russian and preceded the first American pamphlet on him. Mikhail Landor's interpretation of Caldwell, although arguing for his realism, notes his grotesque characters, macabre situations, and "recurrent transitions from tragedy to farce." As in France, this dissonant quality in Caldwell's fiction often brought praise from Soviet critics and frequent comparisons to Gogol and Chekhov, despite the occasional prudish reservations about the excesses of instinctual conduct. In other countries, critics have likewise tended to assume that the confusions and waywardness of Caldwell's imagined world were meant to be just that. Giordano De Biasio of Italy argued that Caldwell's universe "is the product of a vigorous and conscious aesthetic," and the English critic Paul West insisted that it is in this antic, exaggerated, monstrous quality of his work that its real significance lies: "We are jolted, it is true, but meaningfully."[25] Although almost all of these critics sensed a decline in the power of Caldwell's fiction in the forties, it did not appear to erase or contaminate for them the interest of the works of his best period. Thus Caldwell's international reputation seems to rest firmly on just the same issues where it has been shakiest nationally, on the acceptance of a high degree of consciousness in his seemingly primitive style, and on the effect of his mingling of incongruous and distorted attitudes toward his subject.

American critics did indeed have rather more grounds for their confusion about Caldwell's artistic purposes, because they had easy and immediate access not just to the full qualitative range of Caldwell's writing and his copious public comments on it, but also to the popular marketing of his work and to the kind of literary offspring it

25. Deming Brown, *Soviet Attitudes Toward American Writing* (Princeton, 1962), 120, 124, 132, 73, 71; Anatoly A. Kaduk, "The Craftsmanship of Erskine Caldwell's Realistic Short Story," *Pembroke Magazine*, XI (1979), 37; Mikhail Landor, "Erskine Caldwell in the Soviet Union," in *Critical Essays*, ed. MacDonald, 264, 265; Kaduk, "The Craftsmanship," 31–32; Landor, "Erskine Caldwell in the Soviet Union," 265; De Biasio, "Who Is Afraid of the Jeeter Lesters?" 91; Paul West, *The Modern Novel* (2 vols.; London, 1963), II, 290.

appeared to spawn. Some of this confusion may be observed in the comments on Caldwell of a very sympathetic critic like George Snell, who, in his *Shapers of American Fiction*, commented ambiguously that Caldwell's style "was the product of either a fortunate natural virtuosity or a cunning craftsmanship," and also that it was "naïve," "simpleminded," and "evidently natural" though "excellently calculated." Certainly, Caldwell's numerous interviews and public pronouncements on his fiction might have encouraged such a reaction as Snell's, for in them he refused ever to lay aside his simple mask or expose his crafty hand. Unlike Flannery O'Connor, he never defined the operation of the grotesque in southern literature, and unlike Sherwood Anderson, he never was tempted to assume the role of cultural philosopher. He worked consistently to maintain the image of a simple man writing simply about the world as he knew it, and this he did very successfully. His literary language, too, was the essence of simplicity: short sentences, easy syntax, limited vocabulary and frequent repetitions. His characters were sometimes close to simpletons and his plots slight and without complication. In such ways, Caldwell's fiction seemed to invite Snell's epithet "simpleminded," with its hints of foolishness and lack of intellectual acumen. Even his grotesque vision suggested not just an ability to see differences but, to some, an incapacity to reconcile them or work out any larger integration of ideas. The repeated use of the term *natural* for Caldwell's art seems to imply in it a kind of automatic, unthinking element that is the antithesis of the notion of a conscious stylist. There is a pervasive feeling in the reaction of critics in his own country to Caldwell of possibilities unrealized, natural gifts misdirected, and of a lack of intellectual rigor and self-knowledge. Even Cowley, his most encouraging critic, felt that "Caldwell, with an immense natural gift for story telling, made fewer demands on it" than did his contemporaries.[26]

Much of this response clearly stems also from disappointment at Caldwell's later writing career, especially since that career was so long and fertile and since Caldwell himself obstinately insisted that the period from 1950 to 1975 was his "most productive," while for reviewers it merely demonstrated the success of the innovative and lurid marketing of an author whose name was now suggestive of a genre of hillbilly pornography. Indeed, for some time this appeared

26. George Snell, *The Shapers of American Fiction* (New York, 1961), 265–66; Cowley, "Georgia Boy," 326.

to be Caldwell's main legacy to American fiction. In 1982, *The Journal of Popular Culture* published an article, "Sons of *Tobacco Road*: 'Backwoods Novels,'" that cataloged the Caldwell inheritance in dozens of cheap paperbacks with imitative titles, salacious covers, and clearly derivative blurbs about the ribald, lusty, violent, and earthy dregs of society. The titles alone suggest the allusive and associative power of Caldwell's original; among them are *Cabin Road, Shack Road, Shanty Road, Backwoods Shack, Shack Woman, Backwoods Woman, Backwoods Hussy, Backwoods Tramp, Back-Country Wench, Back-Country Woman, Girl Out Back, Gulf Coast Girl, Cracker Girl, Bayou Girl, Swamp Girl, Swamp Brat, Swamp Babe,* and *Swamp Hoyden.* This was clearly part of a calculated marketing strategy by mass paperback publishers, and it suggests that to them, at least, the Caldwell tradition was defined as exotic (meaning southern lower-class) soft-core pornography, with a particular emphasis on dangerously seductive women ("She was no better than she had to be"; "She was as deadly as the untamed swamp that had spawned her"; "Born to trouble . . . and most of it was men").[27] Although rural and small-town poverty was an essential part of these settings, Caldwell's consistent interest in environmental determinism and human irrationality as grounds for the antics of his characters was ignored, as was his concern for economic and social inequities, despite the fact that almost all these titles derive, ironically, from his most socially concerned work.

Although a reputation gleaned from his covers rather than from his books seems likely to distort Caldwell's literary image for some time, there has also been in the United States a more serious critical interest in coupling Caldwell with writers such as Flannery O'Connor and Harry Crews in their common violent comedy and warped spirituality, and in acknowledging and examining the innovations of his literary technique. What seems still to be most absent from Caldwell's reputation, both popular and scholarly, is his central concern with poverty in all its material, moral, social, and spiritual manifestations. No other American writer has made this subject so much his or her province, nor explored so many dimensions of it. Although Dreiser and Steinbeck both examined sympathetically the impetus of poor people to escape from their environment, Caldwell's concern was not with any dynamic movement toward

27. Broadwell and Hoag, "The Art of Fiction LXII," 142; Bill Crider, "Sons of *Tobacco Road*: 'Backwoods' Novels," *Journal of Popular Culture*, XVI (1982), 47–59.

success, no matter how thwarted, like Dreiser's characters, nor even with the energy born of desperation, like Steinbeck's, but with a cycle of entrapment and erratic bursts of activity that led nowhere. Whereas the genuinely proletarian writers like Robert Cantwell, Josephine Herbst, Michael Gold, and Jack Conroy emphasized the stalwart qualities of the poor that fitted them most to be leaders in a new egalitarian society, Caldwell looked candidly at the ravages of both deprivation and original sin that made his characters ludicrous candidates for transformation into such wholesome types. Sherwood Anderson had given dignity and compassion to the buried lives of his characters and offered Caldwell a model of a simple and colloquial style from which he undoubtedly profited, but Caldwell avoided for the most part the private emotional analyses that qualified and softened the starkness of the public and social conduct of Anderson's people.[28]

In the 1930s, when southern poverty became emblematic for the nation of the direness of the times, many novelists turned their attention to striking southern workers as offering the most graphic evidence of both the exploitation of the poor and their innate ability to resist being demeaned by it. Besides Caldwell, at least six authors wrote novels based on one strike by southern mill workers in Gastonia, North Carolina: *Strike!* (1930) by Mary Heaton Vorse, *Call Home the Heart* (1932) by Fielding Burke, *To Make My Bread* (1932) by Grace Lumpkin, *Gathering Storm* (1932) by Myra Page, *Beyond Desire* (1932) by Sherwood Anderson, and *The Shadow Before* (1934) by William Rollins. They all explored variously and sympathetically the conflicts within these poor people between their desire for economic justice and their loyalty to old southern ways and beliefs that worked against any radical social changes. When Caldwell wrote his own oblique version of the Gastonia strike in *God's Little Acre*, he dismissed all notion of sentimental loyalties to religion or family or land in his workers and motivated them instead by a strange mingling of starvation and sexual fantasy in which mill girls kissed the walls of the mill and the men dreamed of seizing control of whatever power it had over them. Yet Caldwell's evocation of hunger and degradation was as dramatic, in his own way, as that of any of the more conventional partisans of the poor and op-

28. See Holman, "Detached Laughter in the South," 87–104; and John Seelye, "Georgia Boys: The Redclay Satyrs of Erskine Caldwell and Harry Crews," *Virginia Quarterly Review*, LVI (1980), 612–26; Broadwell and Hoag, "The Art of Fiction LXII," 154.

pressed, and he continued to write about them long after their brief period of literary ascendancy had ended and they had been largely abandoned by everyone else.

Even among southern writers, for whom poverty, and especially the lurid and extreme condition of the poor whites, was both a social and literary tradition, Caldwell stands virtually alone in his refusal to moderate his depiction of either the grimness of the suffering or the unworthiness of the sufferers. Only Faulkner, in a novel like *As I Lay Dying*, offers him kinship in this, a literary parallel for once conceded by Caldwell in his acknowledgment that "he and I a lot of times were writing the same thing," to which he added, somewhat cryptically, "I didn't know until it was too late."[29]

However, Faulkner's social range was much broader than Caldwell's, and for him poverty was merely one element in a complicated literary universe rather than a key to his moral vision, as it was for Caldwell. Faulkner still had faith in personal acts of charity among his poor and, even in *As I Lay Dying*, faith in a community and families with public consciences and personal loyalties, no matter how compromised they were by private motives. Caldwell's families and communities can no longer be relied on to generate the old loyalties, and though his people have consciences of a kind, they operate in wholly unpredictable ways that tend to alienate them from, rather than admit them to, the common circle of humanity. They are always poised on the far edge of the recognizably familiar. Both Faulkner and Caldwell are heirs to strains of the older southwestern tradition of violent and cruel comedy about poor people, from Augustus B. Longstreet, George W. Harris, and Johnson J. Hooper. However, Caldwell refuses to provide a mediating narrator who relishes the absurd events he relates but also forms a protective barrier between the reader and the cruel farce. Caldwell's narration allows no relief or qualification to the reader's discomfort at the capers of his incorrigible paupers and provides no method for incorporating them into a comfortable view of the world.

The other southern writer who tried to come to terms with the larger meaning of poverty was James Agee, who chose, like Caldwell, to experiment outside fiction with a new hybrid documentary form of words and photographs. While Agee and Walker Evans were living among Alabama tenant farmers in the summer of 1936, collecting material for *Let Us Now Praise Famous Men*, Caldwell

29. Tharpe, "Interview with Erskine Caldwell," 68.

and Margaret Bourke-White were pursuing their odyssey through Georgia, Mississippi, Alabama, Tennessee, Arkansas, South Carolina, Louisiana, and Florida in preparation for *You Have Seen Their Faces*. Of the many picture-texts produced in depression America to chart the lives of the poor, these two are unique for the personal intrusiveness of their authors, Agee becoming an anguished character in his text, Caldwell openly admitting that he is creating fictional dialogue for the real characters in the photographs. Both attempted by these very different methods to penetrate the false authenticity of the documentary genre, and both pushed beyond the mere recording of social conditions to question the significance of the lives of the poor. Agee challenged the partisans and reformers, who felt they knew what was best for the poor, to see the dignity and holiness that mingled with the shame of such lives. Caldwell insisted on creating, through his captions, people who asserted their eccentricities and misbehavior as much as their poverty. What Lionel Trilling professed to find least convincing in Agee's people could never be said of Caldwell's—that they had "no human unregenerateness in them, no flicker of malice or meanness, no darkness or wildness of feeling."[30] Whereas Agee abased himself, with his middle-class background and Harvard education, reverently at the altar of poverty, Caldwell approached the poor curiously, strongly predisposed to the kind of large-scale social reforms Agee questioned, but open to the ironic and ridiculous aspects of their lives as well.

Caldwell's sense of the moral turpitude of the poor and their simultaneous right not to suffer poverty because of it was echoed in the early work of Carson McCullers, especially in *The Heart Is a Lonely Hunter;* but she later turned away from the economic and societal dimension of her grotesque characters to more purely private and psychological concerns. For Caldwell, although there was a similar movement in his later fiction into the sexual problems of the middle class, the great bulk of his work was devoted to what might be called the undeserving poor. He explored the vulnerability of women and the exploitation of blacks with sympathetic insights into the operation of power over powerlessness; but the real zest in his writing, even while on these topics, comes from the more complicated victims of poverty—the poor who are never merely

30. Lionel Trilling, "Greatness with One Fault in It," *Kenyon Review,* IV (Winter, 1942), 102.

innocent victims in any situation that involves them. Caldwell utterly rejected the notion that poor people must be virtuous in order to deserve relief from their poverty, and equally the reformer's notion that such relief would make decent citizens out of wily rogues. His residual Presbyterian vision of human nature saw all mortals as undeserving and irrational, yet only the poor and vulnerable were forced to add further material deprivation to their innate depravity. Caldwell was as certain of the political and social injustice of this in the physical sphere of the world as he was of the absurd mystery of human conduct in the pursuit of the metaphysical. Together, his fiction and nonfiction make a case for the urgent remedy of what is correctable in human affairs and turn a sardonic eye on what is, by nature, incorrigible. Flannery O'Connor later explored similar territory among the southern poor, although with an emphasis on very different redemptive possibilities from Caldwell. Physical suffering is vindicated in her work as a means to spiritual transcendence, whereas Caldwell looks with a jaundiced eye on his characters' quaint pursuit of divinity, but takes their worldly suffering very seriously indeed. Though in his later work Caldwell lost the stimulus of the intellectual context of the Great Depression and tried rather unsuccessfully to broaden his fictional realm, in his major work of the 1930s and 1940s he created a dissonant and defiant literary vision of poverty and social powerlessness. He simultaneously invoked naturalistic theories and undermined them; he was disconcertingly simple in his narration yet complex in his meaning; he relished vulgarity and reviled the circumstances it was forced to dwell in; and his fiction finally refused, much like the poor themselves, to accommodate itself to any comfortable category, either aesthetic or political.

# Bibliography

NOTE: Works marked with an asterisk are reprinted in Scott MacDonald, ed., *Critical Essays on Erskine Caldwell* (Boston, 1981).

## WORKS BY ERSKINE CALDWELL

*Afternoons in Mid-America: Observations and Impressions.* Illustrations by Virginia Caldwell. New York, 1976.

*All Night Long.* New York, 1942.

*All-Out on the Road to Smolensk.* New York, 1942.

*American Earth.* 1931; rpr. New York, 1946.

*Annette.* New York, 1973.

*Around About America.* New York, 1964.

*The Bastard.* 1929; rpr. London, 1958.

"Caldwell to Lieber." Letter. *New Masses,* January 30, 1934, p. 21.

*Call It Experience: The Years of Learning How to Write.* New York, 1951.

*Certain Women.* Boston, 1957.

*Claudelle Inglish.* Boston, 1958.

*Close to Home.* New York, 1962.

*Deep South: Memory and Observation.* New York, 1968.

*The Earnshaw Neighborhood.* New York, 1971.

*Episode in Palmetto.* New York, 1950.

Foreword to *On the Plantation,* by Joel Chandler Harris. Athens, Ga., 1980.

*Georgia Boy.* New York, 1943.

"The Georgia Cracker." *Haldeman-Julius Monthly,* November, 1926. Reprinted in Sutton, William A. *Black Like It Is/Was: Erskine Caldwell's Treatment of Racial Themes.* Metuchen, N.J., 1974.

*God's Little Acre.* 1933; rpr. New York, 1934.

*Gretta.* Boston, 1955.

*Gulf Coast Stories.* Boston, 1956.

*A House in the Uplands.* New York, 1946.

*In Defense of Myself.* Portland, Me., [1929].

*In Search of Bisco.* New York, 1965.

*Introduction to *American Earth.* 1931; rpr. New York, 1950.

Introduction to *The Cock's Funeral,* by Ben Field. New York, 1937.

Introduction to *God's Little Acre.* 1933; rpr. New York, 1934.

*Introduction to *God's Little Acre.* 1933; rpr. New York, 1949.

*Introduction to *A House in the Uplands*. 1946; rpr. New York, 1949.
*Introduction to *Kneel to the Rising Sun*. 1935; rpr. New York, 1951.
*Introduction to *Tobacco Road*. 1932; rpr. New York, 1948.
*Jackpot: The Short Stories of Erskine Caldwell*. New York, 1940.
*Jenny by Nature*. New York, 1961.
*Journeyman*. New York, 1935.
*Kneel to the Rising Sun and Other Stories*. 1935; rpr. New York, 1951.
*A Lamp for Nightfall*. New York, 1952.
*The Last Night of Summer*. New York, 1963.
*Love and Money*. New York, 1954.
*Miss Mamma Aimee*. New York, 1967.
*Moscow Under Fire: A Wartime Diary*. London, 1942.
*"Mr. Caldwell Protests." Letter. *New Republic*, June 27, 1934, pp. 184–85.
"A Night in November/Beverly Hills, California." *Georgia Review*, XXXVI
    (1982), 102–11.
*Place Called Estherville*. New York, 1949.
*Poor Fool*. New York, 1930.
Review of *Folk Beliefs of the Southern Negro*, by Newbell Niles Puckett.
    Charlotte *Observer*, August 15, 1926, p. 9.
Review of *The Negro in American Life*, by Jerome Dowd. Charlotte *Ob-
    server*, November 21, 1926, p. 10.
*"Ripe for Revolution." *New Masses*, VIII (December, 1932), 26–27.
*The Sacrilege of Alan Kent*. Portland, Me., 1936.
*Some American People*. New York, 1935.
*Southways*. 1938; rpr. London, 1953.
*Summertime Island*. New York, 1968.
*The Sure Hand of God*. New York, 1947.
*This Very Earth*. New York, 1948.
*Tobacco Road*. New York, 1932.
*"Tobacco Roads in the South." *New Leader*, June 13, 1936, p. 4.
*Tragic Ground*. New York, 1944.
*Trouble in July*. New York, 1940.
[Untitled]. *New Masses*, January 16, 1934, p. 13.
*We Are the Living*. New York, 1933.
*The Weather Shelter*. New York, 1969.
*With All My Might*. Atlanta, 1987.
*Writing in America*. New York, 1967.

WITH MARGARET BOURKE-WHITE
*North of the Danube*. New York, 1939.
*Russia at War*. London, 1942.
*Say, Is This the U.S.A.* New York, 1941.
*You Have Seen Their Faces*. New York, 1937.

## OTHER SOURCES

Aaron, Daniel. *Writers on the Left: Episodes in American Literary Communism.* New York, 1961.

Agee, James, and Walker Evans. *Let Us Now Praise Famous Men.* 1941; rpr. Boston, 1960.

Arnold, Edwin T., ed. *Conversations with Erskine Caldwell.* Jackson, Miss., 1988.

"Authors' Field Day: A Symposium on Marxist Criticism." *New Masses,* July 3, 1934, pp. 27–36.

Bakhtin, Mikhail. *Rabelais and His World.* Translated by Helene Iswolsky. Cambridge, Mass. 1968.

*Basso, Hamilton. "Sunny South." *New Masses,* June 11, 1935, p. 25.

*Beach, Joseph Warren. Excerpt from *American Fiction, 1920–1940.* New York, 1941.

Beckett, Samuel. *Waiting for Godot.* New York, 1954.

*Benedict, Stewart H. "Gallic Light on Erskine Caldwell." *South Atlantic Quarterly,* LX (August, 1961), 390–97.

*Bode, Carl. "Erskine Caldwell: A Note for the Negative." *College English,* XVII (October, 1955), 357–59.

Bourke-White, Margaret. *Portrait of Myself.* New York, 1963.

Braun, Sidney D., and Seymour Lainoff, eds. *Transatlantic Mirrors: Essays in Franco-American Literary Relations.* Boston, 1978.

Broadwell, Elizabeth Pell, and Ronald Wesley Hoag. "The Art of Fiction LXII: Erskine Caldwell." *Paris Review,* LXXXVI (1982), 127–57.

———. "A Writer First: An Interview with Erskine Caldwell." *Georgia Review,* XXXVI (1982), 83–101.

Brooks, Cleanth. "What Deep South Literature Needs." *Saturday Review,* September 19, 1942, pp. 8–9.

Brown, Deming. *Soviet Attitudes Toward American Writing.* Princeton, 1962.

*Burke, Kenneth. "Caldwell: Maker of Grotesques." *New Republic,* April 10, 1935, pp. 232–35.

Burnett, Whit. Review of *We Are the Living,* by Erskine Caldwell. *Books,* September 24, 1933, p. 8.

Caen, Herb. "Letter to Victor Dalmas." *Pembroke Magazine,* XI (1979), 30–31.

*Caldwell, I[ra] S[ylvester]. "Mr. Caldwell Writes." Augusta *Chronicle,* March 17, 1935, p. 4.

*"Caldwell's Collapse." *Time,* August 30, 1948, pp. 82–84.

*Canby, Henry Seidel. Introduction to *The Pocket Book of Erskine Caldwell Stories.* New York, 1947.

Cargill, Oscar. *Intellectual America: Ideas on the March.* 1941; rpr. New York, 1968.

Clemens, Samuel Langhorne [Mark Twain]. *The Adventures of Huckleberry Finn.* 1886; rpr. New York, 1923.

Coindreau, Maurice Edgar. "Lettres Étrangères." *Nouvelle Revue Française,* July 1, 1934, pp. 125–29.

―――. "Lettres Étrangères." *Nouvelle Revue Française,* November 1, 1936, pp. 908–12.

*―――. Preface to *Poor Fool.* In *The Time of William Faulkner: A French View of Modern American Fiction.* Translated by George McMillan Reeves. Columbia, S.C., 1971.

Collins, Carvel. "Erskine Caldwell at Work: A Conversation with Carvel Collins." *Atlantic,* CCII (July, 1958), 21–27.

Comsa, Ioan. "Caldwell's Stories: Common Reader Response, Analysis and Appreciation at Home and Abroad." *Pembroke Magazine,* XI (1979), 51–58.

*Conroy, Jack. "Passion and Pellagra." *New Masses,* VII (April, 1932), 24–25.

Cook, Sylvia Jenkins. "Caldwell's Fiction: Growing Towards Trash?" *Southern Quarterly,* XXVII (1989), 49–58.

*―――. "Erskine Caldwell and the Literary Left Wing." *Pembroke Magazine,* XI (1979), 132–39.

―――. *From Tobacco Road to Route 66: The Southern Poor White in Fiction.* Chapel Hill, 1976.

Cooper, C. L. Review of *In Search of Bisco,* by Erskine Caldwell. *Saturday Review,* May 1, 1965, p. 39.

*Couch, W. T. "Landlord and Tenant." *Virginia Quarterly Review,* XIV (Spring, 1938), 309–12.

*Cowley, Malcolm. "Fall Catalogue." *New Republic,* November 24, 1937, pp. 78–79.

*―――. "Georgia Boy: A Retrospect of Erskine Caldwell." In *Pages.* Edited by Matthew J. Bruccoli. Detroit, 1976.

*―――. "The Two Erskine Caldwells." *New Republic,* November 6, 1944, pp. 599–600.

*Cowley, Malcolm, and T. K. Whipple. "Two Judgments of *American Earth.*" *New Republic,* June 17, 1931, pp. 130–32.

Crider, Bill. "Sons of *Tobacco Road:* 'Backwoods' Novels." *Journal of Popular Culture,* XVI (1982), 47–59.

Dahlberg, Edward. "Erskine Caldwell and Other 'Proletarian' Novelists." *Nation,* March 8, 1933, pp. 265–66.

*―――. "Raw Leaf." *New Republic,* March 23, 1932, pp. 159–60.

*Daniels, Jonathan. "American Lower Depths." *Saturday Review of Literature,* October 14, 1944, p. 46.

*―――. "From Comedy to Pity." *Saturday Review of Literature,* June 18, 1938, p. 7.

Dardis, Tom. *Some Time in the Sun.* New York, 1976.

*Davidson, Donald. "Erskine Caldwell's Picture Book." *Southern Review*, IV (1938–39), 15–25.

———. "The Trend of Literature: A Partisan View." In *Culture in the South*. Edited by W. T. Couch. Chapel Hill, 1935.

De Biasio, Giordano. "Who Is Afraid of the Jeeter Lesters?" *Pembroke Magazine*, XI (1979), 89–99.

Devlin, James E. *Erskine Caldwell*. Boston, 1984.

Editorial. *New Masses*, January 16, 1934, p. 3.

Eliot, T. S. "From Poe to Valéry." In Eliot, *To Criticize the Critic and Other Writings*. New York, 1965.

Ellison, Ralph. *Going to the Territory*. New York, 1986.

*"Erskine Caldwell." Augusta *Chronicle*, March 14, 1935, pp. 1, 8.

*Farrell, James T. "The Author of 'Tobacco Road' Takes Us Again to Georgia." New York *Sun*, February 7, 1933, p. 22.

*———. "Heavenly Visitation." *New Masses*, April 2, 1935, pp. 32–33.

Faulkner, William. *Faulkner at Nagano*. Tokyo, 1956.

*Ferguson, Otis. "Caldwell's Stories." *New Republic*, July 6, 1938, p. 258.

Ford, Hugh. *Published in Paris: American and British Writers, Printers, and Publishers in Paris, 1920–1939*. New York, 1975.

*Frohock, W. M. "Erskine Caldwell: Sentimental Gentleman from Georgia." *Southwest Review*, XXXI (Autumn, 1946), 351–59.

Godden, Richard L. "Does Anybody Live in There? Character and Representative, Type and Cartoon in Caldwell's *Trouble in July*." *Pembroke Magazine*, XI (1979), 102–12.

Gold, Michael. "Go Left, Young Writers!" (editorial). *New Masses*, IV (January, 1929), 3–4.

Goodin, George. *The Poetics of Protest: Literary Form and Political Implication in the Victim-of-Society Novel*. Carbondale, Ill., 1985.

Gossett, Louise Y. *Violence in Recent Southern Fiction*. Durham, N.C., 1965.

*Gray, Richard J. "Southwestern Humor, Erskine Caldwell, and the Comedy of Frustration." *Southern Literary Journal*, VIII (Fall, 1975), 3–26.

Gwynn, Frederick L., and Joseph L. Blotner, eds. *Faulkner in the University: Class Conference at the University of Virginia, 1957–58*. Charlottesville, 1959.

Hackett, Alice Payne. *70 Years of Best Sellers, 1895–1965*. New York, 1967.

*Halper, Albert. "Caldwell Sees America." *New Masses*, December 10, 1935, pp. 22–23.

Halpert, Stephen, ed., with Richard Johns. *A Return to "Pagany": The History, Correspondence, and Selections from a Little Magazine, 1929–1932*. Boston, 1969.

Harpham, Geoffrey Galt. *On the Grotesque: Strategies of Contradiction in Art and Literature*. Princeton, 1982.

Henderson, Philip. *The Novel Today: Studies in Contemporary Attitudes.* London, 1936.

Hoag, Ronald Wesley, and Elizabeth Pell Broadwell. "Erskine Caldwell on Southern Realism." *Mississippi Quarterly,* XXXVI (1983), 577–84.

Hoffman, Frederick J., Charles Allen, and Carolyn F. Ulrich. *The Little Magazine: A History and Bibliography.* 2nd ed. 1947; rpr. New York, 1967.

Holman, C. Hugh. "Detached Laughter in the South." In *Comic Relief: Humor in Contemporary American Literature.* Edited by Sarah Blacher Cohen. Urbana, 1978.

Hubbell, Jay B. *Who Are the Major American Writers? A Study of the Changing Literary Canon.* Durham, N.C., 1972.

Jacobs, Robert D. "*Tobacco Road:* Lowlife and the Comic Tradition." In *The American South: Portrait of a Culture.* Edited by Louis D. Rubin, Jr. Baton Rouge, 1980.

*Jarrell, Randall. "Ten Books." *Southern Review,* I (1935–36), 401–404.

Johnson, Gerald W. *South-Watching: Selected Essays by Gerald W. Johnson.* Edited by Fred Hobson. Chapel Hill, 1983.

Kaduk, Anatoly A. "The Craftsmanship of Erskine Caldwell's Realistic Short Story." *Pembroke Magazine,* XI (1979), 31–44.

Kayser, Wolfgang. *The Grotesque in Art and Literature.* Translated by Ulrich Weisstein. Toronto, 1966.

Kazin, Alfred. *On Native Grounds: An Interpretation of Modern American Prose Literature.* New York, 1942; abr. ed.; Garden City, N.Y., 1955.

Kinlock, L. M. Review of *Trouble in July,* by Erskine Caldwell. *Library Journal,* February 1, 1940, p. 17.

Klevar, Harvey. "Some Things Holy in a Godforsaken Land." *Pembroke Magazine,* XI (1979), 65–76.

Korges, James. *Erskine Caldwell.* Minneapolis, 1969.

*Kubie, Lawrence S. "'God's Little Acre': An Analysis." *Saturday Review of Literature,* November 24, 1934, pp. 305–306.

*Landor, Mikhail. "Erskine Caldwell in the Soviet Union." *Soviet Literature,* III (1969), 183–86.

Lester, Julius. "James Baldwin—Reflections of a Maverick." *New York Times Book Review,* May 27, 1984, p. 23.

Letter. *New York Times Book Review,* July 1, 1984, p. 27.

Lewis, Edward E. "Letter to Victor Dalmas." *Pembroke Magazine,* XI (1979), 121.

*MacDonald, Scott. "An Evaluative Check-List of Erskine Caldwell's Short Fiction." *Studies in Short Fiction,* XI (1978), 81–97.

*———. "Repetition as Technique in the Short Stories of Erskine Caldwell." *Studies in American Fiction,* V (1977), 213–25.

*Macleod, Norman. "A Hardboiled Idealist." *New Masses,* VII (July, 1931), 18.

McMillan, Dougald. *"transition": The History of a Literary Era, 1927–1938.* New York, 1976.

Martin, Jay. "Erskine Caldwell's Singular Devotions." In *A Question of Quality: Popularity and Value in Modern Creative Writing.* Edited by Louis Filler. Bowling Green, 1976.

Matthiessen, F. O. *From the Heart of Europe.* New York, 1948.

Mott, Frank Luther. *Golden Multitudes: The Story of Best Sellers in the United States.* New York, 1947.

Newman, Frances. *The Short Story's Mutations: From Petronius to Paul Morand.* New York, 1924.

Noble, Donald R. "Erskine Caldwell: A Biographical Sketch." *Pembroke Magazine,* XI (1979), 165–78.

O'Connor, Flannery. Introduction to *Wise Blood.* 1952; 2nd ed. New York, 1962.

Owen, Guy. "The Apprenticeship of Erskine Caldwell: An Examination of *The Bastard* and *Poor Fool.*" In *A Fair Day in the Affections: Literary Essays in Honor of Robert B. White, Jr.* Edited by Jack D. Durant and M. Thomas Hester. Raleigh, 1980.

———. "'The Bogus Ones': A Lost Erskine Caldwell Novel." *Southern Literary Journal,* XI (1978), 32–39.

———. "Erskine Caldwell and D. H. Lawrence." *Pembroke Magazine,* XI (1979), 18–21.

———. "Erskine Caldwell's Unpublished Poems." *South Atlantic Bulletin,* XLIII (1978), 53–57.

———. "Folk Motifs in Erskine Caldwell's Cyclorama of the South." *North Carolina Folklore Journal,* XXVII (1979), 80–87.

———. "*The Sacrilege of Alan Kent* and the Apprenticeship of Erskine Caldwell." *Southern Literary Journal,* XII (1979), 36–46.

Peacock, R. *Criticism and Personal Taste.* Oxford, 1972.

Pells, Richard H. *Radical Visions and American Dreams: Culture and Social Thought in the Depression Years.* New York, 1973.

*"People* v. *Viking Press, Inc.,* et al." 264 N.Y.S. 534 (1933).

Peterson, Theodore. *Magazines in the Twentieth Century.* 1964; 2nd ed. Urbana, 1972.

Pugh, David. "Reading Caldwell Today: Perceiving Craft and Culture." *Pembroke Magazine,* XI (1979), 122–30.

*Rascoe, Burton. "Caldwell Lynches Two Negroes." *American Mercury,* XLIX (April, 1940), 493–99.

Review of *Georgia Boy,* by Erskine Caldwell. *Time,* May 3, 1943, p. 104.

Review of *Georgia Boy,* by Erskine Caldwell. *Weekly Book Review,* April 25, 1943, p. 5.

*Rolfe, Edwin. Review of *God's Little Acre,* by Erskine Caldwell. *New Masses,* VIII (February, 1933), 26.

Rubin, Louis D., Jr. "Trouble on the Land: Southern Literature and the

Great Depression." In *Literature at the Barricades: The American Writer in the 1930s*. Edited by Ralph F. Bogardus and Fred Hobson. University, Ala., 1982.

*Ruhl, Arthur. "Seventeen Tales by Erskine Caldwell." *Saturday Review of Literature*, June 8, 1935, p. 5.

*Sale, Richard B. "An Interview in Florida with Erskine Caldwell." *Studies in the Novel*, III (Fall, 1971), 316–31.

Schücking, Levin L. *The Sociology of Literary Taste*. Translated by Brian Battershaw from 3rd rev. German ed. Chicago, 1966.

Schwartz, Edward P. "Caldwell 'On-the-Road' and Censorship Interlude." *Pembroke Magazine*, XI (1979), 85–87.

Seelye, John. "Georgia Boys: The Redclay Satyrs of Erskine Caldwell and Harry Crews." *Virginia Quarterly Review*, LVI (1980), 612–26.

Simons, Marlise, "A Talk with Gabriel García Marquez." *New York Times Book Review*, December 5, 1982, p. 60.

Smith, C. Michael. "The Surprising Popularity of Erskine Caldwell's South." *Journal of Popular Culture*, XVI (Winter, 1982), 42–46.

*Smith, Harrison. "Comic Citizens of the South." *Saturday Review of Literature*, September 10, 1949, pp. 14–15.

*———. "Well-Controlled Anger." *Saturday Review of Literature*, May 18, 1946, pp. 8–9.

Smith, Thelma M., and Ward L. Miner. *Transatlantic Migration: The Contemporary American Novel in France*. 1955; rpr. New York, 1968.

Snell, George. *The Shapers of American Fiction*. New York, 1961.

Staats, Marilyn Dorn. "Erskine Caldwell at Eighty-One: An Interview." *Arizona Quarterly*, XLI (1985), 247–57.

Stott, William. *Documentary Expression and Thirties America*. New York, 1973.

Sutton, William A. *Black Like It Is/Was: Erskine Caldwell's Treatment of Racial Themes*. Metuchen, N.J., 1974.

*Sykes, Gerald. "The Poetry of Unfeeling." *Nation*, October 21, 1931, pp. 436–37.

Terrie, Henry. "Erskine Caldwell's *Journeyman*: Comedy as Redemption." *Pembroke Magazine*, XI (1979), 21–30.

Tharpe, Jac. "Interview with Erskine Caldwell." *Southern Quarterly*, XX (1981), 64–74.

*Thompson, James J., Jr. "Erskine Caldwell and Southern Religion." *Southern Humanities Review*, V (Winter, 1971), 33–44.

Thorp, Willard. *American Writing in the Twentieth Century*. Cambridge, Mass., 1960.

Thurber, James. *The Thurber Carnival*. New York, 1945.

*Tinkle, Lon. "Crumbled Georgia Crackers." *Saturday Review of Literature*, August 28, 1948, pp. 12–13.

*"'Tobacco Road' Winds Its Way into Congress." New York *Herald Tribune*, April 7, 1936, p. 14.

Trilling, Lionel. "Greatness with One Fault in It." *Kenyon Review,* IV (Winter, 1942), 99–102.

Turnbull, Andrew, ed. *The Letters of F. Scott Fitzgerald.* New York, 1963.

*Van Doren, Carl. "Made in America: Erskine Caldwell." *Nation,* October 18, 1933, pp. 443–44.

*Van Doren, Dorothy. "Out of Georgia." *Nation,* June 25, 1938, p. 730.

Van Gelder, Robert. Review of *Some American People,* by Erskine Caldwell. New York *Times,* December 15, 1935, p. 9.

Wade, Donald. "Sweet Are the Uses of Degeneracy." *Southern Review,* I (1935–36), 449–66.

Warren, Robert Penn. "Some Recent Novels." *Southern Review,* I (1935–36), 624–29.

West, Paul. *The Modern Novel.* Vol. II of 2 vols. London, 1963.

Weybright, Victor. "Georgia Boy—A Recollection from the Inner Sanctum." *Pembroke Magazine,* XI (1979), 115–20.

*"What Will Good People of Jefferson County Say of This?" Augusta *Chronicle,* March 4, 1935, p. 4.

Wolseley, Ronald E. *Understanding Magazines.* Ames, 1965.

*Wright, Richard. "Lynching Bee." *New Republic,* March 11, 1940, pp. 351–52.

# Index